Lecture Notes of the Institute for Computer Sciences, Social Informatics and Telecommunications Engineering 338

More information about this series at http://www.springer.com/series/8197

Seng W. Loke · Zhi Liu ·
Kien Nguyen · Guoming Tang ·
Zhen Ling (Eds.)

Mobile Networks and Management

10th EAI International Conference, MONAMI 2020
Chiba, Japan, November 10–12, 2020
Proceedings

 Springer

Editors
Seng W. Loke
Deakin University
Melbourne, VIC, Australia

Zhi Liu
Shizuoka University
Shizuoka, Japan

Kien Nguyen
Chiba University
Chiba, Japan

Guoming Tang
Peng Cheng Laboratory
Shenzhen, China

Zhen Ling
Southeast University
Nanjing, China

ISSN 1867-8211   ISSN 1867-822X (electronic)
Lecture Notes of the Institute for Computer Sciences, Social Informatics
and Telecommunications Engineering
ISBN 978-3-030-64001-9   ISBN 978-3-030-64002-6 (eBook)
https://doi.org/10.1007/978-3-030-64002-6

This Springer imprint is published by the registered company Springer Nature Switzerland AG
The registered company address is: Gewerbestrasse 11, 6330 Cham, Switzerland

Preface

We are delighted to introduce the proceedings of the European Alliance for Innovation (EAI) International Conference on Mobile Networks and Management (MONAMI 2020). This conference has brought together researchers, developers, and practitioners from around the world, aiming to provide an interdisciplinary platform to share recent results on mobile networks and management technologies. Particularly, MONAMI 2020 puts special focus on IoT and mobile edge computing (MEC), which is an essential component of the upcoming 5G architecture and of fundamental importance to the future mobile computing systems.

The technical program of MONAMI 2020 consisted of 19 full papers in oral presentation sessions at the main conference tracks. The conference tracks were: Track 1 – The application of artificial intelligence for smart city; Track 2 – Advanced technology in edge computing; Track 3 – Recent advances in mobile communications and computing; and Track 4 – Emerging technologies and applications in mobile networks and management. Aside from the high-quality technical paper presentations, the technical program also featured four keynote speeches, which were: i) Prof. Jiangchuan Liu from Simon Fraser University, Canada; ii) Prof. Mianxiong Dong from Muroran Institute of Technology, Japan; iii) Prof. Jianping Wang from City University of Hong Kong, Hong Kong; and iv) Prof. Yusheng Ji from National Institute of Informatics, Japan.

Coordination with the general chairs, A/Prof. Xun Shao, Prof. Kui Wu, and A/Prof. Tan Hwee Pink, was essential for the success of the conference. We sincerely appreciate their constant support and guidance. It was also a great pleasure to work with such an excellent Organizing Committee team and we thank them for their hard work in organizing and supporting the conference. In particular, the Technical Program Committee (TPC), led by our TPC co-chairs, Prof. Seng Loke, A/Prof. Zhi Liu, and A/Prof. Kien Nguyen, who completed the peer-review process of technical papers and made a high-quality technical program. We are also grateful to conference manager, Kristina Petrovicova, for her support and all the authors who submitted their papers to the MONAMI 2020 conference.

We strongly believe that the MONAMI conference provides a good forum for all researchers, developers, and practitioners to discuss all science and technology aspects that are relevant to mobile networks and management technologies. We also expect that future MONAMI conferences will be as successful and stimulating as indicated by the contributions presented in this volume.

October 2020

Xun Shao
Kui Wu
Tan Hwee Pink
Guoming Tang
Zhen Ling

Organization

Steering Committee

Imrich Chlamtac   University of Trento, Italy

Organizing Committee

General Co-chairs

Xun Shao	Kitami Institute of Technology, Japan
Kui Wu	University of Victoria, Canada
Tan Hwee Pink	Singapore Management University, Singapore

TPC Co-chairs

Seng Loke	Deakin University, Australia
Zhi Liu	Shizuoka University, Japan
Kien Nguyen	Chiba University, Japan

Sponsorship and Exhibit Chairs

Xun Shao	Kitami Institute of Technology, Japan
Xianfu Chen	VTT Technical Research Center, Finland

Local Chairs

Kien Nguyen	Chiba University, Japan
Keping Yu	Waseda University, Japan

Workshops Chair

Zhen Ling   Southeast University, China

Publicity and Social Media Chairs

Wei Zhao	Anhui University of Technology, China
Nguyen Huu Thanh	Hanoi University of Science and Technology, Vietnam

Publications Chair

Guoming Tang   Peng Cheng Laboratory, China

Web Chair

Phi Le Nguyen   Hanoi University of Science and Technology, Vietnam

Technical Program Committee

Vojislav Misic	Ryserson University, Canada
Hasegawa Go	Tohoku University, Japan
Hideki Tode	Osaka Prefecture University, Japan
Reza Malekian	Malmo University, Sweden
Jianping Wang	City University of Hong Kong, Hong Kong
Majid Ghaderi	University of Calgary, Canada
Michiharu Takemoto	NTT, Japan
Susumu Takeuchi	NTT, Japan
Ali Saberi	Iranian Researchers Network, Iran
Xiaoyan Yin	Northwest University, China
Zhen Ling	Southeast University, China
Guoming Tang	Peng Cheng Laboratory, China
Hitoshi Asaeda	National Institute of Information and Communications (NICT), Japan
Yuuich Teranishi	National Institute of Information and Communications (NICT), Japan
Yuming Jiang	Norwegian University of Science and Technology, Norway
Niroshinie Fernando	Deakin University, Australia
Heli Zhang	Beijing University of Posts and Telecommunications, China
Alvin Valera	Victoria University of Wellington, New Zealand
Yuki Koizumi	Osaka University, Japan
Israat Haque	Dalhousie University, Canada
Thomas Kunz	Carleton University, Canada
Robin Ram Mohan Doss	Deakin University, Australia
Javier Rubio Loyola	CINVESTAV, Mexico
Alexandre Santos	University of Minho, Portugal
Lucio Studer Ferreira	Lusiada University, Portugal
Yoshiaki Taniguchi	Kindai University, Japan
Tuan Phung Duc	University of Tsukuba, Japan
Junbo Wang	Sun Yat-sen University, China
Bo Gu	Sun Yat-sen University, China
Eum Suyong	Osaka University, Japan
Noriaki Kamiyama	Fukuoka University, Japan
Jinho D. Choi	Deakin University, Australia
Wei Zhao	Anhui University of Technology, China
Yu Gu	Hefei University of Technology, China
Lu Chen	Kyoto Institute of Technology, Japan
Ryohei Banno	Tokyo Institute of Technology, Japan
Wanli Xue	Deakin University, Australia
Ziji Ma	Hunan University, China

Contents

The Application of Artificial Intelligence for Smart City

A Lightweight Deep Learning Algorithm for Identity Recognition

Yanjie Cao[1], Zhiyi Zhou[1], Pengsong Duan[1($\boxtimes$)], Chao Wang[1], and Xianfu Chen[2]

[1] School of Software, Zhengzhou University, Zhengzhou, China
{caoyj,duanps}@zzu.edu.cn, zhou_zhi_yi@163.com, austin423@126.com
[2] VTT Technical Research Centre of Finland, Espoo, Finland
xianfu.chen@vtt.fi

Abstract. The challenges in current WiFi based gait recognition models, such as the limited classification ability, high storage cost, long training time and restricted deployment on hardware platforms, motivate us to propose a lightweight gait recognition system, which is named as B-Net. By reconstructing original data into a frequency energy graph, B-Net extracts the spatial features of different carriers. Moreover, a Balloon mechanism based on the concept of channel information integration is designed to reduce the storage cost, training time and so on. The key benefit of the Balloon mechanism is to realize the compression of model scale and relieve the gradient disappearance to some extent. Experimental results show that B-Net has less parameters and training time and is with higher accuracy and better robustness, compared with the previous gait recognition models.

Keywords: Identity recognition · WiFi · Channel state information · Deep learning

1 Introduction

In recent years, identity recognition has been widely researched [8,10]. Different from the traditional biometrics used for identity recognition, such as fingerprint and iris, gait has attracted extensive attention due to the unique characteristics of long distance, non-contact, and not easy to disguise and so on [3]. Cameras [14], acceleration sensors [19], ground sensors [1] and other devices are used for collecting gait data. Nevertheless, these sensors need to be either highly sensitive and accurately located or worn by the monitored target. In contrast, a device-free approach is often more economical and convenient. However, such an approach may invade people privacy and is often susceptible to illumination. The authors in proposed to use Radio Frequency (RF) technology (such as the Doppler radar). But the dependence on a specialized hardware limits the deployment. On the other hand, WiFi is a promising alternative which utilizes the existing ubiquitous inhouse WiFi signal, frees people from any potable device, as well as avoids the influence of illumination and unnecessary personal

© ICST Institute for Computer Sciences, Social Informatics and Telecommunications Engineering 2020
Published by Springer Nature Switzerland AG 2020. All Rights Reserved
S. W. Loke et al. (Eds.): MONAMI 2020, LNICST 338, pp. 3–18, 2020.
https://doi.org/10.1007/978-3-030-64002-6_1

privacy invasion [4,6]. As a result, researchers begin to focus on WiFi-based identification. Shi et al. conducted a comprehensive analysis on the disturbance characteristics of CSI data based on daily behaviors such as walking and quiescence of human body, and realized the identity recognition function [5,12]. In the WiFi environment, Wang et al. realized user identification function by collecting and analyzing the disturbance effect of gait on CSI data [13]. Zeng et al. proposed an identification method, WiWho, which used multipath elimination and bandpass filtering to remove noise, and extracted gait characteristics from WiFi CSI data for identification, with an accuracy rate of 92% to 80% in a group of 2 to 6 people [17]. In the WiFi-ID method proposed by Zhang et al., disturbance characteristics of the spectrum of WiFi CSI data collected by human gait were utilized to achieve an identification rate of 93% to 77% in the case of 2–6 people [18]. Xin et al. proposed a gait based identification method, FreeSense, which processed the collected CSI data by principal component analysis, discrete wavelet transform and dynamic time normalization, respectively, achieving an identification rate of 94.5% to 88.9% in the case of 2 to 6 people [15]. The above work has achieved certain effects in WiFi based identification research. However, CSI describes the combined effects, caused by scattering, fading, doppler frequency shift and power attenuation, of transmitted signals [11]. Hence, traditional manual feature extraction method requires plenty of data preprocessing, whereas the extracted features are insufficiently effective to improve identification accuracy. Since CSI can characterize multipath propagation at subcarrier level, when behavior occurs, the CSI changes of subcarriers of different antenna pairs are related [2]. Therefore, we uses deep learning to extract spatiotemporal characteristics of CSI data and proposes in this paper a simple but effective gait recognition framework, B-Net, which has the potential of realizing automatic identity recognition. Compared with traditional manual feature extraction methods, B-Net extracts gait characteristics by taking the frequency energy graph as the input, which is converted from the original data. In particular, a Balloon mechanism is designed for autonomous gait feature extraction. We highlight the advantages of a B-Net: first, it gets rid of the tedious and meticulous data preprocessing such as denoising and artificial feature extraction; and second, it implements zeroburden identification, requiring no personal devices.

The main contributions of this paper are summarized as follows.

- We propose that the original CSI data from WiFi signal can be reconstructed and used for individual gait recognition.
- We propose a Balloon mechanism to make the network model of B-Net consume less storage and operation resources.
- We establish a data set based on WiFi signal for gait identification. WiFi devices collect gait data from volunteers of different genders, ages, heights and weights.
- In order to evaluate the performance of B-Net, we conduct extensive experiments under various parameter settings. Experimental results show that the system achieves improved performance. Particularly, the identification

accuracy of the system with a group of 50 people reaches 98.8%, which significantly reduces the number of participants and training time compared with conventional models.

The rest of this paper is organized as follows. In Sect. 2, we detail the B-Net architecture and analyze the CSI characteristics. We present the experimental results and discuss the open problems in Sect. 3. We finally draw conclusions in Sect. 4.

2 B-Net Architecture

In this section, we first overview the B-Net and then introduce the main modules.

2.1 Overview of B-Net

The structure-Net architecture is shown in Fig. 1, including data processing module, Deep feature extraction module and classification module. Data acquisition module: the system sets up a WiFi monitoring environment with a single emitter and a single receiver, which continuously collect the CSI data from different volunteers walking in the area. Data preprocessing module: it is responsible for preprocessing the obtained original CSI data by converting the data into frequency energy diagram, which is applicable to the convolutional layer. Balloon block: as the core algorithm of B-Net, the Balloon block derives the relation model of identity and CSI amplitude fluctuation through a compressed model with a small number of parameters, and extracts effective features from the preprocessed data. Classification module: according to different frequency energy graphs corresponding to different volunteers, the neural network is trained.

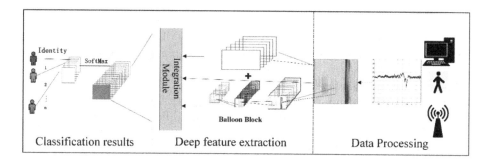

Fig. 1. Overview of B-Net.

2.2 Data Analysis Aonnd Representati

We assume that $X(f,t)$ and $Y(f,t)$ are, respectively, the frequency domain representations of transmitting and receiving signals at the WiFi carrier frequency f, that is,

$$Y(f,t) = H(f,t)X(f,t) \tag{1}$$

where

$$H(f,t) = \sum a_n e^{-j2\pi f\tau_n} + \sum a_m(t)\xi(f)e^{-j2\pi f\tau_m(t)} \tag{2}$$

with f being the carrier Frequency and $H(f,t)$ being the Channel Frequency Response (CFR) of the carrier. Due to the multipath effect, CFR can be represented as in Eq. 2, where $\sum a_n e^{-j2\pi f\tau_n}$ is the channel frequency response under static environment and $\sum a_m(t)\xi(f)e^{-j2\pi f\tau_m(t)}$ is the dynamic CFR value changing with time t. The CSI value of the kth subcarrier is expressed by $H(f_k)$,

$$H(f_k) = \| H(f_k) \| e^{j\angle H(f_k)}, k \in [1,k] \tag{3}$$

where the amplitude and phase of the subcarrier are $\|H(f_k)\|$ and $\angle H(f_k)$, respectively. When collecting the CSI on subcarriers in WiFi signal, each CSI is a complex matrix of size $c*r*n$, where a fixed constant c represents the number of space streams, and r is the number of antennas on commercial routers. In this paper, the CFR value of a given antenna pair and a given OFDM subcarrier is called CSI stream, and hence there are $c*r*n$ CSI streams in the time series of CSI.

Current gait recognition studies usually organize CSI data into one-dimensional time series. The problem is that information in different subcarriers is redundant. Thus an optimal subcarrier selection algorithm is proposed in this paper to screen subcarrier signals with the best quality. Principal Component Analysis (PCA) is also applied to reduce the dimension of CSI data. The effects from different actions on signals are different, and the characteristics exhibit in not only the time dimension, but also the frequency dimension. Therefore, difference among the subcarriers is also one of the important features for action recognition.

Figure 2 shows the influence of the same walking individual on different subcarriers. From experiments, it can be found that sensitivities of the first subcarrier, the 15th subcarrier and the 30th subcarrier are different. This phenomenon also exists in other subcarriers. The reason is that a subcarrier is sensitive to the movements of a particular part of the body, for example the arm or the leg, depending on whether the subcarrier wavelength and action size are comparable. Therefore, it is possible that different subcarriers contain different information when the same behavior occurs. As shown in Fig. 3, the energy distribution of subcarriers with different frequencies is evenly distributed during transmission, and the received energy distribution of each subcarrier varies significantly due to channel gain. Observing the similar distribution of different frequency of different pixel values in image, we propose a multidimensional CSI data organization method, namely, the frequency energy graph, in which the length of time and the number of subcarriers are taken as length and width. Since the CSI received by different antennas to some extent reflects spatial position of the individual entering line-of-sight path, the number of receiving antennas is also taken as a dimension of frequency energy graph, which corresponds to color channel dimension of the ordinary RGB picture. After preprocessing original data at the receiving end, the corresponding frequency energy graph is constructed, whose format is similar to a RGB image.

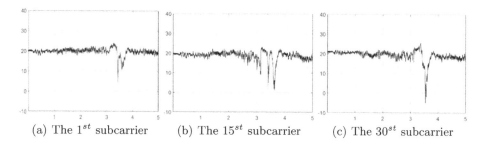

(a) The 1st subcarrier   (b) The 15st subcarrier   (c) The 30st subcarrier

Fig. 2. Sensitivities of different subcarriers to the same action.

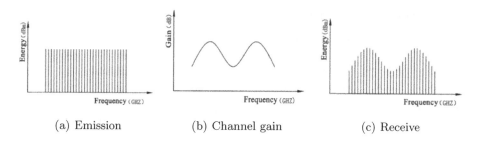

(a) Emission   (b) Channel gain   (c) Receive

Fig. 3. Influence of wireless channel on subcarrier energy distribution.

Figure 4 shows the corresponding frequency energy graphs of CSI signals of volunteer A and volunteer B randomly selected from the data set in three different test cycles. By comparing the frequency energy diagram, it can be found that gait of the detected people shows unique individual characteristics on the frequency energy diagram. As can be seen from Fig. 4, there is a visible similarity between the three frequency energy graphs corresponding to the gait of one volunteer, whereas the frequency energy graphs corresponding to the gait of volunteer A and volunteer B have obvious discernibility. Compared with traditional data organization method, frequency energy graph contains both the time relationship on a single subcarrier and the interrelationship between different subcarriers. The first row are three groups of data randomly selected from volunteer A data set, while the second row are three groups of data randomly selected from volunteer B data set.

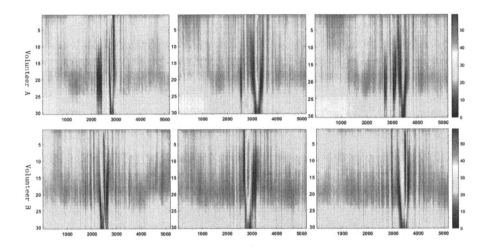

Fig. 4. The frequency energy diagram corresponding to different gait.

2.3   Network Architecture

Considering the timeliness and complexity of frequency energy graph obtained after processing the gait data, we propose a deep neural network model with a Balloon module. The function of each module is discussed as follows:

B-Net model combines one-dimensional convolutional kernel and three-dimensional convolutional kernel to realize feature extraction and channel information integration of data flow in the network. As being commonly known, increasing convolution kernel size increases the computation amount of the convolution operation. The larger the convolution kernel at the same sliding step, the higher the computation. From experiments, it is found that a larger convolution kernel receptive field size can be obtained by multiple small convolution kernel stacks. Using a small convolution kernel can obtain more abundant features than using a large convolution kernel, and make the decision function more discriminative. In addition, a three-dimensional convolution kernel is sufficient to capture the feature changes. The superposition of multilayer small convolutional kernel is equivalent to a single large convolutional kernel. However, with a deeper network, extra nonlinear ReLU function and diversity of features make the network larger in capacity and stronger in classification ability. The use of a large convolution kernel should be avoided from the perspective of model compression. How to use fewer parameters to get a deeper network is the objective of this paper. Overall, the model designed in this paper adopts the combination of a three-dimensional convolution kernel and a one-dimensional convolution kernel to process the data. Note that the three-dimensional convolution kernel is mainly used to extract the features in frequency energy graph. The one-dimensional convolution kernel is shown in Fig. 5, where W and H are the length and width of the feature graph, and D is the number of feature graphs and channels. Although there is only one parameter, when this parameter is applied to a multichannel characteristic graph, it is equivalent to a linear combination of different channels. One-dimensional convolution learns the relationship between feature graphs and has the effect of decoupling, which reduces the number of parameters without compromising the model expressiveness.

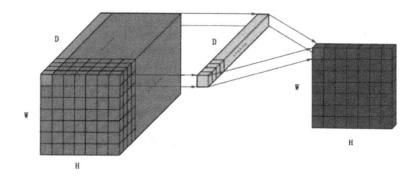

Fig. 5. One-dimensional convolution kernel diagram.

The one-dimensional convolution kernel is shown in Fig. 5, where W and H are the length and width of the feature graph, and D is the number of feature graphs and channels. Although there is only one parameter, when this parameter is applied to a multichannel characteristic graph, it is equivalent to a linear combination of different channels. One-dimensional convolution learns the relationship between feature graphs and has the effect of decoupling, which reduces the number of parameters without compromising the model expressiveness.

Nowadays, increasing the number of layers to improve accuracy has become the mainstream. However, in model training process, the number and size of convolution cores in the convolutional layer directly determine computational parameters of the layer and the amount of data input to the next layer. Blind stacking of network layers will result in an explosive increase in the computational amount. The primary goal of this paper is to build a CNN architecture with a simple structure, fewer parameters and comparable accuracy. In view of the above objectives, we design the Balloon mechanism. Figure 6 is a schematic diagram of Balloon mechanism. Among them, the review channel is inspired by the fact that human beings need to carry out visual input to the original graphics for many times when learning the knowledge of graphics, and a mechanism to simulate human beings' review behavior is designed. After the channel dimension of the original frequency domain, energy graph is increased by a one-dimensional convolution kernel, feature fusion is carried out with the output feature graph of each layer. The fusion model can still achieve high classification accuracy on the basis of a small number of neurons. At the same time, because the feature map of each layer is added with the part of identity mapping, connection matrix degradation caused by layer deepening is reduced. After fusion, the feature map will complete crosschannel interaction and information integration through one-dimensional convolution kernel, so that the feature map can retrieve the original information from frequency energy map and reduce the dimension of feature map input to the next layer. Through review channel, each layer of convolutional network can access "low-level" features from the original data, so that the model can still guarantee good learning ability in the case of few convolutional cores. Classical convolutional neural networks usually increase the maximum pooling layer after convolutional layer to carry out downsampling, which is used to reduce the number of parameters and prevent model from overfitting. However, the characteristic density of frequency energy diagram in this paper is large, hence the classification accuracy is reduced by a pooling operation. Therefore, B-Net does not include a pool layer, but a regularization layer is added to fix the input of each neuron on the same distribution. Regularization layer speeds up the model training and uses a larger learning rate to train the network, hence reducing network retraining time. Finally, considering that the introduction of nonlinear factors can make the model more expressive, the linear rectifier function Relu is employed for activation.

2.4   Classification

B-Net aims to create a model that divides the gait type hypothesis into Y $(1, 2 \ldots, k)$ kinds to predict the possible identity based on the input frequency energy diagram x. The purpose of B-Net model is to solve a multiclassification problem, so it is more appropriate to use the Softmax function, which maps the inputs to real numbers between 0 and 1, and normalizes the guaranteed sum to 1. The probability of each output category $\tilde{y}_i$ is calculated as

$$\tilde{y}_i = P(y|X) = \frac{\exp(z_y)}{\sum_{y=1}^{k} \exp(z_y)} y \in [1, k] \tag{4}$$

where z_y is the result of global pooling on the output. Global pooling operation can not only make the transformation between extracted feature map and final classification result more simple and natural, but also eliminate the need for a large number of training parameters, thus improving robustness and antioverfitting ability of the model. After obtaining $\tilde{y}_i$, Adam optimizer is used to minimize cross entropy loss between the predicted probability and the real one, which is given by

$$L = -\sum y_i \log(\tilde{y}_i) \tag{5}$$

3   Experiments and Evaluations

In this section, we use real gait data to verify the accuracy of the proposed lightweight neural network model through experiments.

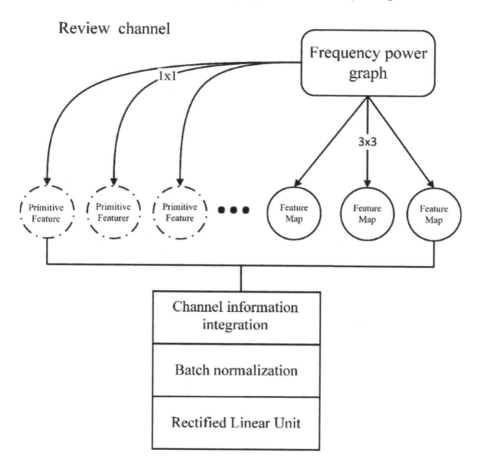

Fig. 6. Schematic diagram of Balloon mechanism.

3.1 Dataset Descriptions

In order to validate the performance from the model under different structures, we chose a relatively empty laboratory as shown in Fig. 7 for the experiments of multiperson gait recognition. Gait CSI data of 50 volunteers were collected as the training set and also as the test set. The volunteers, consisting of both male and female, ranged in ages from 18 to 30, ensuring the data diversity. During the data collection, each volunteer walked back and forth along the line-of-sight path between the vertical transmitter and the receiver for 5 s, and repeated the walking 80 times.

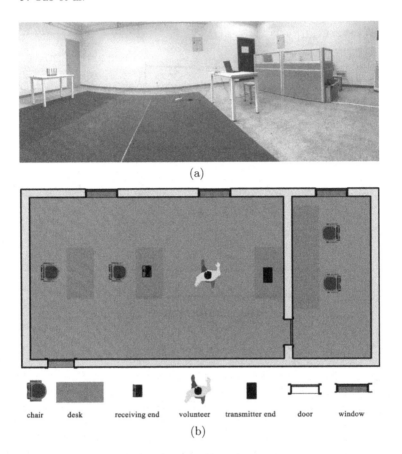

Fig. 7. Data acquisition environment.

3.2 Experiment Setup

In experiments, we used a TP_LINK AC1750 wireless router as the transmitter
and a ThinkPad X201 portable computer terminal as the receiver. ThinkPad
X201 is equipped with Intel 5300 802.11n WiFi NIC network card for receiving CSI data. The transmitter and receiver have 1 and 3 detectable antennas,
respectively, forming 3 (1×3) CSI data streams. Each CSI data stream consists
of 30 subcarriers, which are modulated by OFDM. Therefore, 90 $(1 \times 3 \times 30)$ CSI
data streams were collected. In this paper, we carried out all experiments at the
5 GHz frequency to ensure data integrity and accuracy, and the sampling rate of
CSI packets at the receiver was set to 1000 packets per second. The size of the
sliding window was selected as $T = 600$ ms and the size of the sliding step was
set as $d = 200$ to construct data samples and generate different frequency energy
graphs. The overlap between the sliding window and the step size can ensure
the continuity of data segmentation and help extracting feature information.

3.3 Key Performance Indicators

The multiperson gait recognition by the proposed B-Net system was evaluated by the accuracy, recall, precision and F_1 score. Specifically,

- Accuracy: the proportion of all correct predictions in the total number of predictions, which is given as

$$Accuracy = \frac{TP + TN}{TP + TN + FN + TN} \tag{6}$$

- Precision: the proportion of positive value of correct prediction to the total positive value of prediction, which defined by

$$Precision = \frac{TP}{TP + FN} \tag{7}$$

- Recall rate: the proportion of predicted positive value to the total actual positive value given as

$$Recall = \frac{TP}{TP + FP} \tag{8}$$

- F_1 score: the evaluation index of comprehensive recall rate and precision, which is used to comprehensively reflect the whole index,

$$F_1 = \frac{2TP}{2TP + FP + FN} \tag{9}$$

In above, TP (True Positive) represents the number of samples that are classified to be positive and actually positive ones, FP (False Positive) represents the number of samples that are classified to be positive but actually negative ones, FN (False Negative) represents the number of samples that are classified to be negative but actually positive ones, and TN (True Negative) represents the number of samples that are classified to be negative and actually negative ones.

3.4 Experimental Results

In order to explore the influence of different review channels on the experimental results, we designed two different review channels, namely, a Source link channel and a Fully link channel. A Source link channel represents that each network layer containing a Balloon mechanism accepts only the frequency energy graph raised by a one-dimensional convolution kernel. A Fully link channel represents that the nth network layer containing Balloon mechanism accepts n−1 feature graphs raised by a one-dimensional convolution kernel. As shown in Fig. 8, the walking data sets of 50 volunteers were used to train the neural networks with a Source link channel structure and a Fully link channel structure.

In Fig. 8, the horizontal axis represents the change in the number of network layers, while the vertical axis represents accuracy of the model in identifying data set. Meanwhile, the size of the model is marked at each marker in the figure. It can be seen from the figure that both the Source link channel and the Fully link channel can maintain small model size. Moreover, with the increase of network layers, the accuracy of the Fully link channel case is better than that of the Source link channel case, but with a higher increasing rate. The purpose of this paper is to build a lightweight network. In other experiments, we used a Source link channel network.

Each layer of the Balloon mechanism in B-Net neural network carried out a crosschannel information integration processing after fusing the feature graph and reviewing the channel information. Information integration across channels is a kind of data dimensionality reduction in nature and has a certain decoupling function. At the same time, information integration processing can greatly reduce the number of training parameters, and hence an integration channel is the key to a lightweight model. To verify the effects of channel compression on model size and accuracy, we took a 3-layer Balloon network as an example, and the number of neurons in each layer of convolutional operation was set to 32, 64 and 128.

Table 1. Comparisons of experimental results of different compression channels.

Compression channel number	Model parameter number	Model size	Accuracy	Rate/model size
8/16/32	42260	0.6M	95	1.58
16/32/64	54154	0.748M	98	1.31
32/16/8	99298	1.3M	96.7	0.743
16/16/16	51522	0.71M	96.6	1.36
32/32/32	141282	1.8M	98	0.54
64/64/64	274562	3.4M	97.9	0.28

As shown in Table 1, channel compression number represents the number of feature graphs of the three-layer network after compression. This experiment compared the network with different compression degree and accuracy. The ratio of accuracy to model size is used as the key performance indicator for evaluating the model efficiency. It can be seen that each layer, as shown in the first and second rows of Table 1, got better results as the number of channels increased. The number of parameters of the model in the third row was much larger than that in the second row, but achieved lower accuracy. The reason behind is that the feature levels extracted by the convolution operation of each layer are different. The shallow convolution operation extracts "low-level" features of the data, which loses less information after dimensionality reduction. Deep convolution extracts more special and complex features, and dimension reduction of these features destroys the feature structure and causes the information loss. Results in Rows 4 to 6 show that the increase of parameters and model accuracy

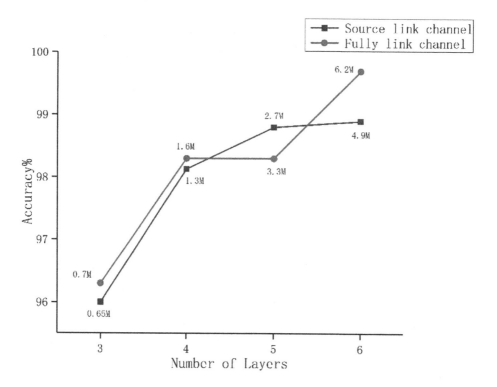

Fig. 8. Comparison of different channel structures.

consumed a large amount of storage space, and accuracy degrades when the number of parameters increased to a certain extent.

This experiment tells that the accuracy of the model relates to the parameter number. Increasing the number of parameters to improve model accuracy results in the storage consumption. Layer by layer compression using the Balloon mechanism saves model storage space while ensuring the accuracy. In addition to the comparison with other models, the experiment of gait data set of 50 people was taken as an example in the hall environment, using a GRU cyclic neural network [7], a full convolutional neural network FCN [9], a WiID model [16] and a Source link channel B-Net containing five layers of Balloon layer. In the experiment, GRU contained two GRU layers, FCN was composed of three convolutional layers, and the setting of WiID followed. All the above models showed good ability in the identification of 10 15 people from the data set. As can be seen from Fig. 9, the recognition accuracy, precision, recall rate and F1 score of GRU and WiID models all decreased significantly as the number of identification increased to 50. Although the evaluation criteria of FCN model are less attenuated, it can be seen that the model size is much larger than B-Net. Table 2 illustrates that B-Net can extract gait characteristics contained in CSI information more completely and accurately by using a frequency energy graph and a Balloon mechanism, and consumes less storage resources. Its recognition performance was the best among the four, reaching 98.8% in accuracy, and the best in the comparison experiment of gait recognition based on Wi-Fi sensing.

Table 2. Experimental results of different models with 50 samples.

Model	Accuracy%	Recall rate%	Precision%	F_1 score	Model size
GRU	75.7	75.6	76	0.758	3.12M
WilD	65.6	65.4	66.0	0.657	2.2M
FCN	93.0	93.2	94.1	0.936	14M
B-Net	98.8	98.8	98.9	0.988	2.7M

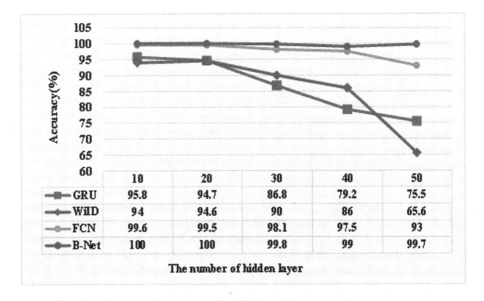

Fig. 9. Comparison of different models.

4   Conclusion

We propose a simple and efficient neural network model, named as B-Net, which can be used to identify WiFi signals from different individuals. Facing the challenges of long training time, large computation and poor performance of traditional deep neural networks, we design a compact neural network to identify CSI of different individuals. The proposed model can not only simplify the training complexity but also ensure good training performance. Compared with the state-of-the-art deep learning methods for gait recognition, the proposed approach has higher recognition rate and operational efficiency. Additionally, B-Net gets rid of the dependence of hand-coded features and realizes end-to-end identity recognition. Further work will be based on B-Net and combine the idea of migration learning to investigate a generalized model for different indoor environments.

References

1. Al-Naimi, I., Wong, C., Moore, P., Chen, X.: Multimodal approach for non-tagged indoor identification and tracking using smart floor and pyroelectric infrared sensors. Int. J. Comput. Sci. Eng. **14**(1), 1–15 (2017)
2. Ali, K., Liu, A.X., Wang, W., Shahzad, M.: Keystroke recognition using WiFi signals. In: The 21st Annual International Conference on Mobile Computing and Networking, pp. 90–102 (2015)
3. Connor, P., Ross, A.: Biometric recognition by gait: a survey of modalities and features. Comput. Vis. Image Underst. **167**, 1–27 (2018)
4. Gu, Y., et al.: EmoSense: computational intelligence driven emotion sensing via wireless channel data. IEEE Trans. Emerg. Top. Comput. Intell. **4**(3), 216–226 (2019)
5. Gu, Y., Wang, Y., Liu, Z., Liu, J., Li, J.: SleepGuardian: an RF based healthcare system guarding your sleep from afar. IEEE Netw. **34**(2), 164–171 (2019)
6. Gu, Y., Zhang, X., Liu, Z., Ren, F.: BeSense: leveraging WiFi channel data and computational intelligence for behavior analysis. IEEE Comput. Intell. Mag. **14**(4), 31–41 (2019)
7. Kyunghyun, C., et al.: Learning phrase representations using RNN encoder-decoder for statistical machine translation. arXiv:1406.1078 (2014)
8. Lin, N., et al.: Contactless body movement recognition during sleeping via WiFi signal. IEEE Internet Things **7**(3), 2028–2037 (2019)
9. Long, J., Shelhamer, E., Darrell, T.: Fully convolutional networks for semantic segmentation. In: IEEE Conference on Computer Vision and Pattern Recognition (CVPR) (2015)
10. Mastali, N., Agbinya, J.I.: Authentication of subjects and devices using biometrics and identity management systems for persuasive mobile computing: a survey paper. In: 2010 Fifth International Conference on Broadband and Biomedical Communications (IB2Com) (2010)
11. Ohara, K., Maekawa, T., Matsushita, Y.: Detecting state changes of indoor everyday objects using Wi-Fi channel state information. Proc. ACM Interact. Mob. Wearable Ubiquit. Technol. **1**(3), 1–28 (2017)
12. Shi, C., Liu, J., Liu, H., Chen, Y.: Smart user authentication through actuation of daily activities leveraging WiFi-enabled IoT. In: The 18th ACM International Symposium, pp. 1–10 (2017)
13. Wang, W., Liu, A.X., Shahzad, M.: Gait recognition using WiFi signals. In: ACM International Joint Conference Pervasive Ubiquitous Computing, pp. 363–373 (2016)
14. Wu, Z., Huang, Y., Wang, L., Wang, X., Tan, T.: A comprehensive study on cross-view gait based human identification with deep CNNs. IEEE Trans. Pattern Anal. Mach. Intell. **39**(2), 209–226 (2017)
15. Xin, T., Guo, B., Wang, Z., Li, M., Yu, Z., Zhou, X.: Freesense: indoor human identification with WiFi signals. In: IEEE Global Communications Conference (GLOBECOM), pp. 1–7 (2016)

16. Yu, X., Chen, W., Wand, D.: A deep learning algorithm for contactless human identification. J. Xi'an Jiaotong Univ. **53**(04), 128–133 (2019)
17. Zeng, Y., Pathak, P.H., Mohapatra, P.: WiWho: WiFi-based person identification in smart spaces. In: 15th ACM/IEEE International Conference on Information Processing in Sensor Networks (IPSN), pp. 1–12 (2016)
18. Zhang, J., Wei, B., Hu, W., Kanhere, S.S.: WiFi-ID: human identification using WiFi signal. In: 2016 International Conference on Distributed Computing in Sensor Systems (DCOSS), pp. 75–82 (2016)
19. Zhang, Y., Pan, G., Jia, K., Lu, M., Wang, Y., Wu, Z.: Accelerometer-based gait recognition by sparse representation of signature points with clusters. IEEE Trans. Cybern. **45**(9), 1864–1875 (2015)

A Novel Neural Network Model for Demand Prediction of Bike-Sharing

Fan Wu[1]([✉]), Si Hong[1], Wei Zhao[2], Xiao Zheng[2], Xun Shao[3], and Wen Qiu[3]

[1] School of Management Science and Engineering,
Anhui University of Technology, Ma'anshan 243032, China
dragonwufan@126.com
[2] School of Computer Science and Technology,
Anhui University of Technology, Ma'anshan 243032, China
[3] School of Regional Innovation and Social Design Engineering,
Kitami Institute of Technology, Kitami 090-8507, Japan

Abstract. Accurate demand prediction of bike-sharing is a prerequisite to reduce the cost of scheduling and improve the users' satisfaction. However, it is very difficult to make the prediction absolutely accurate due to the stochasticity and nonlinearity in the bike-sharing system. In this paper, a model called pseudo-double hidden layer feedforward neural network is proposed to approximatively predict the practical demand of bike-sharing. In this neural network, an algorithm called improved particle swarm optimization in extreme learning machine is proposed to define its learning rule. On the basis of fully mining the massive operational data of "Shedd Aquarium" bike-sharing station in Chicago (USA), the demand of this station is predicted by the model proposed in this paper.

Keywords: Demand prediction · Bike-sharing · Pseudo-double hidden layer feedforward neural network · Extreme learning machine · Improved particle swarm optimization

1 Introduction

With the development of sharing economy, bike-sharing systems have rapidly emerged in major cities all over the world. Bike-sharing can be described as a short-term bicycle rental service for inner-city transportation providing bikes at unattended stations. It has become one of the most important low-carbon travel ways. Compared with traditional rental service, bike-sharing won't be limited by the boxes at bike-stations. It provides more convenient service, but generates more complicated problems. For instance, the layout of bike-sharing stations is more flexible and the capacities of stations will no longer be fixed, leading to big fluctuant demands for the stations. Some new characteristics are exhibited, such as the uneven distribution of users' demand in time and space. It makes the prediction of bike-sharing more complicated.

© ICST Institute for Computer Sciences, Social Informatics and Telecommunications Engineering 2020
Published by Springer Nature Switzerland AG 2020. All Rights Reserved
S. W. Loke et al. (Eds.): MONAMI 2020, LNICST 338, pp. 19–29, 2020.
https://doi.org/10.1007/978-3-030-64002-6_2

Accurate demand prediction of bike-sharing can effectively improve user experience and enhance brand's competence, which was elaborated in Xu et al. (2019). Several interesting factors affecting demand have been studied. We refer to El-Assi et al. (2017) and Ermagun et al. (2018) for a survey on the main problem and methods arising in bike-sharing systems. The key is to have an effective forecasting method. The existing demand prediction methods can be mainly divided into two types. The traditional one is based on statistical analysis. ZH et al. (2019) used a statistical physics method to define demand fluctuation and established different bike-sharing systems in different periods. Based on the ordinary least square, geographically weighted regression (GWR) and semi-parametric geographically weighted regression methods, Yang et al. (2019) proposed a methodology to estimate a shared-bike trip using location-based social network data and conducted a case study in Nanjing, China. Negahban (2019) proposed a novel methodology combining simulation, bootstrapping, and subset selection that harnessed useful partial information in every bike drop-off observation (even if it is subject to censoring). It estimated true demands in situations where data cleaning approaches commonly used in the bike-sharing literature failed due to lack of valid data. Cheng et al. (2019) devised a trip advisor that recommended bike check-in and check-out stations with joint consideration of service quality and bicycle utilization. Then, it predicted user demands of each station to obtain the success rate of rental and return in future. The other is based on artificial neural networks. Among these literatures, we mention Yang et al. (2018) and Yi et al. (2019) which proposed a deep learning approach using convolutional neural networks to predict the daily bicycle pickups at both city and station levels. Lin et al. (2018) proposed a novel graph convolutional neural network with data-driven graph filter (GCNN-DDGF) model. It can learn hidden heterogeneous pairwise correlations between stations to predict station-level hourly demands in a large-scale bike-sharing network. Xu et al. (2018) developed a dynamic demand forecasting model for bike-sharing by deep learning. The comparison results suggested that the LSTM NNs provide better prediction accuracy than both conventional statistical models and advanced machine learning methods for different time intervals. Chang et al. (2019) developed a novel prediction framework integrating AIS and artificial neural network forecasting techniques. The prediction performance is verified compared with other models. Feng et al. (2017) studied the Markov chain population model to predict bicycles demands among different travel stations and verified their effectiveness. Kim (2018) studied the influence of weather conditions and time characteristics on demands for bike-sharing. Furthermore, deep learning and its combination with a variety of new heuristic algorithms have been applied in various engineering practices (Benkedjouh et al. 2015; Wu et al. 2018; Cao et al. 2018; Hu et al. 2020), but rarely applied in demand prediction of bike-sharing.

In addition, those methods have some limitations as follows.

(1) In order to improve the accuracy of prediction by means of deep learning, most works mainly achieved their goals by adding the number of hidden layers. It means to increase the structure complexity of neural network, which would exponentially increase the running time of the method and amplify signal noise in data.

(2) Current researches on deep learning pay too much attention to the accuracy and convergence rate of learning targets by some methods, such as early stopping, adding noise to gradient (e.g. adjusting batch size and learning rate) or constantly adding

new regulators to train targets for improving the generalization of the samples. It is worth mentioning that accelerating gradient descent sometimes leads to worse generalization.

Considering these limitations, a novel neural network model for demand prediction of bike-sharing is proposed, which is called pseudo-double hidden layer feedforward neural network. In this model, an algorithm called improved particle swarm optimization in extreme learning machine is proposed to optimize initial weights and bias of the neural network and improve the prediction accuracy of this model.

2 Pseudo-double Hidden Layer Feedforward Neural Network

2.1 Network Structure

Generally speaking, pseudo-double hidden layer feedforward neural network (PDLFN) is a biologically inspired computational model, which consists of processing elements (called neurons) and connections between them with coefficients. The structure of PDLFN is different from the single hidden layer feedforward neural network (SLFN) and the double hidden layer feedforward neural network (DLFN). As shown in Fig. 1, it includes one input layer, "two" hidden layers and one output layer. The hidden layers consist of V layer and B layer. Compared with SLFN and DLFN, V layer is a special hidden layer. By means of V layer, PDLFN can directly process original data (e.g. multivariate time series) to produce the final results.

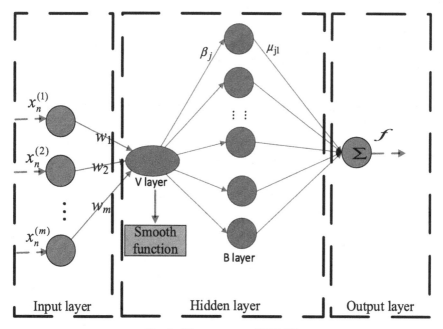

Fig. 1. The structure of PDLFN

Compared with DLFN, the special neuron of V layer in PDLFN is no longer with a bias value and an activation function in traditional sense, but with a smooth function. The smooth process referred to as V layer smooth is defined as follows. Assume that there are N samples. The n-th ($1 \leq n \leq N$) sample is denoted as $X_n = (x_n^{(1)}, x_n^{(2)}, \ldots, x_n^{(m)})^{\mathrm{T}}$, where $x_n^{(i)}$ denotes the i-th component of X_n, corresponding to the i-th neuron in the input layer ($1 \leq i \leq m$). The weight of the input layer to V layer is denoted as $W_i = (w_1, w_2, \ldots, w_m)^{\mathrm{T}}$. V layer smoothing is denoted as $f_V(X_n)$.

$$f_V(X_n) = X_n' = \frac{\sum\limits_{i=1}^{m} w_i \bullet x_n^{(i)}}{\sum\limits_{i=1}^{m} w_i} \tag{1}$$

Except V layer, the other parts of PDLFN are similar to the SLFN. With the gradient descent method, the weights and biases are dynamically modified to achieve the expected learning effect.

The traditional BP learning algorithm has some limitations. For example, the network structure can't be determined easily, and the learning speed is too slow. To overcome these limitations, Huang (2015) proposed an improved learning algorithm called extreme learning machine (ELM). With ELM, we only need to determine the number of neurons in the hidden layers without considering the structure.

The outputs of PDLFN can be represented as follows.

$$f_{J\_out}(X_n) = \sum_{j=1}^{J} \mu_j \cdot T(f_V(X_n) \cdot \beta_j + B_j) \tag{2}$$

In this formula, β_j is the j-th ($1 \leq j \leq J$) input weight of neurons between V layer and B layer. B_j is the bias value of the j-th neuron in B layer. μ_j is the output weight of the j-th neuron in B layer. $T(x)$ is the excitation function, which can be set as "Sig", "Sin" or "Hardlim", etc. In this paper, the excitation function is uniformly set as "tansig". It means the excitation function is a hyperbolic tangent function in the "Sig" functions. The formula is shown in Eq. (3).

$$T(x) = \frac{2}{1 + e^{-x}} - 1 \qquad (-1 < T(x) < 1) \tag{3}$$

2.2 Learning Rule

Improved particle swarm optimization in ELM (IPSO-ELM) is adopted for learning mechanism of pseudo-double hidden layer feedforward neural networks. The influence of initial random bias and weight on prediction accuracy is reduced by improving particle swarm method to optimize the initial threshold and weight of extreme learning machine.

2.2.1 Improved Particle Swarm Optimization

Particle swarm optimization is a swarm intelligence algorithm that simulates the regularity of a bird population. It is based on the concepts of population and evolution, through the cooperation and competition among individuals. And the search for the optimal solution of complex space is realized. Suppose that in a dimensional search space D, the total number of particles is N, where the i-th particle is represented as a D dimensional vector $X_i = (x_{i1}, x_{i2}, \ldots, x_{iD}), i = 1, 2, \ldots, N$. The velocity of the i-th particle is also a D-dimension vector $Vi = (v_{i1}, v_{i2}, \ldots, v_{iD}), i = 1, 2, \ldots, N$. The individual extremum searched before the i-th particle is $Pbest = (p_{i1}, p_{i2}, \ldots, p_{iD}), i = 1, 2, \ldots, N$. And the global extreme value of particle swarm is $gbest = (g_1, g_2, \ldots, g_D)$.

In standard PSO, particles update their velocity and position according to the following formulas:

$$v_{ij}(t+1) = w * v_{ij}(t) + c_1 * r_1(t)[p_{ij}(t) - x_{ij}(t)] + c_2 * r_2(t)[p_{gj}(t) - x_{ij}(t)] \quad (4)$$

$$x_{ij}(t+1) = x_{ij}(t) + v_{ij}(t+1) \quad (5)$$

where c_1 and c_2 are learning factors, r_1 and r_2 uniform random numbers within the range of [0, 1]. The first part in formula (4) represents the velocity before the particle, which ensures the global convergence of the algorithm. The second and third parts make the algorithm have local convergence ability. It can be seen that inertia weight w represents inheritance degree of the original velocity. The global convergence ability increases with w. Therefore, in this paper, a compression factor combined with a dynamic inertia weight updating speed and weight is adopted to ensure that the algorithm has strong global search ability in an early stage. This can guarantee local fine search ability in the later stage, and achieve fast convergence. Its formula is shown as follows:

$$v_{ij}(t+1) = \left(w_{max} - \frac{(w_{max} - w_{min}) * t}{T_{max}} \right) * v_{ij}(t)$$
$$+ c_1 r_1(t)[p_{ij}(t) - x_{ij}(t)] + c_2 r_2(t)[p_{gi}(t) - x_{ij}(t)],$$
$$t < \frac{2T_{max}}{3} \quad (6\text{-}1)$$

$$v_{ij}(t) = \lambda * v_{ij}(t) + c_1 r_1(t)[p_{ij}(t) - x_{ij}(t)]$$
$$+ \ c_2 r_2(t)[p_{gi}(t) - x_{ij}(t)],$$
$$\frac{2T_{\max}}{3} \leq t \leq T_{\max} \tag{6-2}$$

where λ is the compression factor

$$\lambda = \frac{2}{\left|2 - \beta - \sqrt{\beta(\beta - 4)}\right|} \ (\beta = c_1 + c_2)$$

$T_{\max}$ denotes the maximum iteration number. t denotes the current iteration number. And $w_{\max}/w_{\min}$ denotes the maximum/minimum inertia weight.

2.2.2 IPSO-ELM Learning Process

The optimized flow chart of the improved particle swarm optimization algorithm for the extreme learning machine is shown in Fig. 2.

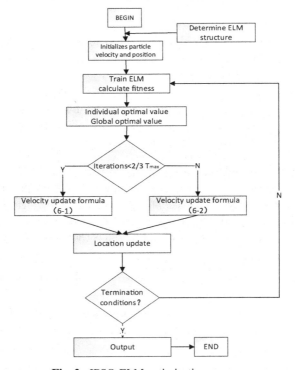

Fig. 2. IPSO-ELM optimization process

The pseudocode is as follows:

Step 1 : BEGIN

Step 2 : Initializing particle x= rand()、v =rand(); Tmax; times_iter;

Step 3 : Train ELM, fun_value = train_error; Record individual optimum p_best、global optimal g_best;

Step 4 : While fun_value> = 0.001

        if times_iter < 2/3*Tmax

            v = formula（5-1）;

        elseif times_iter <= Tmax

            v= formula（5-2）;

            Update particle state；

            times_iter += 1;

            return to Step 3;

        else

            turn to Step 5;

Step 5 :Print g_best;fun_value;

Step 6 : END

---

3 Demand Prediction Model of Bike-Sharing

3.1 Prediction Period

In the bike-sharing system, its self-regulating ability has often met the demand for renting during peak time. In the scheduling problem, the user behavior during a peak period is one of main factors affecting the scheduling scheme. Thus, we discuss the demand prediction during a peak time as our scenario.

3.2 The Prediction Model

The demand prediction model of bike-sharing based on pseudo-double hidden layer feedforward neural network is given in Fig. 3.

3.3 Evaluation Criterion

In order to test the effectiveness of the pseudo-double hidden layer neural network combined with the improved PSO-ELM prediction model, the following error analysis method is selected in this paper, mean squared error (*MSE*). The formula is shown below.

$$MSE = \frac{1}{n} \sum_{i=1}^{n} (Z_i - A_i)^2 \tag{7}$$

where A_i represents the final predicted value. Z_i is the measured value.

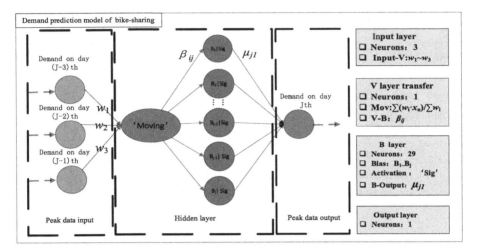

Fig. 3. Demand prediction model of bike-sharing based on PDLFN

4   Empirical Analysis

4.1   Data Collection

The data used in this section is from the official website of Divvy Bike in Chicago, USA. The original data amount is up to 2 million pieces (including 7 data features such as vehicle travel distance, user age, station number, etc.), we select Shedd Aquarium station (station_id = "3") as the study case column. In this paper, a total of 121 samples from April 1, 2018 to June 30, 2018 are selected as the training set. 30 samples from July 2018 are used as prediction sets.

In order to determine the distribution of the peak period in bike-stations, the distribution of bike rent in April is first drawn in Fig. 4.

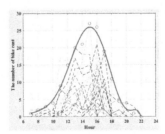

Fig. 4. Rent in April

We can note that the peak period of borrowing bikes is generally distributed from 13 pm to 17 pm, laying a foundation for this paper to select the peak time.

4.2 Prediction Result

In order to verify the performance of the improved particle swarm optimization algorithm, the fitness evolution curves before and after the improvement is shown in Fig. 5 and Fig. 6.

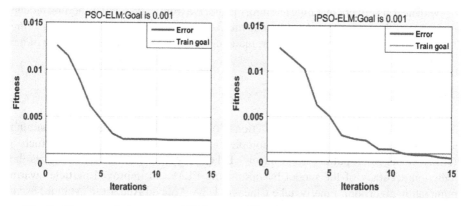

Fig. 5. Fitness evolution curve of PSO   **Fig. 6.** Fitness evolution curve of IPSO

It can be seen that the global search ability of particle swarm is effectively improved by changing particle velocity through compression factor and dynamically adjusting inertia weight. Our particle swarm algorithm is more capable of jumping out of the local optimal solution and finding a better solution in the later stage.

Then, combined with the proposed PDLFN and the improved particle swarm algorithm, a prediction model based on PSO-ELM neural network was established. In this model, the activation function of neurons in B layer is 'Sig', and the TYPE value is 0 (representing fitting). Finally, 29 neurons in B layer are determined by the trial algorithm. The predicted results are shown in Fig. 7.

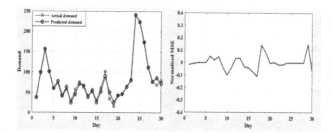

Fig. 7. Pseudo-double hidden layer-IPSO-ELM

In addition, in summarizing the experimental consideration on how to improve the prediction accuracy, it is found that the model proposed in this paper has the following two advantages:

(1) To solve the problem of demand prediction for bike-sharing, the method proposed in this paper to improve the prediction accuracy based on network structure is more effective than that to improve the prediction accuracy based on ELM improved by the optimization algorithm, and the implementation path is simpler and more efficient.

(2) In classification, fitting with time sequence features of large sample data, combined with neural network machine learning method is a frontier way, but by adding hidden layers of the network constantly to achieve the predetermined accuracy, overfitting phenomenon will inevitably occur, reducing the generalization performance of the model.

5 Conclusion

Aiming at the problem of demand prediction of bike-sharing, by referring to the learning method of multiple hidden layers in complex neural networks, the paper constructs a PDLFN model of "input layer - V layer - B layer - output layer", and improves the prediction accuracy of the model by optimizing ELM and improved particle swarm optimization algorithm. Finally, take Chicago, USA ("Shedd Aquarium" station) as an example for analysis, apply Newton interpolation method for processing of individual default values of data. It can be seen from the experimental results that the PDLFN model proposed has high prediction accuracy and good generalization ability. Generally speaking, compared with the existing methods to improve the prediction accuracy of the demand prediction model of bike-sharing, the method proposed in this paper is more concise and efficient, which has certain reference value in the research of demand prediction of bike-sharing.

References

Xu, H., Duan, F., Pu, P.: Dynamic bicycle scheduling problem based on short-term demand prediction. Appl. Intell. **49**(5), 1968–1981 (2019). https://doi.org/10.1007/s10489-018-1360-6

El-Assi, W., Salah Mahmoud, M., Nurul Habib, K.: Effects of built environment and weather on bike sharing demand: a station level analysis of commercial bike sharing in Toronto. Transportation **44**(3), 589–613 (2017). https://doi.org/10.1007/s11116-015-9669-z

Ermagun, A., Lindsey, G., Loh, T.H.: Bicycle, pedestrian, and mixed-mode trail traffic: a performance assessment of demand models. Landscape Urban Plann. **17**, 92–102 (2018)

Yang, F., Ding, F., Qu, X., Ran, B.: Estimating urban shared-bike trips with location-based social networking data. Sustainability **11**, 3220 (2019)

Negahban, A.: Simulation-based estimation of the real demand in bike-sharing systems in the presence of censoring. Eur. J. Oper. Res. **277**(1), 317–332 (2019)

Cheng, P., Hu, J., Yang, Z.D., Shu, Y.C., Chen, J.M.: Utilization-aware trip advisor in bike-sharing systems based on user behavior analysis. IEEE Trans. Knowl. Data Eng. **31**(9), 1822–1835 (2019)

Yang, H., Xie, K., Ozbay, K., Ma, Y., Wang, Z.Y.: Use of deep learing to predict daily usage of bike sharing. Transp. Res. Rec. **2672**(36), 92–102 (2018)

Ai, Y., Li, Z.P., et al.: A deep learning approach on short-term spatiotemporal distribution forecasting of dockless bike-sharing system. Neural Comput. Appl. **31**(5), 1665–1677 (2018). https://doi.org/10.1007/s00521-018-3470-9

Lin, L., He, Z.B., Peeta, S.: Predicting station-level hourly demand in a large-scale bike sharing network: a graph convolutional neural network approach. Transp. Res. Part C Emerg. Technol. **97**, 258–276 (2018)

Xu, C.C., Ji, J.Y., Liu, P.: The station-free sharing bike demand forecasting with a deep learning approach and large-scale datasets. Transp. Res. Part C Emerg. Technol. **95**, 47–60 (2018)

Chang, P.C., Wu, J.L., Xu, Y., et al.: Bike sharing demand prediction using artificial immune system and artificial neural network. Soft. Comput. **23**(2), 613–626 (2017). https://doi.org/10.1007/s00500-017-2909-8

Feng, C., Hillston, J., Reijsbergen, D.: Moment-based availability prediction for bike-sharing systems. Perform. Eval. **117**, 58–74 (2017)

Kim, K.: Investigation on the effects of weather and calendar events on bike sharing according to the trip patterns of bike rentals of station. J. Transport Geogr. **66**, 309–320 (2018)

Benkedjouh, T., Medjaher, K., Zerhouni, N., Rechak, S.: Health assessment and life prediction of cutting tools based on support vector regression. J. Intell. Manuf. **26**(2), 213–223 (2015). https://doi.org/10.1007/s10845-013-0774-6

Wu, Q., Ding, K., Huang, B.: Approach for fault prognosis using recurrent neural network. J. Intell. Manuf. **31**(7), 1621–1633 (2018). https://doi.org/10.1007/s10845-018-1428-5

Hu, H., Liu, Z., An, J.: Mining mobile intelligence for wireless systems: a deep neural network approach. IEEE Comput. Intell. Mag. **15**(1), 24–31 (2020)

Tamura, S., Tateishi, M.: Capabilities of a four-layered feedforward neural network: four layers versus three. IEEE Trans. Neural Netw. **8**(2), 251–255 (1997)

Cao, Y.-J., et al.: Recent advances of generative adversarial networks in computer vision. IEEE Access **7**, 14985–15006 (2018)

Jiawei, H., Kamber, M.: Data Mining: Concepts and Techniques. Morgan Kaufmann Publishers Inc, San Francisco (2001)

Huang, G., Huang, G.B., Song, S.J., You, K.Y.: Trends in extreme learning machines: a review. Neural Netw. **61**, 32–48 (2015)

Bottleneck Feature Extraction-Based Deep Neural Network Model for Facial Emotion Recognition

Tian Ma[1]([envelope]), Kavuma Benon[1], Bamweyana Arnold[1], Keping Yu[2,3], Yan Yang[1], Qiaozhi Hua[4], Zheng Wen[5], and Anup Kumar Paul[6]

[1] College of Computer Science and Technology, Xi'an University of Science and Technology, Xi'an 710054, China
matian@xust.edu.cn
[2] Global Information and Telecommunication Institute, Waseda University, Shinjuku, Tokyo 169-8050, Japan
[3] Shenzhen Boyi Technology Company Ltd., Shenzhen 518125, China
[4] Computer School, Hubei University of Arts and Science, Xiangyang 441000, China
[5] School of Fundamental Science and Engineering, Waseda University, Tokyo 169-8050, Japan
[6] Department of Electronics and Communications Engineering, East West University, Dhaka 1212, Bangladesh

Abstract. Deep learning is one of the most effective and efficient methods for facial emotion recognition, but it still encounters stability and infinite feasibility problems for faces of different races. To address this issue, we proposed a novel bottleneck feature extraction (BFE) method based on the deep neural network (DNN) model for facial emotion recognition. First, we used the Haar cascade classifier with a randomly generated mask to extract the face and remove the background from the image. Second, we removed the last output layer of the VGG16 transfer learning model, which was applied only for bottleneck feature extraction. Third, we designed a DNN model with five dense layers for feature training and used the famous Cohn-Kanade dataset for model training. Finally, we compared the proposed model with the K-nearest neighbor and logistic regression models on the same dataset. The experimental results showed that our model was more stable and could achieve a higher accuracy and F-measure, up to 98.59%, than other methods.

Keywords: Emotion recognition · Deep neural network · K-nearest neighbor · Haar features

1 Introduction

Image detection is increasingly and widely applied for different purposes, such as expert evidence, plant identification, tumor recognition, and facial recognition, among others. Due to the new massive rollouts of 5G internet services around the world and the increase

S. W. Loke et al. (Eds.): MONAMI 2020, LNICST 338, pp. 30–46, 2020.
https://doi.org/10.1007/978-3-030-64002-6_3

in demand from previous versions of the internet, we expect to see a steep mobile application usage boom in the global markets, which could generate mobile data traffic and make it possible to mine mobile intelligence [1]. Images are currently becoming one of the most important forms of mobile data. We could do more with such free data, which are generated through the activities in which users engage. In this paper, we focus on facial emotion (FE) recognition in mobile images [2] of different races. As a special field, FE recognition has attracted the attention of several research teams, and many related methods have been proposed.

For example, as suggested by SL Happy [3], salient patches that had discriminative patches were used in each classification of one pair of facial expressions. Similarly, we also used the CK+ data set, but the difference is that our group decided to use the Haar cascade method with randomly generated masks that we matched with the scores of the image. At times, we could also detect the same image via image edge and edge enhancement, as referenced by Xin Wang [5]. Unlike the facial patches method of S L Happy, B. Ryu [6] used a local directional ternary pattern method that has selected connections to edge-based methods in smooth regions of an image. However, if we detect the image, the stability is important in such a procedure [6]. With this in mind, we attempted to refer to a gridding-based algorithm for stability and endeavored to solve infinite feasibility problems, as that histogram-based algorithm uses grid like features and stability levels using that algorithm. And this would make them feasible because we consider infinite pixels instead of one pixel [5]. To obtain the extracted object, even with many different objects of all shapes, color, and posture, we suggested the K-nearest neighbor (KNN) method. However, their emotion recognition (ER) is better, which we only realized by considering the key points. Certain expressions have relative similarity, but the emotion might be different depending on the person. For example, a person with large cheeks might have a similar facial expression while crying, depending on the moment of the image capture. Because facial patches read only the bloated cheeks, this is where we have a different suggestion. With all of these differences, the need exists to find the best parameters or points to be used, create a group of combined subsets with the extracted components, and not use all of the points because it could affect the time computation of the suggested algorithm.

Certain great methods in machine learning have been used to address problems such as detection of facial emotions. In the field of image recognition, the deep neural network (DNN) has become a powerful tool [22] and has also initiated a large research base that attracts many participants. For example, the deep CNN network and new modern advanced techniques have been used in advanced image feature detection developments. From the VGG16 experimental results, it was found that together with continuous deep learning of the convolutional layer learning, the feed-forward neural network that uses the error backpropagation algorithm could learn more object features. These convoluted characteristics gradually become coarser in the process of model training, and the inadequacy of VGG16 in learning convergence occurs because the degree of convergence is weak. In other words, the phenomenon of gradient disappearance is obvious in the latter layers. The feature data of certain convolutional layers do not reflect the extraction of edge detailed features. The final output port directly uses the featured data of the fully connected layer, which is overly dependent on the extraction of edge detailed features.

Certain of those great methods include transfer learning with VGG16 for extraction of features by relying on a 3 × 3 layer filter with a stride. However, in obtaining precise results, because we are using supervised learning methods, we already know the expected results.

To obtained the desired results, in this paper, we used two baseline methods: KNN and the logistic regression method [7, 8]. In the third stage, we took the input data for the DNN, which were the Haar features that we extracted from the convolutional neural network, and subsequently came up with the results. We used all of these steps to improve the algorithmic time and accuracy. The entire process is a combination of traditional methods for detection and extraction that we used together to obtain the final results.

2 Related Work

For a long time, facial detection has gathered high interest from the research community. The major goals have been accuracy, speed in execution, and the amount of resources consumed in executing the task. All of these mentioned factors rely on the training set. The goal is to obtain an algorithm that aligns well with the training set and gives us the desired results accurately and in time, without consuming most of the hardware resources. It has been estimated that by 2024, 90% of the world's smartphones will be using biometric facial recognition features [9]. This trend is already emerging with the key players of private companies and governmental bodies. This effort has resulted in use of biometric technology. It should be noted that biometric facial recognition must be reinforced through both hardware and software. Via activation of sensors [9, 10], biometric facial recognition has different categories, as specified by Zualkernan and Aloul [11], and the main categories are verification and identification. Considering the importance of facial landmark detection, facial expression performance is attracting increasing attention in the field of image classification. The alignment of the face for detecting the position of the eyes has become an important issue, usually performed by horizontal positioning. For facial expression recognition, extraction of features from the face is followed by landmark detection, and feature selection plays an important role in prediction because it directly influences the model accuracy. The precise components of facial tracking were used in infrared illumination in which Kalman filters were applied. By observing the expression changes, Uddin reported a good performance [20]. In reference [21], a relative geometrical separation-based method was portrayed, which used computationally costly Gabor channels for landmark location and following. That method also used consolidated SVM and HMM models as classifiers. Different methods have been suggested such as the Haar classifier method, adaptive skin color method, and many more [12]. Facial recognition has become a fast-growing technology adapted by many governments and companies for different purposes. For example, identification is used by companies such as Alibaba and Facebook and by police departments in China, USA and Europe. Verification on the other side has been rolled out by certain governments in their different endeavors to collect data on their respective populations. However, each of those categories must fulfill the purposes defined as follows.

To explain this issue in our context, we need know the determinants or the parameters to apply for this matter. These parameters include the background of the picture, the clarity of the picture, the position of the Haar-like features, and others. The contribution of the Voila-Jones algorithm framework face detection method obtained its peak point because of the speed of the implementation of Haar features. It is observed that the Haar classifier works quite impressively if the images contain a simple background. For handling large databases such as CK+, the Haar cascade shows its best detection accuracy. Images in which the target object is wearing glasses do not affect the Haar classifier accuracy. Even if images are confined with illumination, this method still works quite impressively. However, in our case, we had to compare with the existing trained dataset. In such a case, we used the linear regression method, which was the picture we input versus the trained dataset. Although certain shortcomings exist in this method, it gives values larger than 1 and less than zero (0), which are outside the bounds of the Haar classifier if we do not consider the gray areas. Therefore, we pivoted to logistic regression, which is similar to linear regression because the aim is to estimate the values of the parameter coefficients. We determined the algorithm that could show the connection between the no input value and the output value; it is the opposite of a linear function if we consider values that are non-linear. This method generally takes any given number and maps it between 0–1 without necessarily exceeding the limit, thus solving the problem mentioned with linear regression. We plotted the 2D graph using the XY plane and plotted the winners and the losers in terms of points. The losers are the ones tending to zero (0), and the winners are those tending to one (1), and we draw the line between them. From the plotted points, we can estimate whether the input picture matches the emotion that we want. With a given form of gradient descent characteristics that we noted with logistic regression, we are satisfied that the estimation can be used as a determinant for our research purpose. The number of iterations were few in our case, which could affect the algorithmic time consumption such that the desired results might not be achieved. This method was designed to use all of the data and compare with trained data by identifying which points are closer to the others. Whenever we need to find the predicted or chosen point (K), in our case, we already have a trained set of data CK+, and we need to import new images in the algorithm. Our method maps the dataset with the new image data and gives us the desired results. Our design was based on the emotions that we selected, which were sad, happy, angry, surprise, disgust and neutral. When we input the picture, it could predict the result although the result accuracy was slightly lacking. Using the Euclidean method of distance, we might apply both linear and nonlinear operations, and thus we chose to use logistic regression [8], which is applied by supplying the parameters of the logistics model, which is generally a binary model.

3 Proposed BFE Model

The name 'Bottleneck' comes from the fact that we use hidden multi-layer perceptions. The overview of the BFE model is shown in Fig. 1. Observation suggests that improving the feature extraction method can enhance the performance of the model, meaning that the first step was to feed the input images into the BFE model for extraction of the faces by the Haar classifier. The Haar classifier uses the AdaBoost and Viola-Jones detection algorithms to detect the important features of the faces by removing unnecessary components of the image. The extracted faces were fed into the VGG16 transfer learning model for bottleneck features. The implantation was performed by removing the last layer of the VGG16 model. After extracting the features from the BFF model, a deep neural network with five dense layers was implemented for training of the model. Finally, the model was tested with random images downloaded from the internet.

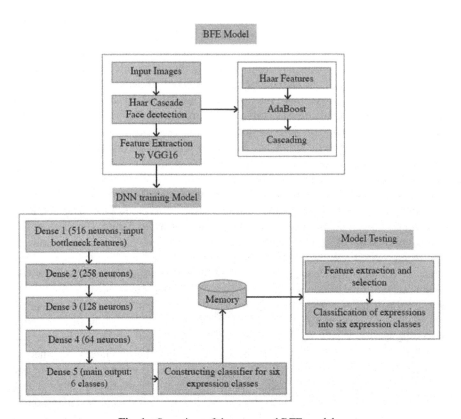

Fig. 1. Overview of the proposed BFE model.

3.1 Haar Cascade Face Extraction

The Haar cascade classifier is based on the ability to analyze pixels in the image into squares by a function. This method uses "integral image" concepts to group the different portions of the image and map the "features" detected. This method also uses the AdaBoost learning algorithm, which chooses a small number of useful features from a large set that have been stored to supply us with valid results for the classifier. The method also uses cascading techniques to detect a face in an image. The Haar cascade classifier is based on the Viola-Jones detection algorithm, which is already trained and has a wide range of faces and non-face components that were previously analyzed in its construction, can be easily accessed, and have a significant comparison with any image that we want to classify.

Haar Features

Haar features are refer to pixels, which in this case are in the form of 0 s and 1 s can also take on the value of −1 if we consider the gray areas [13]. Because we are interested in extracting the face, we apply these pixels in a piece-by-piece manner on the different components of the face, which we refer to as the ROI (region of interest) and is performed by moving them. And then move the pixel again. In this case, we extract the important features and remove the unimportant ones using a 24 × 24 window. As shown in Fig. 2, certain Haar representation are based on their shapes and values, where 0 s represent the white regions and 1 s represent the black shaded region.

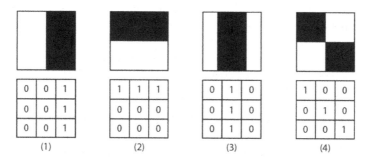

Fig. 2. Haar representations as shapes and numbers.

Although the number of pixels is usually large, we attempt to consider methods such as integral images [14], which reduce the pixels significantly and are applied on the next layer of analysis later.

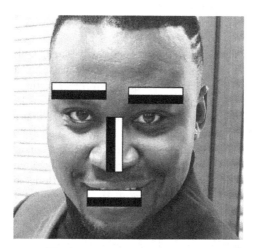

Fig. 3. Haar application on a face.

When we use the Haar algorithm, the windows repeatedly take different shapes of the 0 s and 1 s as they move towards the other pixels. In this case, we used an algorithm that also relies on the integral image in computer vision, which has been suggested by Jones and Viola [1, 15], in which we have had to reduce the pixels significantly but with maximum effect. We applied this approach to differentiate the cat face from the person's face, even when we place them together in the same picture. The major advantage of this method as a base method for any facial recognition algorithm is that it is not affected by certain small factors such as the age of a person or the background behind a person. The Haar features are the eyes, nose, and mouth, as shown in Fig. 3, which exclude people wearing masks and images with background. This method is one of the pioneering methods used in facial detection because it is quick, and the processes it uses to classify the image reduce the algorithmic time. The applications can be found in common technology gadgets such cameras because it is widely used in almost all new facial-recognition phone cameras.

AdaBoost
As discussed above for the Haar features of 24 × 24 base resolution windows, there are approximately 160,000 features that need to be calculated. Additionally, a few features might be useful for more facial recognition systems. Therefore, such notably large features are needed for training, and use of all features can lead to poor results and high GPU and processing times. To remove these unnecessary features, AdaBoost was selected to choose the important relevant features that are needed and used in training. AdaBoost is used to select the best features generated by the Haar method [23]. When the relevant features are found, a weighted combination of all of these features is put to use in assessing and deciding any given window and whether it contains a face or not. Every relevant feature selected that was named as a weak classifier by AdaBoost is treated as fine if it can perform better than random guessing [24]. For detection of a face segment, each of these weak classifiers is relevant. The weak classifier output is binary if the classifier can detect a portion of the face or not.

Cascading
By breaking down a large problem into small and easily manageable modules, the Viola-Jonas algorithm is a famous algorithm that has long been in use and aids in the cascade for the Haar classifier. Boosting calculation requires strong classifiers to make the strategy function well, but for certain situations, we might encounter weak learners, which we can consolidate, and this situation encourages us to characterize that the closer the output, the closer the value to 1. When we used the Haar classifier for almost all cases, we removed the background of the images because we are most concerned with the human faces, especially for emotion recognition. For a 24 × 24 image window, 2,500 relevant features are needed and are processed by AdaBoost. AdaBoost aids in the process of obtaining these important 2,500 features for all 160,000 features. In this method for an input image, the fixed 24 × 24 windows must move all over the image to obtain 2,500 features for each partial window. A simple linear combination of all outputs is built and used to check whether the thresholds of the outputs are inside or outside of a limit. The Viola-Jones method follows a simple principle of scanning the detector through the similar image, and the detector scans with a new size every time. Although an image contains one or more faces, it is obvious that an excessively large amount of the scanned subwindows will still be negatives (non-faces). Therefore, the algorithm should focus

more heavily on discarding non-faces quickly and spend additional on time on probable face regions. Hence, a single strong classifier formed out of the linear combination of all best features is not satisfactory for evaluating each window because of computation costs. Instead of calculating 2,500 features for each single window, we use the idea of cascading and perform a sampling of 2,500 features into x different cascades. In this manner, we can linearly detect whether a face appears or not in different cascades. If a single cascade finds a face in an image, then the image is passed on to the next cascade. If no face is found in a cascade, we can move to the next window after dropping that window. This process reduces the time complexity. The job of each stage is to determine whether a given subwindow definitely contains or does not contain a face. The Viola-Jones face detection algorithm is trained, and the weights are stored on the disk. The next step is to take the features from the file and apply them to our image. If a face is detected, we obtain its corresponding location.

3.2 Feature Extraction

In our quest to recognize the face, the current method available is the Siamese network, which can sometimes translate to "connected". In this case, we already have a trained set that is relatively small, and thus the computation time is not as high, and all we have to do is to compare the input with the existing trained set. We must take the embedding of each image and put it through a neural network to obviously compare their Euclidean distance. This is an improvement over the standard CNN because it requires many images to be trained in the training set. However, on the positive side, certain existing datasets have been supplied [3, 4] to cater to such issues, although they might not be as large as those that are secretively used by large companies in the game. The algorithm requires us to enter two images and compare them by obtaining the sigmoid [8], which can be translated to the similarity between those two images. However, in certain cases, we can pivot to the triple loss [16], where we can input two images that are slightly similar and attempt to find the difference between the three images by first comparing the almost similar images. For example, image A, B and C are the chosen images. We consider A as an anchor image, B as a positive image, and C as a negative image. By applying the Euclidean distance, we can compare the anchor image and the positive image and subsequently compare the anchor and the negative image. Our aim is to plot these images and retain a secret number, or what we would consider a fingerprint, for the collection of images that have been well compared. The major disadvantage is that if we are given a notably large dataset, we might run into problems with computational time. If we need to train 3 images per time, then if we have a 240 million image dataset, that process can take a long time. For this reason, Google introduced an algorithm that can maximize the positive images and minimize the negative images in the process of comparing them to the anchor image. Given the base formula for triple loss $d(a, p)$ and $d(a, n)$, where a is the anchor image or what we consider as the true image on which we base our judgement, and P and n represent positive and negative, respectively, if we rely only on this algorithm, we could find ourselves in more trouble if we need to compute a larger dataset. The solution is to maximize the positives and minimize the negatives.

After extracting the face via Haar cascading, we need to extract the features. To find the bottleneck features, we opted to choose the transfer learning mechanism because transfer learning obtains a better accuracy in taking on highly trained and weighted neural networks. We used VGG16 in Fig. 4 as the transfer learning mechanism, which was discovered in the ImageNet competition in 2015. The input given to the first convolution layer (conv1) is fixed to a 224 × 224 RGB image size. The image passes through a stack of convolutional (conv.) layers, where the filters were used with a small receptive field of 3 × 3 (which is the smallest size used to capture the notion of left/right, up/down, center). One of the configurations also uses selected 1 × 1 convolution filter, which can be viewed as a linear transformation of the input channels (followed by non-linearity). The convolution stride is fixed to 1 pixel. The spatial padding of each conv. layer input is set such that the spatial resolution is preserved after an assessment, i.e., the padding is 1 pixel for 3 × 3 conv. layers. Spatial pooling is applied by five max-pooling layers, which follow certain of the convolution layers (not all of the conv. layers are followed by max pooling). Max pooling is performed over a 2 × 2 pixel window with stride 2. Three fully connected (FC) layers follow a stack of convolutional layers (which have a different depth in architecture). It should be noted that we didn't remove any FC8 layers. The model just removes the top layer of the VGG16, as it is designed for 16 outcomes and the model has 6 outcomes. The first two layers have approximately 4096 channels each, and the third layer performs approximately 1000-way ILSVRC classification, meaning that it contains a staggering 1000 channels (per class). The final layer is the soft-max layer. The configuration of the fully connected layers is the same in all networks. All hidden layers are equipped with rectification (ReLU) non-linearity. It is also noted that none of the networks (except for one) contain local response normalization (LRN). Such normalization does not improve the performance on the ILSVRC dataset, but it can result in a large amount of memory consumption and additional computing time.

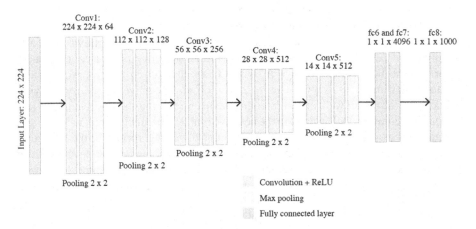

Fig. 4. VGG16 CNN transfer learning model.

A convolution neural net (CNN) was used in feature extraction from the face, and VGG16 was used as a CNN architecture. This method was used to win the ILSVR (ImageNet) competition in 2014 and is considered to be one of the most effective and efficient vision model architectures to date. The most unique characteristic of VGG16 is that instead of using a large number of hyperparameters, it focuses on more convolution layers of a 3×3 filter with a stride 1, supplementing it with the same padding and max-pool layer of a 2×2 filter of stride 2. This method follows this style of convolution and max-pool layers consistently throughout the entire architecture. In the end, this method has 2 fully connected layers followed by a softmax layer for output. The '16' in the VGG16 refers to its 16 layers that have weights. This network is quite large and has approximately 138 million parameters. We took advantage of the VGG16 model for our facial recognition model by removing the last output layer of the model and replacing it with our model. Before feeding the training data into the VGG16 model for the bottleneck feature, we generated more image data extracted from Haar cascading by the Keras image data generator, which increases the size of the images for better accuracy with little variation. The generating systems worked by flipping the images horizontally and vertically or by applying variations in the brightness of the image. We used batch size 1, and after predicting the bottleneck feature, we reshaped the trained data into 568×51200 and saved the data features and labels as NumPy array files for training purposes.

4 DNN Training Model

After we obtained the features in Sect. 3, we implemented these extracted features into our deep neural network (DNN) model, which has five dense layers. The basic knowledge of DNN suggests that many dense layers should be present between the input and output [18, 19] to achieve a better-trained model. The following Table 1 shows the mathematical framework of the DNN model, where x represents the input bottleneck features extracted from the VGG16, and y denotes the emotion labels. In line 4, Ψi defines the mapping function of Di layers, and Wi indicates the random weights generated by the Keras framework library.

In line 3, L represents the layer number (for this model, $L = 5$), and $\Phi(z\_i)$ represents as the activation functions, where z_i obtain the activation (in our case, for the first four layers, we used "ReLU" activation, and in the last layer, we used "softmax" activation). In the first dense layer, we feed every bottleneck feature of each image into 512 neurons. We used dropout as a type of regularization that randomly eliminates certain units and their connections during training, with the intention of reducing the degree to which hidden units co-adapt, thus combatting overfitting. We feed the output of the first dense layer into three consecutive dense layers with 256, 128, and 64 output neurons. In the last layer, we used the "softmax" activation function, which turns the output of the fourth dense layer logits into probability distributions of a list of potential six outcomes. When the model outcomes are greater than two, we used categorical cross-entropy and the popular deep learning "adam" optimizer during the compilation process. In the fitting of trained data with labels, we used 40 number epochs with 100 batch size and saved the training model and weights in hierarchical data format files.

Table 1. Algorithm table for DNN model.

Algorithm: DNN model
1:    **function** *DNN(x, y)*
2:        $x_1 \leftarrow x$
3:        **for** $i \in \{1, \ldots, L\}$ **do**
4:            $z_i \leftarrow \Psi_i (D_i (W_i, x_i))$
5:            $x_{i+1} \leftarrow \Phi(z_i)$
6:        **for** $i \in \{L, \ldots, 1\}$ **do**
7:            $W_i \leftarrow W_i$
8:            **if** $i = L$ **and** type = *classification* **then**
9:                $e_L \leftarrow x_{L+1} - y$
10:            $W_i \leftarrow W_i - \eta \nabla w_i \, J\,(x, y)$
11:    **return** y

5   Experimental Results and Analysis

To validate the proposed methodology, we referred to the Cohn-Kanade (CK) dataset. In the following subsections, we briefly describe the database and present the experimental results and discussion. In Sect. 5.1 we discuss the dataset and details of the images used and generated, and in Sect. 5.2, we show the results of the model and discuss details of the results found.

5.1   Dataset

In our experiment, we used 568 frontal face images of six different emotions, which are converted into grayscale and have a resolution of 350×350. Certain original images were printed, scanned, and digitized. We used the CK+ dataset for training, which was created using the faces of 100 university-level students [25]. This dataset consists of students ranging in age from 18 to 30 years in which 65% were female, 15% were African-American, and 3% were Asian or Latino. As shown in Fig. 5, the trained images with six emotions, i.e., anger, disgust, happy, neutral, sadness, and surprise, are shown from the top to the bottom of the figure. It should be however noted that we didn't use fear in Paul Ekman's 6 basic emotions. As we replaced it with neutral and the reason for that is when we have surprise and fear in images, it is hard to differentiate them. And this is because the reaction on the face is somewhat the same so we wanted to give a broader perspective by introducing a new facial emotion category where each row of the figure represents an emotion. For our study, we used the Haar classifier to extract the faces from these images and cropped the faces to the data directory files. The cropped dataset is saved in the training data directory. During VGG16 feature extraction, we generated more images to increase the data because it yields good accuracy by flipping the images horizontally and zooming in and out by the Keras image generator library.

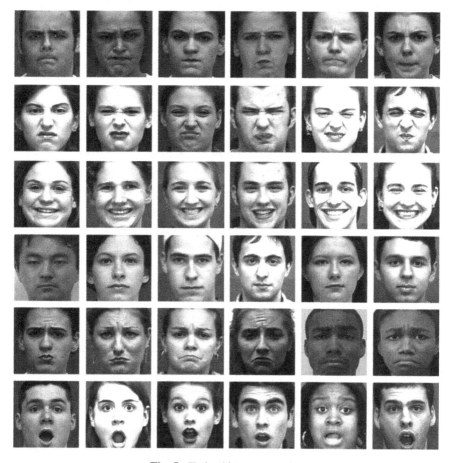

Fig. 5. Trained images sample.

5.2 Experimental Results and Discussion

In this stage, we compared our BFE-based deep neural network (DNN) with two baseline methods, i.e., logistic regression and K-nearest neighbors (KNN) [17]. The accuracy and F-measure of the BFE-based deep neural network (DNN) model are quite impressive.

Table 2. Accuracy comparison.

Model	Accuracy	F-measure
BFE-based DNN model	98.59%	98.59%
K-nearest neighbors	83.09%	80.57%
Logistic regression	89.88%	89.81%

The accuracy and F-measure comparison among the models are shown in Table 2. From this table, it can be easily observed that our BFE-based DNN model produced satisfactory predictions over the two benchmarking models.

Table 3. Confusion matrix for DNN model.

Predicted Class / Original Classes	Neutral	Anger	Disgust	Happy	Sadness	Surprise
Neutral	100	0.0	0.0	0.0	0.0	0.0
Anger	0.0	92.0	0.0	0.0	0.0	0.0
Disgust	0.0	0.0	100	0.0	0.0	0.0
Happy	0.0	0.0	0.0	100	0.0	0.0
Sadness	0.0	8.0	0.0	0.0	100	0.0
Surprise	0.0	0.0	0.0	0.0	0.0	100

Table 3 shows the confusion matrix for the proposed deep neural network (DNN) model. The model predicts almost all of the emotions correctly at 100% accuracy. For the "Anger" emotion, the DNN model predicted with 92% accuracy, and it is the only predicted class in which the model fails to predict with full accuracy. During the training procedure, the training log loss was 21.77% and the testing log loss was 45.45% for alpha value 1. To compare the performance of the outcome, we also generated two other confusion matrices based on the K-nearest neighbors and logistic regression models. This method was designed to take all of the data and compare them with the trained data by finding which points are closer to the others. Whenever we need to find the predicted or chosen point (K), in our case, we already have a trained set of data CK+, and we need to import new images into the algorithm. The primary process was to map the dataset with the new image data and obtain the desired results. Our process was based on the emotions we selected, which were sad, happy, angry, surprise, disgust and neutral. Therefore, when we input the picture, it could predict the result, although the result accuracy was slightly lacking.

For the K-nearest neighbor model, we used 99 n-neighbors, and the "sigmoid" function was also used in the classifier to calibrate the characteristics of the CK data sets. As shown in Table 4, we used the same data sets and features for these two models. It can be observed that the model can correctly predict "happy" facial expressions 100%, and the model we used to predict almost all of the emotions can predict correctly. As shown, this K-nearest neighbor failed to predict the "anger" and "sadness" emotions of these data. The other predicted class accuracy was less than 80% without the surprise emotions.

Table 4. Confusion matrix for K-nearest Neighbors model.

Predicted Class / Original Classes	Neutral	Anger	Disgust	Happy	Sadness	Surprise
Neutral	76.5	0.0	6.5	0.0	0.0	0.0
Anger	8.7	0.0	22.6	0.0	0.0	0.0
Disgust	4.9	0.0	64.5	0.0	0.0	0.0
Happy	1.1	0.0	0.0	100.0	0.0	0.0
Sadness	5.5	0.0	6.5	0.0	0.0	5.4
Surprise	3.3	0.0	0.0	0.0	0.0	94.6

Therefore, to evaluate the accuracy of the model more closely, we decided to test another model for the CK data set because the K-nearest neighbor models fail to predict two of six classes. Logistic regression predicted six out of six classes for the following dataset. The accuracy of the model is also quite impressive compared with that of K-nearest neighbors. For logistic regression, we used stochastic gradient descent learning and implemented regularized linear models. The confusion matrix of logistic regression is shown in Table 5. As shown in the table, the model correctly predicted "happy" facial expressions with 100% accuracy, similar to the two models discussed above, but its predictions of "sadness" are also less accurate. The model showed a bias for the "Neutral" facial expression because the logistic regression model predicted 50% of "sadness" and 2.3% of "surprise" face emotions as "neutral" emotions. We also tested random images from the Google image dataset, and the model perfectly categorized the emotions associated with the test images.

Table 5. Confusion matrix for logistic regression model.

Predicted Class / Original Classes	Neutral	Anger	Disgust	Happy	Sadness	Surprise
Neutral	83.2	0.0	0.0	0.0	50.0	2.3
Anger	7.8	88.9	3.8	0.0	25.0	0.0
Disgust	3.0	0.0	92.3	0.0	0.0	0.0
Happy	0.0	0.0	0.0	100.0	0.0	0.0
Sadness	5.4	11.1	3.8	0.0	25.0	4.7
Surprise	0.6	0.0	0.0	0.0	0.0	93.0

6 Conclusion

Mobile data are useful for user behavior analysis [26] to enhance mobile intelligence, especially image data for emotion recognition. In this paper, we propose a novel bottleneck feature extraction pre-processing method, which improves on the traditional random facial emotion recognition method. In the BFE pre-processing model of bottleneck features, we used the Haar classifier to extract the faces of the images, the AdaBoost element algorithm was used to select important features, and the Viola-Jones detection algorithm was used in the cascade to focus on rapid discard of non-faces and spend more time on the possible face areas. In the feature extraction stage, we used the famous transfer learning VGG16 model. Finally, we used the bottleneck features generated by the BFE pre-processing method in a DNN training model with five dense layers.

Given the current mobile computing paradigm, most of the computing is done from the cloud, and the exchanging data is somewhat very busy or crowded. In such cases, we need to find the methods which are a little bit quicker. And the solution would be to shift from cloud to local devices. The cloud means is great but a little expensive in the long-run. So, it would be better ways, that we run some algorithms and work locally on the machine, and then send to the cloud when some tasks have been done locally.

We found that the BFE pre-processing method is suitable by simply looking at the training model results. The accuracy and F-measure of the model are outstanding, and the score on the test data is 98.59%. Although we used small-size data, the proposed model showed great feature selection ability and thus supplied good results. For benchmarking, we compared this model with the K-nearest neighbors and logistic regression neural network with the same features and dataset. The comparison results show that the test results of the two benchmark test modes are better. However, the natural images have a complex background, and it is difficult to extract faces from them. In the future, BFE is expected to offer robust bottleneck features for complex input images. We also believe that this BFE technique can be used in any circumstance that works with or will work with images.

Acknowledgments. This work was supported by the National Natural Science Foundation of China (61834005), the Enterprise Joint Fund Project of Shaanxi Natural Science Basic Research Plan (2019JLM-11-2), the Shaanxi Key Laboratory of network data analysis and intelligent processing, and the Japan Society for the Promotion of Science (JSPS) Grants-in-Aid for Scientific Research (KAKENHI) under Grant JP18K18044.

References

1. Han, H., Liu, Z., An, J.: Mining mobile intelligence for wireless systems: a deep neural network approach. IEEE Comput. Intell. Mag. **2**, 24–31 (2020)
2. Hossain, M.S., Muhammad, G.: An emotion recognition system for mobile applications. IEEE Access **5**, 2281–2287 (2017). https://doi.org/10.1109/ACCESS.2017.2672829
3. Eleftheriadis, S., Rudovic, O., Pantic, M.: Joint facial action unit detection and feature fusion: a multi-conditional learning approach. IEEE Trans. Image Process. **25**(12), 5727–5742 (2016). https://doi.org/10.1109/TIP.2016.2615288
4. Happy, S.L., Routray, A.: Automatic facial expression recognition using features of salient facial patches. IEEE Trans. Affect. Comput. (2015) https://doi.org/10.1109/TAFFC.2014.238 6334
5. Ryu, B., Rivera, A.R., Kim, J., Chae, O.: Local directional ternary pattern for facial expression recognition. IEEE Trans. Image Process. **26**(12), 6006–6018 (2017). https://doi.org/10.1109/TIP.2017.2726010
6. Celis, D., Rao, M.: Learning facial recognition biases through VAE latent representations. In: FAT/MM 2019 - Proceedings of the 1st International Workshop on Fairness, Accountability, and Transparency in MultiMedia, Co-Located with MM 2019, pp. 26–32 (2019). https://doi.org/10.1145/3347447.3356752
7. Shen, X., Gu, Y.: Nonconvex sparse logistic regression with weakly convex regularization. IEEE Trans. Sig. Process. **66**(12), 3199–3211 (2018). https://doi.org/10.1109/TSP.2018.282 4289
8. Zhang, C., et al.: Multi-gram CNN-based self-attention model for relation classification. IEEE Access **7**, 5343–5357 (2019). https://doi.org/10.1109/ACCESS.2018.2888508
9. Chen, S., Pande, A., Mohapatra, P.: Sensor-assisted facial recognition: an enhanced biometric authentication system for smartphones. In: MobiSys 2014 - Proceedings of the 12th Annual International Conference on Mobile Systems, Applications, and Services, pp. 109–122 (2014). https://doi.org/10.1145/2594368.2594373
10. Gu, Y., Wang, Y., Liu, T., Ji, Y., Liu, Z., et al.: EmoSense: computational intelligence driven emotion sensing via wireless channel data. IEEE Trans. Emerg. Top. Comput. Intell. (2019). https://doi.org/10.1109/TETCI.2019.2902438
11. Kiaee, N., Hashemizadeh, E., Zarrinpanjeh, N.: Using GLCM features in Haar wavelet transformed space for moving object classification. IET Intell. Transp. Syst. **13**(7), 1148–1153 (2019). https://doi.org/10.1049/iet-its.2018.5192
12. Sharifara, A., Rahim, M.S.M., Navabifar, F., Ebert, D., Ghaderi, A., Papakostas, M.: Enhanced facial recognition framework based on skin tone and false alarm rejection. In: ACM International Conference on Pervasive Technologies Related to Assistive Environments, Part F1285, pp. 240–241 (2017). https://doi.org/10.1145/3056540.3064967

13. Viola, P., Jones, M.: Robust real-time object detection. Int. J. Comput. Vis. **57**, 137–154 (2001)
14. Liu, F., Shen, C., Lin, G.: Deep convolutional neural fields for depth estimation from a single image. In: Proceedings of the IEEE Computer Society Conference on Computer Vision and Pattern Recognition (2015). https://doi.org/10.1109/cvpr.2015.7299152
15. Facciolo, G., Limare, N., Meinhardt-Llopis, E.: Integral images for block matching. Image Process. Line (2014). https://doi.org/10.5201/ipol.2014.57
16. Karpathy, A.: CS231n convolutional neural networks for visual recognition. Stanford University (2016)
17. Brace, N., Kemp, R., Snelgar, R., Brace, N., Kemp, R., Snelgar, R.: Discriminant analysis and logistic regression. In: SPSS for Psychologists (2016). https://doi.org/10.1007/978-1-137-57923-2_11
18. Vasuki, A., Govindaraju, S.: Deep neural networks for image classification. In: Deep Learning for Image Processing Applications (2017)
19. Singh, V., Shokeen, V., Singh, B.: Face detection by haar cascade classifier with simple and complex backgrounds images using opencv implementation. Int. J. Adv. Technol. Eng. Sci. **1**(12), 33–38 (2013)
20. Valstar, M.F., Pantic, M.: Combined support vector machines and hidden markov models for modeling facial action temporal dynamics. In: Lew, M., Sebe, N., Huang, T.S., Bakker, E.M. (eds.) HCI 2007. LNCS, vol. 4796, pp. 118–127. Springer, Heidelberg (2007). https://doi.org/10.1007/978-3-540-75773-3_13
21. Islam, M.F., Rahman, M.M.: Metal surface defect inspection through deep neural network. In: 2018 International Conference on Mechanical, Industrial and Energy Engineering, ICMIEE 2018, Khulna, Bangladesh, p. 258 (2018)
22. Ma, S., Bai, L.: A face detection algorithm based on Adaboost and new Haar-Like feature. In: 2016 7th IEEE International Conference on Software Engineering and Service Science (ICSESS). IEEE (2016)
23. Wu, B., et al.: Fast rotation invariant multi-view face detection based on real adaboost. In: 2004 Proceedings of the Sixth IEEE International Conference on Automatic Face and Gesture Recognition. IEEE (2004)
24. Wang, Y., et al.: Real time facial expression recognition with adaboost. In: 2004 Proceedings of the 17th International Conference on Pattern Recognition, ICPR 2004. IEEE (2004)
25. Lemaître, G., Nogueira, F., Aridas, C.K.: Imbalanced-learn: a python toolbox to tackle the curse of imbalanced datasets in machine learning. J. Mach. Learn. Res. **18**(1), 559–563 (2017)
26. Yu, G., Zhang, X., Liu, Z., Ren, F.: BeSense: leveraging WiFi channel data and computational intelligence for behavior analysis. IEEE Comput. Intell. Mag. **14**(4), 31–41 (2019). https://doi.org/10.1109/MCI.2019.2937610

Human Activity Recognition Using MSHNet Based on Wi-Fi CSI

Fuchao Wang$^{(\boxtimes)}$, Pengsong Duan, Yangjie Cao, Jinsheng Kong, and Hao Li

School of Software, Zhengzhou University, Zhengzhou, China
wfc117@163.com, {duanps,caoyj,jskong}@zzu.edu.cn, lh442401597@163.com

Abstract. In recent years, with the prominent population aging problem, health conditions of aged solitaries are inherently gaining more and more attentions. Among the techniques allowing real-time health monitoring, activity perception has become an important and promising eld in both academia and industry. In this paper, a human activity perception recognition model, named MSHNet (Multi-Stream-Hybrid-Network) based on Deep Learning is proposed to solve the problems of difficulty in extracting perceptual features of Wi-Fi signals and low recognition accuracy in traditional Machine Learning methods. MSHNet adopts passive wireless sensing technology, it uses commercial off-the-shelf Wi-Fi devices to collect Channel State Information (CSI) based on underlying physical equipment and automatically extracts human activity features characterized by amplitude in CSI. Then MSHNet aggregates the data streams of the same receiving antenna using the wireless signal transceiving characteristics of Multiple Input Multiple Output (MIMO) and trains the aggregated data streams respectively. At last, the voting mechanism is adopted to select the best training result. The experimental results demonstrate that MSHNet's results on the public dataset have reached the state-of-the-art and on the datasets of four environments collected by ourselves the average recognition accuracy rate has reached 97.41%, satisfying the daily activity monitoring of the elderly, especially those living alone.

Keywords: Human activity recognition · Wi-Fi · CSI · MIMO · Voting mechanism

1 Introduction

Recently, with the aging of the population, it is a long-term obligation of society and families to protect the health of the elderly, especially those who living alone and independently [9]. The detection and recognition of falls [14] and certain diseases, such as Parkinson's disease [29], can be realized by monitoring the daily activities of people. In order to realize human activity monitoring and recognition, researchers mainly use APT, which is obtain information such as the

---

Supported by Zhengzhou University.

S. W. Loke et al. (Eds.): MONAMI 2020, LNICST 338, pp. 47–63, 2020.
https://doi.org/10.1007/978-3-030-64002-6_4

current position, activity and action trajectory of the target through hardware or software, to realize analysis and understanding of the current activity of the target. There are mainly three kinds of APTs: computer vision, special sensors and wireless sensing technology.

Computer vision technology [8, 16, 24] has high recognition accuracy and wide application range, but its shortcomings are obvious, which is easily affected by illumination and obstacles, invasion of user privacy, and existence of blind spot. Special sensors technology [18, 22, 27] uses special sensors or wearable devices to collect relevant human actions, thus realizing human activity perception. They can realize fine-grained activity perception with high accuracy, but their installation and maintenance usually require high cost, therefore preventing this technique to be widely used.

Wireless sensing technology overcomes the shortcomings of the aforementioned technologies and has gained increasing attention in recent years. It further consists of RF-based and Wi-Fi-based approaches. RF-based [11, 35] requires special equipment to be customized, and the cost is usually relatively high, so it is not suitable for large-scale installation. In recent years, with the widespread deployment of Wi-Fi hotspots [1], using Wi-Fi signals to implement some wireless sensing applications [4, 5, 10] has attracted great attention of researchers. By utilizing the ubiquitous in-house Wi-Fi signals, freeing the personel from any on-body equipment, as well as avoiding the effect of illumination and unnecessary personal privacy invasion.

Initially, researchers realized indoor localization, gesture recognition and simple motion detection based on Received Signal Strength (RSS) in Wi-Fi signals. Due to RSS contains too single information to recognize fine-grained human activity, Channel State Information (CSI) has emerged to replace it. The raw CSI is not sufficient to represent human activity, in practical applications, researchers often use Machine Learning method to extract features from CSI manually, but this method is easy to cause feature loss and requires experts in signal field. With the development of Deep Learning, researchers use Deep Learning methods to automatically extract features from CSI and achieve better results.

In Deep Learning, for time series data, such as human activity data, RNN and its variants are often used for feature extraction. Recently, Convolution Neural Network (CNN) has shown excellent performance in processing time series data. Full convolution network (FCN) [31], residual network (ResNet) [31] and multi-scale convolution network (MCNN) [7] have full advantages in the processing of time series data. Inspired by these two network structures, this paper combines RNN's variant Bi-directional LSTM (BLSTM) with Temporal Convolution Network (TCN) to improve feature extraction and recognition performance, and proposed a Multi-Stream Hybrid Network (MSHNet) as shown in Fig. 1, which is used to realize automatic feature extraction and autonomous learning in human activity recognition perception based on CSI. MSHNet firstly extracts the amplitude information from CSI, and then according to the Multi Input Multi Output (MIMO) characteristics of Wi-Fi signals, it aggregates the data streams of different antennas and trains the aggregated data streams respectively. Finally, it adopts the voting mechanism to select the classification results. Experiments demonstrate that MSHNet results are superior to the current several Deep Learning methods, and its accuracy rate in the experimental environment reaches 97.41%.

The contributions of this paper are summarized as follows:

- MSHNet is proposed to extract deep features of raw CSI obtained from Wi-Fi signals, and we conducted a lot of experiments to verify MSHNet is the best network structure.
- Based on the MIMO characteristics of Wi-Fi signals, this paper proposes a voting mechanism to improve the accuracy of activity recognition of MSHNet.
- On the public dataset, we compared the results of MSHNet and other models. The results demonstrate that MSHNet has best performance.
- To evaluate MSHNet's performance in other environments, we collect datasets from different environments and conduct training. The experimental results demonstrate that MSHNet has good environmental adaptability.

The remaining of this paper is organized as follows: Sect. 2 provides related work and progress of Wi-Fi sensing. We will introduce MSHNet architecture and analyze the function of each part in Sect. 3, followed by experimental results and evaluation in Sect. 4. We finally conclude the work in Sect. 5.

2   Related Work

Bahl et al. proposed—RADAR, an indoor localization system based on Wi-Fi RSS, which is the first research work based on wireless Wi-Fi sensing and provides a new idea for wireless Wi-Fi contactless sensing [4]. Nuzzer realized simple action detection based on RSS, but it can only identify whether there are actions in the environment, and cannot distinguish different actions [26]. WiGest used the influence of gestures on RSS to identify different gestures [3]. Due to multipath and fading effects in the process of signal propagation, RSS will be unstable and contain a large amount of noise during collection, resulting in limited performance, which is difficult to apply to fine-grained activity recognition.

However, in 2011, Halperin et al. released the CSI Tool [13], which greatly facilitates the extraction of CSI based on physical layer from commercial off-the-shelf Wi-Fi devices. CSI contains abundant and stable amplitude and phase information [13], which enables to be applied in finer-grained human activity monitoring and recognition systems, such as sleep monitoring [5], fall detection [14], gesture recognition [20], identity recognization [34], activity recognition [6,12,33], etc.

Affected by multipath effect, CSI contains environment and other noises, so the raw CSI is not sufficient to represent different human activities. In practice, the commonly used processing method is to manually extract relevant features from the raw CSI to distinguish different human activities [30]. However, manually extract features not only requires experts in relevant fields, but also easily ignores some features, resulting in unsatisfactory results. With the development of Deep Learning, a large number of Deep Learning models have been applied in Wi-Fi sensing fields to automatically extract features and improve recognition performance. For Sleep monitoring, CBMR is based on CSI and uses Deep Learning model to realize single sleep monitoring, achieving better results [5]. In [36], authors combine CSI and Deep Learning model to realize number gesture recognition. In human activity recognition, Long short-term memory (LSTM) network was used to automatically extract features from CSI, which is superior to the traditional Machine Learning method of manually extract features [33]. ABLSTM model was used to extract features from the raw CSI data for action recognition in [6], achieving satisfactory performance.

To avoid hand-crafted feature extraction, we proposed a hybrid neural network model—BLSTM-TCN by combining BLSTM and TCN with deep learning knowledge. BLSTM simultaneously extracts features from the past and feature of human activity data to improve the classification performance of different human activities. TCN is a new type of time series feature extraction network and has good performance in some applications. In order to realize high-performance human activity recognition, we proposed MSHNet model, which first extract the amplitude from CSI, and then according to the MIMO characteristics of Wi-Fi signals, it aggregates and trains the data streams received by different antennas, and adopts a voting mechanism for the training results. The experimental results demonstrate that MSHNet we designed has very good performance not only on public dataset, but also on our own datasets.

3   MSHNet Architecture

This section introduces the overall process of MSHNet, as shown in Fig. 1. In Sects. 3.1 and 3.2, we focus on Wi-Fi signal characteristics and voting mechanism, In Sect. 3.3 network model construction and technologies are introduced.

3.1   Channel State Information

Channel State Information (CSI) is used to estimate channel attributes of communication links in orthogonal frequency division multiplexing (OFDM) technology [32]. Assuming physical space (including environmental objects and people) is described as a wireless channel, refraction, diffraction and scattering phenomena will occur when signals propagate in the wireless channel. Therefore, the received signals are the superposition of multipath signals. CSI data integrates the time delay, amplitude attenuation and phase shift effects of all signals propagating in wireless channels. In the frequency domain, a wireless channel having a plurality of transmit and receive antennas is described as $y = Hx + \theta$, where y, x, θ and H represent the reception vector, transmission vector, noise vector and channel matrix respectively. Channel matrix is the estimation of CSI.

In OFDM, CSI is presented in the form of subcarriers, and CSI of a single subcarrier can be described by the following mathematical expression $h = |h|e^{jsin\alpha}$, where $|h|$ represent amplitude and α represents phase. CSI provides a more fine-grained description of wireless channels.

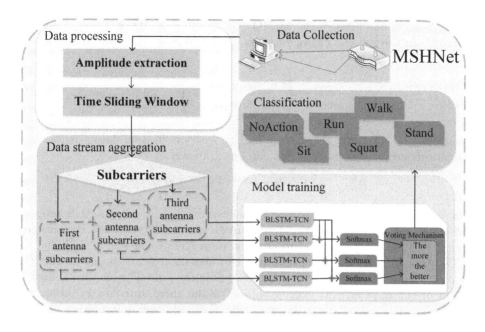

Fig. 1. The structure of MSHNet.

3.2 Multiple Input Multiple Output and Voting Mechanism

Multiple Input Multiple Output (MIMO) represents multiple transmit antennas and multiple receive antennas in a wireless signal transceiving system. MIMO uses multiple antennas to improve signal data throughput and transmission distance without increasing bandwidth and total transmission power. The CSI Tool used in this paper is a MIMO wireless signal under 802.11n standard. Figure 2 is a 2×3 MIMO system model. Assuming that there are N_t transmit antennas

Fig. 2. MIMO system model.

and N_r receive antennas in the MIMO system, all data streams (i.e., channel matrix H) in the wireless channel can be expressed as a matrix of $N_t \times N_r$:

$$H = \begin{pmatrix} H_{11} & \cdots & H_{1N_r} \\ \vdots & \ddots & \vdots \\ H_{N_t1} & \cdots & H_{N_tN_r} \end{pmatrix} \tag{1}$$

Under 802.11n standard, there are n CSI subcarriers in each data stream. All CSI subcarriers in each data stream can be expressed as

$$H_{N_tN_r} = \{h^{N_tN_r,1}, h^{N_tN_r,2}, \cdots, h^{N_tN_r,n}\} \tag{2}$$

refraction, diffraction and scattering phenomena will occur when signals propagate in wireless channel, resulting in multipath effect. Different data streams go through different paths, so that receive antennas receive different CSI [2,23].

The transmission and reception of Wi-Fi signals are carried out in MIMO mode, so multiple antennas receive multiple data streams. The amplitude information of the data streams corresponding to the three antennas is shown in Fig. 3. From the figure, it can be seen that the amplitude information of different data streams are all affected by human activity, moreover, owing to the subcarriers in the data streams tend to fade independently in OFDM, it provides an opportunity to study different data streams separately, and provides a basis for the voting mechanism to be used for the results of different antenna training. All the received data streams are treated as a whole in [6,33]. In this paper, the data received by different antennas are aggregated, and then the aggregated data streams are studied separately. MSHNet uses BLSTM-TCN model to train each data stream separately, and then uses voting mechanism to select the training results of all data streams. The experimental results reach the expectation, and the method provides a new idea for subsequent Wi-Fi signals research.

3.3   Network Model Construction

Bi-directional Long Short-Term Memory. Traditional Recurrent Neural Network (RNN) processing long sequence data will cause gradient vanishing and explosion. To solve those problems, Hochreiter and Schmidhuber proposed a variant of RNN called long short-term memory network (LSTM) in [15]. LSTM uses some gates with memory cells to solve the phenomena of gradient vanishing and explosion. LSTM introduces a connection of cell states, which are used to store information that needs to be memorized. Therefore, LSTM can handle the long-term information dependence in the sequence well. The internal structure of LSTM is shown in Fig. 4.

At time t, LSTM reads data C_{t-1}, h_{t-1}, and X_{t-1}, then updates and outputs information through forget gate f_t, input gate i_t, and output gate O_t in the cell. f_t decides which information to discard from the cell state. i_t has two functions, one is to find the cell state that needs updating, and the other is to update the

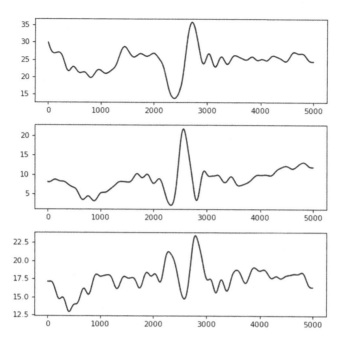

Fig. 3. Amplitude information of different antenna subcarriers. These three diagrams show that the amplitude information contained in the data stream received by different antennas is different, and each antenna has its own characteristics, which provides a basis for the voting mechanism to be used for the data stream training results of different antennas.

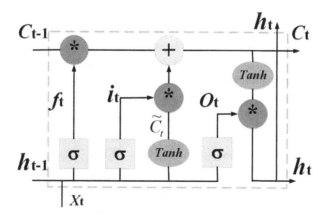

Fig. 4. The structure of LSTM.

information into the cell state. The internal mathematical calculation of LSTM can be described as

$$
\begin{aligned}
f_t &= \sigma(W_f \cdot [h_{t-1}, X_{t-1}] + b_f), \\
i_t &= \sigma(W_i \cdot [h_{t-1}, X_{t-1}] + b_i), \\
\widetilde{C}_t &= \tanh(W_c \cdot [h_{t-1}, X_{t-1}] + b_c), \\
C_t &= \sigma(f_t * C_{t-1} + i_t * \widetilde{C}_t), \\
O_t &= \sigma(W_o * [h_{t-1}, X_{t-1}] + b_o), \\
h_t &= O_t * \tanh(C_t).
\end{aligned}
\tag{3}
$$

Where W_f, W_i, W_c, W_o and b_f, b_i, b_c, b_o respectively represent corresponding weight and bias. $\sigma(\cdot)$ and $\tanh(\cdot)$ represent sigmoid and tanh activation functions, respectively. h_t indicates the hidden state of cells. C_t represents the updated cell state.

Traditional RNN and its variants can only remember the past information when extracting data features. However, for sequence data, the feature information is also of great significance to the current moment. Therefore, Bi-directional recurrent neural network (Bi-RNN) is proposed [25], which can extract not only the past information but also the feature information, Bi-RNN can be defined as follows:

$$
h_t = \overrightarrow{h_t} \bigoplus \overleftarrow{h_t}
\tag{4}
$$

Temporal Convolution Network. Temporal Convolution Network (TCN) is used to solve the classification of time series data. The validity of TCN in time series data classification is fully proved in [19]. In [19], let $X_t \in \Re^{F_0}$ be the input feature vector of length F_0 for time step t ($0 < t \leq T$). Note that the length of time T is fixed in this paper. The true label for each time series is given by $y_t \in \{1, \cdots, C\}$, where C is the number of classes.

Consider L convolutional layers. We apply a set of 1D filters on each of these layers that capture how the input signals evolve over the course of an action. According to [19], the filters for each layer are parameterized by tensor $W^l \in \Re^{F_l \times d \times F_{l-1}}$ and biases $b^l \in \Re^{F_l}$, where $l \in \{1, \cdots, L\}$ is the layer index and d is the filter duration. For the l-th layer, the i-th component of the (unnormalized) activation $\hat{E}_t^l \in \Re^{F_l}$ is a function of the incoming (normalized) activation matrix $\hat{E}_{l-1}^l \in \Re^{F_{l-1} \times T}$ from the previous layer

$$
\hat{E}_{i,t}^l = Relu(b_i^l + \sum_{t'=1}^{d} \langle W_{i,t',\cdot}^l, E_{\cdot,t+d-t'}^{l-1} \rangle)
\tag{5}
$$

for each time t where $Relu(\cdot)$ is a Rectified Linear Unit.

When extracting data features, LSTM extracts potential information in chronological order, while TCN extracts potential information layer by layer. Considering the difference between the two, we designed a hybrid network—BLSTM-TCN as shown in Fig. 5. On the left side of Fig. 5, we use TCN to extract data features, each 1D convolution layer is followed by Batch Normalization (BN) [17], Activation and Dropout layer [28]. BN layer prevents data distribution from changing during model training and accelerates the convergence and training speed [17], and Dropout layer prevents model from overfitting [28]. To make full use of the low-dimensional information and improve the model performance, BLSTM-TCN refers to the residual mechanism in [31] and concats the features extracted from the first TCN block with the features extracted from the second and third TCN blocks respectively. At the end of the left is the global average pooling, which regularizes the structure of the entire network to prevent overfitting, and reduces the data dimension and parameter amount [21]. On the right side of Fig. 5 is a Bi-directional Recurrent Neural Network based on LSTM, the purpose of which is to extract the past and future information of data simultaneously. The BLSTM-TCN model finally concats the features extracted from the left and right sides.

In the model training part of Fig. 1, the aggregated data streams are respectively input into BLSTM-TCN for training. In order to obtain best performance, all data streams are respectively concat with training results of different data streams after being trained by BLSTM-TCN, and then input into Softmax layer for classification. Finally, voting mechanism is used to select the results, if the results are different, the classification results of the data streams with the highest training accuracy are selected as the result.

4 Experiment and Evaluation

In this section, we experimentally confirm the effectiveness of the proposed MSH-Net using real human activity data. Firstly, the dataset we used is described in Sect. 4.1. The evaluation metrics in Sect. 4.2. Finally, the experimental results are presented and discussed in detail in Sect. 4.3.

4.1 Dataset Description

Four datasets are used in this paper, one is public dataset, and the others are the datasets of different environments that we collected.

The public dataset [33] was collected in an indoor office area where the transmitter (Tx) and receiver (Rx) are 3 m apart in line-of-sight (LOS) condition. The Rx is equipped with a commercial Intel 5300 NIC. During data collection, each subject starts moving and doing an activity within a period of 20 s in LOS condition, while in the beginning and at the end of the time period the subject remains stationary. The whole data collection process is recorded by the camera to label the data. The dataset includes 6 persons, 6 activities, denoted as "Lie down, Fall, Walk, Run, Sit down, Stand up" and 20 trials for each one.

To comprehensively evaluate the impact of environment on MSHNet performance, we collected our own datasets. We considered four environments, i.e., Data Collection Room (DCRoom), Conference Room (CRoom), Exhibition Room (ERoom) and Psychology Consultation Room (PCRoom). The layout of

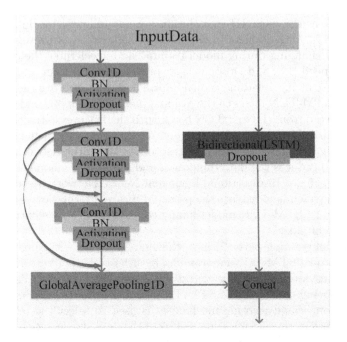

Fig. 5. The structure of BLSTM-TCN.

the four environments is shown in Fig. 6. We use the same equipment in the four environments. The TP_LINK AC1750 wireless router as the Tx, and a desktop computer equipped with an Intel 5300 802.11n Wi-Fi NIC as the Rx. In the process of data collection, each subject has been doing an action repeatedly. We take 5s as a segment to collect data. To make the data more diversified, we collected 10 subjects, each with six common activities, including "noAction, Walk, Run, Sit down, Stand up and Squat". Each action was repeated 10 times. For the case of noAction, we divide it into two kinds of situations, one is that there is someone in the environment and the other is no one. To improve the robustness of MSHNet, we arranged non-subjects to move freely on the non-LOS (outside the red circle in Fig. 6) during data collection.

The sampling rate of all datasets is 1 kHz and Rx has three antennas, each receiving 30 subcarriers, so the amplitude extracted from the raw CSI is 90 dimensions. Note that an Intel 5300 NIC can only be connected with three antennas, if multiple 5300 NICs are used to expand more antennas, it is difficult to achieve synchronous communication between different NICs, therefore, in this paper, we only use one 5300 NIC (i.e. only three receiving antennas). In addition, we use a time sliding window size of $T = 800$ ms to segment data in this paper.

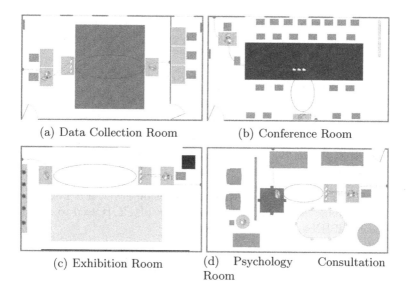

(a) Data Collection Room   (b) Conference Room

(c) Exhibition Room   (d)   Psychology   Consultation
                            Room

Fig. 6. Layout of the four environments.

4.2   Evaluation Metrics

To evaluate MSHNet performance, we use the following four metrics. The first is the most commonly used Accuracy, and others are Precision, Recall and F1. Take current category as a True or Positive (TP) example and non-current category as a False or Negative (FN) example. TP refers to the number of samples that current category is correctly judged as current category; FN refers to the number of samples that current category is judged as non-current category; FP refers to the number of sample that Non-current category is incorrectly judged as current category; and TN refers to the number of samples that non-current category is correctly judged as non-current category. The confusion matrix of TP, FN, FP and TN is shown in Table 1.

Table 1. The confusion matrix of TP, FN, FP and TN.

		Predict label	
		Positive	Negative
True label	True	TP	FN
	False	FP	TN

Accuracy indicates the proportion of both current category and non-current category that are correctly predicted, it can defined as

$$Accuracy = \frac{TP + TN}{TP + FP + FN + TN}. \tag{6}$$

Precision is defined as the ratio of the number of correctly predicted as current category to the number of predicted as both current category and non-current category, which is computed as

$$Precision = \frac{TP}{TP + FP}. \tag{7}$$

Recall refers to the proportion that current category is truly predicted when the true label is current category, which is computed as

$$Recall = \frac{TP}{TP + FN}. \tag{8}$$

To avoid extreme situations in which the precision or recall is 1 and the other one is 0, the harmonic average of precision and recall, F1, is used to evaluate the performance of MSHNet, which is computed as

$$F1 = \frac{2 \times Precision \times Recall}{Precision + Recall}. \tag{9}$$

The above formulas can solve a two-class problem, but a multi-class classification is required in this paper. Since the number of each huamn activity in our dataset is relatively balanced, the average F1 value can be defined as

$$F1 = \frac{2}{k} \frac{N_k}{N_{total}} \sum_k \frac{Precision_k \times Recall_k}{Precision_k + Recall_k}, \tag{10}$$

where k is class index of human activity, N_k is the number of samples of k-th class, and N_{total} is the total number of dataset. $Precision_k$ and $Recall_k$ are the Precision and Recall of human activity of k-th class, respectively.

4.3   Experimental Results

Comparison of Results of Different Structural Models. To choose the best model structure, this paper has done a series of comparative experiments. Comprises the following five experiments:

- Training all data streams by using BLSTM-TCN model (All streams);
- Without voting mechanism, i.e. the training results of different data streams are concated and then classified;
- The training results of all data streams are not concated on the training results of different data streams (Without all streams);
- Without Dropout;
- The low-dimensional features extracted from the first TCN block are not concated (Without residual).

It can be seen from the Table 2 that MSHNet has the best results on the four metrics of Accuracy, Precision, Recall and F1, so the paper finally determines MSHNet as the best model structure, and it also shows that adding Dropout, adding low-dimensional features and voting mechanism can improve the generalization performance and classification accuracy of the model.

Table 2. Comparison of results of different structural models.

	Precision	Accuracy	Recall	F1
All streams	0.9581	0.956	0.9606	0.9593
Without voting mechanism	0.9567	0.9508	0.9549	0.9558
Without all streams	0.9402	0.9275	0.9391	0.9396
Without Dropout	0.9694	0.9663	0.9706	0.97
Without residual	0.9627	0.9585	0.9641	0.9634
MSHNet	**0.9762**	**0.9741**	**0.9773**	**0.9767**

Comparison of Different Model Results on Public Dataset. The confusion matrix can represent the classification performance of the model for each category. This paper takes Long short-term memory [33] and ABLSTM [6] as benchmark experiments. Table 3, Table 4, and Table 5 are respectively the confusion matrices of Long short-term memory, ABLSTM and MSHNet on the public dataset.

From the confusion matrices, MSHNet not only performs well in the overall classification performance, but also achieves the best performance in each category, which mainly due to the fact that BLSTM and TCN show more powerful advantages in feature extraction of sequence data after mixing, and the voting mechanism we designed further improves the performance of MSHNet. The accuracy of Sit down in MSHNet's confusion matrix is slightly lower than other actions, because Sit down and Stand up are very similar in action characteristics.

Random Forest and Hidden Markov Model are mentioned in [33], both of which extract features manually and then use Machine Learning for training and classification. Table 3, Table 4, and Table 5 all use Deep Learning method for automatic feature extraction. The results are obvious, Automatic feature extraction by Deep Learning method can not only reduce labor cost but also improve classification performance.

Table 3. Confusion matrix of long short-term memory's classification results [33].

		Predict					
		Lie down	Fall	Walk	Run	Sit down	Stand up
Actual	Lie down	**0.95**	0.01	0.01	0.01	0.00	0.02
	Fall	0.01	**0.94**	0.05	0.00	0.00	0.00
	Walk	0.00	0.01	**0.93**	0.04	0.01	0.01
	Run	0.00	0.00	0.02	**0.97**	0.01	0.00
	Sit down	0.03	0.01	0.05	0.02	**0.81**	0.07
	Stand up	0.01	0.00	0.03	0.05	0.07	**0.83**

Table 4. Confusion matrix of ABLSTM's classification results [6].

		Predict					
		Lie down	Fall	Walk	Run	Sit down	Stand up
Actual	Lie down	**0.96**	0.00	0.01	0.00	0.02	0.01
	Fall	0.00	**0.99**	0.00	0.01	0.00	0.00
	Walk	0.00	0.00	**0.98**	0.02	0.00	0.00
	Run	0.00	0.00	0.02	**0.98**	0.00	0.00
	Sit down	0.01	0.01	0.01	0.00	**0.95**	0.02
	Stand up	0.01	0.00	0.00	0.00	0.01	**0.98**

Table 5. Confusion matrix of MSHNet's classification results.

		Predict					
		Lie down	Fall	Walk	Run	Sit down	Stand up
Actual	Lie down	**1.00**	0.00	0.00	0.00	0.00	0.00
	Fall	0.00	**1.00**	0.00	0.00	0.00	0.00
	Walk	0.00	0.00	**1.00**	0.00	0.00	0.00
	Run	0.00	0.00	0.00	**1.00**	0.00	0.00
	Sit down	0.00	0.00	0.00	0.00	**0.97**	0.03
	Stand up	0.00	0.00	0.00	0.00	0.00	**1.00**

Comparison of MSHNet Results in Different Environments. To verify the adaptability of MSHNet in different environments, this paper collects datasets in four environments: DCRoom, CRoom, ERoom and PCRoom, and trains with MSHNet. The four evaluation metrics (Accuracy, Precision, Recall, F1) of different environments are shown in Fig. 7 and Table 6 shows the accuracy and overall classification performance of each action in the four environments. As can be seen from Fig. 7 and Table 6, DCRoom has the best results, because DCRoom is an ideal experimental environment with the least obstacles and thus has the least influence on the action characteristics. There are relatively few non-experimental related items in CRoom and ERoom. The PCRoom experimental environment is the most complex, and there are many non-experimental related objects, so the results are relatively slightly worse. However, on the whole, static objects in different environments have little influence on the results, and the activities of non-subjects on non-LOS also have little influence.

The experimental results in different environments show that MSHNet has good adaptability in different environments, and has good performance for individual activity monitoring.

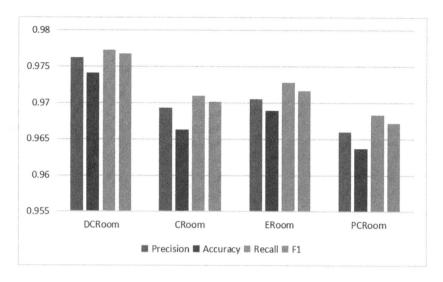

Fig. 7. Comparison of MSHNet results in different environments.

Table 6. Accuracy of different activities in different environments.

	noAction	Run	Sit down	Squat	Stand up	Walk	Overall
DCRoom	1.00	0.9722	1.00	1.00	0.9375	0.9538	0.9772
CRoom	1.00	0.9444	1.00	1.00	0.9125	0.9538	0.9684
ERoom	1.00	0.9583	1.00	1.00	0.9125	0.9538	0.9702
PCRoom	1.00	0.9305	0.9848	1.00	0.925	0.9583	0.9664

5   Conclusion

In this paper, an MSHNet deep neural network model is proposed for the daily health monitoring of elderly people who living alone and independently. The model not only achieves the best performance on public dataset, but also achieves good results on datasets collected in different environments by ourselves. However, MSHNet is only for single person, so in future work, we will mainly study human activity monitoring in multi-person situation. In addition, the paper does not use the phase information of CSI, so we will study the relationship between phase and human activity in the future. For multi-environment situations, we hope that the model trained in one environment can adapt to other environments quickly, which is also the focus of our future research.

References

1. Cisco Mobile, VNI, Cisco visual networking index global mobile data traffic forecast update 2016–2021, pp. 1–17. Cisco Visual Networking Index, San Jose, USA (2017)

2. Abdelnasser, H., Samir, R., Sabek, I., Youssef, M.: MonoPHY: mono-stream-based device-free WLAN localization via physical layer information. In: IEEE Wireless Communications and Networking Conference (WCNC 2013) (2013)
3. Abdelnasser, H., Youssef, M., Harras, K.A.: WiGest: a ubiquitous WiFi-based gesture recognition system. In: IEEE Conference on Computer Communications, pp. 1472–1480 (2015)
4. Bahl, P., Padmanabhan, V.N.: RADAR: an in-building RF-based user location and tracking system. In: Proceedings of the Nineteenth Annual Joint Conference of the IEEE Computer and Communications Societies, INFOCOM 2000. IEEE (2000)
5. Cao, Y., et al.: Contactless body movement recognition during sleep via WiFi signals. IEEE Internet Things J. **7**(3), 2028–2037 (2019)
6. Chen, Z., Zhang, L., Jiang, C., Cao, Z., Cui, W.: WiFi CSI based passive human activity recognition using attention based BLSTM. IEEE Trans. Mob. Comput. **18**(11), 2714–2724 (2019)
7. Cui, Z., Chen, W., Chen, Y.: Multi-scale convolutional neural networks for time series classification. CoRR abs/1603.06995 (2016)
8. Du, J., Zheng, Z., Li, G., Ying, S., Ju, Z.: Gesture recognition based on binocular vision. J. Yangtze Univ. (3), 1–11 (2018)
9. Ghasemzadeh, H., Jafari, R.: Physical movement monitoring using body sensor networks: a phonological approach to construct spatial decision trees. IEEE Trans. Ind. Inform. **7**(1), 66–77 (2011)
10. Gu, Y., et al.: EmoSense: computational intelligence driven emotion sensing via wireless channel data. IEEE Trans. Emerg. Top. Comput. Intell. https://doi.org/10.1109/TETCI.2019.2902438
11. Gu, Y., Wang, Y., Liu, Z., Liu, J., Li, J.: SleepGuardian: an RF-based healthcare system guarding your sleep from afar. IEEE Netw. (2019). https://doi.org/10.1109/MNET.001.1900235
12. Gu, Y., Zhang, X., Liu, Z., Ren, F.: BeSense: leveraging WiFi channel data and computational intelligence for behavior analysis. IEEE Comput. Intell. Mag. **14**(4), 31–41 (2019)
13. Halperin, D., Hu, W., Sheth, A., Wetherall, D.: Tool release: gathering 802.11n traces with channel state information. ACM SIGCOMM Comput. Commun. Rev. **41**(1), 53–53 (2011)
14. Han, C., Wu, K., Wang, Y., Ni, L.M.: WiFall: device-free fall detection by wireless networks. IEEE Trans. Mob. Comput. **16**(2), 581–594 (2017)
15. Hochreiter, S., Schmidhuber, J.: Long short-term memory. Neural Comput. **9**(8), 1735–1780 (1997)
16. Hong, T.K.N., Fahama, H., Belleudy, C., Pham, T.V.: Low power architecture exploration for standalone fall detection system based on computer vision (2015)
17. Ioffe, S., Szegedy, C.: Batch normalization: accelerating deep network training by reducing internal covariate shift. CoRR abs/1502.03167 (2015)
18. Lara, O.D., Labrador, M.A.: A survey on human activity recognition using wearable sensors. IEEE Commun. Surv. Tutor. **15**(3), 1192–1209 (2013)
19. Lea, C., Vidal, R., Reiter, A., Hager, G.D.: Temporal convolutional networks: a unified approach to action segmentation. In: Hua, G., Jégou, H. (eds.) ECCV 2016. LNCS, vol. 9915, pp. 47–54. Springer, Cham (2016). https://doi.org/10.1007/978-3-319-49409-8_7
20. Li, H., Yang, W., Wang, J., Xu, Y., Huang, L.: WiFinger: talk to your smart devices with finger-grained gesture. In: Proceedings of the 2016 ACM International Joint Conference on Pervasive and Ubiquitous Computing (2016)

21. Lin, M., Chen, Q., Yan, S.: Network in network. Computer Science (2013)
22. Ma, C., Li, W., Gravina, R., Cao, J., Li, Q., Fortino, G.: Activity level assessment using a smart cushion for people with a sedentary lifestyle. Sensors **17**(10), 2269 (2017)
23. Perahia, E., Stacey, R.: Next Generation Wireless LANs: 802.11 n and 802.11 ac. Cambridge University Press, Cambridge (2013)
24. Ramakic, A., Bundalo, Z., Bundalo, D.: A method for human gait recognition from video streams using silhouette, height and step length. J. Circuits Syst. Comput. **29**(7), 2050101:1–2050101:18 (2020)
25. Schuster, M., Paliwal, K.K.: Bidirectional recurrent neural networks. IEEE Trans. Sig. Process. **45**(11), 2673–2681 (1997)
26. Seifeldin, M., Saeed, A., Kosba, A.E., El-Keyi, A., Youssef, M.: Nuzzer: a large-scale device-free passive localization system for wireless environments. IEEE Trans. Mob. Comput. **12**(7), 1321–1334 (2013)
27. Selvabala, V.S.N., Ganesh, A.B.: Implementation of wireless sensor network based human fall detection system **30**, 767–773 (2012)
28. Srivastava, N., Hinton, G., Krizhevsky, A., Sutskever, I., Salakhutdinov, R.: Dropout: a simple way to prevent neural networks from overfitting. J. Mach. Learn. Res. **15**, 1929–1958 (2014)
29. Wang, T., et al.: Recognizing parkinsonian gait pattern by exploiting fine-grained movement function features. ACM Trans. Intell. Syst. Technol. **8**, 1–22 (2016)
30. Wang, W., Liu, A.X., Shahzad, M., Ling, K., Lu, S.: Device-free human activity recognition using commercial WiFi devices. IEEE J. Sel. Areas Commun. **35**(5), 1118–1131 (2017)
31. Wang, Z., Yan, W., Oates, T.: Time series classification from scratch with deep neural networks: a strong baseline, pp. 1578–1585 (2017)
32. Wu, K., Jiang, X., Yi, Y., Min, G., Ni, L.M.: FILA: fine-grained indoor localization. In: Proceedings of the IEEE INFOCOM, pp. 2210–2218 (2012)
33. Yousefi, S., Narui, H., Dayal, S., Ermon, S., Valaee, S.: A survey of human activity recognition using WiFi CSI. CoRR abs/1708.07129 (2017). http://arxiv.org/abs/1708.07129
34. Zhang, J., Wei, B., Hu, W., Kanhere, S.S.: WiFi-ID: human identification using WiFi signal. In: International Conference on Distributed Computing in Sensor Systems, pp. 75–82 (2016)
35. Zhao, M., et al.: Through-wall human pose estimation using radio signals. In: IEEE/CVF Conference on Computer Vision and Pattern Recognition, pp. 7356–7365 (2018)
36. Zhou, Q., Xing, J., Li, J., Yang, Q.: A device-free number gesture recognition approach based on deep learning. In: 2016 12th International Conference on Computational Intelligence and Security (CIS) (2016)

Advanced Technology in Edge Computing

Cache-Enhanced Task Offloading for eIoT with Mobile Edge Computing

Zhifeng Li[1], Jie Bai[1], Haonan Zhang[4], Wei Bai[2,3]($\boxtimes$), Yongmin Cao[1], Liwen Wu[1], Jianying Dong[1], and Yanshan Deng[1]

[1] State Grid Jibei Tangshan Power Supply Company, Tangshan 063000, China
[2] Electric Power Intelligent Sensing Technology and Application State Grid Corporation Joint Laboratory, Beijing, China
baiwei@geiri.sgcc.com.cn
[3] Global Energy Interconnection Research Institute Co., Ltd., Beijing 102209, China
[4] Beijing University of Posts and Telecommunications, Beijing, China

Abstract. With the continuous development and improvement of 5G networks, many emerging technology architectures have been introduced to support 5G service requirements. As one of them, mobile edge computing can meet the exponentially increasing computing requirements, and with its advantages of being more efficient, smarter, and more flexible, it can be well adapted to smart grid scenarios. However, most of the existing research contents of the eIoT focus on the research of computing offloading and content caching separately, ignoring the problem of reusability of some computing results. This paper considers the certain content caching capabilities of the MEC system itself, and aims to design a cache-enhanced MEC eIoT. The model includes offloading, calculating and backhaul for uncached task and downloading of cached content. On the other hand, the problem of task diversity and inspection robot mobility is fully analyzed. Subsequently, we studied the impact of caching capabilities on computing power to get the best MEC server parameter information. Based on the above research, this paper proposes a cache enhanced offload strategy and a collaborative scheduling algorithm to optimize the total delay of all tasks of the inspection robot in the eIoT. Simulation results show that the strategy can effectively reduce the computational offloading latency.

Keywords: eIoT · Collaborative caching · MEC · Computing offloading

1 Introduction

eIoT technology has developed rapidly in recent years, and a variety of inspection robot applications have emerged. This trend is expected to continue in the coming years [1]. With the advent of the Internet of Things (IoT) era, intelligent inspection robot terminals must become an indispensable part of it. Communication technologies that provide lower latency and more reliable services are an effective support for eIoT and play a

S. W. Loke et al. (Eds.): MONAMI 2020, LNICST 338, pp. 67–78, 2020.
https://doi.org/10.1007/978-3-030-64002-6_5

significant role in facilitating the commercialization of eIoT. In order to meet the computing needs of emerging applications, the introduction of MEC that provide auxiliary computing is a widely accepted model of current research institutions [2]. However, the computing power, coverage, and energy costs of current MEC servers are still being continually optimized, posing a challenge for MEC-enabled eIoT. Therefore, we propose a cache-enhanced MEC computing offloading strategy to address the challenges in the eIoT [3].

MEC is characterized by location awareness, delay sensitivity and mobile support [4]. The design of MEC needs to comprehensively consider the joint optimization of the location, communication quality and computing resources between distributed mobile devices and MEC servers [5, 6]. A variety of task processing performance can be improved through a federated design with the caching [7]. Recent research has made a lot of efforts and achievements in achieving a more reasonable eIoT structure. For instance, in [8], the author designed an integrated model for computing offloading, content caching, and resource allocation, using MEC's computing power and storage resources to reduce task offloading latency. In [4], the author proposes a distributed content distribution network based on MECs, and analyzes the distribution characteristics of service devices and terminals in the system to develop a grouping-based and hierarchical caching strategy for higher energy efficiency. The author of [9] considered the problem of user mobility, and extended the edge cache to MEC to implement more flexible context-aware cache decision, which proved that the scheme has higher throughput than the traditional scheme. The work in [10] proposed a new scheme where mobile edge computing resources are utilized for enhancing edge caching capability in 5G network, and introduced a concept of eIoT cache cloud to further utilize the cache resources of smart inspection robot to improve cache utilization. A novel theoretical framework that weighs the computational, caching, and communication resources of mobile edge networks reveals the fundamental benefits of computing and caching in content delivery eIoT in [3].

At present, for popular AR and multimedia transformation applications, there is a problem of repeated calculation of computing tasks [10]. Similarly, in the scenario of a service eIoT, there are always numerous identical computing tasks on the same short-distance road segment, and the same task key value is offloaded to the MEC server by different inspection robot. After a complex operation, the same result is fed back to the task requester. When the resource requirements of these high-frequency identical tasks are superimposed, it becomes a cost that cannot be ignored [7]. In this paper, we describe the MEC-assisted task calculation and unloading process in the eIoT. Using the storage capacity of the MEC server to cache the high hit rate calculation results can reduce the resource consumption of the repetitive operation. In order to avoid the high price brought by strengthening the server configuration, the interaction between cache capacity and computing task volume is studied. The cache-enhanced computing offload strategy and collaborative scheduling algorithm is implemented in the eIoT proposed in this paper, which reduces the computational latency of multi-tasking and provides a better experience for intelligent inspection robot.

The rest of the paper is organized as follows, Sect. 2 discusses in details our system model. Section 3 presents our cache-enhanced offloading strategy and collaborative scheduling algorithm, while Sect. 4 presents our performance evaluation. Then we conclude the paper and in Sect. 5.

2 System Model

In this section, we will model the proposed network. A cache-enhanced MEC system that provides services to inspection robot terminals, as shown in Fig. 1.

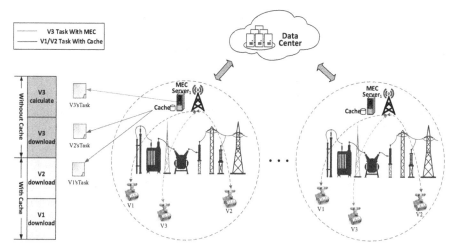

Fig. 1. System model of cache-enhanced vehicular networks

2.1 Transmission Model

Most of the existing research on MEC ignore the backhaul latency in returning calculation results. However, as the number of tasks increases, a series of task types with large amount of backhaul data (such as AR/VR, video transcoding, etc.) appear. Therefore, our transmission model considers not only the upload delay but also the delay of return result [11]. Thanks to the further promotion of 5G communication technology, it can also better support the information transmission of the eIoT.

In the transmission model, a mode in which a base station and a MEC server are deployed in cooperation is used, and the combination is recorded as Access Point (AP). Furthermore, based on the existing 5G version specification, the inspection robot can communicate with AP [1].

During the one-way road patrol, the distance between the robot and AP can be obtained according to the following formula

$$d_{on}(t) = \sqrt{r^2 + \left(\frac{L}{2} - vt_{on}\right)^2} \tag{1}$$

where r is the horizontal distance between the road and the base station inspected by the inspection robot, L is the coverage distance of the AP and the speed of the robot is v. t_{on} is the duration of the robot within the current AP coverage, which can be obtained by

$$t_{on} = \frac{L}{v} \tag{2}$$

In addition, during the change of d_{on}, the data rate R_{V2I} of the task offloading and the backhaul calculation result can be derived as

$$R_{V2I}(t) = B_{V2I} \log_2 \left(1 + \frac{P_t d_{on}^{-\delta}(t) h^2}{N_0} \right) \tag{3}$$

Let B_{V2I} and δ denote the channel bandwidth and path loss exponent respectively. The transmission model takes both the uplink and the downlink, so the transmission power P_t and the channel fading coefficient h should be considered in two cases [9].

High-speed mobility is an important feature in eIoT, which causes d_{on} changing faster. Therefore, the average transmission rate $\overline{R_{V2I}}$ is used to measure the uplink and downlink data rate of the inspection robot terminal and it can be given by

$$\overline{R_{V2I}} = \frac{\int_0^{t_{on}} R_{V2I}(t) dt}{t_{on}} \tag{4}$$

2.2 Computation Model

Typically, a task can be modeled as a profile with three parameters including d_c, d_{up}, t_{max}. The three parameters represent the task input-data size, computation intensity, and maximum allowable delay respectively. d_c and d_{up} are linear as similar to much existing research,

$$d_c = \alpha d_{up} \tag{5}$$

The task complexity index α is usually greater than 1. When some latency-sensitive or computation-intensive tasks are generated, the requester may not finish these tasks on time due to limited processing capacity of the on-board unit, i.e.,

$$t_{local} < t_{max} \tag{6}$$

the local calculation latency t_{local} exceeds maximum tolerance latency [9]. Thus, we introduced a MEC server system equipped with a multi-core CPU that can provide auxiliary calculations for multiple inspection robot terminals simultaneously. Since the computing resources of the MEC are usually subject to payment, the inspection robot terminal also has to obtain a specified CPU cycles by paying an unequal fee.

2.3 Caching Model

The MEC server has a certain storage capacity as a computing device deployed to the edge of the network. Moreover, as part of the AP, the MEC server can be directly connected to a dedicated caching device [13]. Based on its cache capability, the AP stores some task results. When the requester hits the content stored in the cache, the calculation result can be directly obtained. Let c denote the cache action [4, 13].

$$c_n \in \{0, 1\}, n \in \mathcal{N} \tag{7}$$

here, $c_n = 1$ indicates the action of the task n hitting the cached content, and $c_n = 0$ is the opposite. Under the limited cache capacity,

$$C \le \sum_{n \in \mathcal{N}} c_n d_{n,dl} \tag{8}$$

C and $d_{n,dl}$ represent the total caching amount at the current AP and the calculation result data amount of task n, respectively.

3 Cache-Enhanced Offloading Scheme and Collaborative Scheduling Algorithm

Based on the model discussed in Sect. 2, this section designs the cache-enhanced computational offloading scheme. The scheme calls for increased utilization of MEC. In addition, caching reusable results can increase the scalability of the system and reduce resource consumption, latency, and cost. Then we propose a collaborative scheduling algorithm to guide the task requester to do joint computing offloading.

3.1 Cache-Enhanced Offloading Scheme

First, the cache-enhanced offloading scheme is applicable to scenarios where multi-robot terminals carry multitasking. When robot terminal i meets the conditions described in Eq. (7), we record i as a task requester, $i \in \mathbb{SV}$ $\mathbb{SV} = \{1, \ldots, i, \ldots, SV\}$. The requester needs the MEC-assisted computing task $n \in \mathcal{N}, \mathcal{N} \triangleq \{1, 2, \ldots N\}$. In order to describe the key information of the task n, we denote $T_n = \{d_{n,up}, d_{n,dl}, c_n, t_{i,max}\}$ [5]. Indeed, a requester may carry multiple different tasks. The set and number of vehicles who need to execute task n at the random system task state X,

$$SV_n(X) \triangleq \sum_{i \in \mathbb{SV}} I[X_i = n] \tag{9}$$

where $I[\cdot]$ denotes the indicator function. Next, the requester i starts the operation of offloading the task n.

$$\overline{R_{i,n,up}} = \frac{\int_0^{t_{on}} R_{i,n,up}(t)dt}{t_{on}} \tag{10}$$

$$t_{i,n,up} = \frac{d_{i,n,up}}{R_{i,n,up}} \qquad (11)$$

$R_{i,n,up}(t)$ represents the instantaneous transmission rate of the n-type task offloading process on the terminal i. The transmission power of the robot terminal is P_t and the offloading average rate $\overline{R_{i,n,up}}$ can be derived according to (4)–(5). The latency of this process is recorded as $t_{i,n,up}$. Then, the AP determines whether the result has been cached according to the relevant key values of the received task. If $c_n = 0$, the MEC server provides the operating frequency $f_{m,i,n}$ to the requester for calculation. After the time $t_{i,n,ex}$, the result is transmitted back to the requester through the AP [12]. Under the influence of α, the operation delay $t_{i,n,ex}$ and the backhaul delay $t_{i,n,dl}$ can be presented as

$$t_{i,n,ex} = \frac{\alpha d_{i,n}}{f_{m,i,n}} \qquad (12)$$

$$t_{i,n,dl} = \frac{d_{i,n,dl}}{R_{i,n,dl}} \qquad (13)$$

On the other hand, when $c_n = 1$, the MEC server does not perform repetitive computing on the current task, which is beneficial to provide more idle resources for uncached tasks [3]. In summary, the total latency of computing offloading can be expressed as

$$t_{i,n} = (1 - c_n)t_{i,n,up} + t_{i,n,dl} + t_{i,n,ex} \qquad (14)$$

In this paper, how to get task popularity and cache high hit rate content is not our focus since caching is a technology to enhance MEC computing offloading. This scheme ensures that the MEC server has sufficient computing power, and reduces the delay for part of robot terminals. When considering the task requester set $\mathbb{SV}$, the problem of optimizing the total latency can be formulated as

$$\mathbf{P1} : \min_{C} \sum_{i \in \mathbb{SV}} \sum_{n \in \mathcal{N}} t_{i,n}$$

$$\text{s.t.} \begin{cases} C1 : C \leq \sum_{n \in \mathcal{N}} c_n d_{n,dl} \\ C2 : t_{i,n,local} < t_{i,n,max} \\ C3 : \sum_{n \in \mathcal{N}} \left((1 - c_n)t_{i,n,up} + t_{i,n,dl} + t_{i,n,ex}\right) \leq t_{i,n,max}, \\ \forall i \in \mathbb{SV} \end{cases} \qquad (15)$$

Specifically, $C1$ indicates that the cached result cannot contain all task types, which is determined by the actual conditions. $C2$ is a prerequisite for task offloading. If the cache-enhanced scheme still could not guarantee that the task is completed within the maximum tolerance delay, other calculation methods need to be considered, and $C3$ ensures that the situation does not occur. By solving the problem $\mathbf{P1}$, we optimize the total latency.

3.2 Collaborative Scheduling Algorithm

Task offloading should take into account the impact of pricing strategies. The number of computing resources provided by the MEC server for the robot terminal is positively correlated with the pricing [10]. As the price of the payment increases, it will inevitably gain a stronger computing power and a lower processing delay. According to the different needs of users, we can set the peak amount of payment for it. In other words, when the computing resources are in short supply, the unit resource price of the MEC server rises, and the resources required by some users to complete the current task reach the upper limit of their ability to pay. Such users choose to sacrifice the calculation delay to reduce the tariff or use other auxiliary. Way (such as D2D calculation). Such users choose to sacrifice the calculation latency to reduce the tariff or use other auxiliary methods (Such as D2D scheme).

Our collaborative scheduling algorithm can jointly consider the utility value and the delay tolerance parameter to improve the availability of the cache enhanced offloading strategy. Specifically, the utility value U is used to describe the relationship between resources and costs can be given by

$$U_{i,n} = \varphi(f_{m,i,n}) - \omega(P_n, f_{m.i.n}) \tag{16}$$

where $U_{i,n}$ is a utility function [17]. For task n, the MEC server provides the corresponding $f_{m,i,n}$ computation capacity. Task requester always expect a higher QoE, while $f_{m,i,n}$ is directly related to it.

$$\begin{aligned} \varphi(f_{m,i,n}) &= \beta(t_{i,n,local} - t_{i,n,up} - t_{i,n,dl} - t_{i,n,ex}) \\ &+ \gamma(ln(\rho f_{m,i,n} + \in)) \\ &= \beta\left(\frac{d_{i,n}}{f_i} - \frac{d_{i,n,up} + d_{i,n,dl}}{R_{V2I}} - \frac{d_{i,n}}{f_{m,i,n}}\right) \\ &+ \gamma(ln(\rho f_{m,i,n} + \in)) \end{aligned} \tag{17}$$

In (17), we use the processing latency to describe the total utility value $\varphi(f_{m,i,n})$. ρ is a utility coefficient that saves unit delay, and γ is a utility coefficient that saves computational resources. $\omega(P_n, f_{m.i.n})$ represents the payment for MEC server, where the parameter P_n is the price of the unit resource.

Obviously, the utility function of terminal i is mainly related to computation capacity allocated by RSU and $f_{m,i,n}$ is the main influencing factor [10]. According to the configuration of the MEC server, the maximum resource is F_m, so that $f_{m,i,n} \leq F_m$. Bringing (16) into (17), we derive the maximum value of the utility function. The second-order derivative of $U_{i,n}$ with respect to $f_{m,i,n}$ is

$$\frac{\partial^2 U_{i,n}}{\partial^2 f_{m.i.n}} = -2\beta \frac{1}{f_{m.i.n}^3} \tag{18}$$

Because all the values of parameters in (17) are positive, the second-order derivative of the utility function is lower than zero, namely, $\frac{\partial^2 U_{i,n}}{\partial^2 f_{m.i.n}} < 0$ [10]. It shows that the utility function has a maximum value. And the optimal solution $f_{m,i,n}^*$ can be solved by

$\frac{\partial U_{i,n}}{\partial f_{m,i,n}} = 0$. The requester i has an ideal effect value $U_{i,n}^*$ in the unloading calculation. When $U_{i,n}^* > U_{i,n}$, we have to consider other auxiliary calculation methods. The specific algorithm design is as follows. The detail steps about the proposed collaborative scheduling algorithm is described as Algorithm 1.

Table 1. Joint selection algorithm process

Algorithm 1 Joint Selection Algorithm
1: Initialization:
a)The request robots $\mathbb{SV} = \{1,\dots,i,\dots,SV\}$
b)Set caching action $c_n = 0, \text{n} \in \mathcal{N}$
c)The P_n
2: **for** i in **SV do**
3:    **for** n in N **do**
4:      Scan $d_{i,n,up}$
5:      **if** $d_{i,n,up}$ has cached, **then**
6:        Set $c_n = 1$;
7:      **end if**
8:      Calculate $U_{i,n}$ by (14)-(17)
9:      **if** $U_{i,n} > U_i^*$ and $t_{i,n,local}$ satisfy constrain (6), **then**
10:        Calculate $t_{i,n}$ by (14)
11:      **else if**
12:        Set $f_{m,i,n} = f_{m,i,n}^*$
13:        Calculate $t_{i,n}$
14:        **if** $t_{i,n} > t_{i,n,local}$, **then**
15:          Set $t_{i,n} = t_{i,n,local}$
16:        **end if**
17:      **end if**
18:    **end for**
19: **end for**
20: Output: Offloading strategy and the optimal total latency

4   Simulation Result and Discussion

In this section, the performance of the cache enhanced offloading scheme and the collaborative scheduling algorithm are illustrated by comparing the simulation results. In this simulated scenario, each AP cover a range of 200 m [16]. We set transmission power P_t of the vehicle and the AP is 1.3 W and 2 W, respectively, and data is transmitted through the wireless bandwidth of 10 M [16]. The power spectral density of additive white Gaussian noise $N_0 = -100$ dBm, and the channel fading coefficient $h = 4$ [12]. The computational complexity index $\alpha = 1.05$, $\beta = 0.6$, and $\gamma = 0.4$. Since the price P_n of the unit resource is fluctuating, we set the initial value of P_n to 0.5 according to the number of idle resources. With resources become rarer, the P_n is larger.

Compared with the commonly used MEC offloading strategy and partial offloading strategy, the simulation results show that the scheme designed in this paper obtain better performance in latency and scalability for vehicle network. At the beginning, we analyze the situation where an AP covers 40 robot terminals, and each terminal randomly generates computing tasks which size is $5 \times 10^6 bits$ [13]. We simulate the velocity of each robot randomly selected from 10 m/s to 30 m/s. By adjusting the cache capacity, it is possible to store different numbers of high hit rate calculation results, which affects the amount of resources of the required MEC. Figure 2 shows the relationship between the amount of buffer and the required resources. When the buffer reaches $4 \times 10^7 bits$, the slope of the curve is significantly reduced. At this point, the MEC needs to provide $4 \times 10^{10} cycles/s$ processing power for uncached computing tasks.

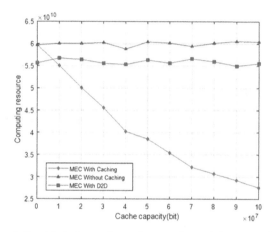

Fig. 2. The relationship between the cache capacity and the computing resource.

Figure 3 depicts the total latency of cache enhanced offloading and popular MEC offloading scheme. Similar to the results shown in Fig. 2, when the cache reaches $4 \times 10^7 bits$, the latency optimization result is quite obvious. Therefore, $C = 4 \times 10^7 bits$ is determined for subsequent research.

Figure 4 and Fig. 5 discuss optimization in multitasking situations. In Fig. 4, it describes the total delay of the three modes in the interval of task data in $[0, 45M]$. Due to the limited computing power of the onboard unit, the D2D mode performance is lower than other modes. With the exhaustion of MEC capabilities, the scheme of offloading some tasks to nearby idle vehicle processing yields lower latency than the scheme that only supports MEC offloading. However, the strategies and algorithms proposed in this paper can save a lot of repetitive task calculation overhead for MEC servers, so the overall performance has always been better than other strategies. Figure 5 describes the total delay in the processing of the task when the number of robot terminals is increasing.

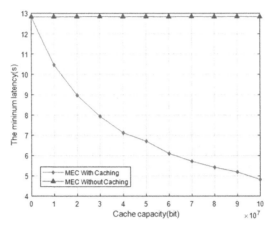

Fig. 3. The minimum latency for computing offloading of MEC with/without caching.

The simulation results are shown in Fig. 4. However, the model proposed by us can save a lot of repetitive calculation overhead for MEC servers, so the overall performance has always been better than other strategies. Figure 5 describes the total latency when the number of robot terminals continues to increase. The results obtained from this simulation are consistent with Fig. 4.

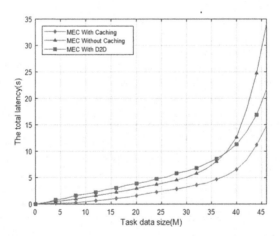

Fig. 4. The total latency of cache-enhanced offloading scheme, without caching and D2D versus the task data size.

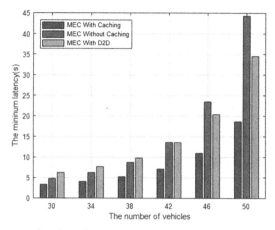

Fig. 5. The total latency of cache-enhanced offloading scheme, without caching and D2D versus the number of robots.

5 Conclusion

This paper focuses on the application of popular MEC technology in smart gird. A cache-enhanced computing task offloading scheme is proposed, which uses cache repetitive task calculation results to optimize system resources and processing latency. At the same time, a collaborative scheduling algorithm is designed to help smart inspection robots to perform optimal calculation and offloading within the limits of their respective payment capabilities. Simulation results verify the effectiveness of our proposal.

Acknowledgement. This paper is supported by Science and Technology Project of State Grid Jibei Electric Power Co., Ltd.; Research and Application of Intelligent Operation Inspection Service Based on Electric Power Wireless Private Network (5201031801CS).

References

1. Shah, V.S.: Deterministic consumer applications enabled policy Architecture of Mobile Edge Computing ecosystem. In: 2017 IEEE 7th Annual Computing and Communication Workshop and Conference (CCWC), pp. 1–7. IEEE (2017)
2. Ren, D., Gui, X., Lu, W., An, J., Dai, H., Liang, X.: GHCC: grouping-based and hierarchical collaborative caching for mobile edge computing. In: 2018 16th International Symposium on Modeling and Optimization in Mobile, Ad Hoc, and Wireless Networks (WiOpt), Shanghai, pp. 1–6 (2018)
3. Wang, X., Han, Y., Wang, C., Zhao, Q., Chen, X., Chen, M.: In-Edge AI: intelligentizing mobile edge computing, caching and communication by federated learning. IEEE Netw. **33**(5), 156–165 (2019)
4. Chen, L., Dong, X., Kuang, X., et al.: Towards ubiquitous power distribution communication: multi-service access and QoS guarantees for IoT applications in smart grid. In: 2019 IEEE Innovative Smart Grid Technologies-Asia (ISGT Asia), pp 894–898. IEEE (2019)

5. Zhang, J., et al.: Joint resource allocation for latency-sensitive services over mobile edge computing networks with caching. IEEE Internet Things J. **6**(3), 4283–4294 (2019)
6. Liu, X., Zhang, J., Zhang, X., Wang, W.: Mobility-aware coded probabilistic caching scheme for MEC-enabled small cell networks. IEEE Access **5**, 17824–17833 (2017)
7. Zhang, K., Leng, S., He, Y., Maharjan, S., Zhang, Y.: Cooperative content caching in 5G networks with mobile edge computing. IEEE Wireless Commun. **25**(3), 80–87 (2018)
8. Zaw, C.W., Ei, N.N., Reum Im, H.Y., Tun, Y.K., Hong, C.S.: Cost and latency tradeoff in mobile edge computing: a distributed game approach. In: 2019 IEEE International Conference on Big Data and Smart Computing (BigComp), Kyoto, Japan, pp. 1–7 (2019)
9. Vu, T.X., Lei, L., Chatzinotas, S., Ottersten, B., Trinh, A.V.: On the successful delivery probability of full-duplex-enabled mobile edge caching. IEEE Commun. Lett. **23**(6), 1016–1020 (2019)
10. Li, M., Rui, L.L., Qiu, X., et al.: Design of a service caching and task offloading mechanism in smart grid edge network. In: 2019 15th International Wireless Communications & Mobile Computing Conference (IWCMC), pp. 249–254. IEEE (2019)
11. Xu, X., Liu, J., Tao, X.: Mobile edge computing enhanced adaptive bitrate video delivery with joint cache and radio resource allocation. IEEE Access **5**, 16406–16415 (2017)
12. Wang, K., Li, J., Wu, J., et al.: QoS-predicted energy efficient routing for information-centric smart grid: a network calculus approach. IEEE Access **6**, 52867–52876 (2018)
13. Wang, D., Lan, Y., Zhao, T., Yin, Z., Wang, X.: On the design of computation offloading in cache-aided D2D multicast networks. IEEE Access **6**, 63426–63441 (2018)
14. Qian, Y., Li, S., Shi, L., et al.: Cache-enabled MIMO power line communications with precoding design in smart grid. IEEE Trans. Green Commun. Netw. **4**(1), 315–325 (2019)
15. Li, Y., Li, C., Wu, G., et al.: Research on high-precision time distribution mechanism of multi-source power grid based on MEC. In: 2019 IEEE International Conference on Communications, Control, and Computing Technologies for Smart Grids (SmartGridComm), pp. 1–5. IEEE (2019)
16. Arun, M., Jenson, D., Nandhini, V.M., et al.: Smart grid robot exclusively designed for high power transmission lines. In: 2019 5th International Conference on Advanced Computing & Communication Systems (ICACCS), pp. 652–654. IEEE (2019)
17. Disyadej, T., Promjan, J., Poochinapan, K., et al.: High voltage power line maintenance & inspection by using smart robotics. In: 2019 IEEE Power & Energy Society Innovative Smart Grid Technologies Conference (ISGT), pp. 1–4. IEEE (2019)

Virtual Edge: Collaborative Computation Offloading in VANETs

Narisu Cha[1] [ID], Celimuge Wu[1(✉)] [ID], Tsutomu Yoshinaga[1] [ID], and Yusheng Ji[2] [ID]

[1] The University of Electro-Communications, Tokyo, Japan
narisu@comp.is.uec.ac.jp, celimuge@uec.ac.jp
[2] National Institute of Informatics, Tokyo, Japan

Abstract. Edge computing can reduce service latency through task offloading. Since computational resources on the edge of the network are scarce, selecting a node with rich computational capability is the key for getting a high-quality service. In this paper, we propose a virtual edge scheme where a node can offload its tasks to a virtual edge node that consists of multiple vehicles in vicinity. The relative vehicle velocity and computational capability are considered in the virtual edge selection. We compare our proposed scheme with several baseline schemes and show the superiority of the scheme.

Keywords: Virtual edge · Edge computing · Computation offloading · VANETs

1 Introduction

Edge computing [1, 2] is a method of selecting nodes that are closer to the end user to offload computation. In the Internet of Vehicles (IoV), in order to improve the network resource utilization efficiency and reduce the response delay, the edge computing has been attracting increasing interest in the past decade due to its capability of conducting computing and data caching near the end users.

In the future, connected vehicle technology will become one of the main important components of an intelligent transportation system. In order to improve traffic safety and alleviate the traffic congestion, various sensors including cameras, radars would be equipped on the vehicles, which generates numerous data. IHS Automotive forecasts that the quantity of vehicles and its in-vehicle equipment could reach nearly two billion on the roads by 2025 and every car will produce up to 30 terabytes of data each day [3]. Due to network bandwidth limitations, traditional cloud-based data processing methods are not suitable for latency-sensitive services in vehicular ad hoc networks (VANETs).

Automatic vehicles on the road can be viewed as edge nodes with computational resources to execute driving tasks such as lane identification, positioning, image processing, and traffic environmental awareness. On the one hand, from the perspective of cost, the owner has the economic capability to purchase a high-performance computer to improve the safety, because the cost of a computer is much cheaper as compared with

S. W. Loke et al. (Eds.): MONAMI 2020, LNICST 338, pp. 79–93, 2020.
https://doi.org/10.1007/978-3-030-64002-6_6

the vehicle. Deploying services and computational resources at the edge of the network is able to avoid transmitting the original data to the cloud and thereby reduce the latency.

Multiple automatic vehicles can collaborate with each other to accomplish some tasks in the scenarios that infrastructure cannot be support adequate resources, such as 3D traffic scene generation, video stream analysis, etc. These applications have the feature that intensive computation can be offloaded to some vehicles in vicinity.

Computation offloading has been studied in mobile edge computing (MEC) including energy-efficient allocation of computing resources [4], binary computation offloading [5], partial computation offloading [6, 8], and stochastic offloading [7]. Most aforementioned works consider that the computation tasks on mobile nodes are aggregated to a node, such as road-side unit (RSU) or base station (BS), which does not consider the use of vehicles as edge nodes.

In [9], Mach and Becvar have reviewed the offloading strategies in the MEC. In [10], Mao et al. concluded the method that uses joint radio and computational resource management to merge the two disciplines of wireless communications and mobile computing seamlessly. Z. Ning et al. have constructed decentralized three-layer vehicular fog computing (FVC) architecture, where moving and parked cars are viewed as fog nodes for processing local traffic data to optimize the network loading balance [11]. Vehicular multi-access networks with collaborative task offloading can guarantee low latency of the application [12]. The optimal policy for the computation offloading to multiple base stations in an ultra-dense sliced RAN is modeled by Markov decision process, and a new algorithm to offload computation based on double deep Q-network is proposed [13]. To tackle the spatial intelligence of vehicular Internet of thing (IoT), the technology of combining decentralized moving edge with multi-tier multi-access edge clustering by Q-learning is discussed in [14]. As automobiles are equipped with stronger processing units, the idea that uses parking or moving vehicles as communication and computation infrastructures has been proposed in [12–17]. Hou et al. [18] found that adjacent moving vehicles have good connectivity between each other and they can form a powerful computation cluster. They described four kinds of application scenarios and three-layer Vehicular fog computing (VFC) paradigm, then verified by real-world vehicular mobility traces and can enlarge available resources and enhance computation capability. There also have been some efforts discussing the joint resource-allocation and computation-offloading [15–23]. However, existing studies do not seriously consider how to efficiently utilize the computing capabilities of moving vehicles in dynamic vehicular networks.

In this paper, we propose virtual edge (VE), a light autonomous cooperative-distributed computing platform established by multiple nodes willing to share computational resources. When there is a need for using the computational resources of other vehicles, a node can construct a VE. The purpose is to alleviate the scarcity of computational resources at the node by using other vehicles' resources and to make the end-user have more computational capability. Our main contributions in the paper are:

- Based on mobile cloud computing, we proposed the concept of virtual edge that can be established on-demand to provide more computational resources for a node, for a better resource utilization and delay reduction.

- A method that quickly establishes VE with short delay in VANETs is proposed and then verified. The method discovers available resources at the vicinity of vehicle nodes in tens of milliseconds and generates stable and efficient edge nodes for providing more computational resources.
- The nodes consisting the VE are selected from the one-hop neighbors of the master node (the node with task establishes a VE) where the relative velocity of vehicles is considered in the VE member selection.

The reminder of the paper is as follows. We first describe system architecture of the virtual edge in Sect. 2. Section 3 describes system model and problem formulation and experimental results are shown in Sect. 4. The last section draws our conclusions.

2 System Architecture

Vehicles are viewed as mobile nodes with available computational resources in the VE architecture. The architecture added a layer on the mobile cloud computing architecture, which has three layers: Cloud, Fog/MEC, virtual edge, as shown in Fig. 1.

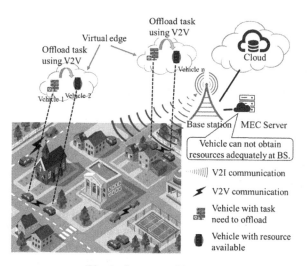

Fig. 1. System architecture.

Cloud layer: Permanent data is stored in the cloud center. For example, Traffic management servers and trusted third authority service are stored in this layer. It is in charge of monitoring global traffic data to optimize the schedule.

Fog/MEC layer: This layer consists of network infrastructures, such as cloudlet server, road-side unit (RSU), smart traffic light, router, access point (AP), and base station (BS). They process local data by collecting, aggregating, controlling and caching, after that, a huge amount of data has been compressed and send it to the cloud.

Virtual Edge: The number of RSUs on the road is limited, and therefore in some cases, it is impossible to connect with the RSU. In this case, the use of available resources for vehicles for computation offloading is more effective than RSU. The vehicle nodes with tasks establish virtual edge on-demand among the idle nodes with available computational resources in vicinity. The lifetime of the connectivity between vehicles is predicted when VE create. After VE is established, it provides more stable computational capability and more bandwidth to the node with a task.

Vehicle node: A vehicle can be used as a router, relay node, or cache to accomplish the computing tasks. Generally, automatic vehicles have more sensing and computational resources than other vehicles. The node that with insufficient computational resources, needs to offload the computation tasks to virtual edge when the vehicle does not obtain the computing resource adequately from the base station.

Virtual edge is established by vehicle nodes to explore lower cost resources when the computational resources provided from BS/RSU do not satisfy the constraint. The architecture proposed is very suitable for dense vehicle scenes, such as urban areas, and can utilize the computational resource of parked vehicles and others running the same direction. Without modifying the cloud and fog/edge layer, the virtual edge can be used as a complement to expand the function of utilizing resources in vicinity. A task needs to be sent to the cloud, when the task cannot be completed at BS/RSU or virtual edge.

3 System Model and Problem Formulation

3.1 System Model

We consider the V2V communications based on dedicated short range communication (DSRC), such as IEEE 802.11p. Basic safety message (BSM) as defined in SAE J2735, including vehicle information such as position, velocity, direction, acceleration and so on. The standard payload of BSM is 39B, smaller than the length of a frame. In our system model, BSM also contains available computation resources like CPU frequency, caching size, available bandwidth etc. According to IEEE 1609.4, each vehicle needs to broadcast a BSM in a certain interval. Each vehicle maintains a BSM table which contains information of vehicles at the vicinity and then computes companion time between connected others directly. VE establishment process could utilize the information of BSM table and companion time in order for a faster creation of VE topology.

These nodes within single-hop communication range show different levels of capabilities, as shown in Fig. 2. In the scenario, vehicles only communicate with each other through V2V communication technology, such as IEEE 802.11p. Assume that vehicle v_2 has a task and needs to be offloaded to the other vehicles. v_1, v_3, v_4, v_5 reside within v_2's communication range. With the movement of vehicles, the connection between vehicles becomes unstable. The duration of the connection between v_2 and v_1 is shorter, because two vehicles are driving in the opposite direction. The connection between v_2 and v_5 is an unstable connection, because v_5 is at the edge of v_2's communication range and the speed difference is large. When selecting a cooperative node, it is important that consider not only the duration time of the connection, but also available computing resources.

The collection $V(t)$ refer to the set of vehicles at time t, where $V(t) = \{v_1, v_2, \ldots, v_{|V(t)|}\}$, $|V(t)|$ is the total number of vehicles at time t. $V_{ve,v}(t)$ refer to the members of VE established by node v at time t and $V_{ve,v}(t) \subseteq V(t)$. Unless otherwise specified, the vehicle set is denoted by $V(t)$.

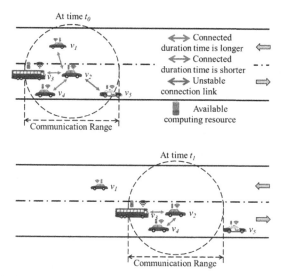

Fig. 2. An example for collaborative node selection; we need to consider the duration of the connection, and the available resources in the selection process.

3.2 Motion Model

Due to the mobility of IoV, establishing a stable VE faces great challenges. In order to return the results of computation offloading before connections between vehicles are broken, the prediction of VE duration time becomes very important. According to the interaction between vehicles, vehicle motion models can be categorized into three types in the literature: macroscopic, mesoscopic and microscopic. Macroscopic and mesoscopic models focused on the analysis results of overall performance by the parameters of the traffic, such as density, flow, arrival rate. Microscopic model describes distance headway of vehicles by the interaction with neighboring vehicles, driving behavior of individual vehicles. In this section, the motion model is a simple motion model belonging to microscopic, similar to in [24]. Below we first introduce three definitions, then introduce the concept of companion time, and use it to calculate the companion time between any two nodes, and finally using companion time to predict the duration time of VE.

Definition 1: Given V is the set of vehicle, $v, u \in V$, we say v and u are connected directly if v and u are reachable within single-hop communication range, and are denoted by $dist(v, u) < r$, where r refers to the communication range of the vehicle.

Definition 2: Given V is the set of vehicle, $\forall v, u \in V$, $\exists v_1, v_2, \ldots, v_n \in V$, $\langle v, v_1 \rangle, \langle v_1, v_2 \rangle, \ldots, \langle v_{n-1}, v_n \rangle, \langle v_n, u \rangle$ are all connected directly, then it is called that V is interconnected.

Definition 3: Given V is the set of vehicle, in the future period T, if $\forall t \in [0, T], \forall v, u \in V$, node v and u are connected, it is called that the duration time of V is at least T.

Following, the companion time of two nodes with direct connection is discussed. Each vehicle is only responsible for computing/updating the companion time for directly connected vehicles. The vector $\vec{P}_v = (p_{x,v}, p_{y,v}, p_{z,v})$, $\vec{v}_v = (v_{x,v}, v_{y,v}, v_{z,v})$, $\vec{a}_v = (a_{x,v}, a_{y,v}, a_{z,v})$, refer to position, velocity, acceleration of vehicle v. The vector $\vec{P}_u = (p_{x,u}, p_{y,u}, p_{z,u})$, $\vec{v}_u = (v_{x,u}, v_{y,u}, v_{z,u})$, $\vec{a}_u = (a_{x,u}, a_{y,u}, a_{z,u})$, refer to position, velocity, acceleration of vehicle u. Three elements represent values in x, y, z directions, respectively. Assuming that the acceleration is a constant before it is updated, the relative position of two vehicles is

$$\vec{P} = \vec{P}_u - \vec{P}_v = (p_{x,u} - p_{x,v}, p_{y,u} - p_{y,v}, p_{z,u} - p_{z,v}) \tag{1}$$

Similarly, relative velocity and acceleration of two vehicles are

$$\vec{a} = \vec{a}_u - \vec{a}_v = (a_{x,u} - a_{x,v}, a_{y,u} - a_{y,v}, a_{z,u} - a_{z,v}) \tag{2}$$

$$\vec{v} = \vec{v}_u - \vec{v}_v = (v_{x,u} - v_{x,v}, v_{y,u} - v_{y,v}, v_{z,u} - v_{z,v}) \tag{3}$$

The relative trajectory of node u is

$$\vec{S} = \frac{1}{2}\vec{a}t^2 + \vec{v}t + \vec{P} \tag{4}$$

Then, the length of relative trajectory can be expressed as

$$\vec{S} \cdot \vec{S} = r^2 \tag{5}$$

where r is the radius of the vehicle's communication range, $(\cdot)$ is an inner product. Obtain from equations above

$$\left(\frac{1}{2}\vec{a}t^2 + \vec{v}t + \vec{P}_u - \vec{P}_v\right) \cdot \left(\frac{1}{2}\vec{a}t^2 + \vec{v}t + \vec{P}_u - \vec{P}_v\right) = r^2 \tag{6}$$

Expand the above formula we get

$$\left(\frac{1}{2}(a_{x,u} - a_{x,v})t^2 + (v_{x,u} - v_{x,v})t + p_{x,u} - p_{x,v}\right)^2 +$$
$$\left(\frac{1}{2}(a_{y,u} - a_{y,v})t^2 + (v_{y,u} - v_{y,v})t + p_{y,u} - p_{y,v}\right)^2 +$$
$$\left(\frac{1}{2}(a_{z,u} - a_{z,v})t^2 + (v_{z,u} - v_{z,v})t + p_{z,u} - p_{z,v}\right)^2 = r^2 \tag{7}$$

In the equation above, variable t is an unknown and others are known. The value of t can be solved, and it is the companion time between node v and u. Companion time of two nodes v and u t multiple relay nodes is

$$t_{\langle v,u \rangle} = \{t_{x_i,x_{i+1}} | i \in \{1, n-1\}, x_1 = v, x_n = u, \; dist(x_i, x_{i+1}) < r\} \tag{8}$$

The duration time of VE is determined by the minimum companion (duration) time between the master node and other nodes, which can be expressed as

$$t_{dur,ve} = \left\{ t_{\langle v,u \rangle} \right\} \tag{9}$$

where node v is master node, $V_{ve,v}$ is the set of nodes included VE. In order to avoid disconnection of nodes frequently, the companion time must be greater than the threshold δ when the node is selected, $t_{\langle v,u \rangle} \geq \delta$. The recommended value of δ

$$\delta = \frac{r}{v_{road}} \tag{10}$$

where v_{road} is the maximum allowable velocity of road.

3.3 Communication Model

The efficiency of the offloading process is affected by the stability of the connection between vehicles in VANETs. We use a simple model to estimate the time of transmissions by dividing the number of the hops with the data size. An example is presented in Fig. 3, where v_2 is the vehicle with a task, and the dashed circle shows the communication range of the node. The hops between v_2 and v_4 varies from 2 to 1, and then becomes to 2. The throughput between v_2 and v_4 varies with the routing length. Figure 4 illustrates the result that the throughput changes for various number of hops under TCP (RENO) flow in the simulation, where the vehicle nodes are running at the velocity of 20 km/hour along the straight road.

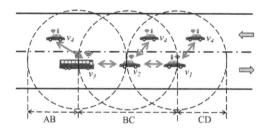

Fig. 3. The throughput varies with the number of hops between source and destination.

3.4 Computation Model

We consider that node v has a computation task $D = \left\{ d_1, d_2, \ldots, d_{|V_{ve,v}(t)|} \right\}$, that can be divided into multiple blocks. Block j is sent from vehicle v to vehicle i over IEEE 802.11p for the execution. Element d_i refer to the cycle number of block i. The variable f_i refers to the available computation resource (i.e., CPU-cycle frequency) on the vehicle i. When the computation task is offloaded onto the vehicle, the processing time t_i can be expressed as

$$t_i = \frac{d_j}{f_i} \tag{11}$$

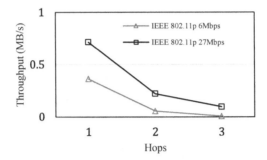

Fig. 4. The throughput of TCP over IEEE 802.11p under the different bitrates.

where $j = 1, 2, \ldots, \left| V_{ve,v}(t) \right|$ and $\forall v_i \in V_{ve,v}$. Since multiple vehicles can process the computation task Simultaneously after received the task, the computation time of VE can be obtained by

$$t_{ve,v} = \left\{ t_i | i = 1, 2, \ldots, \left| V_{ve,v}(t) \right| \right\} \tag{12}$$

3.5 Utility Function

Utility function describes the impact of the number of VE topology changes during task execution on the overall performance. The more the number, the more the impact on the task. The value t_e is VE establishment time that is shown as Fig. 5. In the case where the number of nodes is fixed, t_e can be considered as a constant. To complete computation, the duration time of VE must be larger than the processing time of computation. Therefore, the utility function can be expressed as

$$\left\{ t_{dua,ve} - t_{ve,v} \right\} \tag{13}$$

where $2^{|V(t)|}$ is the power set of V(t), which is the set including all subsets of $V(t)$.

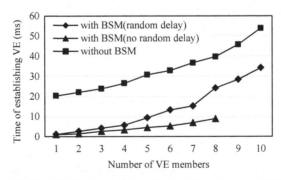

Fig. 5. Time of establishing VE [the method that Basic Safety Message (BSM) without random delay fail to establish VE at 9, 10].

3.6 Complexity

We adopt the utility function above as our objective function, and it is formulated as

$$\left\{ t_{dua,ve} - t_{ve,v} \right\}$$

$$\text{s.t. } t_{dua,ve} \geq t_{ve,v}, \forall V_{ve} \in 2^{|V(t)|}$$

$$t_{\langle v,u \rangle} \geq \delta, \forall u \in V_{ve,v}, \forall V_{ve} \in 2^{|V(t)|} \tag{14}$$

The first constraint guarantees that the results can be returned to the vehicle v. The second constraint guarantees that the member of VE did not disconnect frequently.

We assume that $a_\rightarrow = \{a_i | a_i \in \{0, 1\}, i = 1, 2, \ldots, |V(t)|\}$ where element a_i refer to the vehicle i is whether the member of VE or not. To find the optimal solution of the problem, it is required to search the entire space and the size of the space is $2^{|V(t)|}$. Due to the complexity of the problem, we proposed a simplified method of establishing VE.

The computational capability is used to indicate the potential computational power that VE can provide.

$$A_{cc} = \sum_{i=1}^{n} C_i * T_i \tag{15}$$

where n is times of VE topology changes during the completion of the task. Total computation time T is divided into n stage and T_i is duration time of VE at i th stage. C_i is the computational power of VE at i th stage and it is represented by CPU frequency. The computational power of the VE at each stage is represented by the following formula.

$$C_i = c_i^0 + B * \sum_{j=1}^{m} c_i^j \tag{16}$$

where m is the slave node count in VE, B is the ratio of network transmission rate and memory transfer rate, and c_i^j is the computation power of slave node j at stage i. c_i^0 is the computational power of master node at stage i.

$$A_{cc} = \sum_{i=1}^{n} \left(c_i^0 + B * \sum_{j=1}^{m} c_i^j \right) * T_i$$

$$= c_i^0 * T + B * \sum_{i=1}^{n} \left(\left(\sum_{j=1}^{m} c_i^j \right) * T_i \right) \tag{17}$$

The problem is to select the best VE members to minimize the objective function. The fewer the number of VE topology changes, the smaller the penalty. When the slave node in VE is disconnected, it needs to reselect the nodes for replacement. The fewer the count to replace nodes, the smaller the communication overhead generated by the migration data. The number of members of VE directly affects the computational capability of the VE. However, a large member node will increase the potential risk of the VE's disconnection.

Because in VANETs, the establishment of VE is affected by many factors such as traffic conditions, signal coverage, maximum speed limit of the road, and road layout. In this paper, the simulator is used to explain the impact of many influencing factors on generating VE in VANETs.

4   Performance Evaluations

The discrete event simulator OMNeT++ and the mobility generator SUMO are used to build realistic vehicular scenarios. We compare our scheme with three benchmarks. Simulation process consists of two parts: establishment of VE and VE topology changes. The parameters in the simulation are listed in Table 1. A 2800 m × 2800 m area of Tokyo is used as the map in the simulator. Speed limit on the road is 40 km/hour (14 m/s). There are two opposite directions of traffic flows and their arrival rate is 0.2 vehicle/second. the vehicle begins to establish VE when the task is arrived, after the warm-up process. Vehicles are classified into three categories: master vehicle, slave vehicle and ordinary vehicle. A master vehicle is a vehicle with a task and the slave is without task. Master and slave vehicles participate in establishing VE and task processing while ordinary vehicles do not.

Table 1. Parameters in the simulator

Parameter	Value
Max velocity of vehicle	14 m/s
Antenna frequency	5.9 GHz
Interval of sending BSM	1 s
BSM timeout	2 s
V2V data rate	27 Mbps
Memory data rate	600 Mb/s
Communication range	250 m
Warm-up time	200 s
Simulation time	320 s

For the slave node selection, we have developed four methods: random, the minimum distance first, the maximum available resources first, and the longest drive-through time first.

- Random (rand): randomly select vehicles within the single-hop range.
- Minimum distance first (minDist): setting a higher priority for the vehicles with the minimum distance to master vehicle.
- Maximum available resources first (maxRes): setting a higher priority for the nodes with the maximum available resources.
- Longest drive-thru time first (ourProp): The master node is regarded as a fixed point. The relative speed between the master and slave node is obtained by vector product between the speed of the master node and the slave node. The relative speed is used to calculate the drive-thru time through the one-hop range of the master node.

4.1 VE Establishment

As shown in Fig. 6 that the duration time of VE becomes shorter with the increase of the number of VE members as the more the nodes, the shorter the connection link lifetime between nodes. Although, as the number of slave nodes increases, the computation power obtained according to weighted accumulation above method will increase, as shown in Fig. 7, but the duration time will decrease so that the computational capacity will decrease. Therefore, it is important to find the most suitable VE size according to the vehicular environment.

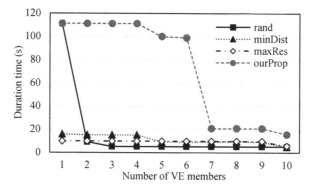

Fig. 6. Duration time of VEs which are consisted of different numbers of members while without VE maintenance.

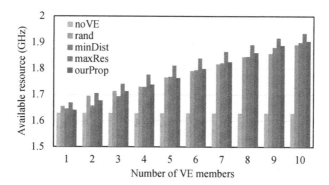

Fig. 7. Computational resources of VEs which are consisted of different numbers of members while without VE maintenance.

4.2 VE Maintenance

Due to the continuity of the cloud service, VE topology change is required in order to satisfy the requested services. The VE will be invalid, when a slave node leaves the communication range of the master node. At this time, the master node automatically maintains the VE, resulting in the change of VE members.

Several metrics are used to compare the performance of schemes in the simulation. In the ideal state, the duration time of the VE equals the service time. However, due to unstable node connection and VE re-establishment time, the duration time of VE is less than the service time, as shown in Fig. 8. Unexpected disconnection is caused by the following reasons: the slave node leaves the communication range of the master node; the failure to receive BSM due to packet losses. The comparison of expected disconnection times for different edge selection methods is shown in Fig. 9.

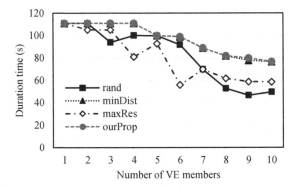

Fig. 8. Duration time of VE which are consisted of different numbers of members.

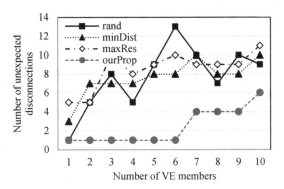

Fig. 9. The number of unexpected disconnections which are consisted of different numbers of members.

Figure 10 and 11 illustrates the number of failures for various number of VE members and the available computational capability, respectively. Available computational capability in the case of VE maintenance is calculated by weighted accumulation. The potential computational capability of VE is stronger than one single node without VE. VE re-creation failed due to the difficulty in finding the enough slave nodes at vicinity. As the slave nodes count in VE increases, the computational capability of VE can be enhanced, but it also causes some difficulties. For example, the prediction of VE's duration becomes more difficult, and the probability of missing VE member increases, as shown Fig. 9 and Fig. 10. Unexpected disconnection during the task execution is harmful to collaborative task offloading. It is very important to maximize computational capability by increasing the number of the slave nodes while minimizing the number of unexpected disconnections. It can be seen from Fig. 9, VE with 6 slave nodes achieves the largest computational resources with the smallest unexpected disconnections. A similar result can be seen from Fig. 10 where VE with 4 slave nodes achieves the largest computational resources with the smallest number of VE re-creations. Due to the lack of vehicles, VE cannot be established successfully, and transmitting tasks to the cloud for execution will take longer delay.

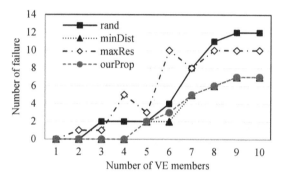

Fig. 10. Number of failures of VE re-formation which are consisted of different numbers of members.

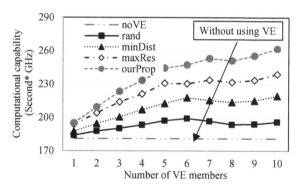

Fig. 11. Obtaining stable services is impracticable in VANET, since the connection is unstable. The product of connection lifetime and computing capability (represented by CPU frequency) is induced to describe the available computational capability of VE.

5   Conclusion

We proposed the concept of virtual edge based on mobile edge computing to solve the shortage of computing capability at the edge of the network. We also proposed a VE selection method where the relative velocity between vehicles is considered. We used computer simulations to evaluate the proposed method by comparing with other baseline approaches. The simulation results show that the proposed method can generate more stable and efficient edge nodes as compared with existing baselines.

Acknowledgment. This research was supported in part by ROIS NII Open Collaborative Research 2020-20S0502, and JSPS KAKENHI grant numbers 18KK0279, 19H04093 and 20H00592.

References

1. Hassan, N., Yau, K.L.A., Wu, C.: Edge computing in 5G: a review. IEEE Access **7**, 127276–127289 (2019)
2. Feng, J., Liu, Z., Wu, C., Ji, Y.: AVE: autonomous vehicular edge computing framework with ACO-based scheduling. IEEE Trans. Veh. Technol. **66**(12), 10660–10675 (2017)
3. Huang, C., Lu, R., Choo, K.R.: Vehicular fog computing: architecture, use case, and security and forensic challenges. IEEE Commun. Mag. **55**(11), 105–111 (2017)
4. You, C., Huang, K., Chae, H., Kim, B.-H.: Energy-efficient resource allocation for mobile-edge computation offloading. IEEE Trans. Wireless Commun. **16**(33), 1397–1411 (2016)
5. Bi, S., Zhang, Y.: Computation rate maximization for wireless powered mobile-edge computing with binary computation offloading. IEEE Trans. Wireless Commun. **17**(6), 4177–4190 (2018)
6. Khalili, S., Simeone, O.: Inter-layer per-mobile optimization of cloud mobile computing: a message-passing approach. Trans. Emerg. Telecommun. Technol. **27**(6), 814–827 (2016)
7. Jiang, Z., Mao, S.: Energy delay tradeoff in cloud offloading for multi-core mobile devices. IEEE Access **3**, 2306–2316 (2015)
8. Wang, Y., Sheng, M., Wang, X., Wang, L., Li, J.: Mobile-edge computing: partial computation offloading using dynamic voltage scaling. IEEE Trans. Commun. **64**(10), 4268–4282 (2016)
9. Mach, P., Becvar, Z.: Mobile edge computing: a survey on architecture and computation offloading. IEEE Commun. Surveys Tutor. **19**(3), 1628–1656 (2017)
10. Mao, Y., You, C., Zhang, J., Huang, K., Letaief, K.B.: A survey on mobile edge computing: the communication perspective. IEEE Commun. Survey Tutor. **19**(4), 2322–2358 (2017)
11. Ning, Z., Huang, J., Wang, X.: Vehicular fog computing: enabling real-time traffic management for smart cities. IEEE Wirel. Commun. **26**(1), 87–93 (2019)
12. Qiao, G., Leng, S., Zhang, K., He, Y.: Collaborative task offloading in vehicular edge multi-access networks. IEEE Commun. Mag. **56**(8), 48–54 (2018)
13. Chen, Xianfu, Zhang, Honggang, Celimuge, Wu, Mao, Shiwen, Ji, Yusheng, Bennis, Mehdi: Optimized computation offloading performance in virtual edge computing systems via deep reinforcement learning. IEEE Internet Things J. **6**(3), 4005–4018 (2019)
14. Wu, C., Liu, Z., Zhang, D., Yoshinaga, T., Ji, Y.: Spatial intelligence toward trustworthy vehicular IoT. IEEE Commun. Mag. **56**(10), 22–27 (2018)
15. Whaiduzzaman, M., Sookhak, M., Gani, A., Buyya, R.: A survey on vehicular cloud computing. J. Netw. Comput. Appl. **40**, 325–344 (2014)

16. Olariu, S., Eltoweissy, M., Younis, M.: Towards autonomous vehicular clouds. ICST Trans. Mobile Commun. Appl. **11**(7–9), 1–11 (2011)
17. Olariu, S., Khalil, I., Abuelela, M.: Taking VANET to the clouds. Int. J. Pervasive Comput. Commun. **7**(1), 7–21 (2011)
18. Hou, X., Li, Y., Chen, M., Wu, D., Jin, D., Chen, S.: Vehicular fog computing: a viewpoint of vehicles as the infrastructures. IEEE Trans. Veh. Technol. **65**(6), 3860–3873 (2016)
19. Wang, C., Liang, C., Yu, F.R., Chen, Q., Tang, L.: Computation offloading and resource allocation in wireless cellular networks with mobile edge computing. IEEE Trans. Wireless Commun. **16**(8), 4924–4938 (2017)
20. Kumar, K., Liu, J., Lu, Y.-H., Bhargava, B.: A survey of computation offloading for mobile systems. Mobile Netw. Appl. **18**(1), 129–140 (2013)
21. Huynh, L.N.T., Pham, Q., Pham, X., Nguyen, T.D.T., Hossain, M., Huh, E.: Efficient computation offloading in multi-tier multi-access edge computing systems: a particle swarm optimization approach. Appl. Sci. **10**(1), 203 (2020)
22. Yan, J., Bi, S., Zhang, Y., Tao, M.: Optimal task offloading and resource allocation in mobile-edge computing with inter-user task dependency. IEEE Trans. Wireless Commun. **19**(1), 235–250 (2020)
23. Xu, X., et al.: An edge computing-enabled computation offloading method with privacy preservation for internet of connected vehicles. Futur. Gener. Comput. Syst. **96**, 89–100 (2019)
24. Zhang, D., Zhang, T., Liu, X.: Novel self-adaptive routing service algorithm for application of VANET. Appl. Intell. **49**, 1866–1879 (2019)

Delay and Energy Aware Computation Task Offloading Strategy in Power Wireless Heterogeneous Networks

Wei Bai[1,2]([✉]), Yang Lu[1,2], Donglei Zhang[1,2], Jawei Li[3], Ping Ma[4],
Shuiyao Chen[5], and WeiPing Shao[5]

[1] Electric Power Intelligent Sensing Technology and Application State Grid
Corporation Joint Laboratory, Beijing, China
baiwei@geiri.sgcc.com.cn
[2] Global Energy Interconnection Research Institute Co., Ltd., Beijing, China
[3] Beijing University of Posts and Telecommunications, Beijing, China
[4] State Grid Shaoxing Electric Power Supply Company Shaoxing, Shaoxing, China
[5] State Grid Zhejiang Electric Power Co., Ltd., Hangzhou, China

Abstract. Mobile Edge Computing (MEC) is regarded as a promising technology that migrates cloud computing platforms with computing and storage capabilities to the edge of the wireless access network, enabling rich applications and services in close proximity to the mobile users (MUs). There are a lot of literatures that have studied computation offloading. Different from them, this paper performs a novel research on multi-level computation offloading taking account into the heterogeneity of computation tasks and computation resource backup pool, and introducing opportunistic networks in multi-access networks simultaneously. Firstly, we describe the computation offloading model. Then, we formulate the multi-level computation offloading problem as a Stackelberg game and demonstrate the existence of the game Nash equilibrium. In order to solve above problem, we design a global optimal algorithm based on game theory. Finally, the performance of the proposed algorithm is verified by comparing with other algorithms. Simulation results corroborate that the algorithm can not only decrease the energy consumption, but also is stable.

Keywords: Mobile edge computing · Stackelberg game · Computation offloading · Multi-access network

1 Introduction

Nowadays, the development of latency sensitive and computation intensive applications such as interactive game and augmented reality is closely related to the development of mobile devices. These applications have attracted a lot of attention because of their ability to spice up and bring convenience to our lives. Nevertheless, mobile devices are often resource constrained [1]. As a result, resource-constrained mobile devices can become strained by latency sensitive and computation intensive applications, causing bottlenecks and making it difficult for

© ICST Institute for Computer Sciences, Social Informatics and Telecommunications Engineering 2020
Published by Springer Nature Switzerland AG 2020. All Rights Reserved
S. W. Loke et al. (Eds.): MONAMI 2020, LNICST 338, pp. 94–110, 2020.
https://doi.org/10.1007/978-3-030-64002-6_7

mobile devices to ensure the required quality of service (QoS) (including energy consumption and/or processing delay [2]. Mobile Edge Computing (MEC) proposed by ETSI (European Telecommunications Standards Institute) can mitigate the need for large amounts of computation from mobile devices, which enables such applications through providing computation resource in close to mobile users and at the edge of the radio access network [3].

Computation offloading is one of the critical issues in MEC system. Generally speaking, computation offloading is made up of three phases, the data uploading, the task execution and the result return. However, since the computation results are very small, the time for returning the computation results is ignored in most literatures [4]. With computation offloading technology, the resource-constrained MUs can save energy and enrich MUs experience by fully or partially offloading computation-intensive tasks to the nearby other MU or MEC server [5].

There are a lot of work that has investigated the computation offloading and resource allocation of MEC. In a multi-user scenario, paper [5] investigated the resource allocation for MEC offloading in cellular networks. Considering a multi-user and multi-server MEC scenario, the authors in [6] proposed a genetic algorithm based computation algorithm in order to solve offloading decision, computation resource allocation and channel allocation. As indicated in [7], the efficiency of the computation offloading and resource allocation depends largely on the decision to offloading strategy. Task offloading and resource allocation in an MEC enabled multi-cell wireless network are studied in [8] with the objective of maximizing the MUs' task offloading gains and it formulate considered problem as a mixed integer nonlinear program. However, the authors did not consider the heterogeneity of MUs computation tasks and the queue latency at the MEC servers. Various from above work, we do a novel research on the computation offloading decision-making and resource allocation in a multi-access network.

In this paper, we study a MEC system in which consider computation resource backup pool among the MEC servers and investigate computation offloading strategy with the objective of maximizing the utility of MUs and the revenue of MEC servers via optimizing offloading decision-making while taking into account heterogeneity of computation tasks, queue delay and opportunistic networks (ONs) in multi-access networks, where, opportunistic networks is a self-organizing network which introduces encountering opportunities brought by node movement to realize communication rather than relying on a complete link between the source node and the target node [9] and the ONs enable MUs to communicate not only with MUs connected by D2D link, but also with computing nodes via movement. First, we denote the system model and formulate the main problem as a Stackelberg game problem. Then, we prove the existence of the game Nash equilibrium. Furthermore, we propose a global optimal algorithm namely computation offloading algorithm to tackle this problem. Eventually, the convergence of the algorithm is studied by simulation. The simulation results show that the algorithm works well comparing with other algorithms, which verifies the effectiveness of the proposed algorithm in terms of maximizing the utility of MUs and the revenue of MEC servers.

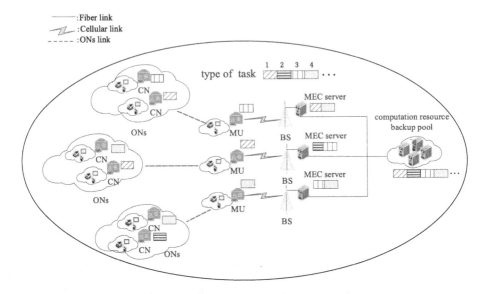

Fig. 1. System model

The remainder of our work is organized as follows. Section 2 gives the system model and problem formulation. In Sect. 3, the proposed joint optimization algorithm is developed. Simulation results and discussions are described in Sect. 4. Finally, we conclude this paper in Sect. 5.

2 System Model

2.1 Network Model

We consider a multi-access network with I mobile users (MUs) and M small base stations (SBSs) as shown in Fig. 1, where all of SBSs is equipped with MEC servers. The set of MUs and MEC servers are denoted by $I = \{1, 2, ..., i, ..., I\}$ and $N = \{1, 2, ..., k, ..., N\}$, in which i and k represent MU i and MEC server k, respectively. Moreover, we suppose that each MU has at most M types of computation tasks to be accomplished, and each task cann't be divided into. Also, the set of computation task types requested by MUs is denoted by $M = \{1, 2, ..., j, ..., M\}$, which include interactive games, face/fingerprint recognition, natural language processing, and so on. In addition, we introduce $p_{i,j}$ to indicate the request probability of the type-j task at MU i taking into account that different computation tasks are randomly requested by MUs at a time, where $0 < p_{i,j} < 1$. As for type-j computation task at MU i, it can be described as three items, i.e., $b_{i,j} = \{L_{i,j}, D_{i,j}, T_{i,j}^{max}\}$, in which $L_{i,j}$ denotes the data size of computation task, $D_{i,j}$ describes the total number of CPU cycles required to complete the computation task measured in Megacycle, $T_{i,j}^{max}$ represents the Quality of Service (QoS) requirement of computation task. Furthermore, the maximum computation capacity of MU i and MEC server k is separately $f_i^{l,max}$ and $f_k^{e,max}$.

In the MEC system, between MU i and MEC server k are connected with cellular link, and each of MUs is capable of communicating with other MUs nearby via opportunistic networks (ONs), which communicates using short-range communication protocols, for example, wifi, bluetooth, and etc. For ease of description, the set of MUs in close to the MU i is described as U and called help users (HUs). Otherwise, let $\delta_{i,j}$ denote offloading decision for type-j computation task at MU i, $\delta_{i,j} = \{-I, -(I-1), ..., -m, -(i+1), -(i-1), ..., 0, 1, 2, ..., k, ...N\}$, $m \in I\backslash i$, $k \in N$. Specifically, $\delta_{i,j} = -m$ if MU i offloads type-j computation task to HUs m, $\delta_{i,j} = 0$ if MU i decides to execute type-j computation task locally by its own CPU, $\delta_{i,j} = k$ if MU i offloads type-j computation task to MEC server k. Next, we will describe the processing delay and energy consumption in the above mentioned cases.

2.2 Local Computing

For $\delta_{i,j} = 0$, MU i chooses to execute type-j computation task by its own CPU. Suppose that the computation capacity of each MU is fixed when computing, but may vary among the MUs. Denote the available computation capacity of MU i as $f_i^l = a_i^l f_i^{l,max}$, $a_i^l \in (0,1]$, which is measured by CPU cycles per second. Therefore, the total delay in this case can be expressed by

$$T_{i,j}^l = \frac{D_{i,j}}{f_i^l} \tag{1}$$

Given e_i^l which denotes the consumed energy of MU i per CPU cycle for local computing, the energy consumption in such case can be given by

$$E_{i,j}^l = D_{i,j} e_i^l \tag{2}$$

2.3 Offload to MEC Servers

For $\delta_{i,j} = k$, MU i decides to offload type-j computation task to MEC sever k. Considering the case where multiple MUs are simultaneously offloaded to the same MEC server k, although the MEC server can purchase computation resources from the network operator, which places a computation resource backup pool (CRBP) in each small cell, there is a queue delay because the purchase of resources requires a certain amount of cost, and the MEC server is rational. In order to compute execution time and queue time of computation task $b_{i,j}$ at the MEC server k, we suppose that the probability of computation task requests at MU i follows a Poisson distribution, and then the arrival of various types of computation tasks at the MEC server k is a Poisson process. After that, we can model the execution and arrival of computation tasks at the MEC server as an $M/M/1$ queue. Therefore, the service time of computation tasks at the MEC server (including execution time and queuing time) follows an exponential distribution with an average service time of $\frac{1}{\sigma^M}$, where $\sigma^M = f_k^{e,max} + f_k^{e,c}$, $f_k^{e,c}$ is the computation resources purchased from network operator. Hereafter, the average time to complete computation task $b_{i,j}$ in this case can be denoted by $t_{i,j} = \frac{D_{i,j}}{\sigma^M - \overline{\lambda_M}}$. Here, $\overline{\lambda_M}$ is the average arrival rate of the computation task $b_{i,j}$ at the MEC server, it can be described as:

$$\overline{\lambda_M} = \sum_{i=1}^{I} \sum_{j=1}^{M} p_{i,j} D_{i,j} X_{\{\delta_{i,j}=k\}} \tag{3}$$

where, $X_{\{\#\}} = 0$ if the condition $\#$ is false, and otherwise $X_{\{\#\}} = 1$. Furthermore, the total delay of computation task $b_{i,j}$ in the case can be calculated by

$$T_{i,j}^k = \frac{L_{i,j}}{R_{i,j}^k} + \frac{D_{i,j}}{\sigma^M - \overline{\lambda_M}} \tag{4}$$

Here, $R_{i,j}^k$ represents the data transfer rate from the MU i to the MEC server k. Moreover, let $P_{i,j}$, $h_{i,k}$ and B_k denote the transmission power of MU i, the channel gain and the channel bandwidth, respectively. $R_{i,j}^k$ can be computed by

$$R_{i,j}^k = B^k \log_2 \left(1 + \frac{P_{i,j}|h_{i,k}|^2}{N_0 + \sum_{i' \in U \setminus i, j' \in M \setminus j, \delta_{i,j}=1} P_{i',j'}|h_{i',k}|^2} \right) \tag{5}$$

where N_0 is the additive white gaussian noise power. Thus, the total energy consumption for offloading to MEC server can be denoted by

$$E_{i,j}^k = P_{i,j} T_{i,j}^k \tag{6}$$

2.4 Offload to Help Users

For $\delta_{i,j} = -m$, MU i decides to offload type-j computation task to help user m. Since there exists a large queue delay for MU i when it decides to offload computation task $b_{i,j}$ to the MEC server during peak hours, the MUs can also choose to offload to a help user with a large amount of idle resources nearby. In this case, the MU i transmits the computation task $b_{i,j}$ to the help user m through the ONs. After that, we assume that each help user can only help one user at a time taking into account the computation resources limitation of MUs', and then the transmission rate can be expressed as

$$R_{i,j}^m = B^m \log_2 \left(1 + \frac{P_{i,j}|h_{i,m}|^2}{N_0} \right) \tag{7}$$

where B^m and $h_{i,m}$ denote the channel bandwidth and the channel gain between MUi and help user m. Let f_i^m represents available computation resource of help user m, the total execution delay can be given by

$$T_{i,j}^m = \frac{L_{i,j}}{R_{i,j}^m} + \frac{D_{i,j}}{f_i^m} \tag{8}$$

Therefore, the total energy consumption in such case can be expressed as

$$E_{i,j}^m = P_{i,j} T_{i,j}^m \tag{9}$$

3 Problem Formulation and Proposed Algorithm

3.1 Problem Formulation

Considering that the MUs and MEC servers are always maintained and operated by some operators, in order to gain revenues from the provision of computation services, the operator adopts a pricing scheme so that the MUs can be charged according to the computation resources they require. In addition, we consider the linear cost function MEC servers that provide resources. The cost of MEC server k that provides x unit resources for computation offload is expressed as

$$C_k(x) = \beta_k^e x + \gamma_k^e \tag{10}$$

where $\beta_k^e > 0$ and γ_k^e represent the coefficients of cost function for MEC server. For ease of analysis, we have $\gamma_k^e = 0$.

Due to the computation resource limitation of the MEC server, there may be competition among the MUs when making offloading decision. Since the MUs' offloading decisions are driven by the pricing scheme, these MUs are indirectly coupled by the computation resource price. Moreover, the computation resource providers, i.e., the MEC servers, are also indirectly coupled through the price during the offloading process.

The MUs can offload the computation task to the help users nearby or the MEC servers remotely, and the MUs' offloading decisions are response to the price advertised by the MEC servers. Therefore, the Stackelberg game is an attractive method to model the multi-level computation offloading [13]. In this game, the MEC server is the leader, and the MUs act as followers through the optimal response to the MEC server strategy. Next, we define the utilities of MUs and the revenue of MEC servers, then model the computation offload problem as a Stackelberg game.

3.2 The Utility of MUs

The utility of MU i accomplishing type-j computation task is defined as

$$
\begin{aligned}
U_{i,j} = & \sum_{k=1}^{N} X_{\{\delta_{i,j}=k\}} \left(\alpha_{i,j} \left(E_{i,j}^l - E_{i,j}^k \right) - \varepsilon_k^e f_k^{e,i} \right) \\
& + \sum_{m=1}^{I} X_{\{\delta_{i,j}=-m\}} \left(\alpha_{i,j} \left(E_{i,j}^l - E_{i,j}^m \right) - \varepsilon_m f_i^m \right) \\
& + \sum_{i'=1,i'\neq i}^{I} X_{\{\delta_{i',j}=-i\}} \left(\varepsilon_i f_{i'}^i - \beta_i f_{i'}^i \right)
\end{aligned}
\tag{11}
$$

Where $\alpha_{i,j}$ is the MU-specific parameter which demonstrates the sensitivity of MU i to the reduction in computation task execution energy consumption, $\alpha_{i,j} > 0$. ε_m and ε_k^e are the prices charged for the MU using the unit computation resource from the help user m and the MEC server k, respectively. β_m and β_k^e are severally corresponding cost. $f_k^{e,i}$ denotes the computation resources allocated by the MEC server k to MU i.

Since the MUs are rational, they maximize their utilities through making the offloading decision. In this case where the price set $\{\varepsilon_m, \varepsilon_k^e, m \in I, k \in N\}$ is given, the optimization problem for MU i can be formulated as

$$\max_{\{\delta_{i,j}, f_k^{e,i}\}} U_{i,j} \quad i \in I, j \in M, k \in N, m \in I$$

$$\text{s.t.} \quad C1 : \max\left(\sum_{k=1}^{N} X_{\{\delta_{i,j}=k\}} T_{i,j}^k, T_{i,j}^l\right) \leq T_{i,j}^{\max}$$

$$C2 : \max\left(\sum_{m=1}^{N} X_{\{\delta_{i,j}=-m\}} T_{i,j}^m, T_{i,j}^l\right) \leq T_{i,j}^{\max} \tag{12}$$

$$C3 : \sum_{m=1}^{I} X_{\{\delta_{i,j}^m=-m\}} + \sum_{k=1}^{N} X_{\{\delta_{i,j}^k=k\}} \leq 1$$

$$C4 : X_{\{\delta_{i,j}=-m\}} = \{0,1\}$$

$$C5 : X_{\{\delta_{i,j}=k\}} = \{0,1\}$$

$$C6 : f_i^m \leq f_m^{l,\max}$$

$$C7 : f_k^{e,i} \leq f_k^{e,\max} + f_k^c$$

where f_k^c is the amount of computation resource bought from the network operator by MEC server k.

The offloading decision of the MU i not only depends on their own offloading demands, but also on the offloading strategies of other MUs, which makes Stackelberg game an appropriate approach to model the decision-making process. The players in this game are the MUs $\{N\}$. The strategy set for MU i can be expressed as $s_i = \{s_{i,-I}, ..., s_{i,-m}, ..., s_{i,1}, ..., s_{i,k}, ..., s_{i,N}\}$, where $s_{i,-m} = \delta_{i,j} f_i^m$, $s_{i,k} = \delta_{i,j} f_k^{e,i}$, $m \in I$, $k \in N$. Therefore, the player's strategic space can be denoted as $s = \{s_1 \times s_2 \times ... \times s_I\}$. Given s_{-i} as the offloading decisions for all MUs besides MU i, the utility of MU i can be given as $U_{i,j}(s_i, s_{-i})$, $i \in I$.

Theorem 1. *The computation task offloading game between the MUs is a concave multi-player game with Nash Equilibrium (NE).*

Proof. In the case where MU i offloads its computation task to help user m or MEC server k, as $f_i^m = [0, f_m^{i,\max}]$, $f_k^{e,i} = [0, f_k^{e,\max} + f_k^c]$. Thus, we have $s_{i,-m} = [0, f_m^{i,\max}]$, $s_{i,k} = [0, f_k^{e,\max} + f_k^c]$, $i \in I$, $m \in I$, $k \in N$. Replacing f_i^m, $f_k^{e,i}$ by $s_{i,-m}$, $s_{i,k}$ in (11), we can obtain $\frac{\partial^2 U_{i,j}}{\partial s_{i,-m}^2} = -\frac{\alpha_{i,j} P_{i,j} D_{i,j}}{s_{i,-m}^3} < 0$, $\frac{\partial^2 U_{i,j}}{\partial s_{i,k}^2} = -\frac{\alpha_{i,j} P_{i,j} D_{i,j}}{s_{i,k}^3} < 0$. For the given all MUs' offloading decisions besides MU i, the

MU i's payoff function $U_{i,j}(s_i, s_{(-i)})$ is strictly convex in terms of the variables $s_{i,-m}$, $s_{i,k}$, which holds for all MUs making offloading decisions. Therefore, the computation task offloading game between MUs is a strictly concave multi-player game, which exits a NE [10].

3.3   The Revenue of MEC Servers

As an offloading service provider, the MEC servers sells computation resources to MUs with the objective of making more profit. Since each of MUs can make any offloading decisions while meeting the specified computation task processing delay constraints, the MEC servers play the non-cooperative price decisions game with each other in order to determine the optimal computation resource price. Therefore, there will be competition between the MEC servers during the offloading process. In addition, when the MEC servers' own computation resources cannot meet the needs of the MUs, the computation resources can be purchased from the network operator. Since the total amount of available computation resources for the MEC servers affects the revenue of each MEC server, the amount of computation resources purchased from the network operator is also the decision of each MEC server in the offloading competition. Considering that competition is not perfect, each of MEC servers makes its offloading decision set (ε_k^e, f_k^c) based on its own available computation resources and the offloading demands, $k \in N$.

Since the computation resources from the network operator are often more expensive than those from the MEC server itself, we have $\varepsilon_k^c \succ \varepsilon_k^e$, $k \in N$. Therefore, each of MEC servers prefers to employing its own available computation resources first. Given the decision sets of other MEC servers, the revenue of employing decision (ε_k^e, f_k^c) for the MEC server k can be denoted as

$$
\begin{aligned}
&U_{mec}^k \left((\varepsilon_k^e, f_k^c), (\varepsilon_{-k}^e, f_{-k}^c) \right) \\
&= \varepsilon_k^e \sum_{i=1}^{I} X_{\{\delta_{i,j}=k\}} f_k^{e,i} - \beta_k^e \min \left(\sum_{i=1}^{I} f_k^{e,i}, f_k^{e,\max} \right) - \varepsilon_k^c f_k^c
\end{aligned}
\tag{13}
$$

Where $\left(\varepsilon_{-k}^e, f_{-k}^c \right)$ is the decision set of MEC servers besides server k. After that, the revenue optimization problem of the MEC server k can be expressed as

$$
\max_{\varepsilon_k^e, f_k^c} U_{mec}^k \left((\varepsilon_k^e, f_k^c), (\varepsilon_{-k}^e, f_{-k}^c) \right)
$$

$$
\begin{aligned}
\text{s.t.} \quad &C1 : \varepsilon_k^c > \varepsilon_k^e \quad k \in N \\
&C2 : f_k^c \geq 0 \quad k \in N \\
&C3 : \beta_k^e > 0 \quad k \in N
\end{aligned}
\tag{14}
$$

Lemma 1. *There exists an upper limit on the selling price of computation resources for each MEC server, i.e., $\varepsilon_k^e \leq \varepsilon_k^{e,\max}$, $k \in N$.*

Proof. For specific computation tasks $b_{i,j}$, we have $U_{i,j} = \alpha_{i,j}\big(E^l_{i,j} - \frac{L_{i,j}}{R^k_{i,j}} - \frac{L_{i,j}D_{i,j}}{f^{e,i}_k}\big) - \varepsilon^e_k f^{e,i}_k$ according to (11) when MU i offloads computation task to the MEC server k. Since the MU i is rational, the MU i can offload computation tasks to the MEC server k only when $U_{i,j} > 0$. Let $Z_{i,j} = E^l_{i,j} - \frac{L_{i,j}}{R^k_{i,j}}$, we can get

$$\varepsilon^e_k < \frac{\alpha_{i,j}Z_{i,j}}{f^{e,i}_k} - \frac{D_{i,j}}{\big(f^{e,i}_k\big)^2}. \text{ Then, let } Q\big(f^{e,i}_k\big) = \frac{\alpha_{i,j}Z_{i,j}}{f^{e,i}_k} - \frac{\alpha_{i,j}D_{i,j}}{f^{e,i}_k\big(\delta^M - \lambda_M\big)}. \text{ Nextly, we}$$

need to prove that $Q\big(f^{e,i}_k\big)$ has a maximum value in order to prove the existence of $\varepsilon^{e,\max}_k$. The first derivative of $Q\big(f^{e,i}_k\big)$ with regard to $f^{e,i}_k$ can be denoted by $\frac{\partial Q\big(f^{e,i}_k\big)}{\partial f^{e,i}_k} = -\frac{V}{\big(f^{e,i}_k\big)^2} + \frac{G\big(2f^{e,i}_k - S\big)}{\big(\big(f^{e,i}_k\big)^2 - Sf^{e,i}_k\big)^2}$, where $V = \alpha_{i,j}Z_{i,j}$, $G = \alpha_{i,j}L_{i,j}$, $S = P_{i,j}L_{i,j}$. Let $H = SV + G$, it can be seen that $\frac{\partial Q\big(f^{e,i}_k\big)}{\partial f^{e,i}_k} > 0$ when $\frac{H - \sqrt{GH}}{V} < f^{e,i}_k < \frac{H + \sqrt{GH}}{V}$. Therefore, the function $Q\big(f^{e,i}_k\big)$ has a maximum value $Q^{i,max}_k$. Taking into account that each of MEC servers is able to offload computation tasks from any MUs under the processing delay constraints, the sufficient condition for MEC servers that is capable of selling its computation resources to the MUs is $\varepsilon^e_k \leq \varepsilon^{e,\max}_k = \max\big(Q^{1,\max}_k, Q^{2,\max}_k, ..., Q^{I,\max}_k\big)$, $k \in N$ (The same reason can be proved $\varepsilon_m \leq \varepsilon^{\max}_m$, $m \in I$). Thus, there is an upper limit for the computation resource selling price of each MEC server.

Lemma 2. *There is an upper limit for the amount of computation resources purchased by each MEC server from network operator, i.e., $f^c_k \leq f^{c,\max}_k$, $k \in N$.*

Proof. According to (13), if the resource requirements on the MEC server k are not exceed its supply capacity, i.e., $\sum_{i=1}^{I} X_{\{\delta_{i,j}=k\}} f^{e,i}_k \leq f^{e,\max}_k$, the MEC server k should not purchase any resources from the network operator so as to maximize its revenue. Otherwise, (13) can be described as $U^k_{mec}\big((\beta^e_k, f^c_k), (\beta^e_{-k}, f^c_{-k})\big) = \varepsilon^e_k \sum_{i=1}^{I} X_{\{\delta_{i,j}=k\}} f^{e,i}_k - \beta^e_k f^{e,\max}_k - \varepsilon^c_k f^c_k$. $U^k_{mec}\big((\beta^e_k, f^c_k), (\beta^e_{-k}, f^c_{-k})\big) \geq 0$ due to that MEC servers are rational. Hence, we have $f^c_k \leq \frac{\varepsilon^e_k \sum_{i=1}^{I} X_{\{\delta_{i,j}=k\}} f^{e,i}_k - \beta^e_k f^{e,\max}_k}{\varepsilon^c_k}$. Since Lemma 1 proves the maximum selling price $\varepsilon^{e,\max}_k$, we can get $f^c_k \leq f^{c,\max}_k = \frac{\varepsilon^{e,\max}_k \sum_{i=1}^{I} X_{\{\delta_{i,j}=k\}} f^{e,i}_k - \beta^e_k f^{e,\max}_k}{\varepsilon^c_k}$.

Theorem 2. *There exits a Nash equilibrium in the game between the computation resource price determination and the network operator resource purchase among the MEC servers.*

Proof. For MEC server k, $k \in I$, its price strategy $\varepsilon^e_k \in (0, \varepsilon^{e,\max}_k]$ and the network operator purchase strategy $f^c_k \in (0, f^{c,\max}_k]$ according to Lemma 1 and Lemma 2. Therefore, the spaces of MEC servers' strategy sets $\{(\varepsilon^e_k, f^c_k), k \in N\}$

are convex, nonempty and compact. Moreover, from (13), it can seen that the revenue function of MEC server k is quasi-concave and continuous in terms of ε_k^e and f_k^c. Hence, the game has a Nash equilibrium [11,12].

3.4   Stackelberg Equilibrium

In the Stackelberg game of MUs computation task offloading process, the leaders are the MEC servers and the followers are the MUs. The MUs' equilibrium strategies in the game are the optimal response to the strategies announced by the MEC servers. According to (12), given strategy sets of the MEC servers, i.e., $\{(\varepsilon_k^e, f_k^c), k \in N\}$, the equilibrium strategy of MU i, i.e., $\left(\delta_{i,j}^*, f_k^{e,i*}\right)$, should meet the following condition:

$$U_{i,j}\left(s_{i,k}^*, s_{i,-k}^*\right) \geq U_{i,j}\left(s_{i,k}, s_{i,-k}^*\right) i \in I, j \in M \tag{15}$$

In like manner, the equalization strategies of the MEC server is based on the optimal strategies for the MUs' known response. The strategy set $(\varepsilon_k^{e*}, f_k^{c*})$ is an equilibrium strategy of the MEC server k, when

$$\begin{aligned}
&U_{mec}^k \left(\left(\varepsilon_k^{e*}, f_k^{c*}\right), \left(\varepsilon_{-k}^{e*}, f_{-k}^{c*}\right), s_k\left(\varepsilon_k^{e*}, f_k^{c*}; \varepsilon_{-k}^{e*}, f_{-k}^{c*}\right)\right) \\
&\geq U_{mec}^k \left(\left(\varepsilon_k^e, f_k^c\right), \left(\varepsilon_{-k}^{e*}, f_{-k}^{c*}\right), s_k\left(\varepsilon_k^e, f_k^c; \varepsilon_{-k}^{e*}, f_{-k}^{c*}\right)\right) k \in N
\end{aligned} \tag{16}$$

The game among MUs and the game among MEC servers have Nash Equilibrium according to Theorem 1 and Theorem 2, separately. Thus, there exists a Stackelberg Equilibrium in the Stackelberg game [13].

3.5   Proposed Algorithm

In order to solve the above computation offloading decision, we propose a distributed algorithm. In the algorithm, each of MEC servers begins by randomly choosing both the amount of computation resources purchased from network operator and its computation resource selling price. Taking into consideration that that each of MEC servers is rational, the price set by MEC server k is greater than or equal to the computation resource cost. Moreover, there exits an upper limit $\varepsilon_k^{e,\max}$ for the computation resource selling price of each MEC server. Therefore, the price of the randomly selected by the MEC server k should be in the interval $[\beta_k^e, \varepsilon_k^{e,\max}]$.

Theorem 3. *In the case where the MEC server k's selling price satisfies $\beta_k^e \leq \varepsilon_k^e \leq \varepsilon_k^c$, if the total computation resource demand from the MUs on the MEC server k is not less than its computation resource capacity upper limit $f_k^{e,\max}$, further lowering the selling price reduces the revenue of the MEC server k, $k \in N$.*

Algorithm 1. Computation offloading algorithm based on Stackelberg game (COAS)

1: Initialization:
   a) The number of MUs I; the computation task, $b_{i,j}$, $i \in I, j \in M$
   b) The computation resource of MU i and MEC server k: $f_i^{l,max}$, $f_k^{e,max}$, $k \in N$
   c) The network operator computation resource selling price ε_k^c;
2: The MEC server k randomly selects its strategy set (ε_k^c, f_k^c);
3: Calculate the demand response of MUs;
4: Repeat
5: **for** MEC server k, $k \in N$ **do**
6:     **if** $\left(\sum_{i=1}^{I} X_{(\delta_{i,j}=k)} f_k^{e,i} \geq f_k^{e,\max} \right)$ & $(\varepsilon_k^e \leq \varepsilon_k^c)$ **then**
7:         Use (13) increase strategy to obtain the optimal price ε_k^{e*};
8:     **else**
9:         Get the optimal ε_k^{e*} by increasing or decreasing the strategies;
10:    **end if**
11:    Update the computation resource demands of the MUs;
12:    **if** $\left(\sum_{i=1}^{I} X_{(\delta_{i,j}=k)} f_k^{e,i} \leq f_k^{e,\max} \& f_k^c > 0 \right)$ ||
        $\left(\sum_{i=1}^{I} X_{(\delta_{i,j}=k)} f_k^{e,i} > f_k^{e,\max} \right)$ &
        $\left(\sum_{i=1}^{I} X_{(\delta_{i,j}=k)} f_k^{e,i} \neq f_k^{e,\max} + f_k^c \right)$ **then**
13:        $f_k^{c*} = \max \left(0, \sum_{i=1}^{I} X_{(\delta_{i,j}=k)} f_k^{e,i} - f_k^{e,\max} \right)$
14:    **end if**
15: **end for**
16: Until $\forall (\varepsilon_k^{e*}, f_k^{c*}) == (\varepsilon_k^e, f_k^c)$, $k \in N$.

According to the announced MEC servers' strategies, MUs are selected by a random order. By solving (12), each selected MU determines its offloading decision and the amount of computation resources that it needs to offload its computation task.

Based on the MUs' response, each MEC server first adjusts its computation resource selling price ε_k^e, $k \in N$. After the adjustment, if the demand for MEC server k still goes beyond its available computation resources, it determines to purchase more computation resources from the network operator. On the contrary, the MEC server k reduces f_k^c until f_k^c reaches 0. The MUs responds to the strategy changes of MEC servers. The MEC servers' strategies are iteratively updated until it is unchanged compared with the last iteration

In order to improve the efficiency of the proposed algorithm, some unrealistic strategies of the MEC server can be left from the iteration, as shown by the following theorem.

Proof. Since $\sum_{i=1}^{I} X_{\{\delta_{i,j}=k\}} f_k^{e,i} \geq f_k^{e,\max}$, according to (13), we can get $U_{mec}^k = $

$\varepsilon_k^e X_{\{\delta_{i,j}=k\}} f_k^{e,i} - \beta_k^e f_k^{e,\max} - \varepsilon_k^c \left(\sum_{i=1}^{I} f_k^{e,i} f_k^{e,\max} \right)$. The revenue of VEC server

k which cuts down computation resource price with the decrease θ is denoted by $U_{mec}^{k'}(\varepsilon_k^e - \theta)$. Taking into account that the each of MUs is rational, the price reduction has attracted more MUs to offload their computation tasks to the MEC server k. Let λ denote the increase in the demand for computation resources from the MUs. Then, we can denote

$U_{mec}^{k'}(\varepsilon_k^e - \theta)$ as $U_{mec}^{k'}(\varepsilon_k^e - \theta) = (\varepsilon_k^e - \theta)\left(\sum_{i=1}^{I} X_{\{\delta_{i,j}=k\}} f_k^{e,i} + \lambda \right) - \varepsilon_k^e f_k^{e,\max} -$

$\varepsilon_k^c \left(\sum_{i=1}^{I} X_{\{\delta_{i,j}=k\}} f_k^{e,i} + \lambda - f_k^{e,\max} \right)$. The difference between them can be given

by $U_{mec}^{k'}(\varepsilon_k^e - \theta) - U_{mec}^k(\varepsilon_k^e) = (\varepsilon_k^e - \varepsilon_k^c)\lambda - \theta\left(\sum_{i=1}^{I} f_k^{e,i} + \lambda \right)$. As $\varepsilon_k^e \leq \varepsilon_k^c$, we get

$U_{mec}^{k'}(\varepsilon_k^e - \theta) < U_{mec}^k(\varepsilon_k^e)$. Therefore, the decrease in the selling price ε_k^e reduces the server k's revenue.

The specific details of the algorithm we proposed are shown in Algorithm 1.

4   Simulation Results and Discussions

In this section, we evaluate the performance of CORA we proposed algorithm. We consider a 400 m * 400 m area, where SBSs and MUs are randomly distributed and the radius of each SBS is set as 100 m. Besides, the channel gain is denoted by d^{α}, where d is the distance between the SBS and the MU, α represents the path loss exponent, of which value is -3. Moreover, other main parameter settings are shown in Table 1 [14,15].

Table 1. The simulation parameters.

Simulation parameters	Value
The bandwidth of each Opportunity network channel B^m	20 MHz
The bandwidth of each Cellular network channel	40 MHz
The transmission power of the MU $P_{i,j}$	200 mW
The type of computation task M	5
The maximum delay of the computation task $T_{i,j}^{\max}$	$[0.2, 1.5]$ s
The computation capacity of the MU $f_i^{l,\max}$	$[1, 2]$ GHz
The computation capacity of the MEC server $f_k^{e,\max}$	$[8, 10]$ GHz

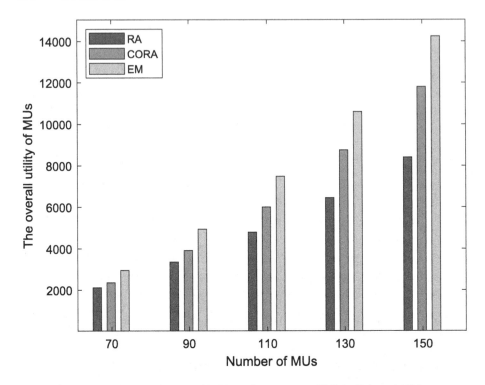

Fig. 2. The comparison of MUs utility among CORA, RA and EM

To prove the effectiveness of the CORA proposed solution, we compare its performance with the other two baseline algorithms as shown in Fig. 2, where EN and RA denotes Enumeration method and random computation offloading scheme, respectively. The MU utility of the CORA algorithm is very close to EN, which should theoretically be the optimal algorithm. However, it should not be overlooked that EN has very high time complexity compared with the CORA. The MUs' utility of the RA scheme is sometimes higher than EN, sometimes otherwise, which is because of its randomness. Therefore, CORA can be considered as the optimal algorithm in terms of both the time complexity and the utility of the MUs.

To further demonstrate the performance of the CORA algorithm, we compare it to two other computation offloading strategies: Proportional Price and Dynamic Price. In Fig. 3, the computation offloading system with the proportional price strategy has the lowest benefit. Since the price in this case is directly proportional to the computation resource cost of the MEC server, it cannot be dynamically adjusted according to the supply and demand situation. That's why these two options get more profit than the proportional price strategy.

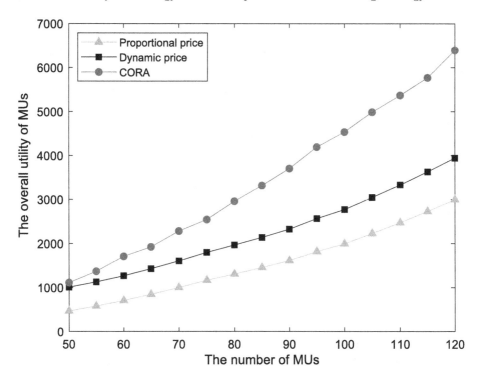

Fig. 3. The overall utility of the MUs with different offloading schemes.

Whereas, due to the limitation of the MEC servers' computation resource capacity, the revenue obtained by the price scheme without BCS cannot be increased with the increase of the number of MUs. In our proposed CORA algorithm, when BCS is used to compensate for insufficient computation resources, the price can be optimally adjusted. Therefore, compared with the other two offloading strategies, the CORA we proposed can gain the highest utility, whether it is a small amount or a large number of MUs.

Figure 4 illustrates the impact of BCS computation resource prices on MEC servers' revenue as the number of MUs increases. It can be seen that all incomes in these cases decrease when the computation resource price rises. Due to the limitation of the MEC server's computation resource, more computation tasks is capable of being offloaded to the BCS as the number of MUs increases. Consequently, the revenue with more MUs is more susceptible to the BCS computation resource and is more likely to decrease as prices increase. Besides, we can find that when the computation price is 0.9, the revenue of 200 MUs is nearly equal to the case where the number of MUs is 160. The reason is that there exits an

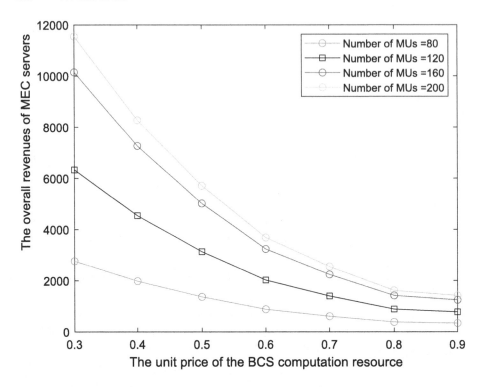

Fig. 4. The overall revenues of the MEC servers affected by BCS resource price.

upper limit for MEC servers' computation resource price according to Lemma 1. The MEC servers may not buy computation resource from the BCS when its price becomes high. In addition, due to computation resource constraints, the number of offloading services for MEC servers is limited. Therefore, in the case of a high BCS price and a large number of vehicles, the benefits obtained by the MEC servers are almost the same.

Figure 5 shows convergence of the proposed algorithm in terms of MUs' utility and is a perfect proof that the system can reach the NE, which can further explain that CORA cannot only get close to the optimal result by the lower time complexity than EM but also it is stable.

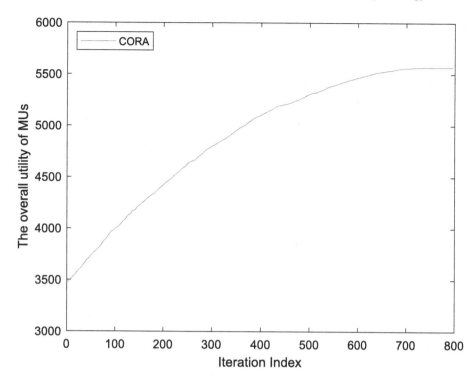

Fig. 5. Convergence of the proposed algorithm

5   Conclusion

In this paper, we design a multi-level computation offloading strategy and consider the heterogeneity of computation tasks and computation resource backup pool while making offloading decision in multi-access networks. Firstly, the computation offloading model is introduced for each computation strategy. Then the main problem is formulated as a Stackelberg game problem, and a global optimal algorithm based on game theory with lower time complexity compared with EM and RA is proposed and the numerical simulation results show the efficiency and stability of the proposed algorithm. For future work, in order to improve the performance of the MEC system, we will consider a resource s allocation and design a more efficient algorithm.

Acknowledgment. This work has been supported by STATE GRID Corporation of China science and technology project" Research and application on key technologies of power wireless heterogeneous network convergence" (5700-201919236A-0-0-00).

References

1. Kan, T., Chiang, Y., Wei, H.: QoS-aware mobile edge computing system: multi-server multi-user scenario. In: 2018 IEEE Globecom Workshops (GC Wkshps), Abu Dhabi, United Arab Emirates, pp. 1–6 (2018)
2. Wang, S., Zhang, X., Zhang, Y., Wang, L., Yang, J., Wang, W.: A survey on mobile edge networks: convergence of computing, caching and communications. IEEE Access **5**, 6757–6779 (2017)
3. Cao, X., Wang, F., Xu, J., Zhang, R., Cui, S.: Joint computation and communication cooperation for energy-efficient mobile edge computing. IEEE Internet Things J. **6**(3), 4188–4200 (2019)
4. Dai, Y., Sheng, M., Liu, J., Cheng, N., Shen, X.: Resource allocation for low-latency mobile edge computation offloading in NOMA networks. In: 2018 IEEE Global Communications Conference (GLOBECOM), Abu Dhabi, United Arab Emirates, pp. 1–6 (2018)
5. Chen, M., Liang, B., Dong, M.: Joint offloading and resource allocation for computation and communication in mobile cloud with computing access point. In: IEEE INFOCOM 2017 - IEEE Conference on Computer Communications, Atlanta, GA, pp. 1–9 (2017)
6. Guo, F., Zhang, H., Ji, H., Li, X., Leung, V.C.M.: Energy efficient computation offloading for multi-access MEC enabled small cell networks. In: 2018 IEEE International Conference on Communications Workshops (ICC Workshops), Kansas City, MO, pp. 1–6 (2018)
7. Yang, Y., Wang, K., Zhang, G., Chen, X., Luo, X., Zhou, M.: Maximal energy efficient task scheduling for homogeneous fog networks. In: IEEE INFOCOM 2018 - IEEE Conference on Computer Communications Workshops (INFOCOM WKSHPS), Honolulu, HI, pp. 274–279 (2018)
8. Tran, T.X., Pompili, D.: Joint task offloading and resource allocation for multi-server mobile-edge computing networks. IEEE Trans. Veh. Technol. **68**(1), 856–868 (2019)
9. Marin, R., Ciobanu, R., Dobre, C.: Improving opportunistic networks by leveraging device-to-device communication. IEEE Commun. Mag. **55**(11), 86–91 (2017)
10. Rosen, J.B.: Existence and uniqueness of equilibrium points for concave N-person games. Econometrica **33**(3), 520–534 (1965)
11. Debreu, G.: A social equilibrium existence theorem. Proc. Natl. Acad. Sci. U.S.A. **38**(10), 886–893 (1952)
12. Zhang, K., Mao, Y., Leng, S., Maharjan, S., Zhang, Y.: Optimal delay constrained offloading for vehicular edge computing networks. In: 2017 IEEE International Conference on Communications (ICC), Paris, pp. 1–6 (2017)
13. Maharjan, S., Zhu, Q., Zhang, Y., Gjessing, S., Basar, T.: Dependable demand response management in the smart grid: a stackelberg game approach. IEEE Trans. Smart Grid **4**(1), 120–132 (2013)
14. Guo, F., Ma, L., Zhang, H., Ji, H., Li, X.: Joint load management and resource allocation in the energy harvesting powered small cell networks with mobile edge computing. In: IEEE INFOCOM 2018 - IEEE Conference on Computer Communications Workshops (INFOCOM WKSHPS), Honolulu, HI, pp. 299–304 (2018)
15. Guo, H., Zhang, J., Liu, J., Zhang, H., Sun, W.: Energy-efficient task offloading and transmit power allocation for ultra-dense edge computing. In: 2018 IEEE Global Communications Conference (GLOBECOM), Abu Dhabi, United Arab Emirates, pp. 1–6 (2018)

Resource Allocation Scheme Design in Power Wireless Heterogeneous Networks Considering Load Balance

Shuiyao Chen[1], Di Zhai[2,3], Wei Bai[2,3(✉)], Haochen Guan[5], Ping Ma[4], and Weiping Shao[1]

[1] State Grid Zhejiang Electric Power Co., Ltd., Hangzhou, China
[2] Electric Power Intelligent Sensing Technology and Application State Grid Corporation Joint Laboratory, Beijing, China
[3] Global Energy Interconnection Research Institute Co., Ltd., Beijing, China
baiwei@geiri.sgcc.com.cn
[4] State Grid Shaoxing Electric Power Supply Company Shaoxing, Shaoxing, China
[5] Beijing University of Posts and Telecommunications, Beijing, China

Abstract. Recently, in heterogeneous smart grids, mobile network traffic and various power interconnection services grow in a high way. Caching the service at the edge of smart grid network is a common optimization method to reduce the heavy network traffic. In this paper, we propose a cooperative resource allocation scheme in heterogeneous smart grid networks. Firstly, the effect of computing and channel resources on the initial latency of the electric services is studied. Secondly, the model of topology and resource distribution in the network is established, with the goal of minimizing the overall network delay. Thirdly, an algorithm combining KM matching and genetic algorithm is proposed to solve the proposed problem. Finally, the simulation results show that the proposed algorithm optimizes the average delay of the smart grid service.

Keywords: Heterogeneours smart grid networks · Overlapped clustering · Resource allocation

1 Introduction

Smart Grid (SG) is a new generation of power generation, transmission and distribution systems that have emerged in recent years. Its purpose is to manage power resources more effectively [1]. In recent years, with the development of mobile network, 5G technology is maturing day by day. 5G technology can match the emerging services of smart grid due to its advantages of large bandwidth, low delay, high reliability and communication capability of massive connections [2]. However, the following is the problem of excessive mobile network traffic. At the same time, for the operation of smart grid business, a reliable, safe and efficient communication is needed [3].

© ICST Institute for Computer Sciences, Social Informatics and Telecommunications Engineering 2020
Published by Springer Nature Switzerland AG 2020. All Rights Reserved
S. W. Loke et al. (Eds.): MONAMI 2020, LNICST 338, pp. 111–124, 2020.
https://doi.org/10.1007/978-3-030-64002-6_8

Uplink service content occupies a major part of mobile network traffic. How to deal with uplink content transmission is one of the key issues to alleviate the high load of smart grid. At present, the combination of edge cache and smart grid is an effective solution [4]. By caching the content of the core network at the edge of the mobile network, users can preferentially obtain the required content at the base station closer to the user equipment. The backhaul link load from the core network to the edge base station is greatly reduced.

With the development of mobile edge computing, base stations in mobile networks have certain computing capabilities. These computing resources can play a role in content caching. In mobile video services, high-quality versions of the same video can be converted to low-quality versions through transcoding. In this way, users' requests for different versions of the same video can be met by combining higher version videos with video transcoding. This idea is reflected in edge caching: when caching a popular content, we do not need to cache all its versions, but only cache the higher-quality versions, thereby increasing the probability of cached content being used, and then greatly the utilization of cache space. Some studies have optimized the overall network delay or transmission rate. Reference [5] gives different locations where content coding occurs and different delivery methods resulting from it, calculates the network delay for the content transmission, and gives an online cache update strategy based on this. Reference [6] used the Starkelberg game algorithm and many-to-many matching algorithm to allocate the buffer and radio resources in the network to achieve higher transmission rates. Reference [7] proposed a cooperative caching strategy, which caches only the initial part of a part of video content, which has reached a higher cache utilization rate, thereby reducing the average network latency. Another part of the research is dedicated to improving the quality of video provided by the network. Reference [8] started with the overall video quality delivered by the network, and studied strategies to maximize video quality under specific channel conditions. The reference [9] paid attention to the QoE performance of the network, and optimized the average video quality provided by the network through a retention-based collaborative caching strategy. In addition, some researchers have optimized energy consumption. Reference [10] gives the energy consumption of video caching, transcoding, and delivery, and it is optimized as a whole using annealing algorithms.

Due to the large number of power equipment, it can be regarded as an ultra-dense scene. With the development of UDN networks, the transmission mode of a user equipment connected to a base station has changed. The grouping method of overlapping packets is applied in a mobile network to improve the signal-to-noise ratio and anti-interference ability of communication between a base station and a user. Reference [11] proposed a user-centric overlapping grouping method, and designed a spectrum allocation scheme based on the graph theory framework, which improved the overall transmission efficiency. Reference [12] proposed a dynamic clustering scheme based on overlapping clusters, which improved the output signal-to-noise ratio. In the cache placement and distribution process, the

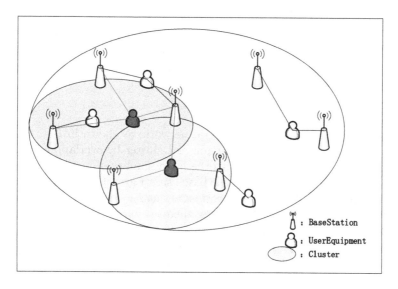

Fig. 1. System model of overlapped clustering in smart grid network

idea of overlapping packets also helps improve the allocation efficiency of cache, computing, and communication resources.

With the development of electric services, the delay of service requirements has gradually increased, and it is difficult for a single node to independently process user video requests. At the same time, because the node density in UDN is relatively large, the idle resource utilization of nodes can effectively improve network performance. In this scenario, this paper proposes a cooperative transcoding and distribution mechanism based on overlapped clustering. First, the strategy of overlapped clustering in ultra-dense networks is considered. Secondly, a mathematical model of node clustering and heterogeneous resource distribution is established. The optimization of the initial buffering time of the video is used to divide the overall network delay optimization problem into two sub-problems: clustering and resource allocation. Thirdly, a resource allocation algorithm combining KM matching and genetic algorithm is proposed. Based on the optimized KM matching algorithm, the nodes in the ultra-dense network are overlapped clustered, and the genetic algorithm is used to allocate the grouped computing and channel resources. Finally, it can be seen through simulation that the proposed algorithm can effectively reduce the average initial buffer delay of the user.

The rest of this article is structured as follows. The second section gives system modeling and problem simulation. The third section gives the KM and genetic algorithm methods. Section 4 lists the simulation results and corresponding analysis. Finally, Sect. 5 summarizes the full article.

2   System Model

In this section, we introduce the system model and formulate grouping and resource allocation issues.

2.1   System Model

This paper considers that in a smart grid network, as shown in Fig. 1, J small base stations are divided into a maximum of I cluster by overlapping clustering to provide services for I users. Due to the large number of power equipment, it can be regarded as an ultra-dense scene based smart grid network. For simplicity, this article represents the set of user equipment as $I = \{1, 2, ..., I\}$ and the set of base stations as $J = \{1, 2, ..., J\}$. Among them, i, j represent the i-th user and the j-th base station, respectively. The connection relationship between each user and the base station is represented by a matrix $X = [x_{ij}]$. When $x_{ij} = 1$, it means that base station j provides service for user i. Conversely, $x_{ij} = 0$ means that the current base station j does not provide service to user i. It is assumed that in the current area, each base station occupies a different frequency band range, and different users are allocated different subcarriers for communication, so the interference between different base stations and users is not considered. A cache and MEC server are deployed at the base station to provide cache and computing resources. The amount of computing resources at the base station is represented by the number of video bits per second that the CPU can transcode, and is denoted as C_j^f. Assuming that the transmission power of each base station in the network is the same, the communication resources of different base stations are mainly compared by bandwidth, and the total subcarrier bandwidth allocated by each base station is represented by W_{ij}. The video content on the network has multiple definition versions. This article describes versions of videos by the bit rate of the video contents, which is represented by the symbol R. The version of the video content requested by user i is represented by the bit rate R_i^s; and the version of the video content cached at the base station is represented by the bit rate R_j^c. Between different versions of the same video, lower-bit-rate video content can be transcoded from higher-bit-rate video content.

In this article, it is assumed that the users always has enough buffer space to support the transmitted video stream to be buffered in the user equipment. After the user sends a request for video content to the base station, each node in the base station group sends video content to the user in the form of a video stream at the same time and stores it in the buffer of the user equipment. During this period, it is assumed that the location of the user remains unchanged, the amount of resources provided by the base station does not change, and the wireless channel status does not change. Therefore, it can be considered that the buffering speed of the video content is constant. On this basis, if the user equipment determines that the video content can be transmitted before the end of playback at the current rate, then the video content can start playing. The time from when a user sends a request to when the video starts playing can be expressed by the user's waiting delay τ_{ij}.

2.2 Problem Formulation

In a smart grid network, when a user is served by only one base station j, for each user i, the delay τ_{ij} from its request for a specialized content to the start of playing the video is mainly composed of the calculated delay and the communication delay, namely:

$$\tau_{ij} = \tau_{ij}^c + \tau_{ij}^t \tag{1}$$

When the base station serve content by way of overlapping clustering, the base station needs to determine the content distribution mode according to its own cache. Different distribution methods can be represented by x_{ij}, R_i^s and R_j^c. When the cached video content at the base station does not match the user's request, or the quality of the cached video content is lower than the user's request, the base station cannot provide services, so $x_{ij} = 0$. When the video content cached at the base station matches, but the video quality is higher than the user's request, that is, $R_i^s < R_j^c$, two processes of video transcoding and distribution are required. When the video content and the quality version cached at the base station are consistent with the user request, only the video distribution process is performed, that is, $R_i^s = R_j^c$. The following will model the calculation delay and communication delay of the base station and describe the optimization problem:

1. Calculation Delay

   The time required for video transcoding at the base station is related to the total amount of computing tasks and the allocated computing resources. The total amount of calculation tasks can be expressed as the product of the difference between the video bit rate before and after transcoding and the video length. The calculation resource is expressed as the number of bits processed by the CPU per second c_j^f. Assume that the user $i \in \mathbb{I}$ requests different versions of the same file. The minimum bit rate requirement for each version is R_i^s. The bit rate of the video version buffered in base station j is R_j^c, and t_v is the total video duration. Therefore, the calculated delay is:

$$\tau_{ij}^c = \frac{t_v \cdot (R_j^c - R_i^s)}{c_{ij}^f} \tag{2}$$

2. Communication Delay

   The communication delay includes two parts which are the uplink upload and downlink transmission, respectively. Assume that the user has sufficient storage space for video caching. In order to avoid interruption during video playback, it is necessary to pre-cache video content of size $\tau_{ij}^t \cdot R_{ij}^r$, τ_{ij}^t is the communication delay when the user requests it, that is:

$$t_v \cdot R_i^s = (t_v + \tau_{ij}^t) \cdot R_{ij}^r \tag{3}$$

$$\tau_{ij}^t = \left(\frac{R_i^s}{R_{ij}^r} - 1\right) \cdot t_v \tag{4}$$

Among them, the frequencies between base stations are different, and each base station allocates its own channel bandwidth to different users according to frequency bands. Therefore, without considering path loss and mutual interference between users, there are:

$$R_{ij}^r = W_{ij} \cdot \log\left(1 + SNR_{ij}\right) \tag{5}$$

$$SNR_{ij} = \frac{P_j^s \cdot |h_{ij}|^2}{\sigma^2} \tag{6}$$

Where W_{ij} is the sub-channel bandwidth allocated by the base station to users, and P_j^s is the maximum transmit power of the base station.

3. Problem Description

In the network, the base stations cooperate in a manner of overlapping clusters. The connection relationship between each user and the base station is represented by a matrix $X = [x_{ij}]$. For the waiting delay of user i τ_i:

$$\sum_{j=1}^{J} x_{ij}(\tau_i - \tau_{ij}^c) \cdot R_{ij}^r = t_v \cdot R_i^s \tag{7}$$

$$\tau_i = \frac{\sum_{j=1}^{J} \left(x_{ij} \cdot R_{ij}^r \cdot \tau_{ij}^c\right) + R_i^s \cdot t_v}{\sum_{j=1}^{J} x_{ij} \cdot R_{ij}^r} \tag{8}$$

Then the minimum average waiting delay of users in the network is:

$$\min \tau = \min \frac{1}{I} \sum_{i=1}^{I} \tau_i$$

$$\text{s.t.} \quad C1 : x_{ij}\left(R_j^c - R_i^s\right) \geq 0$$

$$C2 : \sum_{i=1}^{I} x_{ij} \leq S_j \tag{9}$$

$$C3 : \sum_{i=1}^{I} x_{ij} W_{ij} \leq B_j$$

$$C4 : \sum_{i=1}^{I} x_{ij} c_{ij}^f \leq C_j^f$$

Constraint 1 indicates that the quality of the version of the video cached at the base station should be higher than the quality of the video requested by the user in the overlapping clusters, so that the high-level video can be converted to the low-level through video transcoding. Constraint 2 indicates that the number of users connected to each base station should not exceed the maximum number of access users. Constraints 3 and 4 respectively indicate that the bandwidth allocated by the base station and the computing resources should not exceed the total amount of resources at the base station.

3   Overlapping Clustering and Resource Allocation Algorithm

3.1   Algorithm Design

In this paper, the optimization problem is decomposed into two sub-problems, one is the overlapping clustering problem of the base station, and the other is the problem of base station communication and computing resource allocation. In the overlapping clustering problem, the improved KM algorithm is used to match the user and the base station to find the anchor node of the overlapping cluster. The version of the file requested by the user is cached at the anchor node. Through the anchor node, users can get basic quality of service guarantee. In the resource allocation problem, this paper uses the genetic algorithm to allocate the channel resources and computing resources of the base station.

In the grouping problem, the network topology of the base station and the user can be regarded as a bipartite graph. The bipartite graph can be defined as $G = (V_1, V_2, E)$, where V_1, V_2 is two non-empty subsets, and $V_1 \cap V_2 = \varnothing$. E is the set of edges between V_1, V_2. Since each edge has different weights E, and can be expressed as $E = \{w_{ij}\}$, where $i \in V_1, j \in V_2$ and w_{ij} are weight vectors between vertex i and j. In the scenario of the ultra-dense network considered in this paper, the number of users is not more than the number of base stations, and there is no intersection between the two sets. Therefore, let I, J be V_1, V_2. Consider the delay of one-to-one service between the base station and the user, and use the inverse number of the delay as the weight w_{ij} of the bipartite graph side. Therefore, as long as an optimal match of this bipartite graph is found, the anchor node allocation method with the most benefit (the lowest instantaneous delay) can be obtained. After the assignment of the anchor node and the determination of the caching version of the base station are completed, the grouping result of overlapping clustering can be preliminarily determined according to the caching situation of the small base stations around the user.

The KM algorithm is a typical algorithm for solving the optimal matching problem with weighted bipartite graphs. The top matching is used to convert the optimal matching into the maximum matching problem. In general, when $|V_1| = |V_2|$, the KM algorithm can be used to find the optimal solution. In this article, due to $|J| \gg |I|$, the traditional KM algorithm needs to be improved to adapt it to the needs of specific scenarios. Specifically, since the grouping method in this paper is overlapping clustering, in order to ensure the basic quality of service of users, at least one node needs to be allocated for users. After forming a group, a node is also needed in the group to collect and distribute user information. This node is called an anchor node. In the overlapping clustering problem, a key problem is to find a one-to-one match in the network topology, so that each user owns an anchor node independently. In particular, in the time-delay optimization problem in this paper, it is necessary to ensure that the user's time-delay is the smallest in the subgraph formed after the one-to-one matching. Since the KM algorithm is essentially a process of continuously relaxing restrictions and finding the best match through the Hungarian algorithm, when the number of base station nodes is significantly greater than the number of user nodes, the KM algorithm can also be used to solve. Different from the traditional method, the KM algorithm in this paper will stop when the user equipment finds a matching base station, and the remaining base stations are used as auxiliary nodes when overlapping clusters are assigned to each group for cooperation.

In this paper, the user set first needs to assign initial values to the nodes in the user set I and the base station set J. Here, the top index of the base station set is set to zero, and the top index of the user set is assigned to the largest weight among all connections. Construct a subgraph of a bipartite graph. The subgraph contains all the nodes of the bipartite graph, and the edges satisfy the arbitrary side length weight equal to the sum of the two superscripts. Then look for the augmentation road from i_0 in the subgraph. The set of nodes in $\mathbb{I}$ on the augmented road is added to the set $\mathbb{S}$, and the set of nodes in $\mathbb{J}$ is added to the set $\mathbb{T}$. When the augmentation path is not found and the number of nodes in the set $\mathbb{S}$ is smaller than the number of nodes in the set $\mathbb{I}$, the node top label needs to be adjusted so that the sub-picture contains more edges. That is, the set $\mathbb{S}$ is reduced at the same time, and the top flag of the set $\mathbb{T}$ is increased until all the nodes in the set $\mathbb{I}$ are included in one augmented road, that is, an optimal match is obtained. After finding the optimal match and determining the anchor node, the base station caches the video according to the video version request of the user, and the base station without the user randomly selects the video version for caching. Thereafter, each user determines its own base station grouping according to the reachability and buffering conditions of the surrounding base stations. This results in overlapping clustering results for the network.

After solving the grouping method, in the resource allocation problem, this paper finds a sub-optimal solution through genetic algorithm. Genetic algorithm is an optimization algorithm based on the principle of genetic selection. It is similar to the principle of chromosome generation in biology. It takes all individuals in the group as the object, and under the guidance of randomization technology, efficiently searches a coded parameter space. As the number of iterations increases, the fitness of the individuals in the group gradually increases, and finally converges to a suboptimal solution. Among them, selection, crossover and mutation constitute the genetic operation of the genetic algorithm. The specific operation process includes:

1. Initialization

In the genetic algorithm, the chromosome should contain information about the solution to the optimization problem. Therefore, the possibility of all solutions needs to be presented in the chromosome. Different coding methods can be used to map the solution of the problem to the chromosome through genes, so that each possibility may correspond to a chromosome. In the genetic algorithm, the coding problem is the key of the genetic algorithm. Both the mutation operator and the crossover operator are affected by the coding method. Therefore, the coding problem greatly affects the efficiency of the genetic calculation. Common coding methods are: binary coding, Gray code, floating point coding, multi-parameter cascade coding, multi-parameter cross coding, etc. Among them, the binary coding method uses a binary symbol set $\{0, 1\}$ for coding, and its individual genotype is a binary coding symbol string. Although this coding method is simple to operate, it is not suitable for continuous function optimization. Gray code improves the local search ability of the algorithm on the basis of binary coding, but the accuracy is still greatly restricted. In floating-point encoding, individual gene values are represented by a real number within a certain range. Its high precision is suitable for continuous variable problems.

2. Fitness function

In genetic algorithms, fitness is an important basis for selecting individuals, and it is also an important indicator that reflects the optimization effect of individual corresponding solutions. Therefore, the optimization goal is usually converted into individual fitness according to certain rules. In this paper, the reciprocal of the optimization goal is selected as the fitness.

3. Choose

The selection operation is a process of selecting different individuals according to the performance of the individuals in the parent group to inherit to the next generation. Commonly used selection operators include roulette selection, random competition selection, best retention selection, etc. This article adopts the method of combining the best reserved choice and the roulette choice, to keep multiple copies of the best individual completely, and the remaining individuals are selected through the roulette choice.

4. Crossover

Crossover operation means that two chromosomes produce new individuals by exchanging some genes. Crossover operators include single-point crossover, multi-point crossover, uniform crossover, and arithmetic crossover. Since the method chosen in this paper is the encoding of floating-point numbers, the arithmetic crossover is selected, and a new individual is created by the linear combination of two individuals.

5. Variation

Variation refers to the process in which certain genes in an individual's chromosome are replaced with other alleles. Common mutation operators include basic bit mutation, uniform mutation, boundary mutation, non-uniform mutation and Gaussian approximate mutation. In this paper, the uniform mutation method is used to replace the original gene value with a random number that is evenly distributed within a reasonable range to generate new individuals.

Since genetic algorithm has good global convergence performance of discrete variables under relatively low complexity, it is suitable for solving the resource allocation problem proposed in this paper. In this paper, the communication and computing resources of the network are respectively expressed by two $I \times J$ matrices. The matrix stores the proportion of the resources allocated by the user to the total resources of the base station, and the proportions of frequency band resources and computing resources are w_{ij} and c_{ij} respectively. Since w_{ij} and c_{ij} can be any value within $(0, 1)$ in the algorithm of this paper, the two matrices are merged into a chromosome by means of floating-point encoding. After the chromosome construction is completed, the optimal resource allocation matrix is obtained through chromosome crossing, mutation, and inheritance.

3.2 Algorithm Flow

The algorithm proposed in this paper mainly includes two parts, KM algorithm for base station grouping, and genetic algorithm for resource allocation. The execution process of the algorithm is shown in the following table.

Algorithm 1. Resource Allocation Algorithm Based on KM Matching Algorithm and Genetic Algorithm

---

Input: I, J, B_j, C_j, S_j
Output: Grouping and resource allocation results
 1: Initialization:
      The distance matrix D between the user and the base station, the chromosome S, the top standard value of the base station $q_j=0$, the matching node $I', J'=\varnothing$
 2: **repeat**
 3:     **while** $i \in I$ **do**
 4:         Use the minimum value of the corresponding column in D as the superscript value p_i
 5:         **if** $p_i+q_j \le d_{ij}$ **then**
 6:             $I'=I' + i, J'=J' + j$
 7:         **else**
 8:             Record the difference $g = p_i+q_j - d_{ij}$
 9:         **end if**
10:     **end while**
11:     **if** $i \in I'$ **then**
12:         $p_i=p_i\text{-}g_{\min}$
13:     **end if**
14:     **if** $j \in J'$ **then**
15:         $q_j=q_j+g_{\min}$
16:     **end if**
17: **until** $I'=I$
18: **repeat**
19:     **while** $s \in S$ **do**
20:         Find the corresponding fitness
21:     **end while**
22:     Selection, crossover, mutation
23: **until** Algorithm termination

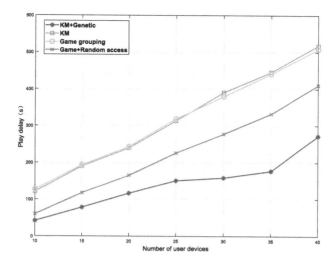

Fig. 2. Relationship between the overall network delay and the number of users

4   Simulation Results and Discussions

In this paper, a mobile network is composed of 60 micro base stations and 10–40 user equipments randomly generated in a 200 m area. The frequency band resources of the base station are divided into multiple sub-channels according to frequency for serving different users. Transcode and distribute the same video on the network. The video is divided into three versions of 32M, 40M and 48M with different bit rates, and the duration is unified to 60 min. Assuming that each user has different video version requirements, the base station chooses to cache the appropriate version according to the grouping situation. Finally, the average waiting time of users in the network is counted to reflect the network performance.

In order to verify the performance of the proposed algorithm, this paper selects four packet transmission methods for comparison, including KM algorithm, game algorithm and other one-to-one grouping algorithms, game and random allocation combined many-to-one grouping algorithm, KM and genetic many-to-many overlapping clustering algorithm. The traditional KM algorithm can find a service node for the user, and from the perspective of the entire network, the average distance of the user is the shortest. By examining the distance between the user and the base station, the game algorithm preferentially selects the user with the closer distance to match with the idle base station, and finally forms a one-to-one allocation of the base station. The combination of game and random access can form a one-to-one allocation, based on the principle of proximity to allow idle base stations to serve the closest users, and then form a base station group, but each small base station can only exist in Within a group. This method and the overlapping clustering algorithm proposed in this paper use genetic algorithm to allocate resources within the group.

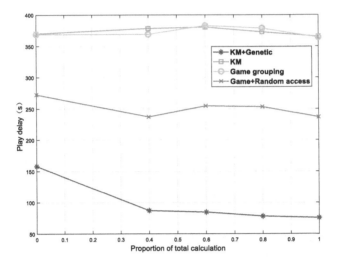

Fig. 3. Relationship between the overall network delay and the base station band resources

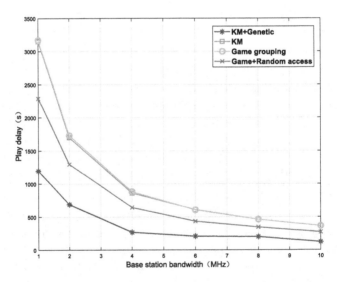

Fig. 4. Relationship between the overall network delay and the base station computing resources

In order to consider the relationship between the number of users and network performance, this article changes the value of the number of users and compares the delay performance under the four comparison algorithms. As shown in Fig. 2, when the number of users increases, the delay of each algorithm increases. Among them, the one-to-one grouping algorithm has poor performance due to certain resource idleness. The combination of game and random access has better performance, but when the number of users increases, the speed of performance reduction is still greater. The overlapping clustering algorithm proposed in this paper can optimize the overall performance according to the actual situation, and the adjustment space for resource allocation is larger, so the performance is better and the impact of the increase of users is relatively small.

Considering the impact of communication and computing resources on the performance of the algorithm, as can be seen from Fig. 3, with the increase of frequency band resources, the delay of the algorithm generally decreases, and the delay performance of the network increases first and then tends to be stable. Specifically, the latency of the two one-to-one grouping algorithms is still relatively high. When the network's frequency band resources are insufficient, the performance declines quickly, making it difficult to guarantee the quality of service that users get. The many-to-many overlapping clustering algorithm proposed in this paper has the least impact on the total delay when the frequency band resources are small, so it shows certain advantages.

In terms of computing performance, as shown in Fig. 4, the one-to-one grouping algorithm has relatively fixed resources, so it fluctuates less with changes in computing resources. With the reduction of computing resources, the amount of resources that can be used for transcoding in the two multi-pair packet algorithms is reduced, which has a greater impact on the final delay performance. However, the resource allocation algorithm proposed in this paper still has certain performance advantages.

5 Conclusion

This paper proposes a resource allocation algorithm based on overlapping clustering for transcoding and distribution of multi-version video. This article considers the optimization problem in two phases. Firstly, the KM matching algorithm is used to select the anchor node corresponding to the user, and the overlapping cluster is completed. The second stage uses the genetic algorithm to allocate resources within the group to achieve global optimization. The simulation results show that the algorithm has good delay performance in the video transcoding distribution of small base stations, especially in the scenario with less resources.

Acknowledgment. This work has been supported by STATE GRID Corporation of China science and technology project "Research and application on key technologies of power wireless heterogeneous network convergence" (5700-201919236A-0-0-00).

References

1. Trajano, A.F.R., de Sousa, A.A.M., Rodrigues, E.B., de Souza, J.N., de Castro Callado, A., Coutinho, E.F.: Leveraging mobile edge computing on smart grids using LTE cellular networks. In: 2019 IEEE Symposium on Computers and Communications (ISCC), pp. 1–7 (2019)

2. Meng, S., Wang, Z., Tang, M., Wu, S., Li, X.: Integration application of 5G and smart grid. In: 2019 11th International Conference on Wireless Communications and Signal Processing (WCSP), pp. 1–7 (2019)
3. Monhof, S., Bocker, S., Tiemann, J., Wietfeld, C.: Cellular network coverage analysis and optimization in challenging smart grid environments. In: 2018 IEEE International Conference on Communications, Control, and Computing Technologies for Smart Grids (SmartGridComm), pp. 1–6 (2018)
4. Cosovic, M., Tsitsimelis, A., Vukobratovic, D., Matamoros, J., Anton-Haro, C.: 5G mobile cellular networks: enabling distributed state estimation for smart grids. IEEE Commun. Mag. **55**(10), 62–69 (2017)
5. Tran, T.X., Pandey, P., Hajisami, A., Pompili, D.: Collaborative multi-bitrate video caching and processing in mobile-edge computing networks. In: 2017 13th Annual Conference on Wireless On-demand Network Systems and Services (WONS), pp. 165–172. IEEE (2017)
6. Xu, X., Liu, J., Tao, X.: Mobile edge computing enhanced adaptive bitrate video delivery with joint cache and radio resource allocation. IEEE Access **5**, 16406–16415 (2017)
7. Kumar, S., Franklin, A.A.: Consolidated caching with cache splitting and transrating in mobile edge computing networks. In: 2017 IEEE International Conference on Advanced Networks and Telecommunications Systems (ANTS), pp. 1–6. IEEE (2017)
8. Liang, C., He, Y., Yu, F.R., Zhao, N.: Video rate adaptation and traffic engineering in mobile edge computing and caching-enabled wireless networks. In: 2017 IEEE 86th Vehicular Technology Conference (VTC-Fall), pp. 1–5. IEEE (2017)
9. Mehrabi, A., Siekkinen, M., Ylä-Jääski, A.: QoE-traffic optimization through collaborative edge caching in adaptive mobile video streaming. IEEE Access **6**, 52261–52276 (2018)
10. Xie, R., Li, Z., Wu, J., Jia, Q., Huang, T.: Energy-efficient joint caching and transcoding for HTTP adaptive streaming in 5G networks with mobile edge computing. China Commun. **16**(7), 229–244 (2019)
11. Lin, Y., Zhang, R., Li, C., Yang, L., Hanzo, L.: Graph-based joint user-centric overlapped clustering and resource allocation in ultradense networks. IEEE Trans. Veh. Technol. **67**(5), 4440–4453 (2017)
12. Feng, S., Feng, W., Mao, H., Lu, J.: Overlapped clustering for comp transmissions in massively dense wireless networks. In: 2014 IEEE International Conference on Communication Systems, pp. 308–312. IEEE (2014)

A Secure Crowdsourcing-Based Indoor Navigation System

Liang Xie, Zhou Su$^{(\boxtimes)}$, and Qichao Xu

School of Mechatronic Engineering and Automation, Shanghai University,
Shanghai 200444, People's Republic of China
zhousu@ieee.org

Abstract. At present, the crowdsourcing-based indoor navigation system has attracted extensive attention from both the industry and the academia. The crowdsourcing-based indoor navigation system commendably solves the deficiencies (e.g., high cost, low accuracy, etc.) of traditional navigation methods. Unfortunately, the system that relies on crowdsourced data is vulnerable to the collusion attack, which may threaten the security of the system. In this paper, a novel crowdsourcing-based secure indoor navigation system is proposed. Specifically, we first propose a novel reputation mechanism. Then, we employ the offensive and defensive game to model the interactions between the fog service platform and responders. Next, the optimization problem of the system is established to maximize the total utility of the system. Finally, the simulation results demonstrate that the proposed system can effectively encourage responders to provide positive navigation services.

Keywords: Crowdsourcing · Collusion · Indoor navigation · Reputation mechanism · Offensive and defensive game

1 Introduction

With the rapid expansion of technologies such as internet of things (IoTs) [1], the navigation system has received extensive attention from academia and industry, since it can bring unprecedented convenience to people's travel. At present, mobile smart devices are equipped with global positioning system (GPS) for precise navigation in outdoor. However, GPS signals are attenuated and distorted when they pass through the walls and various obstacles of the building, resulting in that GPS is not suitable for indoor environments. In order to realize the stability and accuracy of the navigation system within the indoor environment, the indoor navigation enabled by crowdsourcing technology has emerged. Specifically, the crowdsourcing-based indoor navigation technology presents the following advantages: 1) The crowdsourcing-based indoor navigation system does not require the deployment of a large number of sensors, which greatly reduces manpower. 2) The crowdsourcing-based indoor navigation technology is a real-time interactive technology that can provide mobile users with real-time navigation services.

© ICST Institute for Computer Sciences, Social Informatics and Telecommunications Engineering 2020
Published by Springer Nature Switzerland AG 2020. All Rights Reserved
S. W. Loke et al. (Eds.): MONAMI 2020, LNICST 338, pp. 125–137, 2020.
https://doi.org/10.1007/978-3-030-64002-6_9

Although the crowdsourcing-based indoor navigation system can solve the deficiencies of traditional indoor navigation [2], security is a serious problem due to the system that depends on crowdsourced data is vulnerable to the collusion attack [3,4]. Specifically, malicious responders collude with requesters who deliberately offer the positive feedback, which can contribute to the increase of their reputation. The attack of collusion behavior may cause many detrimental effects on the crowdsourcing-based indoor navigation system. For the fog platform: it disrupts the credibility of the reputation mechanism [5] and reduces the feasibility of the fog server platform. For the normal requesters: the attack of collusion behavior leaks the privacy of normal requesters and threatens the requester's personal secure. For the normal responders: the attack of collusion behavior reduces the probability of getting a task in the future.

In order to tackle the above challenges, a secure crowdsourcing-based indoor navigation system is proposed in this paper. The main distributions are summarized as follows:

- Firstly, we propose a novel crowdsourcing-based security indoor navigation system that does not require professional equipment on site to offer fundamental location services for requesters.
- Secondly, we build an attack model in conjunction with the system background and propose a novel reputation incentive mechanism based on the behaviors of responders, which ensures the security of the system.
- Thirdly, we use the offensive and defensive game to model the interactions between the fog server platform and responders. The optimization problem of the system is established to maximize the total utility of the system. The stable equilibrium solution of the game is obtained by solving the replicator dynamic equation and using the Jacobian matrix analysis method.

The rest of this paper is organized as follows: related work is reviewed in Sect. 2. In Sect. 3, we introduce the system model. In Sect. 4, we construct the offensive and defensive game model. Extensive simulations are conducted to evaluate the performance of the proposed incentive mechanism in Sect. 5. Finally, we conclude the paper in Sect. 6.

2   Related Work

In order to achieve the stability and accuracy of indoor positioning and navigation system, domestic and foreign scholars have put forward a large number of indoor navigation technologies in recent years. Zhuang et al. [6] proposed two WiFi-based crowdsourcing positioning systems, which autonomously update the database according to the dynamic changes of the indoor environment. Xiang et al. [7] proposed a new mobile application framework that relies on crowdsourcing technology to provide location-based services. Li et al. [8] proposed two incentive mechanisms to encourage people to participate in the crowdsourcing-based indoor navigation system. Chi et al. [9] proposed a privacy protection mechanism combining differential privacy protection and K anonymity, which can

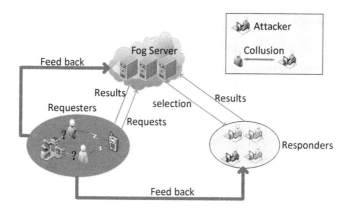

Fig. 1. Network model.

effectively protect the privacy of the users. Moreover, through the privacy protection mechanism, the trade-off between privacy protection and service quality is solved. Wang *et al.* [10] proposed a new method based on co-location edges, which can effectively defense the attack of attackers and improve the security of the crowdsourcing-based indoor navigation system. In summary, the above researches mainly focus on how to encourage mobile users to participate in the system. However, as the real, the security of the crowdsourcing-based indoor navigation system is the most important issue. In order to preserve the system, we propose a reputation incentive mechanism and construct the offensive and defensive game to maximize the utility of the system.

3   System Model

In this section, we propose the indoor navigation system consisting of four parts: network model, social relationship model, reputation mechanism, and attack model.

3.1   Network Model

As shown in Fig. 1, our network model is composed of the following three entities: requesters, fog server and responders.

– **Requesters** are a group of mobile users who have the requirement for navigation. We define the set of requesters as $\mathcal{U} = \{u_1, u_2, \ldots, u_I\}$. Specifically, when they broadcast tasks, the platform feeds back the navigation path provided by the responders to the requesters. After completing the task, the requesters need to pay the fee α, where the responders obtain $\delta\%$ of the fee, the platform acquires $1 - \delta\%$. Moreover, the requesters need to feed back the reputation value R to the platform and the responders. However, the requesters may be bribed by the attackers to help them attack the system.

- **Responders** are a group of mobile users who respond to a request when requesters issue a task. We define the set of responders as $V = \{v_1, v_2, \ldots, v_J\}$.
- **Fog server platform** is a completely trusted platform in the system. Meanwhile, the platform has the following functions: firstly, the platform is the connection centre between the responders and the requesters. Secondly, Fog server platform has supervision and detection abilities. If the platform choices supervision strategy, the collusion behavior of the responders can be detected with the probability of P.

3.2   Social Relationship Model

For each location request service, it is important to choose responders since the strengths and weaknesses of responders directly affect their service level. Without loss of generality, responders who have an intimate social relationship with the requester can provide better service for the requester. The social relationships between requester i and responder j, denoted as $f(i,j)$, which are defined as

$$f(i,j) = \frac{|I_i \cap I_j|}{|I_i \cup I_j|}, \tag{1}$$

where $f(i,j) \in [0,1]$. we define I_i as a social relationship set, which is denoted by $I_i = [O_{i,1}, \ldots, O_{i,n}, \ldots, O_{i,N}]$. $O_{i,n}$ is special relationships such as friends. When these relationships exist, $O_{i,n} = 1$, otherwise $O_{i,n} = 0$.

Case 1:

$$f(i,j) = \frac{|I_i \cap I_j|}{|I_i \cup I_j|} > HL. \tag{2}$$

The social relationship between requester u_i and responder v_j is intimate. HL is defined as the bounds for social relationships.

Case 2:

$$f(i,j) = \frac{|I_i \cap I_j|}{|I_i \cup I_j|} < HL. \tag{3}$$

The social relationship between requester u_i and responder v_j is unfamiliar.

3.3   Reputation Incentive Mechanism

In the indoor navigation system, the platform provides location services to requesters by selecting responders with the highest reputation value. Moreover, based on the reputation value R of the platform, requesters determine whether or not to request the platform. Therefore, some responders with low reputation value may illegally increase their reputation by colluding with the requesters.

We propose a novel reputation incentive mechanism to ensure the security of the system.

Case 1: When responders provide positive services. The reputation value R of the platform is updated by

$$R = (1 + \epsilon) * R_0, \tag{4}$$

where R_0 is the initial reputation value. ϵ is the increment of reputation. In this case, we use the reputation incentive coefficient ϵ to reward responders who choose normal strategy, prompting them to persistently choose normal strategy to ensure the security of the system.

Case 2: When responders provide negative services, the reputation value R of the platform is calculated by

$$R = (1 - \lambda) * R_0, \tag{5}$$

where $\lambda \in [0, 1]$ represents the degree of collusion. A larger λ indicates a greater degree of collusion, resulting in a greater loss of reputation value. In this case, we use the degree of collusion of the attacker as a punishment coefficient to reduce the reputation value of the attacker and thereby reducing their utility. In this way, the attack willingness of attacker is reduced, which ensures the security of the system.

3.4   Attacker Model

We divide the attack model into the following categories based on several factors that affect the ability of collusion:

1) Collusion with strangers in social relationships
    We define Ω as a collusive requester whose social relationship with the attackers is unfamiliar. When the attackers collude with Ω to attack reputation mechanism m times and the number of Ω is n ($n \in [0, N]$, $m \in [0, M]$, $N \geqslant 1$, $M \geqslant 1$), attackers collaborate with Ω to issue m times false mission requests. Then, Ω feeds back to the attackers with a higher reputation value, so as to influence the selection of normal requesters in the next stage.

2) Collusion with people who are socially intimate
    We define $\Omega^\star$ as a collusive requester whose social relationship with the attackers is intimate. When the attackers collude with the $\Omega^\star$ to attack reputation mechanism m times and the number of $\Omega^\star$ is n ($n \in [0, N]$, $m \in [0, M]$, $N \geqslant 1$, $M \geqslant 1$), attackers collaborate with $\Omega^\star$ to issue m times false mission requests.

4 Offensive and Defensive Game

4.1 Problem Formulation

Responders are categorized into two categories: the normal responders and the attackers. The attackers collude with the requesters with a probability x, and illegally increase their profits with a degree of collusion λ. The collusion level λ follows

$$\lambda = \frac{1}{1 + e^{-[f(i,j)*g(C_u, N_u)]}}, \tag{6}$$

where $\lambda \in [0,1]$ is proportional to the capacities of attackers. ω is the accuracy of the path provided by the attackers. $g(C_u, N_u)$ is the frequency of attacks, defined as

$$g(C_u, N_u) = \sigma_1 C_u + \sigma_2 N_u, \tag{7}$$

where N_u is the number of requesters who collude with the attackers. C_u is the times of attacks. σ_1 is the importance of the number of colluding requesters in the attacks frequency. σ_2 is the importance of the times of attacks in the attack frequency.

The attacker also can disguise himself as a normal responder to reduce the probability of being supervised by the platform. The quality of the navigation path provided by the attackers, denoted as β, which is defined as

$$\beta = \begin{cases} \beta_{min}, & \text{if the destination is inconsistent,} \\ \frac{\int_A^B h(x,y,z)\,dl}{\int_A^B h'(x,y,z)\,dl}, & \text{if the destination is consistent.} \end{cases} \tag{8}$$

A is the starting point of the path and B is the end point of the path. $h(x, y, z)$ is the shortest trajectory from point A to point B. $h'(x, y, z)$ is the trajectory from point A to point B provided by the attacker. The normal responder's β is equal to 1, because the normal responder's target is to improve his utility. When the attackers choose the wrong navigation path, the value of β is β_{min}.

The fog service platform has the functions of supervision and detection in the system. When the platform chooses the supervision strategy, it has a probability P to successfully supervise the collusion behavior of the attackers. If detected, the attackers need to pay the illegal cost. Otherwise, the attackers will receive illegal income, which is the platform losses. The probability of platform successful supervision P follows

$$P = (1 - \beta\lambda). \tag{9}$$

When the platform supervision fails, it is considered that the attackers choose the non-collusion strategy.

4.2 Utility Function

The offensive and defensive game matrix is shown in Table 1.

Table 1. The offensive and defensive game matrix

		Fog serve platform	
		(y)supervision	(1-y)non-supervision
Responders	(x)collusion	$U_a(x,y), U_d(x,y)$	$U_a(x,1-y), U_d(x,1-y)$
	(1-x)non-collusion	$U_a(1-x,y), U_d(1-x,y)$	$U_a(1-x,1-y), U_d(1-x,1-y)$

(1) When the responders choose the collusion strategy and the degree of collusion is λ, as well as the platform chooses the supervision strategy:

Different from the traditional definition of utility, we introduce the reputation incentive mechanism and divide the utility into current utility and future utility. The utility of the responders is defined as

$$U_a = U_a^m + U_a^n, \tag{10}$$

where U_a is the total utility of the responders. U_a^m is the current utility of the responders, and U_a^n is the future utility of the responders.

The current utility of the responders is defined as

$$U_a^m(x,y) = \sum_{k=1}^{k_d} [\delta\alpha_k - \lambda\beta_k c_1 - PW\lambda + (1-P)S\lambda], \tag{11}$$

where k_d is the total number of tasks. W represents the cost of attacker when the attack fails. S represents the attacker's profits when the attack is successful. c_1 represents the unit cost of the responders who choose the collusion strategy.

The future utility of the responders follows

$$U_a^n(x,y) = \delta e^{\varphi R}, \tag{12}$$

where R represents the reputation value of the platform. $\varphi > 0$ represents a positive correlation coefficient between reputation value and future utility.

Substituting Eq. (11) and Eq. (12) into the Eq. (10), the total utility of the responders can be rewritten as

$$U_a(x,y) = \sum_{k=1}^{k_d} [\delta\alpha_k - \lambda\beta_k c_1 - PW\lambda + (1-P)S\lambda] \\ + \delta e^{\varphi(1-\lambda)R_0}. \tag{13}$$

We design a novel reputation incentive mechanism that links future utility, so as to encourage responders to choose the non-collusion strategy.

The utility of the platform is defined as

$$U_d = U_d^m + U_d^n, \tag{14}$$

where U_d is the total utility of the platform. U_d^m is the current utility of the platform, and U_d^n is the future utility of the platform.

The current utility of the platform follows

$$U_d^m(x,y) = \sum_{k=1}^{k_d} [(1-\delta)\alpha_k - d_1 + PJ\lambda - (1-P)B\lambda], \tag{15}$$

where d_1 is the cost of the platform when the platform chooses the supervision strategy. J is the profits from platform successful supervision. B is the cost of the platform when attackers collusion successfully.

The future utility is defined by the reputation value of the platform

$$U_d^n(x,y) = (1-\delta)e^{\varphi R}. \tag{16}$$

Substituting Eq. (15) and Eq. (16) into the Eq. (14), the total utility of the platform can be rewritten as

$$U_d(x,y) = \sum_{k=1}^{k_d}[(1-\delta)\alpha_k - d_1 + PJ\lambda - (1-P)B\lambda] \\ + (1-\delta)e^{\varphi(1-\lambda)R_0}. \tag{17}$$

(2) When the responders choose the collusion strategy and the degree of collusion is λ, as well as the platform chooses the non-supervision strategy:
The current utility of the responders is defined as

$$U_a^m(x,1-y) = \sum_{k=1}^{k_d}[\delta\alpha_k - \lambda\beta_k c_1 + S\lambda]. \tag{18}$$

The future utility of the responders is denoted as

$$U_a^n(x,1-y) = \delta e^{\varphi R}. \tag{19}$$

Substituting Eq. (18) and Eq. (19) into the Eq. (10), the total utility of the responders can be rewritten as

$$U_a(x,1-y) = \sum_{k=1}^{k_d}[\delta\alpha_k - \lambda\beta_k c_1 + S\lambda] \\ + \delta e^{\varphi(1-\lambda)R_0}. \tag{20}$$

The current utility of the platform is defined as

$$U_d^m(x,1-y) = \sum_{k=1}^{k_d}[(1-\delta)\alpha_k - d_2 - B\lambda], \tag{21}$$

where d_2 is the cost of the platform when the platform chooses the non-supervision strategy.

The future utility of the platform is denoted as

$$U_d^n(x,1-y) = (1-\delta)e^{\varphi R}. \tag{22}$$

Substituting Eq. (21) and Eq. (22) into the Eq. (14), the total utility of the platform can be rewritten as

$$U_d(x,1-y) = \sum_{k=1}^{k_d}[(1-\delta)\alpha_k - d_2 - B\lambda] \\ + (1-\delta)e^{\varphi(1-\lambda)R_0}. \tag{23}$$

(3) When the responders choose the non-collusion strategy and the platform chooses the supervision strategy:

The total utility of the responders is defined as

$$U_a(1 - x, y) = \sum_{k=1}^{k_d} [\delta \alpha_k - c_2] + \delta e^{\varphi(1+\epsilon)R_0}, \tag{24}$$

where c_2 is the cost of the responders who choose the non-collusion strategy.

The total utility of the platform is denoted as

$$U_d(1 - x, y) = \sum_{k=1}^{k_d} [(1 - \delta)\alpha_k - d_1] \\ + (1 - \delta)e^{\varphi(1+\epsilon)R_0}. \tag{25}$$

(4) When the responders choose the non-collusion strategy and the platform chooses the non-supervision strategy:

The total utility of the responders is defined as

$$U_a(1 - x, 1 - y) = \sum_{k=1}^{k_d} [\delta \alpha_k - c_2] + \delta e^{\varphi(1+\epsilon)R_0}. \tag{26}$$

For the platform, it does not need to pay more cost to manage the behavior of responders. The total utility of the platform is denoted as

$$U_d(1 - x, 1 - y) = \sum_{k=1}^{k_d} [(1 - \delta)\alpha_k - d_2] \\ + (1 - \delta)e^{\varphi(1+\epsilon)R_0}. \tag{27}$$

4.3   Game Equilibrium Solution

In the replication dynamic equation, the growth rate of a strategy in the community is equal to the difference between the utility of the strategy and the average utility of the community [11]. Therefore, the replication dynamic equation can be described as

$$\frac{dx}{dt} = x[U_a(x) - \bar{U}_a], \\ \frac{dy}{dt} = y[U_d(y) - \bar{U}_d], \tag{28}$$

where $\bar{U}_a$ and $\bar{U}_d$ are the average utility of the responders and platform, respectively. Based on the replication dynamic equations of the two parties, the equation M can be described as

$$M = \left[\begin{array}{c} \frac{dx}{dt} \\ \frac{dy}{dt} \end{array} \right]. \tag{29}$$

We can get five sets of equilibrium solutions by letting $M = 0$, which are $(0, 0)$, $(0, 1)$, $(1, 0)$, $(1, 1)$, (x^*, y^*). The expression of x^* is

$$x^* = \frac{d_1 - d_2}{P(J + B)\lambda}. \tag{30}$$

The expression of y^* is

$$y^* = \frac{\delta(e^{\varphi(1-\lambda)R_0} - e^{\varphi(1+\epsilon)R_0}) - \lambda\beta c_1 + c_2 + S\lambda}{PK_d(S+W)\lambda}. \tag{31}$$

4.4   Stability Analysis of Equilibrium Solutions

For a group of dynamic characteristic described by a differential equation system, the stability of its equilibrium point is obtained by using the local stability analysis method of the Jacobian matrix.

Case 1: When $[(1-2P)S\lambda - \beta\lambda c_1 + \delta e^{[\varphi(1-\lambda)R_0]}] - (\delta e^{[\varphi(1+\epsilon)R_0]} - c_2) > 0$ and $d_2 > d_1$, the equilibrium point of the system is only $(1, 1)$, i.e., the responders select the collusion strategy, and the fog server platform selects the supervision strategy.

Case 2: When $[(1-2P)S\lambda - \beta\lambda c_1 + \delta e^{[\varphi(1-\lambda)R_0]}] - (\delta e^{[\varphi(1+\epsilon)R_0]} - c_2) < 0$, and $2PJ\lambda + d_2 < d_1$, the equilibrium point of the system is only $(0, 0)$, i.e., the responders select the non-collusion strategy, and the fog server platform selects the non-supervision strategy.

Case 3: When $[(1-2P)S\lambda - \beta\lambda c_1 \delta e^{[\varphi(1-\lambda)R_0]}] - (\delta e^{[\varphi(1+\epsilon)R_0]} - c_2) > 0$ and $2PJ\lambda + d_2 < d_1$, the equilibrium point of the system is only $(1, 0)$, i.e., the responders select the collusion strategy, and the fog server platform selects the non-supervision strategy.

Case 4: When $[(1-2P)S\lambda - \beta\lambda c_1 + \delta e^{[\varphi(1-\lambda)R_0]}] - (\delta e^{[\varphi(1+\epsilon)R_0]} - c_2) < 0$, and $d_2 > d_1$, the equilibrium point of the system is only $(0, 1)$, i.e., the responders select the non-collusion strategy, and the fog server platform selects the supervision strategy.

5   Performance Evaluation

5.1   Simulation Setup

In the simulations, the increment of reputation is selected from the interval $[0, 1]$. The total profit of per task is set to be 0.5. The responder's profit as a percentage of total profit is set to be 0.6. The initial reputation value is set as 0.5. The quality of the navigation path provided by the attackers is set as 0.2. Other parameters in the simulations are given in Table 2 to satisfy our four constraints. The performance of the proposed reputation incentive mechanism is verified by comparing with two mechanisms, namely the fixed mechanism and the linear mechanism.

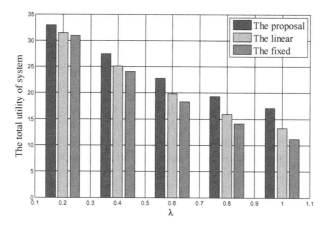

Fig. 2. The impacts of λ on total utility of system.

Table 2. Parameters

Case 1		Case 4	
Parameter	Value	Parameter	Value
S	1	S	1
W	1	W	1
J	1	J	1
B	1	B	1
c_1	0.5	c_1	0.5
c_2	5	c_2	0.5
d_1	0.2	d_1	0.2
d_2	0.4	d_2	0.4
φ	3	φ	4
K_d	10	K_d	10

5.2 Simulation Results

It is shown in Fig. 2 that the impact of λ on total system utility. We compare the proposed mechanism with the fixed mechanism and linear mechanism to verify the effectiveness of the proposed mechanism. From Fig. 2, we can obtain that with the increase of λ, the system utilities obtained by the three mechanisms are gradually reduced, while the utilities based on the proposed mechanism are better than the utilities obtained by the other two mechanisms. The reason is that the offensive and defensive game can effectively motivate responders to pay attention to long-term utilities with reputation incentives and choose the best strategy with reputation incentive. In the fixed mechanism, the attacker chooses the strategy according to the preset probability. In the linear mechanism, the attacker chooses the strategy without considering the reputation mechanism.

Therefore, the performance based on the proposed mechanism is better than the other two mechanisms.

6 Conclusion

In this paper, we have proposed a crowdsourcing-based secure indoor navigation system. Firstly, we have built an attack model in conjunction with the system background, and we have proposed a novel reputation incentive mechanism. Secondly, we have constructed the offensive and defensive game to model the interactions between the fog service platform and responders. By means of game theory, the utility function of both the system and the attacker are maximized. Finally, extensive simulations have validated the effectiveness of our mechanism. For the future work, we plan to take the multi-stage collusion into account to improve the reliability of the crowdsourcing-based indoor navigation system.

Acknowledgements. This work is supported in part by NSFC (nos. U1808207, 91746114), and the Project of Shanghai Municipal Science and Technology Commission, 18510761000.

References

1. Su, Z., Wang, Y., Xu, Q., Zhang, N.: LVBS: lightweight vehicular blockchain for secure data sharing in disaster rescue. IEEE Trans. Depend. Secure. https://doi.org/10.1109/TDSC.2020.2980255
2. Li, W., Su, Z., Zhang, K., Benslimane, A., Fang, D.: Defending malicious check-in using big data analysis of indoor positioning system: an access point selection approach. IEEE Trans. Netw. Sci. Eng. https://doi.org/10.1109/TNSE.2020.3014384
3. Li, W., Su, Z., Zhang, K., Xu, Q.: Abnormal crowd traffic detection with crowdsourcing-based RSS fingerprint position in heterogeneous communications networks. IEEE Trans. Netw. Sci. Eng. https://doi.org/10.1109/TNSE.2020.3014380
4. Wang, Y., Su, Z., Zhang, N., Benslimane, A.: Learning in the air: secure federated learning for UAV-assisted crowdsensing. IEEE Trans. Netw. Sci. Eng. https://doi.org/10.1109/TNSE.2020.3014385
5. Goswami, A., Gupta, R., Parashari, G.S.: Reputation-based resource allocation in P2P systems: a game theoretic perspective. IEEE Commun. Lett. **21**(6), 1273–1276 (2017)
6. Zhuang, Y., Syed, Z., Li, Y., El-Sheimy, N.: Evaluation of two WiFi positioning systems based on autonomous crowdsourcing of handheld devices for indoor navigation. IEEE Trans. Mob. Comput. **15**(8), 1982–1995 (2016)
7. Xiang, L., Tai, T., Li, B., Li, B.: Tack: learning towards contextual and ephemeral indoor localization with crowdsourcing. IEEE J. Sel. Areas Commun. **35**(4), 863–879 (2017)
8. Li, W., Zhang, C., Liu, Z., Tanaka, Y.: Incentive mechanism design for crowdsourcing-based indoor localization. IEEE Access **6**, 54042–54051 (2018)
9. Chi, Z., Wang, Y., Huang, Y., Tong, X.: the novel location privacy-preserving CKD for mobile crowdsourcing systems. IEEE Access **6**, 5678–5687 (2018)

10. Wang, G., Wang, B., Wang, T., Nika, A., Zheng, H., Zhao, B.Y.: Ghost riders: sybil attacks on crowdsourced mobile mapping services. IEEE/ACM Trans. Networking **26**(3), 1123–1136 (2018)
11. Xu, H., Wang, Z., Xiao, W.: Analyzing community core evolution in mobile social networks. In: 2013 International Conference on Social Computing, Alexandria, VA, pp. 154–161 (2013)

Recent Advances in Mobile
Communications and Computing

Throughput Optimal Uplink Scheduling in Heterogeneous PLC and LTE Communication for Delay Aware Smart Grid Applications

Qiyue Li[1,2(✉)], Tengfei Cao[1,2], Wei Sun[1,2], and Weitao Li[1,2]

[1] School of Electrical Engineering and Automation,
Hefei University of Technology, Hefei 230009, Anhui, China
liqiyue@mail.ustc.edu.cn, tfcao@mail.hfut.edu.cn,
{wsun,wtli}@hfut.edu.cn
[2] Engineering Technology Research Center of Industrial Automation,
Hefei 230009, Anhui, China

Abstract. Smart grid is an energy network that integrates advanced power equipment, communication technology and control technology. It can transmit two-way power and data among all components of the grid at the same time. The existing smart grid communication technologies include power line carrier (PLC) communication, industrial Ethernet, passive optical networks and wireless communication, each of which have different advantages. Due to the complex application scenarios, massive sampling points and high transmission reliability requirements, a single communication method cannot fully meet the communication requirements of smart grid, and heterogeneous communication modes are required. In addition, with the development of cellular technology, long term evolution (LTE)-based standards have been identified as a promising technology that can meet the strict requirements of various operations in smart grid. In this paper, we analyze the advantages and disadvantages of PLC and LTE communication, and design a network framework for PLC and LTE communication uplink heterogeneous communication in smart grid. Then, we propose an uplink scheduling transmission method for sampling data with optimized throughput according to the requirements of system delay and reliability. Then, we use the formula derivation to prove the stability and solvability of the scheduling system in theory. Finally, the simulation results show that under the condition of satisfying the delay requirement, our proposed framework can optimally allocate the wireless communication resource and maximize the throughput of the uplink transmission system.

Keywords: Smart grid · Heterogeneous communication · Optimized throughput

1 Introduction

Smart grid is built on the basis of an integrated high-speed two-way communication network through advanced technology to achieve a reliable, safe, economic, and efficient power grid. In addition to ensuring the two-way flow of electric energy among all nodes

S. W. Loke et al. (Eds.): MONAMI 2020, LNICST 338, pp. 141–160, 2020.
https://doi.org/10.1007/978-3-030-64002-6_10

from the power plant to the end-user in the process of power transmission and distribution, smart grid also needs to transmit a large amount of information; to achieve this, power communication technology is required [1, 16]. The application of power communication technology in smart grid can further improve the efficiency and quality of power systems. Establishing an efficient power communication channel can provide rapid feedback concerning user circumstances, enable effective resource use, and address unexpected power grid situations in a timely manner. The channel can also monitor all abnormal parameters in the power grid at the same time, providing a comprehensive technical guarantee for the energy system.

The key factor in the development of smart grid is certainly the communication infrastructure. PLC and LTE have been used to constitute pathways for implementing smart grid [17]. There are many applications of PLC technology in smart grid communication, especially in transmission networks [2]. In the low-speed application scenario, ultranarrowband PLC technology can realize long-distance communication. Additionally, as a multi-channel transmission system, PLC technology has been developed into a multiple input multiple output (MIMO) version, which uses space-time coding to realize transmission diversity and spatial multiplexing, and can greatly improve the stability and transmission efficiency of the system. PLC technology has become quite mature, and related supporting facilities have become more advanced; hence, PLC technology is widely used in power system communication.

With the promotion of distributed generation (DG), consumers have begun to experience the advantages in generating part of the electricity. Then most commonly used types of power generation are photovoltaic panels and wind turbines. The principle of distributed generation is to achieve the goal of efficient, economic and stable power generation in the distribution network system, through directly setting or focusing on the power generation equipment near the load. As far as reliability is concerned, DG is considered to be a form of diversified power generation and has a variety of methods (a hybrid method) to achieve its objectives [14, 18]. DG can generate electricity not only under normal conditions, but also in some special cases [3]. With the development of LTE and 5G, the application of wireless communication in power system communication is increasing [4, 15]. In the distribution network, the network facilities are poor and there are many users, and it is difficult to meet the requirements by a separate communication method. The relationships in DG can be applied to the data communication infrastructure to combine and create redundancy for critical and necessary data communication paths. This is the so-called heterogeneous data communication architecture or hybrid data communication system [5].

At present, research on wired/wireless heterogeneous communication is still limited, mainly focusing on heterogeneous wireless communication. Yasin Kabalci clearly revealed the network and physical structure of smart grid [6]. T. De Schepper proposed the ORCHESTRA framework to manage different devices in heterogeneous wireless networks and introduced capabilities such as packet-level dynamic and intelligent handovers (both inter- and intra technology), load balancing, replication, and scheduling [7]. Zhang developed a set of hybrid communication system simulation models to verify the key system design standard of distributed solar photovoltaic (PV) communication systems [8]. J. Wan proposed a heterogeneous network architecture based on a software-defined network (SDN) for realizing cross-network flexible forwarding of multi-source manufacturing data and optimized the utilization of network resources [9]. M. A. Zarrabian studied the problem of multirate packet delivery in heterogeneous packet- erasure broadcast networks and presented a new analytical framework for characterizing the delivery rate and delivery delay performance of a nonblock-based network coding scheme [10]. Koohifar proposed a hybrid Wi-Fi/LTE aggregated data communication architecture and compared it with the baseline LTE architecture under the smart grid flow profile. The results show that the proposed architecture can improve the performance of the control channel and random access channel [11].

The first method combined PLC and wireless communication in smart grid data transmission was developed in [12]. However, the article only compared the achievable data rates in communication systems and analyzed the advantages of hybrid systems over non-hybrid systems.

There are many devices in the distribution network, that generate a large amount of data, and the throughput that needs to be transmitted is large. Meanwhile, telemetry and remote signal data have transmission delay requirements. Therefore, we must reasonably allocate data to PLC or LTE while meeting the data delay requirements and reliability to maximize system throughput.

This paper proposes a throughput-optimized transmission scheduling framework that meets the smart grid specifications and system requirements. In addition, we prove that the proposed heterogeneous PLC and LTE communication uplink optimized transmission scheduling methods can maximize system throughput and reasonably allocate resources.

Our contributions are as follows:

(1) We propose a framework for heterogeneous communication in smart grid that combines PLC and LTE uplink channels to maximize the throughput of the system.
(2) We prove the stability and solvability of the scheduling system in theory and design an optimization algorithm to solve the scheduling problem of system throughput optimization.
(3) The simulation results show that the optimized transmission scheduling method for heterogeneous PLC and LTE communication can maximize the throughput of the system compared with other typical solutions.

The remainder of this paper is organized as follows. In Sect. 2 a network framework for PLC and LTE communication in smart grid is designed. In Sect. 3, the stability and solution of the system are theoretically proven by reasoning. In Sect. 4, the simulation results show that the optimized transmission scheduling method of heterogeneous PLC and LTE communication can maximize the throughput of the system. Finally, we conclude this paper in Sect. 5.

2 System Model

First, consider the system application scenario shown in Fig. 1. As shown in the figure, the system consists of three parts: N wireless sensor network nodes with different types of sensors, intelligent grid multi interface heterogeneous communication platforms, and remote cloud monitoring equipment. There are three modules in the multi- interface heterogeneous communication platform of the smart grid: the scheduler, PLC module and LTE module. First, different types of sensors collect all kinds of data, including voltage, current, temperature and humidity, control and other data, and then transmit the data to the multi-interface heterogeneous communication platform of smart grid. There are different transmission delay and packet loss rate requirements for the different types of sensors, and these requirements are comprehensively analyzed to achieve the maximum system throughput and to decide whether to use the PLC or LTE of the data.

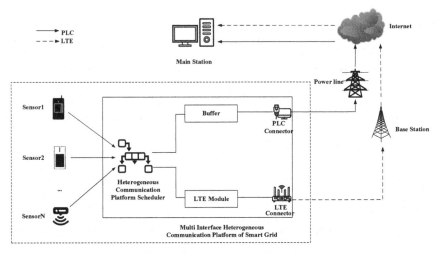

Fig. 1. System structure diagram

These three modules work together to optimize the transmission, which means that to maximize the throughput of the system, the data sampled by different sensors are reasonably distributed to PLC and LTE. Specifically, the workflow of the system is as follows: all kinds of data collected by N different types of sensors are transmitted to the scheduler in the heterogeneous communication platform. It comprehensively analyzes the specific transmission delay and data packet loss rate requirements for each piece of data and reasonably distributes the data to the PLC or LTE. If the data is transmitted by PLC, it will pass through the data buffer, and then it will be transmitted to the remote cloud monitoring system by wire through the PLC interface. If the LTE uplink channel interface is selected, we do not consider the delay, but due to the characteristics of the wireless channel, packet loss may occur.

There is a data buffer in the PLC module, and it is used to temporarily store the transmitted data. When the data are transferred to the front end of the data buffer, the end of the data buffer is simultaneously transferring data to the outside. In the buffer, the data are transmitted in line, according to the principle of "first in, first out", so the data will stay in the data buffer for a period of time. The data buffer will affect the transmission delay of the data. We assume that the transmission data rate r_{PLC} is constant. The total time for data transmission in PLC cannot exceed the system delay requirements.

In the LTE part, the data transmission mode is the space-time multiplexing mode of orthogonal frequency division multiple access (OFDMA), so the transmitted data blocks occupy a certain range on the time axis and on the space axis. As shown in Fig. 2, generally, a resource block (RB) occupies 0.5 ms, which occupies 12 subcarrier channels. We assume that the wireless transmission resource block is limited for a period of time, and the resource block consumed by wireless transmission data during resource allocation cannot exceed this fixed value. At the same time, packet loss of data will occur during wireless transmission, resulting in data transmission failure. Bit error rate P_b during wireless transmission is related to the signal-to-noise ratio threshold and the average signal-to-noise ratio of the platform. Different types of data have different requirements for successful reception rates, and the probability of successful data transmission cannot be less than the corresponding requirements for successful reception rates [19, 20].

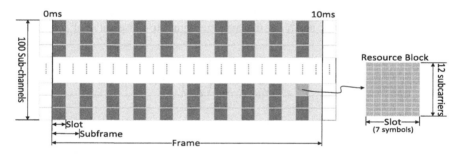

Fig. 2. Schematic diagram of wireless resource blocks

2.1 Problem Formulation

a. Dynamics of PLC data buffer

In the process of wired transmission, the total time needed for data transmission is equal to the total time spent in the data buffer plus the time needed for wired transmission. Let $D_{n,i}$ represent the data size sampled by the n th sensor at the i th timestep; $t_{n,i}$ represents the total time that the amount of data $D_{n,i}$ sampled by the n th sensor at the ith timestep stays in the data buffer during wired transmission. The total time in which the data remain in the data buffer is the ratio of the current buffer depth to the wire transmission rate.

$$t_{n,i} = \frac{m(i)}{r_{PLC}} \tag{1}$$

The depth of the current data buffer is equal to the depth of the data buffer at the previous moment plus the amount of incoming data minus the amount of data transmitted. We use $m(i)$ to represent the depth of sampled data amount $D_{n,i}$ in the buffer at time slot i; $x_{n,i}$ represents the data $D_{n,i}$ is transmitted by PLC or LTE, i.e., decision variable $x_{n,i} = 1$ represents data transmitted by PLC and $x_{n,i} = 0$ represents data transmitted by LTE.

$$m(i + 1) = m(i) + \sum_{n=1}^{N} \left(D_{n,i} \cdot x_{n,i} - r_{PLC} \cdot x_{n,i} \right) \tag{2}$$

b. Bit error rate of wireless transmission

The bit error rate is an index used to measure the accuracy of data transmission in a given time, and the generation of the error code is due to the decay in the signal voltage in the signal transmission, which causes the signal to be damaged in the transmission. In [13], Eq. (3) is used to determine bit error rate P_b during wireless transmission:

$$P_b = \frac{1}{2} \left[1 + \mathrm{erf} \left(\frac{\gamma - \bar{\gamma}}{\sigma \sqrt{2}} \right) \right] \tag{3}$$

In Eq. (1), σ is a fixed parameter, γ represents the signal-to-noise ratio threshold, $\mathrm{erf}(\cdot)$ denotes the error function, and $\bar{\gamma}$ is the average signal-to-noise ratio of the sensor. Additionally,

$$\bar{\gamma} = \frac{P_r}{N_0} = \frac{P_t K}{N_0} \left(\frac{d_0}{d_n} \right)^{\lambda} \tag{4}$$

c. Objective function and constraints

The throughput of a network system is the measure of the network's bearing capacity and transmission performance. In this paper, we try to maximize the throughput of a heterogeneous platform, which is the sum of the data volume of the PLC and LTE in the infinite time domain and is used as the system's throughput, represented by TP.

$$\max \mathrm{Tp} = \sum_{i=1}^{\infty} \sum_{n=1}^{N} D_{n,i} \cdot x_{n,i} + \sum_{i=1}^{\infty} \sum_{n=1}^{N} D_{n,i} \cdot \left(1 - x_{n,i} \right) \cdot \left(1 - P_b \right)^{D_{n,i} \cdot (1 - x_{n,i})} \tag{5}$$

According to the delay and reliability requirements of various types of smart grid communication data, the following constraints hold.

$$\frac{D_{n,i} \cdot x_{n,i}}{r_{PLC}} + t_{n,i} \leq T_{c,n} \tag{6}$$

$$1 - (1 - P_b)^{D_{n,i} \cdot (1 - x_{n,i})} \leq 1 - P_{e,n} \tag{7}$$

$$\frac{\sum_{i=1}^{T} \sum_{n=1}^{N} D_{n,i} \cdot (1 - x_{n,i})}{R_{RB}} \leq Y \tag{8}$$

$$0 \leq X_{n,i} \leq 1, x_{n,i}N \tag{9}$$

Constraint (6) indicates that the total time for data transmission by wire cannot exceed delay requirement $T_{c,n}$ of the nth sensor data.

Constraint (7) means that the bit error rate of data transmitted wirelessly cannot exceed the required bit error rate of data $(1 - P_{e,n})$, and $P_{e,n}$ indicates the successful receiving rate of the data transmitted wirelessly for the n th sensor.

Constraint (8) means that the number of resource blocks consumed by the data transmitted wirelessly in time T does not exceed the number of wireless transmission resource blocks Y, and R_{RB} is the transmission rate of the LTE resource blocks.

Constraint (9) shows that a packet can only be transmitted in either a wired or wireless mode.

In this paper, on the premise of fully considering the delay requirements of the data in wired transmission and the reliability requirements of the data in wireless transmission, we decide to take either 0 or 1 for every $x_{n,i}$, which indicated whether the data of each sensor at each time is transmitted by wire or by wireless, to maximize the total throughput of the system. Obviously, this is a nonlinear 0-1 programming problem with constraints.

3 Problem Solving

The optimization of the heterogeneous platform throughput in an infinite time problem cannot be solved by calculation. In this paper, we use an iterative method and obtain the optimal solution of the current state and the current status by predicting the optimal solution at time NP, which is optimized in the following section.

For the dynamics of the PLC data buffer:

$$m(k + 1) = m(k) + \sum_{n=1}^{N} \left(D_{n,k} \cdot x_{n,k} - r_{PLC} \cdot x_{n,k} \right) \tag{10}$$

We mark as:

$$m(k + 1) = f(m(k), x(k)) = m(k) + \sum_{n=1}^{N} \left(D_{n,k} \cdot x(k) - r_{PLC} \cdot x(k) \right), m(0) = m_0 \tag{11}$$

where $m(k) \in R$, and $x(k) \in R$ represent the depth of the data buffer and the decision variable at time k, respectively. The system's decision volume and data buffer constraints are:

$$m(k) \in [0, M], \ k \geq 0, \tag{12}$$

$$x(k) \in [0, 1], \ k \geq 0, \tag{13}$$

where M is the maximum buffer depth.

Obviously, the mapping f satisfies the following conditions:

A1) $f : R \times R \to R$ is continuous,

A2) $[0, 1] \in R$ is a tight interval and a convex interval, $[0, M] \in R$ is connected, and point $(0, 0)$ is contained in the aggregate $[0, 1] \times [0, M]$;

3.1 Finite Time Domain Problem Reformulation

$$\max \text{Tp} = \sum_{i=0}^{\infty} \sum_{n=1}^{N} \left(D_{n,i} \cdot x(i) + D_{n,i} \cdot (1 - x(i)) \cdot (1 - P_b)^{D_{n,i} \cdot (1-x(i))} \right)$$

TP is denoted as

$$TP^{\infty}(m(0), x(\cdot)) = \sum_{i=1}^{\infty} F(m(i), x(i)) \tag{14}$$

where $F(\cdot, \cdot)$ satisfies the following conditions:

B1) $F(m(i), x) : M \times X \to R$, where R is continuous with respect to independent variables $m(i)$ and x and satisfies $F(0, 0) = 0$ while for any $(m(i), x)M \times X \setminus \{0, 0\}$, there are $F(m(i), x) > 0$.

Due to the existence of time-domain constraints, it is almost impossible to give the exact expressions for analytical solutions to problem (14). To solve this problem, we can rewrite (14) as follows:

$$TP^{\infty}(m(0), x(\cdot))$$
$$= \sum_{i=0}^{T-1} \sum_{n=1}^{N} \left(D_{n,i} \cdot x(i) + D_{n,i} \cdot (1 - x(i)) \cdot (1 - P_b)^{D_{n,i} \cdot (1-x(i))} \right)$$
$$+ \sum_{i=T}^{\infty} \sum_{n=1}^{N} \left(D_{n,i} \cdot x(i) + D_{n,i} \cdot (1 - x(i)) \cdot (1 - P_b)^{D_{n,i} \cdot (1-x(i))} \right) \tag{15}$$

$$\Omega := \{m(i)R|E(m) \leq \alpha, \ \alpha\rangle 0\} \tag{16}$$

where here $E(m(i))$ is a positive definite function such that $E(0) = 0$ and $E(m(i)) > 0$, $\forall m(i) \neq 0$. Assume that such an input $x = \kappa(m)$ in Ω satisfies the following conditions:

C1) $\Omega \subseteq M$,

C2) $\kappa(m)X$ for all $m \in \Omega$,

C3) For all $x \in \Omega$ positive definite function $E(m)$ satisfies the inequality:

$$E(m(s)) - E(m(j)) \leq -\sum_{i=j}^{s} \sum_{n=1}^{N} \left(D_{n,i} \cdot x(i) + D_{n,i} \cdot (1 - x(i)) \cdot (1 - P_b)^{D_{n,i} \cdot (1-x(i))} \right), \ T \geq s \geq j \geq 0 \tag{17}$$

In Ω, because the input $x = \kappa(m)$ makes the data buffer system asymptotically stable, $E(m(\infty)) = 0$, and

$$\sum_{i=T}^{\infty} \sum_{n=1}^{N} \left(D_{n,i} \cdot x(i) + D_{n,i} \cdot (1 - x(i)) \cdot (1 - P_b)^{D_{n,i} \cdot (1-x(i))} \right) \le E(m(T)) \quad (18)$$

Substituting the above formula into (15),

$$\sum_{i=0}^{T-1} \sum_{n=1}^{N} \left(D_{n,i} \cdot x(i) + D_{n,i} \cdot (1 - x(i)) \cdot (1 - P_b)^{D_{n,i} \cdot (1-x(i))} \right)$$
$$+ \sum_{i=T}^{\infty} \sum_{n=1}^{N} \left(D_{n,i} \cdot x(i) + D_{n,i} \cdot (1 - x(i)) \cdot (1 - P_b)^{D_{n,i} \cdot (1-x(i))} \right)$$
$$\le \sum_{i=0}^{T-1} \sum_{n=1}^{N} \left(D_{n,i} \cdot x(i) + D_{n,i} \cdot (1 - x(i)) \cdot (1 - P_b)^{D_{n,i} \cdot (1-x(i))} \right) + E(m(T))$$
$$(19)$$

Therefore, we define the finite time domain objective function as follows:

$$\sum_{i=0}^{\infty} \sum_{n=1}^{N} \left(D_{n,i} \cdot x(i) + D_{n,i} \cdot (1 - x(i)) \cdot (1 - P_b)^{D_{n,i} \cdot (1-x(i))} \right)$$
$$:= \sum_{i=0}^{T-1} \sum_{n=1}^{N} \left(D_{n,i} \cdot x(i) + D_{n,i} \cdot (1 - x(i)) \cdot (1 - P_b)^{D_{n,i} \cdot (1-x(i))} \right) + E(m(T))$$
$$(20)$$

The above is an upper bound on objective function (14) in the infinite time domain. In this way, we transform the optimization problem of the infinite time domain into a finite time domain optimization problem.

3.2 Finite Time Domain Optimization Problem

The optimization problem of quasi infinite time domain nonlinear predictive control for discrete systems can be described as

$$max_{\bar{x}(\cdot)} TP(m(k), \bar{x}(\cdot)) \quad (21)$$

$$TP(m(k), \bar{x}(\cdot)) = \sum_{i=0}^{T-1} \sum_{n}^{N} \left(D_{n,k+i|k} \cdot \bar{x}(k + i|k) + D_{n,k+i|k} \cdot (1 - \bar{x}(k + i|k)) \cdot (1 - P_b)^{D_{n,k+i|k} \cdot (1-x(k+i|k))} \right) +$$
$$E(\bar{m}(k + T|k)) \quad (22)$$

This meets both system dynamics and time domain constraints:

$$m(\tau + i|k) = f(\bar{m}(|k), \bar{x}(|k)) = \bar{m}(|k) + \sum_{n=1}^{N} \left(D_{n,(|k)} \cdot \bar{x}(\tau|k) - r_{PLC} \cdot \bar{x}((\tau|k)), \bar{m}(k|k) = m(k) \right)$$
$$(23)$$

$$x(\tau|k) \in X, \tau \in [k, k + N - 1], \quad (24)$$

$$\bar{m}(\tau|k) \in M, \tau \in [k, k + N - 1], \quad (25)$$

$$\bar{m}(k + T|k) \in \Omega, \tag{26}$$

where T is the limited prediction time domain and $\bar{m}(\tau|k)$ is the predicted state trajectory of the system starting at $m(k)$ under the action of decision variable $\bar{x}(\cdot)$.

If optimization problem (21) has a solution, record it as

$$X^*(k) = \begin{bmatrix} \bar{x}^*(k|k) \\ \bar{x}^*(k+1|k)^T \\ \cdots \\ \bar{x}^*(k+T-1|k) \end{bmatrix}^T$$

We select $x^*(k|k)$ as the optimal solution of original problem (14) at time step k:

$$x^*(k) = \bar{x}^*(k|k) \tag{27}$$

Then:

$$m(k+1) = f\big(m(k), x^*(k)\big) = m(k) + \sum_{n=1}^{N}\big(D_{n,k} \cdot x^*(k) - r_{PLC} \cdot x^*(k)\big) \tag{28}$$

Let us discuss the stability of the prediction data buffer system.

(1) Suppose A1) to A2) and B1) are true,
(2) For nonlinear system (14), there is an input $x = \kappa(m)$, and the domain Ω of the equilibrium point and the positive definite function $E(m)$ satisfy the conditions C1)–C3),
(3) When $k = 0$, optimization problem (21) has a feasible solution,

Without considering external disturbances and model error:

(a) For any time $k > 0$, the optimization problem (21) has a feasible solution,
(b) The closed-loop system is asymptotically stable.

Proof: First, the feasibility of the optimization problem (21) at time k means that it is also feasible at time $(k + 1)$. The buffer depth measured at time k is $m(k)$. It is known from the assumption that there is a feasible solution to the optimization problem at this time, which is recorded as

$$X^*(k) = \begin{bmatrix} \bar{x}^*(k|k) \\ \bar{x}^*(k+1|k) \\ \cdots \\ \bar{x}^*(k+T-1|k) \end{bmatrix} \tag{29}$$

It satisfies control constraint (13), and the corresponding state sequence in the interval $[k + 1, k + T]$ is

$$m^*(k) = \begin{bmatrix} \bar{m}^*(k+1|k) \\ \bar{m}^*(k+2|k) \\ \cdots \\ \bar{m}^*(k+T-1|k) \\ \bar{m}^*(k+T|k) \end{bmatrix} \tag{30}$$

It satisfies state constraints (12) and terminal constraints (26), that is,

$$\bar{m}^*(k+i|k) \in M , i \in [k+1, k+T], \tag{31}$$

$$\bar{m}^*(k+T|k) \in \Omega \tag{32}$$

According to the principal of iteration, we apply the first element of the open-loop control sequence to the system to obtain buffer depth $m(k+1)$ at $(k+1)$. Without considering the model error of external interference, we obtain the following:

$$m(k+1) = \bar{m}^*(k+1|k)$$

With $m(k+1)$ as the initial buffer depth, a candidate solution for selecting open-loop optimization problem (21) at time $(k+1)$ is:

$$X(k+1) = \begin{bmatrix} \bar{x}^*(k+1|k) \\ \cdots \\ \bar{x}^*(k+T-1|k) \\ \kappa(\bar{m}^*(k+T|k)) \end{bmatrix} \tag{33}$$

Obviously, the first $(T-1)$ elements of this candidate solution are the last $(T-1)$ elements of optimal solution (29) at time k, and they all satisfy constraint (13). Since $\bar{m}^*(k+T|k) \in \Omega$ and all m in Ω have $\kappa(m)X$, (33) satisfies control constraint (13).

The prediction state sequence corresponding to (33) is

$$M(k+1) = \begin{cases} \bar{m}(k+i|k+1) = \bar{m}^*(k+i|k), & i \in [1,T] \\ \bar{m}(k+T+1|k+1) = f(\bar{m}^*(k+T|k), \kappa(\bar{m}^*(k+T|k))), & i = T+1 \end{cases} \tag{34}$$

From (32), we obtain

$$\bar{m}(k+i|k+1) \in M , i \in [1, T]$$

That is, the first step, $(T-1)$, of the predicted state sequence satisfies the state constraints. The invariance of class Ω and system $m(k+1) = f(m(k), \kappa(m(k)))$, implies $\bar{m}(k+T+1|k+1) \in \Omega$, that is, the predicted state sequence satisfies state constraints and terminal constraints.

In summary, $X(k+1)$ given by (34) is a feasible solution to the open-loop optimization problem in (21) at time $(k+1)$. Nature (a) is proven.

The stability of the closed-loop system can be proved, but limited to the page length, the specific proof will not be written.

From the recursive formula, we know that Eq. (2) can take the following form:

$$m(k+1) = m(k) + \sum_{n=1}^{N} \left(D_{n,k} \cdot x_{n,k} - r_{PLC} \cdot x_{n,k} \right) = m(1) + \sum_{k=0}^{\infty} \sum_{n=1}^{N} \left(D_{n,k} \cdot x_{n,k} - r_{PLC} \cdot x_{n,k} \right) \tag{35}$$

3.3 Integer Solution

The solution variable of the objective function is relaxed into a continuous variable, and the nonlinear integer programming problem is turned into an easy-to-solve nonlinear programming problem. To find the maximum value of a function under certain conditions, we use the Lagrangian multiplier method to solve the function and establish the Lagrangian function of the nonlinear programming problem according to Eq. (36):

$$L(x_{n,i}, \lambda) = TP + \lambda_1 h_1(x_{n,i}) + \lambda_2 h_2(x_{n,i}) + \lambda_3 h_3(x_{n,i}) + \lambda_4 h_4(x_{n,i}) \quad (36)$$

In Eq. (36), $L(x_{n,i}, \lambda)$ represents a Lagrangian function with respect to $x_{n,i}$, Lagrange multipliers λ, $h_1(x_{n,i})$, $h_2(x_{n,i})$, $h_3(x_{n,i})$ and $h_4(x_{n,i})$ represent the four constraint functions, and λ_1, λ_2, λ_3, λ_4 represent the Lagrangian multipliers corresponding to the constraint function. The specific forms of h_1, h_2, h_3 and h_4 are:

$$h_1(x_{n,i}) = \frac{D_{n,i} \cdot x_{n,i}}{r_{PLC}} + \tau_{n,i} - T_{c,n} \quad (37)$$

$$h_2(x_{n,i}) = P_{e,n} - (1 - P_b)^{D_{n,i} \cdot (1 - x_{n,i})} \quad (38)$$

$$h_3(x_{n,i}) = \frac{\sum_{n=1}^{N} \sum_{i=1}^{I} D_{n,i} \cdot (1 - x_{n,i})}{R_{RB}} - Y \quad (39)$$

$$h_4(x_{n,i}) = x_{n,i} - 1 \quad (40)$$

The KKT conditions are established according to Eqs. (37) to (40), and optimal solution x_{relax} of the relaxed nonlinear programming problem is obtained by combining the correlated equations of the KKT conditions:

$$\frac{d(L(x_{n,i}, \lambda))}{d(x_{n,i})} = \frac{d(TP)}{d(x_{n,i})} + \lambda_1 \frac{d(h_1(x_{n,i}))}{d(x_{n,i})} + \lambda_2 \frac{d(h_2(x_{n,i}))}{d(x_{n,i})} + \lambda_3 \frac{d(h_3(x_{n,i}))}{d(x_{n,i})} + \lambda_4 \frac{d(h_4(x_{n,i}))}{d(x_{n,i})} = 0 \quad (41)$$

$$h_1(x_{n,i}) \le 0, \quad h_2(x_{n,i}) \le 0, \quad h_3(x_{n,i}) \le 0, \quad h_4(x_{n,i}) \le 0 \quad (42)$$

$$\lambda_1, \lambda_2, \lambda_3, \lambda_4 \ge 0 \quad (43)$$

$$\lambda_1 h_1(x_{n,i}) = 0, \lambda_2 h_2(x_{n,i}) = 0, \lambda_3 h_3(x_{n,i}) = 0, \lambda_4 h_4(x_{n,i}) = 0 \quad (44)$$

The branch and bound method is used to obtain the solution variable of the objective function. Either wired or wireless transmission is used for the amount of data according to the solution variable.

We use Algorithm 1 to predict the optimal solution that satisfies the 0-1 constraint at 1-T time:

Objective function maxTp $= \sum_{n=1}^{N} \sum_{i=1}^{T} D_{n,i} \cdot x_{n,i} + \sum_{n=1}^{N} \sum_{i=1}^{T} D_{n,i} \cdot (1 - x_{n,i}) \cdot (1 - P_b)^{D_{n,i} \cdot (1 - x_{n,i})}$ is taken as the problem P − 1;

Algorithm 1: Branch and bound method

Input: x_{relax}: The optimal solution of the relaxation problem with the KKT condition
Z_{relax} : The optimal objective function value of the relaxation problem
ε : Any value within 0 to 1
Output: x_{0-1}: The optimal solution of problem P-1 with 0-1 constraints
Z_{0-1}: The optimal objective function value corresponding to the optimal 0-1 solution of P-1

Initialize k=0, L=0, U $= Z_{relax}$
1. Select any solution x_j that does not meet the 0-1 constraint condition from the optimal solution x_{relax}, that is: $x_j \in (0,1)$;
2. IF $0 \leq x_j < \varepsilon$, then add constraint condition $x_j = 0$ to problem p-1 to form sub-problem I; otherwise, add constraint condition $x_j = 1$ to problem p-1 to form sub-problem II, where ε means any value within 0 to 1;
3. k++, continue to find the solution to the relaxation problem of sub-problem I or sub-problem II, record it as x_k, and record the corresponding optimal objective function value as Z_k;
4. Find the optimal objective function maximum value U as the new upper bound, that is:

$$U = \max\{Z_{k'}|k' = 1,2,\cdots,k\}, x_{k'} \in [0,1];$$

5. Then, from the branches that meet the 0-1 condition, find the maximum value of objective function L as the new lower bound:

$$L = \max\{Z_{k'}|k' = 1,2,\cdots,k\}, x_{k'} \in \{0,1\};$$

6. IF $Z_{k'} <$ L, then cut the corresponding branch;
7. ELSE IF $Z_{k'} >$ L, and does not meet the 0-1 condition, return to step 2;
8. ELSE it means that the optimal objective function value of all branches is equal to the lower bound: $Z_{k'} =$ L,then assign $Z_{k'}$ to Z_{0-1} and $x_{k'}$ to x_{0-1}, and use it as optimal solution of the problem p-1,

Then, we use Algorithm 2 to find the actual optimal solution that satisfies the 0-1 constraint at time 1-I:

Algorithm 2: Throughput scheduling optimization algorithm for heterogeneous PLC and LTE communication uplink

Input: $M(:,1)$: Buffer initial depth
Output: X: The actual optimal solution meeting the 0-1 constraint

Initialization: $m\_init = 10^8$, $X = [0; 0; 0]$
1. The buffer initial depth is $M(:,1)$, let $M(:,1) = m\_init$;
2. FOR $i=1 \rightarrow$ I do;
3. $mk = M(:,i)$;
4.   Let mk be initial state $M(1)$ in buffer state equation (35), and use the Lagrangian multiplier method to find optimal solution x_{relax} of the nonlinear programming problem after time T;
5.   Use algorithm 1 to find a predicted optimal solution x_{0-1} that meets the 0-1 constraint;
6.   Make optimal solution xk at the current moment equal to optimal solution $x_{0-1}(1)$ at the predicted first moment, that is, $xk = x_{0-1}(1)$;
7. $X(:,i) = xk$;
8.   Substitute $X(:,i)$ as the control amount into formula (2) to obtain the depth $M(:,i+1)$ of the buffer at the next moment;
9. $mk = M(:,i+1)$;
10. END

4   Simulation and Experiment

In this section, we will evaluate the performance of our scheduling algorithm. A heterogeneous communication network is considered to be composed of N different types of sensors, one smart grid multiinterface heterogeneous communication platform and one remote cloud monitoring device. Table 1 lists the detailed parameters used to evaluate the network performance. We assume that PLC is not interfered with by the external environment and that the transmission rate, r_{PLC}, is constant. At the same time, we assume that the bit error rate of LTE can be calculated by calculating the average signal-to-noise ratio of the sensor.

Table 1. Simulation parameters

Parameters	Values
Number of RBs	100
Initial buffer depth	10^4 bytes
SNR threshold	11.5 dB
σ	2
Thermal noise variance	1 dB
Maximum transmitting power of sensor	20 dB
Number of packets	100
Reference distance from system to base station	1 m
Actual distance from system to base station	10–200 m
Pathloss exponent	2
Bit error rate of LTE	0.00003%–0.00005%
Transmission rate of PLC	10^4 bytes/s
Resource block transfer rate of LTE	240 bits/s

We use d to represent the average amount of data sampled per second by the sensor.

To evaluate our proposed algorithm, we compare the single PLC/LTE algorithm with the greedy algorithm. The single PLC/LTE algorithm assume that there is only one communication mode of PLC or LTE in the communication transmission. Theoretically, the greedy algorithm does not consider global optimization but only makes a local optimal choice. The greedy algorithm determines the optimal wired/wireless resource allocation method to maximize the local throughput. The simulation results are presented in terms of throughput, buffer depth and packet loss rate of different d.

Figures 3, 4 and 5 show the system throughput of our algorithm at different times. Greedy is the greedy algorithm, Single LTE represents the situation when LTE transmission is considered separately. We can see that the throughput of the system increases with time. The throughput of our algorithm is the largest, the greedy algorithm is second, and the corresponding throughput of single LTE is the smallest.

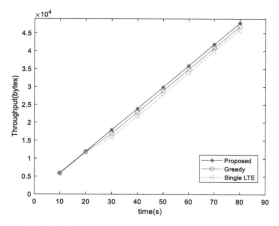

Fig. 3. Throughput (d = 200) at different times

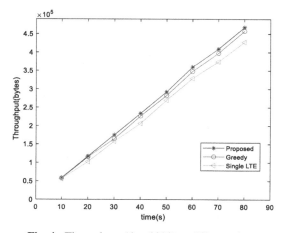

Fig. 4. Throughput (d = 2000) at different times

Figures 6, 7 and 8 show that the buffer depth of our algorithm at different times is more stable than that of the greedy algorithm and single PLC. Greedy is the greedy algorithm, Single PLC represents the situation when PLC transmission is considered separately. First, we can see that with increasing time, the buffer depth of the greedy method, single PLC and our proposed method decreases. The buffer depth of the proposed method decreases slowly, that of the greedy method decreases slowly at first and then quickly, and that of the single PLC decreases quickly. In a certain period of time, the wireless resources are limited. As time goes on, the wireless resources are gradually insufficient. The greedy algorithm can only allocate most communication resources to PLC, so the buffer depth drops rapidly in about 50 s. As time increases, the amount of data collected by the sensors increases. Due to the high wire transmission rate, the buffer depth will be

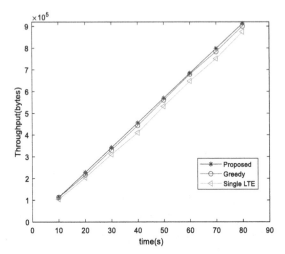

Fig. 5. Throughput (d = 4000) at different times

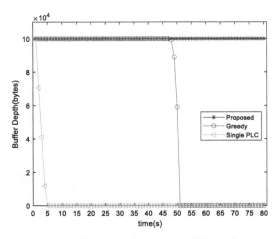

Fig. 6. Buffer depth (d = 200) at different times

reduced. However, our algorithm can schedule the sampled data effectively and allocate the resources to PLC or LTE optimally. Therefore, our algorithm makes the buffer depth change more stable.

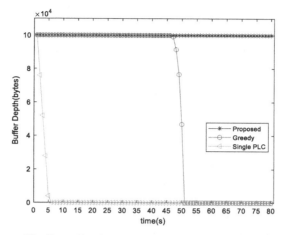

Fig. 7. Buffer depth (d = 2000) at different times

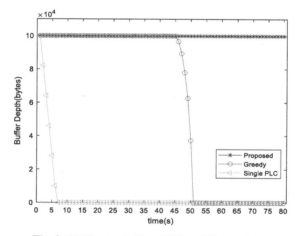

Fig. 8. Buffer depth (d = 4000) at different times

Figures 9, 10 and 11 show the packet loss rate of our algorithm and the greedy algorithm. Obviously, as the sampling time increases, the packet loss rate of a single LTE is constant, and the packet loss rate of both the proposed algorithms and greedy algorithms increases slowly, but our algorithm can reasonably schedule data to the PLC to reduce the packet loss rate. Our algorithm can achieve better results in terms of packet loss rate.

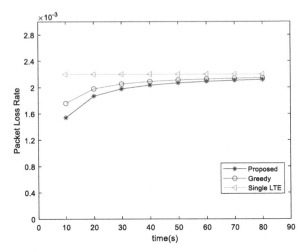

Fig. 9. Packet loss rate (d = 200) at different sampling times

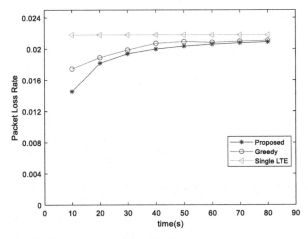

Fig. 10. Packet loss rate (d = 2000) at different sampling times

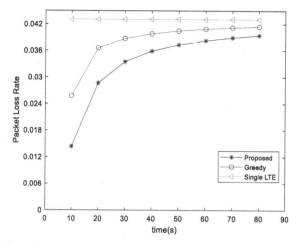

Fig. 11. Packet loss rate (d = 4000) at different sampling times

5 Conclusion

At present, heterogeneous network communication is a difficult problem. Many studies have focused only on wired or wireless communications, and even the research on heterogeneous networks has only focused on how to achieve heterogeneous wireless network communication, there is little research on heterogeneous PLC/LTE. In this paper, we propose a heterogeneous PLC/LTE uplink transmission scheduling method, and establish a heterogeneous communication network system. Then we convert the allocation scheme into a nonlinear programming problem by choosing PLC or LTE to maximize the system throughput. We also prove that the nonlinear problem is solvable and use the branch and bound method to find a 0-1 integer solution. Finally, we compared the performance of our method with other typical solutions. The numerical experimental results show that our algorithm can stabilize the buffer depth and achieve a lower packet loss rate while maintaining maximum system throughput.

References

1. Yang, B., Katsaros, K.V., Chai, W.K., et al.: Cost-efficient low latency communication infrastructure for synchrophasor applications in smart grids. IEEE Syst. J. **12**, 1–11 (2016)
2. Prasad, G., Lampe, L.: Full-duplex power line communications: design and plications from multimedia to smart grid. IEEE Commun. Mag. 2–8 (2019). https://doi.org/10.1109/mcom.001.1900519
3. Energy; Study Data from National Renewable Energy Laboratory Update Knowledge of Energy (Hybrid Communication Architectures for Distributed Smart Grid Applications). Computers Networks Communications (2018)
4. Han, T., Li, S., Zhong, Y., Bai, Z., Kwak, K.: 5G software-defined heterogeneous networks with cooperation and partial connectivity. IEEE Access **7**, 72577–72590 (2019)
5. Barbierato, L., et al.: A distributed IoT infrastructure to test and deploy real-time demand response in smart grids. IEEE Internet Things J. **6**(1), 1136–1146 (2019)

6. Kabalci, Y.: A survey on smart metering and smart grid communication. Renewable Sustain. Energy Rev. **57**, 302–318 (2016)
7. De Schepper, T., et al.: ORCHESTRA: enabling inter-technology network management in heterogeneous wireless networks. IEEE Trans. Netw. Serv. Manage. **15**(4), 1733–1746 (2018)
8. Zhang, J.: Hybrid communication architectures for distributed smart grid applications. Energies **11**(4), 871 (2018)
9. Wan, J., Yang, J., Wang, S., et al.: Cross-network fusion and scheduling for heterogeneous networks in smart factory. IEEE Trans. Ind. Inf. **16**(9), 6059–6068 (2020)
10. Zarrabian, M.A., Tabataba, F.S., Molavipour, S., Sadeghi, P.: Multirate packet delivery in heterogeneous broadcast networks. IEEE Trans. Veh. Technol. **68**(10), 10134–10144 (2019)
11. Koohifar, F., Saputro, N., Guvenc, I., et al.: Hybrid Wi-Fi/LTE aggregation architecture for smart meter communications. In: IEEE International Conference on Smart Grid Communications. IEEE (2015)
12. Leonardo, de, M.: et al. Hybrid PLC/wireless communication for smart grids and internet of things applications. IEEE Internet Things J. **5**(2), 655–667 (2017)
13. Park, J., Tarkhan, A., Hwang, J.N., et al.: Optimal DASH-multicasting over LTE. In: ICC IEEE International Conference on Communications. IEEE (2017)
14. Zhu, A., Guo, S., Liu, B., Ma, M., Yao, J., Su, X.: Adaptive multiservice heterogeneous network selection scheme in mobile edge computing. IEEE Internet Things J. **6**(4), 6862–6875 (2019)
15. Büyükçorak, S., Kurt, G.K., Yongaçoğlu, A.: Inter-network localization frameworks for heterogeneous networks with multi-connectivity. IEEE Trans. Veh. Technol. **68**(2), 1839–1851 (2019)
16. Yang, H., Zhang, J., Qiu, J., Zhang, S., Lai, M., Dong, Z.Y.: A practical pricing approach to smart grid demand response based on load classification. IEEE Trans. Smart Grid **9**(1), 179–190 (2018)
17. Sánchez, P.A., Luna-Ramírez, S., Toril, M., et al.: A data-driven scheduler performance model for QoE assessment in a LTE radio network planning tool. Comput. Netw. 107186 (2020)
18. Gupta, M., Kumar, P.: Recommendation generation using personalized weight of meta-paths in heterogeneous information networks. Eur. J. Oper. Res. **284**(2), 660–674 (2020)
19. Li, Q., Ge, Y., Yang, Y., Zhu, Y., Sun, W., Li, J.: An energy efficient uplink scheduling and resource allocation for M2M communications in SC-FDMA based LTE-A networks. In: Leung, V.C.M., Zhang, H., Hu, X., Liu, Q., Liu, Z. (eds.) 5GWN 2019. LNICSSITE, vol. 278, pp. 124–140. Springer, Cham (2019). https://doi.org/10.1007/978-3-030-17513-9_9
20. Sun, W., Li, Q., Wang, J., Chen, L., Mu, D., Yuan, X.: A radio link reliability prediction model for wireless sensor networks. Int. J. Sens. Netw. **27**, 215 (2018). https://doi.org/10.1504/IJSNET.2018.093960

Distributed Spectrum and Power Allocation for D2D-U Networks

Zhiqun Zou[1]([✉]), Rui Yin[1], Celimuge Wu[2], Jiantao Yuan[3], and Xianfu Chen[4]

[1] School of Information and Electrical Engineering,
Zhejiang University City College, Hangzhou 310015, China
zouzhiqun@zju.edu.cn
[2] Graduate School of Informatics and Engineering,
The University of Electro-Communications, 1-5-1,
Chofugaoka, Chofu-shi, Tokyo 182-8585, Japan
[3] Institute of Ocean Sensing and Networking of the Ocean College,
Zhejiang University, Hangzhou, China
[4] VTT Technical Research Centre of Finland, Espoo, Finland

Abstract. In this paper, a distributed power and spectrum allocation scheme is proposed for *Device-to-Device communication on unlicensed bands* (D2D-U) enabled networks. To make full use of the spectrum resources on the unlicensed bands while guaranteeing the fairness among D2D-U links and the harmonious coexistence with WiFi networks, an online trained *Neural network* (NN) is first utilized on each D2D-U pair to determine the price to use the unlicensed channels according to the channel state and traffic loads. Then, a non-convex optimization problem can be formulated and solved on each D2D-U link to determine the optimal spectrum and power allocation scheme which can maximize the its transmission data rate. Numerical simulation results are demonstrated to verify the performance of the proposed method which enables each D2D-U link to maximize its own data-rate individually under the constraint of the fair coexistence with other D2D-U devices and WiFi networks.

Keywords: D2D-U · Resource allocation · Price model · Neural network

1 Introduction

In order to meet the explosive growth of data transmission demands, the large-scale commercialization of *fifth generation* (5G) mobile networks has brought us better communication experience with lower latency and high transmission rates. As a key technology in 5G systems, *device-to-device* (D2D) communication allows data to be transmitted directly between D2D terminals instead of relaying through the base station, which improves both system *spectrum efficiency* (SE), *energy efficiency* (EE) and *quality-of-service* (QoS) of D2D pairs [1].

The conventional D2D communication mainly reuses the licensed channels with *long-term evolution* (LTE) cellular networks to increase system SE and EE in the licensed bands [2]. However, the licensed spectrum is basically managed by

© ICST Institute for Computer Sciences, Social Informatics and Telecommunications Engineering 2020
Published by Springer Nature Switzerland AG 2020. All Rights Reserved
S. W. Loke et al. (Eds.): MONAMI 2020, LNICST 338, pp. 161–180, 2020.
https://doi.org/10.1007/978-3-030-64002-6_11

mobile communication operators and is expensive. In addition, with the explosive growth of the number of smart terminals, the spectrum resources on the licensed bands are becoming more scarce and D2D communications may cause severe interference to the cellular users. In order to guarantee the transmission performance of the cellular users as well as improve the QoS of D2D users, *Device-to-Device on unlicensed bands* (D2D-U) is proposed to enable D2D communication on unlicensed spectrum [3]. As the unlicensed bands have abundant spectrum resources and are free to use, D2D-U may significantly increase the SE and EE of D2D pairs as well as guarantee the QoS of cellular users [4].

Most existing works have studied on the mode selection, power and spectrum allocation mechanisms for D2D enabled cellular networks. In [5], the impact of mode selection on effective capacity has been investigated via the Markov service process model. Authors in [6] have proposed a centralized optimal mode selection and resource allocation for D2D enabled cellular networks. A distributed joint spectrum sharing and power allocation problem has been modeled as a non-convex optimization problem in [7] and the suboptimal solution is obtained by convex approximation techniques. Similar problem is solved by a price-based model in [8], where a game-theoretic approach is proposed to mitigate interference among D2D pairs in a distributed way. Many machine learning-based methods have also been used to solve related problems in recent years. The authors of [9] have designed a transmit power control strategy to D2D pairs based on a *deep neural network* (DNN) structure, where the SE and interference are taken into account. A deep reinforcement learning-based method is utilized in [10] to maximize the sum rates of D2D links.

Recently, *long-term evolution on unlicensed bands* (LTE-U) system is introduced into the unlicensed spectrum. *listen-before-talk* (LBT) and *duty cycle method* (DCM) access mechanisms have been proposed for LTE-U based cellular users to access the unlicensed spectrum while ensuring the fair coexistence with WiFi networks [11–15]. In [16], the back-off window size based on LBT mechanism is adaptively adjusted according to the WiFi traffic load and available bandwidth on licensed spectrum, which obviously improves the system spectrum efficiency. A Q-learning based scheme is also proposed to adjust the back off window size of LBT in [17]. The performance of DCM mechanism is analyzed in [18,19], where the reinforcement learning based methods are employed to achieve fair coexistence between LTE-U networks and WiFi system. A hybrid mechanism is designed in [20], both LBT and DCM are utilized and the flexible handoff between two mechanisms is achieved to meet fairness constraint.

Only a small amount of work has focused on D2D transmission on unlicensed bands. The conclusion of [21] has proven that D2D-U technologies can significantly mitigate the congestion, conflicts in D2D system and improve the total throughput. In [22], the sub-channel allocation of D2D-U enabled LTE cellular networks has been formulated as a many-to-many matching problem with externality and an iterative sub-channel swap algorithm has been proposed to improve the system performance. A reinforcement learning based scheme is proposed in [23], where a deep Q-network has been utilized to learn the traffic load on the unlicensed spectrum. It allows D2D-U system to model the joint allocation problem as a convex optimization problem.

After thorough investigation, most above mentioned power and spectrum allocation schemes are centralized, which may bring large signaling overhead to the base station and lead to high latency. Besides, most of the work concentrates on maximizing system throughput without considering the difference on traffic loads of different D2D links. In this paper, we first define the unlicensed traffic load according to the number of competing WiFi users when DCM scheme is applied at D2D-U network. A price based model is then proposed and a *Neural network* (NN) is applied to estimate the price to use unlicensed spectrum at each D2D-U link adaptively. In order to guarantee the fairness among D2D-U pairs and the harmonious coexistence with the WiFi networks, the loss function is designed specifically to realize the online unsupervised learning via NN. Afterwards, the spectrum and power allocation can be optimized jointly to maximize the transmission rates with the corresponding price at each D2D-U pair. The main contributions of the paper are summarized as follows.

1. A DCM based channel access model is built for the D2D-U networks to share the unlicensed spectrum with the WiFi networks. According to the *carrier sensing multiple access with collision avoidance* (CSMA/CA) mechanism adapted in WiFi, a novel traffic load on the unlicensed channel is defined.
2. To balance the traffic load and SE of D2D-U pairs while ensuring the fairness, a virtual variable, named as price, is defined, which is related to the traffic load and channel state information of D2D-U links and the traffic load on the unlicensed channel. With the price, the unlicensed spectrum and transmission power allocation can be optimized jointly in a distributed way at each D2D-U pair.
3. Since it is hard to formulate an explicit function to model the relationship between the price and the traffic load and channel state information, an online trained NN with a specific loss function is applied to derive the price at each D2D-U pair adaptively.
4. The centralized optimal solution is presented for comparison. Moreover, the simulation results are provided to verify the effectiveness of the scheme and the theoretical analysis.

The rest of this paper is organized as follows. Section 2 introduces the system model and a novel definition of WiFi traffic load on unlicensed channels. The price based learning model is proposed in Sect. 3 and Sect. 4, respectively. We analyze the simulation results in Sect. 5 and summarize the paper in Sect. 6

2   System Model

In this paper, we study the scenario where multiple D2D-U links share the unlicensed channels with WiFi *Access points* (APs), as shown in Fig. 1, where D2D-U links are able to simultaneously use multiple unlicensed channels and a single unlicensed channel can be shared by more than one D2D-U pair. *Macro base station* (MBS) can obtain the information on the achievable data rates of each D2D-U pair via the control channel on licensed bands.

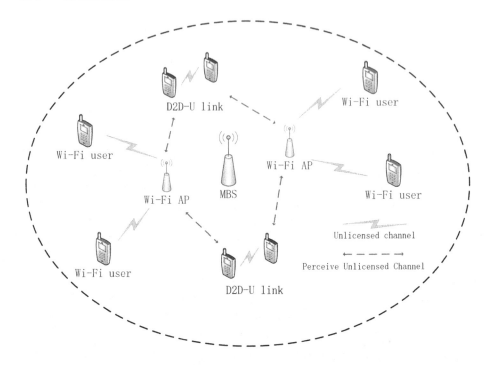

Fig. 1. System model.

To model the system mathematically, we use set $\mathcal{D} = \{d_0, d_1, ..., d_{N-1}\}$ to demonstrate all N D2D-U links in the coverage of the MBS. Moreover, there are M accessible unlicensed channels, denoted by set $\mathcal{U} = \{u_0, u_1, ..., u_{M-1}\}$, which are orthogonal with each other. To consider the fairness among D2D-U links and the harmonious coexistence with WiFi networks, $\mathcal{L}^{\mathcal{D}} = \{l_0^D, l_1^D, ..., l_{N-1}^D\}$ and $\mathcal{L}^{\mathcal{U}} = \{l_0^U, l_1^U, ..., l_{M-1}^U\}$ are used to denote the traffic loads of D2D-U links and WiFi systems on the unlicensed channels, respectively. In addition, WiFi APs adopt the CSMA/CA based *distributed coordination function* (DCF) to access the unlicensed channels while DCM mechanism is applied at D2D-U links to access the unlicensed channels.

2.1 Achievable Data Rates at D2D-U Links

The transmission model when applying DCM mechanism at D2D-U links is shown in Fig. 2, where the time frames on the unlicensed channels are divided into two parts. WiFi users can only transmit data during the first part, which is called 'off period', and the remaining section, named as 'on period', is occupied by D2D-U pairs. We further use $\theta_{i,j} \in [0, 1]$ to represent the proportion used by D2D-U link d_i on unlicensed channel u_j. Then, the achievable data-rate at d_i on unlicensed channels can be calculated by

$$R_i = \sum_{j=0}^{M-1} \theta_{i,j} B_j \log \left(1 + \frac{p_{i,j} h_{i,j}}{N_0 B_j} \right), \tag{1}$$

where B_j is the bandwidth of unlicensed channel u_j, $h_{i,j}$ is the channel power gain of D2D-U pair d_i on u_j and $p_{i,j}$ is the corresponding transmission power. N_0 is the noise power spectrum on unlicensed channel, which is fixed in the manuscript.

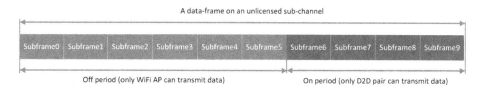

Fig. 2. DCM mechanism.

2.2 WiFi Traffic Load Definition

To ensure the transmission requirements of WiFi users, D2D-U links must decide the duration of 'on period' based on the WiFi traffic load on the unlicensed channels, which means that D2D-U links need to obtain WiFi traffic load before accessing the channels. The conventional traffic load of WiFi networks is mainly decided by the number of competing WiFi users, in [24, 25], the extended Kalman filter has been used to achieve an accurate estimation on the number of active WiFi users. However, the impact of the number of WiFi users on the throughput of the WiFi system is non-linear and D2D-U links cannot directly determine the duration of 'on period' based on the number of WiFi users. Therefore, a novel WiFi traffic load definition is first proposed when the DCM mechanism is applied at the D2D-U pairs.

As WiFi APs adopt binary slotted exponential back-off scheme in DCF, the relationship between the total WiFi throughput on an unlicensed channel and the number of WiFi users could be obtained according to [26], as illustrated in Fig. 3. The size of back-off contention window, denoted as G, is 32 and the maximum back-off contention stage, denoted as m, is set to 3 and 5, respectively. We can observe that, as the number of WiFi users increases, the achievable throughput on the unlicensed channel increases first and then decreases. The reason is that when a large number of WiFi users compete for the same unlicensed channel, the transmission collision probability will increase, resulting in transmission failure and lower throughput.

Herein, we use the number of WiFi users corresponding to the highest throughput, $n_k^{\max}$, to represent the maximum load that the WiFi network can handle on unlicensed channel u_k. If the number of WiFi users in the unlicensed channel is greater or equal to $n_k^{\max}$, the channel u_k is considered inaccessible to D2D-U pairs. Furthermore, in order to define the WiFi traffic load to fit the DCM

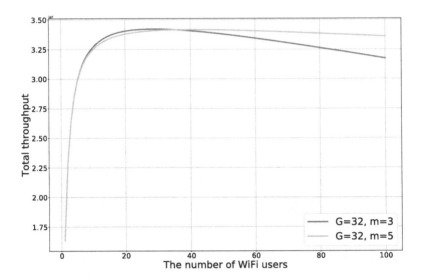

Fig. 3. Relationship between throughput and number of WiFi users.

mechanism, when the throughput of the WiFi network reaches maximum, the average throughput of each WiFi user, $\hat{r}_k^{\max}$, is treated as the basic throughput guarantee of WiFi users. Let $R_k^{\max}$ denote the maximum system throughput on unlicensed channel u_k. Then, $\hat{r}_k^{\max}$ can be calculated as $\hat{r}_k^{\max} = \frac{R_k^{\max}}{n_k^{\max}}$. The basic throughput guarantee means that when D2D-U pairs reuse the unlicensed channels based on DCM mechanism, the average throughput of WiFi users should not be less than $\hat{r}_k^{\max}$.

Then we can calculate the minimum value of the 'off period' based on the above description. For unlicensed channel $u_k \in \mathcal{U}$, let $\hat{r}_k$ represent the average throughput of each WiFi user when no D2D-U links use u_k. On the other hand, when the number of WiFi users is less than $n_k^{\max}$, D2D-U pairs are allowed to use u_k with DCM mechanism and the average throughput of WiFi users is given by

$$\hat{r}_k' = \hat{r}_k(1 - \sum_{i=0}^{N-1} \theta_{i,k}). \tag{2}$$

According to the basic throughput guarantee, we can further achieve

$$\hat{r}_k^{\max} = \frac{R_k^{\max}}{n_k^{\max}} \leq \hat{r}_k'. \tag{3}$$

The relation ship between $\hat{r}_k'$ and $\hat{r}_k^{\max}$ is shown in Fig 4, when $\hat{r}_k'$ locates on the left side of $\hat{r}_k^{\max}$, u_k is available to D2D-U users. In order to adapt to DCM access mechanism, the WiFi traffic load l_k^U on u_k is defined as the minimum 'off period' duration that meets the basic throughput guarantee of WiFi users.

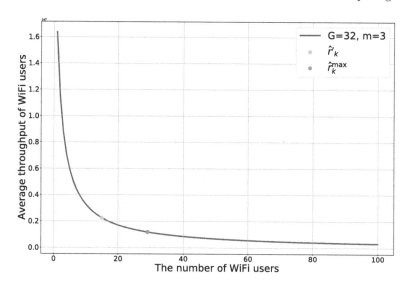

Fig. 4. Relationship between $\hat{r}'_k$ and $\hat{r}^{\max}_k$.

Combining (2) and (3), l^U_k can be given by

$$l^U_k = \frac{\hat{r}^{\max}_k}{\hat{r}_k} \leq 1 - \sum_{i=0}^{N-1} \theta_{i,k}. \tag{4}$$

Since both $\hat{r}^{\max}_k$ and $\hat{r}_k$ can be calculated according to the physical layer parameters of the WiFi networks [26] and the number of WiFi users can be estimated by extended Kalman filter based methods [24, 25], D2D-U links are able to sense the traffic load in the unlicensed channel and then decide their own resource allocation scheme. In next section, the resource allocation model is built for D2D-U links and a priced-based solution is proposed.

3   Distributed Price Based Model

In this section, we first formulate a distributed optimization problem for each D2D-U link to maximize its own data rate. Then, in order to ensure fairness among D2D links, a priced-based solution is proposed to provide D2D-U links with different prices for using unlicensed spectrum under different traffic load and channel state conditions.

3.1   Problem Formulation

For a single D2D link, $d_i \in \mathcal{D}$, to maximize its transmission rates while guaranteeing the performance of WiFi networks, an optimization problem can be formulated as

$$\max_{\{\theta_{i,j}, p_{i,j}\}} \{R_i\}, \tag{5}$$

subject to

$$C1 : \theta_{i,j} \leq 1 - l_j^U, \ \forall j \in [0, M-1], \tag{5a}$$

$$C2 : \sum_{j=0}^{M-1} \theta_{i,j} p_{i,j} \leq p_c, \tag{5b}$$

$$C3 : \theta_{i,j} p_{i,j} \leq p_u, \ \forall j \in [0, M-1], \tag{5c}$$

where $C1$ is to guarantee the fair coexistence with WiFi networks on the unlicensed channels, $C2$ is the total power constraint of d_i and $C3$ is the transmission power limit on the unlicensed channel according to the regulation.

Problem (5) is a non-convex problem but can be converted into a convex optimization problem and solved on each D2D link. In detail, a extra parameter $\eta_{i,j} = \theta_{i,j} p_{i,j}$ is introduced and (1) can be re-expressed as

$$R_i = \sum_{j=0}^{M-1} \theta_{i,j} B_j \log \left(1 + \frac{\eta_{i,j} h_{i,j}}{N_0 B_j \theta_{i,j}} \right), \tag{6}$$

then problem (5) is converted into

$$\max_{\{\theta_{i,j}, \eta_{i,j}\}} \{R_i\}, \tag{7}$$

subject to

$$C1 : \theta_{i,j} \leq 1 - l_j^U, \ \forall j \in [0, M-1], \tag{7a}$$

$$C2 : \sum_{j=0}^{M-1} \eta_{i,j} \leq p_c, \tag{7b}$$

$$C3 : \eta_{i,j} \leq p_u, \ \forall j \in [0, M-1]. \tag{7c}$$

Problem (7) is a convex optimization problem and can be solved by Lagrangian multiplier method. However, optimization problem (7) can only allow a D2D-U link to maximize its own throughput under the constraint of guaranteeing the fair coexistence with WiFi networks without considering the impact on other D2D-U pairs. When multiple D2D-U links share the same unlicensed channel, the possibility of transmission collision is extremely high, which leads to the lose on the performance of the D2D-U transmission. Therefore, the model needs to be improved based on the respective traffic load conditions of D2D-U links, where D2D-U links with heavy transmission tasks could use more spectrum resources while D2D-U links with light transmission tasks require only a small fraction of unlicensed spectrum resources. In next subsection, a priced-based solution is applied to achieve this goal.

3.2   Priced-Based Solution

In the proposed price-based model, each D2D-U link is considered as a consumer and spectrum resources in unlicensed bands are provided to consumers as commodities. The total money which each D2D-U link has are set to the same, which is represented by C. Define the price corresponding to the unlicensed channel u_j for the D2D-U link d_i as $c_{i,j}$ and when d_i transmits data on u_j, the price d_i needs to pay is written as $\theta_{i,j} \times c_{i,j}$. Accordingly, the optimization problem (5) can be expressed with an extra fairness constraint as

$$\max_{\{\theta_{i,j}, p_{i,j}\}} \{R_i\}, \tag{8}$$

subject to

$$C1 : \theta_{i,j} \leq 1 - l_j, \ \forall j \in [0, M-1], \tag{8a}$$

$$C2 : \sum_{j=0}^{M-1} \theta_{i,j} p_{i,j} \leq p_c, \tag{8b}$$

$$C3 : \theta_{i,j} p_{i,j} \leq p_u, \ \forall j \in [0, M-1], \tag{8c}$$

$$C4 : \sum_{j=0}^{M-1} \theta_{i,j} c_{i,j} \leq C. \tag{8d}$$

The above problem is also a non-convex optimization problem and can not be solved in its current formation. Same as in Problem (5), replacing $p_{i,j}$ with $p_{i,j} = \frac{\eta_{i,j}}{\theta_{i,j}}$ and the above problem is converted into

$$\max_{\{\theta_{i,j}, \eta_{i,j}\}} \{R_i\}, \tag{9}$$

subject to

$$C1 : \theta_{i,j} \leq 1 - l_j, \ \forall j \in [0, M-1], \tag{9a}$$

$$C2 : \sum_{j=0}^{M-1} \eta_{i,j} \leq p_c, \tag{9b}$$

$$C3 : \eta_{i,j} \leq p_u, \ \forall j \in [0, M-1], \tag{9c}$$

$$C4 : \sum_{j=0}^{M-1} \theta_{i,j} c_{i,j} \leq C. \tag{9d}$$

Herein, one important key to solve (9) is to find $c_{i,j}$. If $c_{i,j}$ is known, the above problem is a convex optimization problem and the optimal solution can be obtained based on the Lagrangian multiplier method. The Lagrangian function of Problem (9) is constructed as

$$L(\theta_{i,j}, \eta_{i,j}, \mu_j^{(1)}, \mu^{(2)}, \mu_j^{(3)}, \mu^{(4)}) = -R_i + \sum_{j=0}^{M-1} \mu_j^{(1)}(\theta_{i,j} + l_j - 1)$$

$$+ \mu^{(2)}(\sum_{j=0}^{M-1} \eta_{i,j} - C) + \sum_{j=0}^{M-1} \mu_j^{(3)}(\eta_{i,j} - p_u)$$

$$+ \mu^{(4)}(\sum_{j=0}^{M-1} \theta_{i,j} c_{i,j} - C), \tag{10}$$

where $\mu_j^{(1)}$, $\mu^{(2)}$, $\mu_j^{(3)}$ and $\mu^{(4)}$ are the Lagrangian multipliers and the *Karush-Kuhn-Tucker* (KKT) conditions of $L(\cdot)$ are derived based on (10) as

$$\frac{\partial L}{\partial \theta_{i,j}} = 0, \ \forall j \in [0, M-1], \tag{11}$$

$$\frac{\partial L}{\partial \eta_{i,j}} = 0, \ \forall j \in [0, M-1], \tag{12}$$

$$\mu_j^{(1)}(\theta_{i,j} + l_j - 1) = 0, \ \forall j \in [0, M-1], \tag{13}$$

$$\mu^{(2)}(\sum_{j=0}^{M-1} \eta_{i,j} - C) = 0, \tag{14}$$

$$\mu_j^{(3)}(\eta_{i,j} - p_u) = 0, \ \forall j \in [0, M-1], \tag{15}$$

$$\mu^{(4)}(\sum_{j=0}^{M-1} \theta_{i,j} c_{i,j} - C) = 0, \tag{16}$$

$$\mu_j^{(1)} \geq 0, \mu^{(2)} \geq 0, \mu_j^{(3)} \geq 0, \mu^{(4)} \geq 0, \ \forall j \in [0, M-1]. \tag{17}$$

On the basis of KKT conditions, the optimal solutions of $\theta_{i,j}$ and $\eta_{i,j}$ should satisfy

$$\eta_{i,j} = \theta_{i,j} B_j(\frac{\log e}{\mu^{(2)} + \mu_j^{(3)}} - \frac{N_0}{h_{i,j}}), \tag{18}$$

and

$$\log(1 + \frac{\eta_{i,j} h_{i,j}}{N_0 B_j \theta_{i,j}}) - \frac{\eta_{i,j} h_{i,j} \log e}{N_0 B_j \theta_{i,j} + \eta_{i,j} h_{i,j}} = \frac{\mu_j^{(1)} + \mu^{(4)} c_{i,j}}{B_j}. \tag{19}$$

Then, according to (18) and (19), $\eta_{i,j}$ and $\theta_{i,j}$ can be achieved for different d_i and u_j. Since (19) is a transcendental equation, numerical method can be applied to find the solution.

Based on above analysis, $\theta_{i,j}$ and $p_{i,j}$ can be obtained with the known price, $c_{i,j}$, which can be used to ensure the fairness among D2D-U pairs. To adjust prices adaptively to reach the fairness, each D2D-U pair needs to determine the

$c_{i,j}$ based on its own traffic load, channel state information and the WiFi traffic load on the unlicensed channel. Accordingly, we denote $c_{i,j}$ as

$$c_{i,j} = F(l_i^D, l_j^U, h_{i,j} | s^c), \tag{20}$$

where l_i^D represents the transmission task of d_i, $h_{i,j}$ represents the channel power gain on unlicensed channel u_j. The function $F(\cdot)$ is to model the relationship between the price and the traffic loads of the D2D links and the unlicensed channels. When the traffic load of D2D-U link, d_i, is heavy, d_i is encouraged to use unlicensed spectrum with a low price while the price to D2D-U link with less traffic load is high; Moreover, unlicensed channels with low traffic loads or strong channel power gain for the D2D link will need to be paid with low prices while under channels with high traffic loads or poor channel conditions will be expensive. In addition, to mitigate the channel access conflict among D2D-U links, a feedback signal s^c is set on d_i. If d_i collides with other D2D-U links on the channel, s^c is activated and the price should be enhanced accordingly. Therefore, function $F(\cdot)$ should have the following characteristics:

(1). $F(\cdot)$ should decrease monotonically with respect to l_i^D;
(2). $F(\cdot)$ should increase monotonically with respect to l_j^U;
(3). $F(\cdot)$ should decrease monotonically with respect to $h_{i,j}$;
(4). $F(\cdot)$ should increase with the activation of s^c.

As for the fairness among D2D-U links, we define *Expected transmission time* (ETT) as the ratio of a D2D-U link's traffic load to its achievable data rates. Then, the fairness sharing on unlicensed channels among D2D-U links is denoted as that the ETT values of all D2D-U links are equal, which is written as

$$\frac{l_0^D}{R_0} = \frac{l_1^D}{R_1} = \cdots = \frac{l_{M-1}^D}{R_{M-1}}. \tag{21}$$

However, it is difficult to directly build an explicit mathematical model to formulate the function $F(\cdot)$ and achieve (21). To address this issue, an online training *neural network* (NN) architecture is exploited to implement function of $F(\cdot)$ and the loss function for all D2D-U links are provided based on s^c and the assistance of MBS. Specific details of the adopted NN will be given in the next section.

4   Learning Based Method

Because of the strong fitting performance and robustness of NN, the online trained NN is utilized to achieve adaptive adjustment of the prices in a dynamic environment. The structure of the distributed pricing system is illustrated in Fig. 5 where each D2D-U pair holds a NN and determines its own price. The output of NN in d_i can be calculate as

$$\hat{c}_{i,j} = \hat{F}(l_i^D, l_j^U, h_{i,j} | \phi), \tag{22}$$

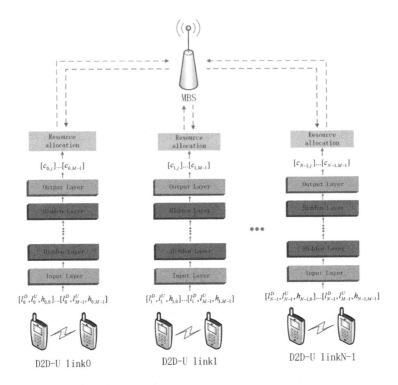

Fig. 5. The structure of NN.

where $\hat{c}_{i,j}$ is the output as well as the price estimated by NN, the input of NN is $[l_i^D, l_j^U, h_{i,j}]$. In particular, before $[l_i^D, l_j^U, h_{i,j}]$ is fed into NN, the data needs to be normalized to avoid problems caused by different orders of magnitude. $\hat{F}(\cdot)$ indicates the forward propagation of NN and ϕ represents all the weights and bias parameters. At each iteration, all the parameters in NN are updated based on the gradient descent algorithm, which is denoted by

$$\phi = \phi - \alpha \frac{\partial Q}{\partial \phi}, \tag{23}$$

where α is the learning rate of NN and Q is the loss function. Since it is hard to achieve global optimal solution of problem (8), we cannot obtain labels and use the supervised learning method to train the network. Therefore, based on (21) and the collision detection, the loss function Q is formulated by two parts to train NN in an unsupervised way. Q_1 and Q_2 are used to represent these two parts, respectively, where Q_1 is defined as:

(1). if $\frac{l_i^D}{R_i}$ is larger than ETT values of $\frac{M+1}{2}$ D2D-U links (when M is odd) or $\frac{M}{2}$ D2D-U links (when M is even), $Q_1 = q$;

(2). if $\frac{l_i^D}{R_i}$ is smaller than ETT values of $\frac{M+1}{2}$ D2D-U links (when M is odd) or $\frac{M}{2}$ D2D-U links (when M is even), $Q_1 = -q$;

(3). else $Q_1 = 0$;

Algorithm 1. Distributed joint spectrum and power allocation at d_i

---

1: Initialize the structure and the parameters of d_i and NN;
2: **while** d_i is transmitting data **do**
3:     Estimate the number of WiFi users with EKF based method;
4:     Estimate the traffic load $\mathcal{L}^\mathcal{U}$ on unlicensed spectrum based on (4);
5:     Normalize the input of NN;
6:     The prices of all unlicensed channels are calculated based on (22);
7:     Problem(8) is solved to get the resources allocation scheme of d_i;
8:     Calculate the loss value on the basis of (24);
9:     d_i trains the NN based on gradient descent algorithm in (23);
10: **end while**

---

where q is the adjustment step size of the price and is set to a tiny positive value. Q_2 corresponds to conflict feedback s^c, which is defined as:

(1). if d_i collides with other D2D-U links, Q_2 is set to v_1;
(2). else $Q_2 = v_2$;

In order to mitigate the transmission collision among D2D-U links quickly in actual operation, v_1 is set to a larger positive value to significantly increase the price of the unlicensed channel when collision happens. v_2 is a negative value which aims at decreasing prices to allow D2D-U links to use more spectrum resources when no collision happens. Herein, the value Q_1 can be provided by MBS and Q_2 can be decided on d_i according to its transmission collision situation. Accordingly, the target of NN output is denoted as $T = \hat{c}_{i,j} + Q_1 + Q_2$ and Q can be calculated by

$$Q = (T - \hat{c}_{i,j})^2 = (Q_1 + Q_2)^2. \tag{24}$$

Furthermore, to keep the convergence of NN and the stability of output, we use Sigmoid function to limit the output value in a certain range according to the actual conditions. The activation function of the output layer is set to be $w \times$ Sigmoid$(\cdot)$, which limits the output in $[0, w]$. Based on the above interpretation on the proposed NN, the process of the joint power and spectrum allocation algorithm for a single D2D-U link, $d_i \in \mathcal{D}$, is summarized in Algorithm 1. It is noteworthy that each D2D-U link holds a NN independently to determine the price corresponding to the utilization on the unlicensed channels. When the neural networks of D2D-U links converge, the system has reached an equilibrium. When the traffic load of D2D-U links or WiFi system changes, neural networks will converge to a new equilibrium adaptively.

5   Numerical Results

In this section, the simulation results are demonstrated to verify the performance of the proposed distributed D2D-U communication scheme. In the simulation setup, the relevant parameters of NN are demonstrated in Table 1 and

Table 1. Parameters of NN.

Parameters	Value
α	0.0001
Number of hidden layers	2
Number of neurons	32/32
Active function	tanh/tanh/tanh/$w \times$ sigmoid
Max value of output w	10
Fairness-based loss q	0.01
Conflict multiplication loss v_1	0.03
Maximum throughput loss v_2	-0.03

Table 2. Parameters of D2D-U links.

Parameters	Value
Total power control p_c	35 dBm
Power control on one unlicensed channel p_u	23 dBm
AWGN noise power N	-95 dBm
Total assets C	1

the parameters related to the D2D-U and WiFi networks are given in Table 2. Since the real-time performance of the algorithm is required in practice, we use shallow fully connected neural networks to reduce algorithm complexity and for quickly convergence during online training processing.

5.1 Effectiveness on the Proposed NN

We first verify the effectiveness on the proposed scheme, assuming that there are two D2D-U links, d_1 and d_2, and two independent unlicensed channels, u_1 and u_2. The traffic load of d_1 is set to be larger than d_2 and the WiFi traffic load on unlicensed channel u_1 is set to be less than that on u_2. Then the output prices from the NNs of two D2D-U links on two unlicensed channels are illustrated in Fig. 6. It can be observed that the prices of u_1 and u_2 is much more cheaper for d_1 with heavy transmission tasks, which implies that d_1 is encouraged to use more unlicensed spectrum resources. In addition, since the WiFi traffic load on u_1 is lighter than that on u_2, the value of $c_{1,1}$ is smaller than $c_{1,2}$ and d_1 will select the unlicensed channel u_1 in the first place.

As for d_2, since u_1 has priority to be selected by d_1 with much less price, to avoid transmission collision, $c_{2,1}$ is trained larger than $c_{2,2}$ and d_2 will mainly use u_2 for transmission. Figure 7 shows the fairness between d_1 and d_2, where we can observe that as the prices converge, $\frac{l_1^D}{R_1}$ is equal to $\frac{l_2^D}{R_2}$ and the fairness between d_1 and d_2 is achieved.

5.2   Verification on the Fairness

To further illustrate the fairness of the proposed algorithm, the performance of D2D-U system with more D2D-U links and unlicensed channels is analyzed and the result is compared with centralized algorithm which concentrates on maximizing system throughput. In the centralized algorithm, price based model is

Fig. 6. The price determined by D2D-U links.

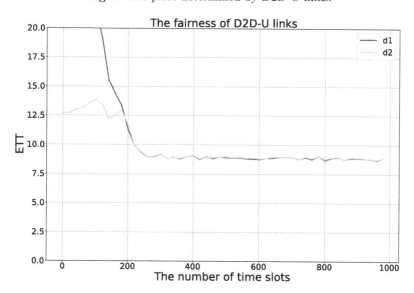

Fig. 7. The transmission fairness among D2D links.

not applied and all the parameters are collected at MBS. A joint optimization problem is then built and solved to maximize the throughput of D2D-U system while guaranteeing the harmonious coexistence with the WiFi networks. The ETT value comparison of two schemes is shown in Table 3. When the normalized traffic load of D2D-U links is '1', the actual traffic load is 10e8bits. It can be found that the proposed price based distributed method can adaptively allocate resources at the D2D-U pairs with respect to the traffic load and channel conditions to guarantee the fairness. On the other hand, the centralized algorithm is far from achieving the fairness.

The fair coexistence with WiFi networks by the proposed scheme is depicted in Fig. 8, where the actual WiFi traffic load is normalized based on the basic WiFi throughput guarantee calculated in (3). Simulation result shows that after the convergence of the price, the WiFi throughput is basically equal to the basic WiFi throughput guarantee. Due to the set of v_2 which encourages D2D-U links to use more spectrum resources with less collision, there are a little transmission collision which leads to the tiny impairment to the WiFi system throughput.

Table 3. The comparison of transmission fairness.

Users number	Normalized traffic load	ETT(price-based)	ETT(max throughput)
1	0.8	8.779	14.010
2	0.6	8.788	10.508
3	0.4	8.750	7.005
4	0.2	8.810	3.503

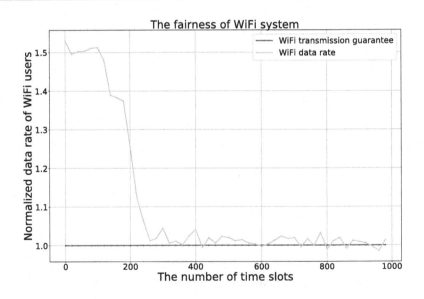

Fig. 8. Achieved fairness of WiFi system.

5.3 Achievable Data Rates

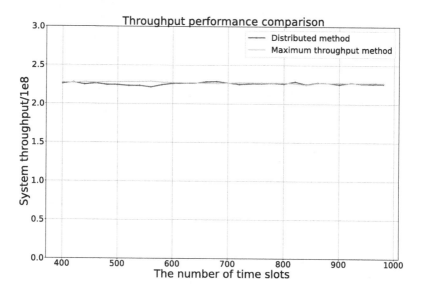

Fig. 9. The comparison of system throughput between price based method and maximum throughput method.

Figure 9 demonstrates the total achievable data rates of D2D-U links with centralized and proposed scheme, respectively. From the figure, we can observe that the data rates obtained by the proposed are close to that by the centralized scheme, which indicates that the proposed method can almost maximize the system performance while ensuring the fairness of D2D-U pairs. Besides, the details of D2D-U link power allocation is illustrated in Fig. 10, where the unlicensed channel traffic load on u_0 and u_1 is low and on u_2 and u_3 is high. The abscissa of Fig. 10 is different unlicensed channels and the ordinate is $\eta_{i,j}$ of related D2D-U pairs and unlicensed channels. It can be observed that in the price based model, the D2D-U link with more traffic load reuses the spectrum resources of more ideal channels and the D2D-U link with less traffic load chooses to reuse more crowded channels. While in the centralized method, the change of D2D-U traffic load has no effect on its power allocation scheme. Therefore, simulation results justify that the proposed method can guarantee the fairness among D2D-U pairs with least lose on the data rates comparing with the centralized optimal solution.

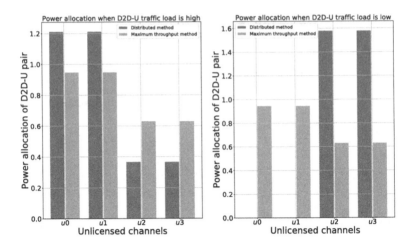

Fig. 10. The comparison of power allocation between price based method and maximum throughput method.

6   Conclusion

In this paper, in order to reuse the spectrum resources on the unlicensed bands to improve the transmission performance of D2D-U system, a distributed power and spectrum allocation mechanism with adaptive price adjustment scheme is proposed. An unsupervised online learning structure is employed on each D2D-U link to estimate the prices of all perceived unlicensed channels. Then the power and spectrum optimization models can be established and solved by D2D-U links to access the unlicensed spectrum. Numerical simulation proves that the proposed algorithm allows D2D-U link to maximize data-rate while ensuring the fairness of WiFi system and the fairness among all D2D-U users.

Acknowledgements. The authors gratefully acknowledge the financial support of the National Natural Science Foundation of China (Grant No. 61771429), Zhejiang University City College Scientific Research Foundation (No. JZD18002).

References

1. Doppler, K., Rinne, M., Wijting, C., Ribeiro, C., Hugl, K.: Deviceto-device communication as an underlay to LTE-Advanced networks. IEEE Commun. Mag. **47**(12), 42–49 (2009)
2. Yu, G., Xu, L., Feng, D., Yin, R., Li, G., Jiang, Y.: Joint mode selection and resource allocation for device-to-device communications. IEEE Trans. Commun. **62**(11), 3814–3824 (2014)
3. Wu, Y., Guo, W., Yuan, H., Li, L., Wang, S., Chu, X., Zhang, J.: Device-to-device meets LTE-unlicensed. IEEE Commun. Mag. **54**(5), 154–159 (2016)
4. Liu, R., Yu, G., Qu, F., Zhang, Z.: Device-to-device communications in unlicensed spectrum: mode selection and resource allocation. IEEE Access **4**, 4720–4729 (2016)

5. Shah, S., Rahman, M., Mian, A., Imran, A., Mumtaz, S., Dobre, O.: On the impact of mode selection on effective capacity of device-to-device communication. IEEE Wireless Commun. Lett. **8**(3), 945–948 (2019)

6. Yu, G., Xu, L., Feng, D., Yin, R., Li, G.: Joint mode selection and resource allocation for device-to-device communications. IEEE Trans. Commun. **62**(11), 3814–3824 (2014)

7. Yin, R., Zhong, C., Yu, G., Zhang, Z., Wong, K., Chen, X.: Joint spectrum and power allocation for d2d communications underlaying cellular networks. IEEE Trans. Veh. Technol. **65**(4), 2182–2195 (2016)

8. Yin, R., Yu, G., Zhang, H., Zhang, Z., Li, G.: Pricing-based interference coordination for d2d communications in cellular networks. IEEE Trans. Wireless Commun. **14**(3), 1519–1532 (2015)

9. Lee, W., Kim, M., Cho, D.: Transmit power control using deep neural network for underlay device-to-device communication. IEEE Commun. Letters **8**(1), 141–144 (2019)

10. Moussaid, A., Jaafar, W., Ajib, W., Elbiaze, H.: Deep reinforcement learning-based data transmission for D2D communications. In: 2018 14th International Conference on Wireless and Mobile Computing, Networking and Communications (WiMob). pp. 1–7. IEEE (2018)

11. QualComm, Extending LTE advanced to unlicensed spectrum, White Paper, San Diego, CA, USA (2013)

12. Huawei, U-LTE: Unlicensed spectrum utilization of LTE, White Paper, Shenzhen, China (2014)

13. Study on licensed-assisted access to unlicensed spectrum (Release 13), document 3GPP, Sophia Antipolis Cedex, France, TR 36.889 (2015)

14. Sun, X., Dai, L.: Towards fair and efficient spectrum sharing between lte and wifi in unlicensed bands: fairness-constrained throughput maximization. IEEE Trans. Wireless Commun. **19**(4), 2713–2727 (2020)

15. Cui, Q., Ni, W., Li, S., Zhao, B., Liu, R., Zhang, P.: Learning-assisted clustered access of 5G/B5G networks to unlicensed spectrum. IEEE Wireless Commun. **27**(1), 31–37 (2020)

16. Yin, R., Yu, G., Maaref, A., Li, G.: LBT-based adaptive channel access for LTE-U systems. IEEE Trans. Wireless Commun. **15**(10), 6585–6597 (2016)

17. Maglogiannis, V., Naudts, D., Shahid, A., Moerman, I.: A Q-learning scheme for fair coexistence between LTE and Wi-Fi in unlicensed spectrum. IEEE Access **6**, 27278–27293 (2018)

18. de Santana, P.M., de Sousa, V.A., Abinader, F.M., de C. Neto, J.M.: DM-CSAT: a LTE-U/Wi-Fi coexistence solution based on reinforcement learning. Telecommun. Syst. **71**(4), 615–626 (2019). https://doi.org/10.1007/s11235-018-00535-7

19. Neto, J., Neto, S., Santana, P., Sousa, V.: Multi-cell LTE-U/Wi-Fi coexistence evaluation using a reinforcement learning framework. Sensors **20**(7), 1855–1877 (2020)

20. Liu, S., Yin, R., Yu, G.: Hybrid adaptive channel access for LTE-U systems. IEEE Trans. Veh. Technol. **68**(10), 9820–9832 (2019)

21. Andreev, S., Galinina, O., Pyataev, A., Johnsson, K., Koucheryavy, Y.: Analyzing assisted offloading of cellular user sessions onto D2D links in unlicensed bands. IEEE J. Sel. Areas in Commun. **33**(1), 67–80 (2015)

22. Zhang, H., Liao, Y., Song, L.: D2D-U: device-to-device communications in unlicensed bands for 5G system. IEEE Trans. Wireless Commun. **16**(6), 3507–3519 (2017)

23. Zou, Z., Yin, R., Chen, X., Wu, C.: Deep Reinforcement Learning for D2D transmission in unlicensed bands. In: 2019 IEEE/CIC International Conference on Communications Workshops in China (ICCC Workshops). pp. 42–47 IEEE (2019)
24. Bianchi, G., Tinnirello, I.: Kalman filter estimation of the number of competing terminals in an IEEE 802.11 network. IEEE Infocom **2**, 844–852 (2003)
25. Qin, F., Dai, X., Mitchell, J.E.: Effective-SNR estimation for wireless sensor network using kalman filter. Ad Hoc Netw. **11**(3), 944–958 (2013)
26. Bianchi, G.: Performance analysis of the IEEE 802.11 distributed coordination function. IEEE J. Sel. Areas Commun. **18**(3), 535–547 (2000)

Graph-Based Terminal Ranking for Sparsification of Interference Coordination Parameters in Ultra-Dense Networks

Junxiang Gou[1,3], Lusheng Wang[1,3(✉)], Hai Lin[2], and Min Peng[1,3]

[1] Ministry of Education, School of Computer Science and Information Engineering,
Key Laboratory of Knowledge Engineering with Big Data,
Hefei University of Technology, 230601 Hefei, China
wanglusheng@hfut.edu.cn
[2] Ministry of Education. School of Cyber Science and Engineering,
Key Laboratory of Aerospace Information Security and Trusted Computing,
Wuhan University, 430072 Wuhan, China
[3] Anhui Province Key Laboratory of Industry Safety and Emergency Technology,
230601 Hefei, China

Abstract. In the future mobile communication system, inter-cell interference becomes a serious problem due to the intensive deployment of cells and terminals. Traditional interference coordination schemes take long time for optimization in ultra-dense networks. Meanwhile, due to the increase of factors affecting communication and in order to better meet the communication needs of each terminal, an interference coordination scheme needs to fully consider multiple characteristic parameters of the terminal, which will further increase the scheme's computational time. Therefore, we should compress all the data through sparsification of parameters before optimization. There are many terminal parameters, and the essence of sparsification of parameters is to rank terminals. In this paper, a graph-based terminal ranking scheme is designed. First, each terminal can be represented by its multiple parameters. Then, all terminals are used as the vertexes in the graph to form a complete weighted graph, and edge weights represent the degree of dissimilarity between terminals. A ranking of terminals is obtained by finding a minimum Hamiltonian path in the graph. Finally, the ranking of all parameter sequences is obtained according to terminals ranking, which makes the sparsity of all parameter sequences better. Simulation results show that the proposed scheme can accomplish sparsification of parameter sequences effectively, especially when the number of sequences increases. In addition, compared with the optimal coordination of traditional scheme, this scheme improves the fairness of the system while ensuring high system capacity, and dramatically reduces the computational time of interference coordination.

Keywords: Ultra-dense networks · Inter-cell interference coordination · Sparsification · Hamiltonian path · Approximation algorithm

© ICST Institute for Computer Sciences, Social Informatics and Telecommunications Engineering 2020
Published by Springer Nature Switzerland AG 2020. All Rights Reserved
S. W. Loke et al. (Eds.): MONAMI 2020, LNICST 338, pp. 181–197, 2020.
https://doi.org/10.1007/978-3-030-64002-6_12

1   Introduction

With the commercialization of the fifth generation (5G) mobile communication system, the research on 6G wireless network will also be launched to meet the requirements of the intelligent information society in 2030 [1]. Compared with 5G, 6G will have super flexibility in the utilization of time-frequency-space resources, providing higher speed, greater capacity and ultra-low delay for applications faster than 5G in the future [2]. Ultra-dense networks (UDNs) are widely used as an effective way to increase system capacity. The intensive deployment of cells and terminals will result in intra-cell and inter-cell interference. Intra-cell interference can be avoided through clever design of transmission signals, while inter-cell interference is regarded as the main limiting factor of cellular system performance, so interference coordination will become a very important issue in ultra-dense networks [3].

In the existing researches on interference coordination, most of the literatures considered two parameters of the useful signal power and interference signal power of the terminal, and then maximized the average spectral efficiency of the network according to Shannon formula [4–6]. [7] considered the transmitting power of the terminal, inter-cell interference could be reduced by controlling power of the user at the edge of cell. Due to the increase of terminal business types, different business requirements correspond to different data rates, so the minimum data rate requirement of users was also an important parameter [8], and [9] converted the data rate requirement of users into the number of resource blocks required by users. There are a large number of mobile terminals in the cellular network, or most of the terminal devices are moving, so we should also consider the impact of terminal mobility on the network [10]. [11] proposed mobility management based on contextual information awareness. In addition, when there are terminals with low power in actual network scenes, better channels should be allocated for them, otherwise user experience will be affected. Therefore, the battery power of terminals is also an important influencing factor. To sum up, in the future mobile communication system, in order to meet the communication needs of each terminal as much as possible, interference coordination scheme need to fully consider the various factors influencing the terminal. In other words, multiple characteristic parameters of the terminal should be considered in interference coordination. Therefore, it is of great significance to study interference coordination scheme for terminal multi-parameter case.

Traditional inter-cell interference coordination schemes take long time in the ultra-dense network, especially with the increase of terminal parameters, the interference coordination time will be further increased. [12] considered interference coordination problem in the two-layer heterogeneous network, an almost blank subframe (ABS) was introduced and the original resource allocation problem was modeled as a generalized allocation problem (GAP) by fixing the ABS ratio. Then the ant colony algorithm was used to solve the problem, which can significantly improve throughput of the system. [13] studied interference coordination in ultra-dense networks from a user-centric perspective. On the one hand, the user kept away from the main interference sources to ensure that its ideal signal to interference plus noise ratio (SINR). On the other hand, the QoS requirements of users could be satisfied through priority allocation of resources. And then an iterative resource allocation scheme based on graph coloring algorithm was proposed, which proved that this scheme could improve the system spectral efficiency and the proportion of users meeting QoS requirements. [14] considered the joint optimization of mobile station unloading and interference coordination in ultra-dense heterogeneous networks, and a heuristic algorithm was proposed to solve the problem step by step. Compared with the traditional frequency-domain interference coordination scheme, this scheme could improve the signal to noise ratio and data rate of mobile stations. [15] studied energy consumption and interference coordination in ultra-dense networks, and the goal was to maximize the energy efficiency of the worst user in the cell. The original problem was transformed by relaxation method and introduction of new parameters, then the transformed problem could be solved by fractional programming and Lagrangian dual decomposition method, and finally, the solution was rounded to get the original solution. The scheme ensured good load balance and energy efficiency in ultra-dense networks.

Some researchers have tried to use intelligent methods to solve the problem of interference coordination. [16] studied interference management problem in dense small cellular networks. Base stations determined downlink transmission power by autonomously sensing the surrounding interference, aiming to minimize the total transmission power, thus forming a competitive relationship between base stations. Then the interference coordination problem was modeled as a partially observable Markov decision process, and multi-agent reinforcement learning was used to solve the problem. Finally, it was proved that this method could reduce the power consumption, and improve network performance. In [17], the problems of beamforming, power control and interference coordination in downlink cellular networks were studied, which were jointly modeled as a non-convex optimization problem to maximize the sum of signal-to-noise ratios of all users. Then deep reinforcement learning be used to solve the problem, which could greatly improve sum-rate capacity of the network. [18] provided a new way of thinking for solving interference coordination in multi-cell downlink communication, which was to make full use of the beneficial influence of intra-cell interference and inter-cell interference. Under different coordination overhead, three schemes are proposed to make full or partial use of inter-cell and multi-user interference in the paper. All three schemes considered incomplete channel state information and therefore used probabilistic and deterministic optimization methods to minimize the total transmitted power. Finally, the paper also verified that the power consumption of these schemes is lower than that of existing schemes.

In order to reduce the time of interference coordination scheme in ultra-dense networks, we prefer to compress data first and then carry out interference coordination. Data compression refers to the use of less data to represent the original huge data, that is, the sparse representation of data [19]. In other words, the implicit information in the data can be reflected in a small number of coefficients, reducing the redundancy of data. Wavelet transform is a time-frequency analysis method with multi-resolution characteristics [20]. The high-frequency coefficients of wavelet coefficients are mostly zero or very small while the low-frequency coefficients with relatively large modulus reflect the contour information of the signal. Therefore, we can use a small amount of low-frequency coefficients to express the original signal sparsely. In order to make a small amount of low-frequency coefficients in the wavelet domain reflect various characteristics of the original data better, the data should be ranked according to certain rules, that is, the ranked data has better sparsity. The process of ranking is called sparsification of data.

According to the above analysis, sparsification of data is a key step to reduce the computational time of interference coordination scheme. [21] proposed a grouping and sorting method, which only considered useful signal power and interference signal power of the terminal, and two parameters were related to the terminal position. When multiple and random parameters of the terminal are considered, such as terminal business requirements, the performance of the scheme will be significantly reduced. [6] proposed and proved a fast matching scheme. By ranking two terminal parameter vectors, the optimal interference coordination could be achieved by using reverse matching. However, this scheme required the objective function to meet certain conditions. Sparsification of multiple parameters essentially means to rank multiple parameter sequences differently, so that multiple parameter sequences have better sparsity. But as the number of parameter sequences increases, the scheme of ranking each parameter sequence separately will make the first ranked sequence have poor sparsity. So we consider to rank multiple parameter sequences simultaneously. At the same time, due to the essence of sparsification of multiple parameters is to rank terminals, we rank terminals according to certain rules, and then get the new ranking of each parameter sequence according to the ranking of terminals. As a result, we put forward graph-based terminal ranking scheme. The idea of the scheme is to regard terminals as the vertexes in the graph, the weight of each side express the degree of dissimilarity between terminals. Terminal ranking problem can be converted to a problem of traversing all vertexes once and only once in the graph, that is, finding a Hamiltonian path in the graph. This is a classical mathematical problem in graph theory, so it can be solved quickly with the help of relevant algorithms.

The rest of this paper is arranged as follows. Section 2 describes the system model. In Sect. 3, we introduce the terminal ranking scheme based on graph and its application. In Sect. 4, the performance of the method is simulated. Finally, the conclusion is drawn in Sect. 5.

2   System Model

We consider a communication system containing multiple cells. Assuming that M characteristic parameters are used to describe each terminal, the corresponding matrix of all characteristic parameters can be expressed as

$$\mathbf{CP} = \{CP_{m,n} \,|\, m = 1, 2, \cdots, M; n = 1, 2, \cdots, N\}$$

where N represents the total number of terminals in the system. The optimization problem of inter-cell interference coordination can be expressed as

$$\max f(\mathbf{CP}) \tag{1}$$

where $f(\cdot)$ is the objective function of the optimization of the interference coordination problem, which can be capacity, throughput, etc. The above problems are usually NP hard, and the solution space is determined by N. Considering that the solution space of this problem is very large, the time to obtain an approximate optimal solution should be extremely long, so that traditional search algorithms are difficult to find a near-optimal solution within an acceptable computational time.

As shown in Fig. 1, multilayer wavelet decomposition is performed for each row in $\mathbf{CP}$ to retain the wavelet transformation coefficients of each layer and the scaling transformation coefficients of the last layer to form a new matrix $\mathbf{CPW}$. Only the scaling transformation coefficients are retained to form a new matrix, written as

$$\mathbf{CPS} = \{CPS_{m,n} \,|\, m = 1, 2, \cdots, M; n = 1, 2, \cdots, NS\}$$

where NS is the length of the remaining scaling transformation coefficient vector of N after the wavelet decomposition of layer L, which can be approximately expressed as $NS \approx N/2^L$.

The parameters after the above wavelet decomposition processing are used for the interference coordination optimization problem, and can be expressed as

$$\max f(\mathbf{CPS}) \tag{2}$$

Since the solution space of (2) is determined by NS, which is much smaller than (1), the computational time must be greatly reduced.

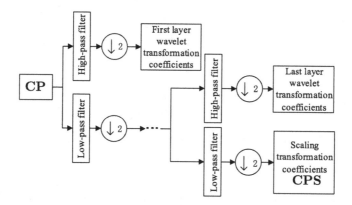

Fig. 1. Discrete wavelet transform process.

In the process of wavelet decomposition, the terminal characteristic information represented by the original parameter matrix should not be discarded too much, and the original parameter matrix information extracted by the retained scaling transformation coefficients is closely related to the rank of these parameters. These parameters describe the characteristics of terminals, and the ranking of parameters is determined by the ranking of terminals. So we are committed to designing a terminal ranking method.

This paper adopts graph theory to model the problem. Terminals are the vertexes of the graph, vertex set $\mathbf{V} = \{v_n | n = 1, 2, ..., N\}$ represents N terminals, edge set $\mathbf{E} = \{(v_i, v_j) | i, j = 1, 2, \cdots, N, i \neq j\}$ represents the degree of difference between any two terminals, and the weight of edge (v_i, v_j) is denoted as $w_{i,j}$. Considering that there is only one terminal sequence and there are multiple parameters affecting its ordering, the numerical values of multiple characteristic parameters can be used to solve ranking problem of terminal sequence. The weight of each side is the Euclidean distance calculated according to parameter values between terminals, which is expressed as $w_{i,j} = (\sum_{m=1}^{M} (\overline{CP}_{m,i} - \overline{CP}_{m,j})^2)^{\frac{1}{2}}$, where $\overline{}$ represents the normalization processing of corresponding parameter values. After the above processing, the scenario is represented as an undirected complete graph $G = (\mathbf{V}, \mathbf{E})$. Then the graph theory knowledge is used to find a ranking strategy of the terminal, written as $A = \{A(n) | n = 1, 2..., N\}$, where $A(n)$ is the terminal number that ranked the n-th position. Therefore, the sparsity of the characteristic parameter matrix after ranking is better.

The smaller the distance between two terminals, the closer the corresponding characteristic parameters of two terminals are. The sequential arrangement of the terminals with close Euclidean distance can make the parameter vector redundant as far as possible, and the scaling transformation coefficients can be extracted easily. Therefore, the ranking result of terminals should satisfy the requirement that the distance between any two adjacent terminals should be as small as possible, then the terminal ranking problem is transformed into the problem of finding the minimum Hamiltonian path, which is expressed as

$$A^* = \underset{A}{argmin} \sum_{n=1}^{N-1} w_{A(n),A(n+1)} \tag{3}$$

where A^* is the optimal ranking strategy of terminals.

3   Graph-Based Terminal Ranking Method

3.1   The Proposed Method for the Minimum Hamiltonian Path

Formula (3) indicates that solving the minimum Hamiltonian path is an NP hard problem [22], which cannot be solved in polynomial time. We can get a minimum Hamiltonian cycle and then remove an edge to get a Hamiltonian path (usually removing the edge with the largest weight).

There are two common algorithms to find the minimum Hamiltonian cycle of a complete graph. One is search algorithm, such as simulated annealing algorithm, genetic algorithm, etc. The other is approximation algorithm, such as nearest neighbor algorithm, double spanning tree algorithm and Christofides algorithm. The upper limit of approximation ratio is $\frac{1}{2}(\lceil \log_2 N \rceil + 1)$, 2 and 1.5 respectively [23–25]. Among them, the search algorithm can get an approximate optimal solution, but when the number of terminals is very large, the search process takes too long time, which violates our original intention of reducing the time of the interference coordination scheme. Therefore, we prefer to use approximation algorithm to get a better solution of the above problems in a short time. The approximation ratio is used to measure approximation algorithms running in polynomial time and ensure the ratio of the cost of approximation algorithm to optimal cost [26].

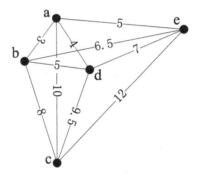

Fig. 2. Complete weighted graph.

The detailed steps of the three approximation algorithms are described below, and each of them is used to solve the complete graph shown in Fig. 2. In order to compare the advantages and disadvantages of the solutions of the three algorithms, we use the exhaustive method to calculate that the optimal solution in Fig. 2 is *abcdea* with weight of 32.5, and the worst solution is *acebda* with weight of 37.5.

Nearest Neighbor Algorithm(NNA)

Step 1. Select any point $v_1 \in \mathbf{V}$, use $\mathbf{H}$ to store the minimum Hamiltonian cycle found and initialize it as $\mathbf{H} = \{v_1\}$, and set the unselected vertices as $\tilde{\mathbf{V}} = \mathbf{V} \backslash \mathbf{H}$;

Step 2. Set $\mathbf{H} = \{v_1 v_2 \cdots v_i\}$, pick the next point $v_j^* = argmin\ w_{i,j}$, the new
$${v_j \in \tilde{\mathbf{V}}}$$
minimum Hamiltonian cycle is denoted as $\mathbf{H} = \{v_1 v_2 \cdots v_i v_j^*\}$, and update the set $\tilde{\mathbf{V}}$;

Step 3. If $\tilde{\mathbf{V}} = \emptyset$, stop, obtain an approximate minimum Hamiltonian cycle, denoted as $\mathbf{H} = \mathbf{H} + \{v_1\} = \{v_1 v_2 \cdots v_N v_1\}$. Otherwise, go to Step 2.

Taking the complete graph in Fig. 2 as an example, and set a as the starting point, a Hamiltonian cycle *abdeca* with weight of 37 can be obtained. The solving process is shown in Fig. 3, where the bold line represents the selected edge and the arrow represents the selection order of each vertex.

Thus, it can be seen that when the nearest neighbor algorithm is used to solve the problem, the edge with the lowest current weight is selected each time to get the next vertex, which will make the selection of the last two edges unique. If one of the edges has a large weight, the approximate solution will be poor. Therefore, the approximate solution obtained by nearest neighbor algorithm may have a certain gap from the optimal solution.

Double Spanning Tree Algorithm(DSTA)

Step 1. Find a minimum spanning tree T of complete graph G;

Step 2. Double its edges to get an Euler diagram G^*;

Step 3. Find an Eulerian cycle $\mathbf{E_v}$ of G starting from some vertex v, that is, a cycle that goes through each edge of the graph once and only once;

Step 4. Starting from v and visiting each vertex of G along $\mathbf{E_v}$. In this process, once a duplicate vertex is encountered, it is skipped straight to the next vertex, until all the vertices have been accessed.

Taking Fig. 2 as an example, a minimum spanning tree is first obtained, as shown in the thick line in Fig. 4, and then double its edges to obtain an Euler diagram, as shown in Fig. 4. Then an Eulerian cycle starting from point a is *aeadabcba*, and the final Hamiltonian cycle is *aedbca* with the weight of 35.

Because there are many Eulerian cycles, the Hamiltonian cycles obtained are not unique. However, some distant points will not appear continuously in any closed trace (such as *ac*, *ec*), so these poor edges will not appear in the final Hamiltonian cycle, which guarantees the performance to a certain extent.

Christofides Algorithm(CA)

Step 1. Find a minimum spanning tree T of complete graph G;

Step 2. Set the set of odd-degree vertexes in T as $\hat{\mathbf{V}}$, find the minimum-weight perfect matching of the derived subgraph of $\hat{\mathbf{V}}$ (that is, the match that contains all vertices and has the minimum sum of matching edge weights), add these matching edges to T to get Euler diagram G^*;

Step 3. Find an Eulerian cycle $\mathbf{E_v}$ of G starting from some vertex v, that is, a cycle that goes through each edge of the graph once and only once;

Step 4. Starting from v and visiting each vertex of G along $\mathbf{E_v}$. In this process, once a duplicate vertex is encountered, it is skipped straight to the next vertex, until all the vertices have been accessed.

Taking Fig. 2 as an example, a minimum spanning tree is first obtained, as shown in the bold line in Fig. 5. Find out the odd-degree vertexes, as shown circled vertexes in Fig. 5. Find its minimum-weight perfect matching as $\{ae, cd\}$, add matching edges to T to get Euler diagram G^*. An Eulerian cycle from point a is *aeadcba*, and finally Hamiltonian cycle is *aedcba* with the weight of 32.5.

Similar to double spanning tree algorithm, Christofides algorithm also uses the minimum spanning tree and Euler diagram, which can avoid selecting the edge with large weight. Christofides algorithm can obtain an Euler diagram by

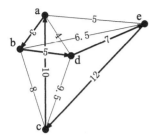 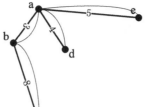 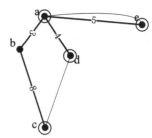

Fig. 3. The optimal solu-   **Fig. 4.** Euler diagram in   **Fig. 5.** Euler diagram in
tion obtained by NNA.   DSTA.   CA.

adding a small number of matching edges, so that the final approximate solution
may be better and the time required to find Eulerian cycle is lower.

3.2   Application of the Proposed Method for Inter-Cell Interference Coordination

In the future, the number of terminals in ultra-dense networks is usually large,
and the service transmission delay of terminals is usually small. After confirming
which terminals have service transmission, resource management needs to be
completed within a very short time, that is, corresponding to the millisecond
resource management cycle. Therefore, the above algorithm cannot be directly
applied to rank the terminals within the resource management cycle.

Further considering the characteristics of terminal mobility, position, power,
business flow and so on in these scenarios, the change period is usually much
larger than the millisecond level. Therefore, we can adopt a terminal ranking
process with a larger level of cycle to rank all terminals in the system. Then,
when the terminals requiring business transmission are processed in a resource
management cycle, the ranking is not needed anymore. Instead, the ranking
of these terminals can be obtained directly from the ranking of all terminals,
which solves the problem that terminals ranking cannot be completed in resource
management cycle of milliseconds.

The specific process is shown in Fig. 6. First, the parameters matrix of terminals is updated in real time according to their constant change. When a large
cycle update is reached, the graph-based terminal ranking method proposed in
this paper will be used to rank all the terminals in the system, so as to obtain a
long cycle of terminal ranking results. Then, during each resource management
cycle, terminals requiring coordinated interference are identified according to
business requirements, and the order of these terminals is determined based on
the ranking results of the long cycle. Final, the matrix formed by these terminal
characteristic parameters is transformed by discrete wavelet transform, and the
scaling transformation coefficients are used for interference coordination. Since
the length of the scaling transformation coefficient vector is much smaller than
the number of these terminals, the computational time of interference coordination can be greatly reduced.

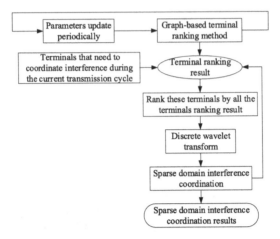

Fig. 6. Application of terminal ranking method to interference coordination.

Note that this process may involve the optimization objective function calculated by scaling transformation coefficients, may also involve in adopting discrete wavelet inverse transform to return the interference coordination result corresponding to the scaling transformation coefficients to the terminal coordination result, etc. But these are necessary steps in interference coordination scheme. This paper focus on the terminal ranking in order to adopt the best way to extract the scaling transformation coefficients of the terminal characteristic parameters, so the steps involved in interference coordination are not described in detail here.

In the application scheme shown in Fig. 6, it is necessary to ensure that the large cycle is much larger than the small cycle, so as to make the proposed scheme effective. The update cycle of terminal parameters is much larger than a resource management cycle, so that several or dozens of resource management processes can be effectively carried out within a large cycle. If the terminal parameters are updated frequently, the proposed scheme is no longer applicable. Therefore, the proposed scheme is suitable for communication scenarios in which the terminal is moving at low and medium speeds and the transmission service is relatively stable. In addition, the number of terminals in each cell is very large, but the large cycle is only relative to one resource management cycle. In each large cycle, not all terminals will participate in interference coordination all the time, so it is not necessary to directly handle all terminals in the cell indiscriminately. Although this is done by base station with very powerful computing power, it will undoubtedly add to the computational burden of base station. Therefore, how to dynamically manage the terminal to be ranked within each large cycle will be a practical application problem, which will further reduce the power consumption of base station.

4   Performance Evaluation

4.1   Simulation Parameters and Performance Indicators

This paper simulates a two-cell scenario, and scenario parameters are as follows: cell radius is 200 m, distance of base station is 220 m, carrier frequency is 2.0 GHz, transmitting power of terminal is 21 dBm, the power of AWGN is 174 dBm/Hz, bandwidth per resource blocks is 180 kHz, signal transmission model use close-in free space reference distance pathloss (CI-FSPL) model [27]. The proposed scheme is independent of the number of terminals and their characteristic parameters. Theoretically, the number of terminals in each cell can be set arbitrarily. However, due to the limited computing capacity of the hardware devices used in the simulation, we set the number of terminals in each cell to 500, and these terminals are uniformly distributed. The number of terminals that can be arranged for transmission varies within each resource management cycle, but the number of resource blocks that can be used by each cell within that cycle is fixed in each simulation, plotted on the X-axis of some figures, and varies between 200 and 1000. Assuming that the network is saturated, that is, all resource blocks are fully used in each cell. The interference coordination problem between two cells is mathematically reduced to a two-dimensional matching problem. The wavelet basis of discrete wavelet transform is Sym2, and the number of decomposition layers is 3.

Terminal characteristic parameters consider useful signal power, interference signal power, and terminal business requirements, among which useful signal power and interference signal power are determined by the terminal position and network parameters. Different terminals have different business requirements and need to use different number of resource blocks to meet their own data transmission. Therefore, the business requirements of terminals are transformed into the number of resource blocks required by terminals, which is represented by integer between $[1, 10]$, and generated randomly in simulation. In the following simulation, two parameters are used to refer to the useful signal power and interference signal power of terminals. The number of terminals to be coordinated in each cell within a resource management cycle is consistent with the number of resource blocks. Adopting three parameters refers to increasing the business requirements of terminals. The number of terminals in each cell that acquire transmission opportunities within a resource management cycle varies from 50 to 250, and these terminals divide the entire resource block in a random manner.

In this paper, four performance indicators are used to measure the proposed method, namely, Gini index, reconstruction error, capacity per resource block and Jain's fairness index. System capacity corresponds to the total capacity of all terminals allocated resources in the corresponding resource management period in the system. To facilitate comparison, we further take an average of system capacity to get the capacity per resource block. Jain's fairness index is the value obtained by plugging the capacity of these terminals into the Jain's fairness calculation formula [28]. These two are common indicators and will not be repeated here. The following is a brief description of the calculation of Gini index and reconstruction error in this paper.

Gini index is one of the important parameters to measure sequence sparsity [29], **CPW'** represents the matrix formed by each row in **CPW** is arranged in ascending order, and the Gini index corresponding to the coefficients of the m-th row is calculated as

$$GI_m = 1 - 2 \sum_{n=1}^{NS} \frac{CPW'_{m,n}}{\sum_{n=1}^{NS} CPW'_{m,n}} \left(\frac{NS - n + \frac{1}{2}}{NS} \right) \tag{4}$$

Gini index is between [0,1), which corresponds to the distribution of the wavelet coefficients of the matrix after the wavelet transform. The sparsity of the original parameter matrix **CP** is better, the more zero value (or approaching zero value) in the wavelet coefficient matrix obtained by the wavelet transform, the larger the Gini index of each row of the matrix **CPW** will be. Gini index of each row is calculated according to formula (4), and its average value is calculated as the performance indicator in this paper.

The reconstruction error reflects the gap between the reconstructed signal and the original signal [30], reconstruction error of **CP** is expressed as

$$\delta = \frac{1}{M} \sum_{m=1}^{M} \sqrt{\frac{1}{N} \sum_{n=1}^{N} \left(\overline{CP}_{m,n} - \overline{\overline{CP}}_{m,n} \right)^2} \tag{5}$$

where $\overline{\overline{CP}}_{m,n}$ represents the value after normalization by row of corresponding elements in the matrix $\overline{\overline{CP}}$ reconstructed by the inverse transformation of **CPS**. The sparsity of the original parameter matrix is better, which indicates that the more high-frequency coefficients in the wavelet coefficients after the discrete wavelet transform tend to zero, and the low-frequency coefficients can better reflect the characteristics of the original matrix. Therefore, the error between the matrix that is reconstructed back to primitive domain with a small amount of low-frequency coefficients and the original matrix is smaller.

4.2   Simulation Results and Analysis

Figure 7 and Fig. 8 show the Gini index and reconstruction errors of the proposed method, and compare them with the no-ranking method. The corresponding performance of three Hamiltonian path algorithms for terminal ranking is better than that of no-ranking method, which indicates that the sparsity of parameter matrix is greatly improved after ranking. It can also be seen that the performance of the three algorithms for solving Hamiltonian path differs little. In comparison, the Gini index of the Nearest neighbor algorithm is slightly better, and the reconstruction error of the Christofides algorithm is slightly worse. In addition, when the number of decomposition layers is too large, the reconstruction error of the nearest algorithm will suddenly increase. By comparing the two sub-graphs of two figures, when the number of parameter sequences increases, the scheme of ranking the parameter sequences separately will lead to poor sparsity of the first ranking sequence, thus verifying the effectiveness of the scheme of ranking multiple sequences simultaneously.

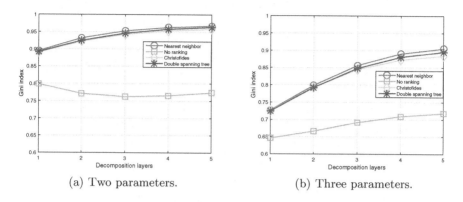

(a) Two parameters.

(b) Three parameters.

Fig. 7. Gini index.

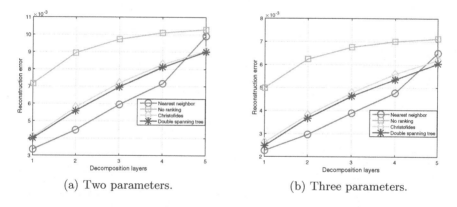

(a) Two parameters.

(b) Three parameters.

Fig. 8. Reconstruction errors.

Figure 9 and Fig. 10 show the performance improvement after applying the terminal ranking method proposed in this paper to interference coordination. It can be seen from Fig. 9 that capacity per resource block is not significantly affected by the removal of wavelet coefficients in interference coordination, which is better than directly using wavelet decomposition without ranking to reduce the problem size. It can be seen from Fig. 10 that the fairness of terminals is greatly improved due to the use of wavelet transform. However, the ranking scheme in this paper will make the fairness somewhat lower, which is lower than the method of using wavelet transform directly without ranking. By comparing the subgraphs in two figures, it is found that the sparsity of considering one parameter more makes the capacity per resource block of the network

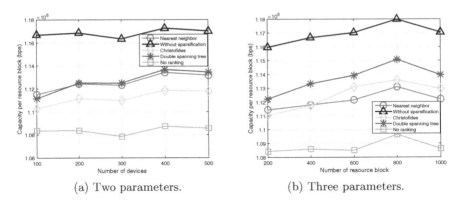

(a) Two parameters.   (b) Three parameters.

Fig. 9. Capacity per resource block.

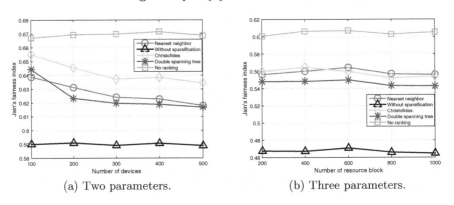

(a) Two parameters.   (b) Three parameters.

Fig. 10. Jain's fairness index.

slightly increase, and the difference of the capacity per resource block of various algorithms slightly decrease. At the same time, it is found that the sparsity of considering one parameter more will lead to a slight decrease in the fairness of terminals, and the difference of the fairness of each algorithm will also be slightly reduced.

The scheme proposed in the paper improves the sparsity of parameter matrix as much as possible by ranking terminals. Compared with no-ranking method, the randomness of terminals makes the sparsity of the original parameter matrix very poor, which results in wavelet transformation coefficients with large modulus are too many, and the scaling transformation coefficients can't approximately reflect the variation characteristics of the original parameter matrix. The result of sparse-domain interference coordination using the scaling transformation coefficients no longer corresponds to the approximate optimal coordination strategy in the original domain. Therefore, the proposed scheme is superior to the no-ranking scheme in each performance indicator. Of course, this scheme will introduce more time consuming in the process of terminal ranking. In order to ensure that the resource management process is completed within milliseconds, we will carry out terminal ranking and interference coordination respectively. As shown in Fig. 6, terminal ranking is completed before interference coordination and does not take up time in the resource management cycle. Therefore, we compare the time cost of terminal ranking and interference coordination respectively.

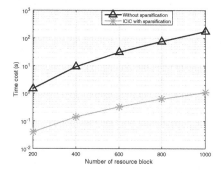 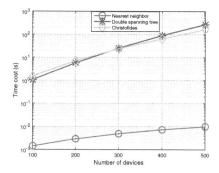

Fig. 11. Time cost of interference coordination.   **Fig. 12.** Time cost of terminal ranking.

Figure 11 compares the computational time of the interference coordination optimization. As can be seen, the use of wavelet transform can significantly reduce the size of the problem, so that the time cost of interference coordination is only one percent of magnitude of the traditional scheme. As can be seen from Fig. 12, the nearest neighbor algorithm has the minimum time cost, because it only ranks according to the relative size between sequence values. When the number of terminals is small, the Christofides algorithm is more time-consuming than the double spanning tree algorithm. Because the step of minimum-weight perfect matching of the odd-degree vertexes in Christofides algorithm introduces a lot of time. But when the number of terminals is increased, the Christofides algorithm is less time-consuming than the double spanning tree algorithm. This is because the total number of edges of an Euler diagram constructed in Christofides algorithm is much less than the double spanning tree algorithm, so that it may take less time to find Eulerian cycle.

5   Conclusion

This paper studied sparsification of interference coordination parameters. On the one hand, we considered multiple characteristic parameters of the terminal to better meet the service requirements of each terminal. On the other hand, in order to reduce the computational time of scheme, a large amount of original data was sparsely represented before interference coordination. Therefore, this paper proposed a graph-based terminal ranking scheme. Terminals and its parameters corresponded to the vertexes and edge weights in the graph, respectively. And then the terminal ranking problem could be turned into finding a Hamiltonian path problem in the graph, which could be solved with the help of the correlation graph theory algorithms. Based on the proposed scheme, this paper also designed a two-period interference coordination framework with practical value. Simulation results showed that the proposed scheme could greatly reduce the computational time of interference coordination and keep the better performance in all aspects.

Acknowledgement. This document is the results of the research project funded by the Fundamental Research Funds for the Central Universities of China under grant no. PA2019GDQT0012. It was also supported in part by the Applied Basic Research Program of Wuhan City, China, under grant 2017010201010117.

References

1. David, K., Berndt, H.: 6G vision and requirements: is there any need for beyond 5G? IEEE Veh. Technol. Mag. **13**(3), 72–80 (2018)
2. Yang, P., Xiao, Y., Xiao, M., Li, S.: 6G wireless communications: vision and potential techniques. IEEE Netw. **33**(4), 70–75 (2019)
3. Teng, Y., Liu, M., Yu, F.R., Leung, V.C., Song, M., Zhang, Y.: Resource allocation for ultra-dense networks: a survey, some research issues and challenges. IEEE Commun. Surveys Tuts. **21**(3), 2134–2168 (2019)
4. Zhao C., Xu X., Gao Z., Huang L.: A coloring-based cluster resource allocation for ultra dense network. In: IEEE ICSPCC, pp. 1–5. IEEE, Hong Kong (2016)
5. Georgakopoulos P., Akhtar T., Kotsopoulos S.: On game theory-based coordination schemes for mobile small cells. In: IEEE CAMAD, pp. 1–5. IEEE, Limassol, Cyprus (2019)
6. Zha, Z., Wang, L., Huang, C., Kai, C.: Quick matching for interference coordination in ultra-dense networks. IEEE Wireless Commun. Lett. **9**(1), 47–50 (2020)
7. Essassi S., Siala M., Hamila R., Hasna M.O., Cherif S.: Power control and RB allocation for LTE uplink. In: IWCMC, pp. 417–421. IEEE, Paphos (2016)
8. Chen Z., Tang Y.: A resource collaboration scheduling scheme in ultra-dense small cells. In: ICCSE, pp. 401–405. IEEE, Houston, TX (2017)
9. Huang, P., Kao, H., Liao, W.: Cross-tier cooperation for optimal resource utilization in ultra-dense heterogeneous networks. IEEE Trans. Veh. Technol. **66**(12), 11193–11207 (2017)
10. Zhu, J., Zhao, M., Zhou, S.: An optimization design of ultra dense networks balancing mobility and densification. IEEE Access. **6**, 32339–32348 (2018)
11. Calabuig, D., et al.: Resource and mobility management in the network layer of 5g cellular ultra-dense networks. IEEE Commun. Mag. **55**(6), 162–169 (2017)
12. Jiang L., Che H., Sun W., Liu J.: Resource allocation method for inter-cell interference coordination in heterogeneous networks with almost blank subframe. In: ICTIS, pp. 875–879. IEEE, Liverpool, United Kingdom, TX (2019)
13. Qu D., Zhou Y., Tian L., Shi J.: User-centric qos-aware interference coordination for ultra dense cellular networks. In: IEEE GLOBECOM, pp. 1–6. IEEE, Washington, DC (2016)

14. Qu D., Xie S., Sun B., Zhou Y.: Joint MS offloading and interference coordination for heterogeneous ultra dense networks. In: WCSP, pp. 1–6. IEEE, Xi'an, China (2019)

15. Zheng, J., Gao, L., Zhang, H., Zhu, D., Wang, H., Gao, Q., Leung, V.C.: Joint energy management and interference coordination with max-min fairness in ultra-dense hetnets. IEEE Access. **6**, 32588–32600 (2018)

16. Wang, Y., Feng, G., Wei, F., Qin, S., Liang, Y.: Interference coordination for autonomous small cell networks based on distributed learning. In: IEEE ICC, pp. 1–6. IEEE, Dublin, Ireland (2020)

17. Mismar, F.B., Evans, B.L., Alkhateeb, A.: Deep reinforcement learning for 5G networks: joint beamforming, power control, and interference coordination. IEEE Trans. Commun. **68**(3), 1581–1592 (2020)

18. Wei, Z., Masouros, C., Wong, K., Kang, X.: Multi-cell interference exploitation: enhancing the power efficiency in cell coordination. IEEE Trans. Wireless Commun. **19**(1), 547–562 (2020)

19. Lv C., Wang Q., Yan W., Zhao R., Chen J.: A sparse representation method of 2-D sensory data in wireless sensor networks. In: IEEE International Instrumentation and Measurement Technology Conference Proceedings, pp. 1–6. IEEE, Taipei (2016)

20. Daubechies, I.: Ten lectures on wavelets, 2nd edn. Society for Industrial Applied Mathematics, Philadelphia (1992)

21. Zhang, S., Wang, L., Kai, C., Wang, W.: Sparse-domain interference coordination scheme in ultra-dense networks. In: IEEE ICCC, pp. 1119–1123. IEEE, Chengdu, China (2018)

22. Garey, M.R., Johnson, D.S., Tarjan, R.E.: The planar hamiltonian circuit problem is NP-complete. SIAM J. Comput. **5**(4), 704–714 (1976)

23. Bellmore, M., Nemhauser, G.L.: The traveling salesman problem: a survey. Oper. Res. **16**(3), 538–558 (1968)

24. Rosenkrantz, D.J., Stearns, R.E., Lewis, P.M.: An analysis of several heuristics for the traveling salesman problem. SIAM J. Comput. **6**(3), 563–581 (1977)

25. Christofides N.: Worst-case analysis of a new heuristic for the travelling salesman problem. Report 388, Graduate School of Industrial Administration, CMU (1976)

26. Brecklinghaus, J., Hougardy, S.: The approximation ratio of the greedy algorithm for the metric traveling salesman problem. Oper. Res. Lett. **43**(3), 259–261 (2015)

27. 5GCM Homepage, http://www.5gworkshops.com/5GCM.html

28. Shi, H., Prasad, R.V., Onur, E., Niemegeers, I.: Fairness in wireless networks: issues, measures and challenges. IEEE Commun. Surveys Tuts. **16**(1), 5–24 (2014)

29. Zonoobi, D., Kassim, A.A., Venkatesh, Y.V.: Gini index as sparsity measure for signal reconstruction from compressive samples. IEEE J. Sel. Topics Signal Process. **5**(5), 927–932 (2011)

30. Jagtap A.S., Shriram R., Patil H.T.: Comparison of decomposition and reconstruction of 2D signal using slantlet transform and DCT. In: IEEE ICCSP, pp. 0593–0597. IEEE, Chennai (2017)

An Efficient Protocol for Tag-Information Sampling in RFID Systems

Xiujun Wang[1]($\boxtimes$)(iD), Yan Gao[1](iD), Yangzhao Yang[2](iD), Xiao Zheng[1](iD), Xuangou Wu[1](iD), and Wei Zhao[1](iD)

[1] School of Computer Science and Technology, Anhui University of Technology, Maanshan 243032, China
wxj@mail.ustc.edu.cn
[2] Research Institute of Cyberspace Security of CETC, Beijing, China
forester@mail.ustc.edu.cn

Abstract. Given a population S of N tags in an RFID system, the tag-information sampling problem is to randomly choose K distinct tags from S to form a subset T, and then inform each tag in T of a unique integer from $\{1, 2, ..., K\}$. This is a fundamental problem in many real-time analysis applications in RFID systems. Because it enables rapidly selecting a random subset T and collecting the tag-information from T. However, existing protocols for this problem are far from satisfactory due to high communication costs. In this paper, our objective is to solve this problem by using a small communication cost. We first obtain a lower bound on communication cost, denoted by C_{lb}, for this problem. Then we design a protocol, denoted by P_{s}, to solve this problem, and prove that the communication cost of P_{s} stays within a factor of 2 of C_{lb}. Extensive simulations verifies the advantages of P_{s} comparing with other protocols.

Keywords: IoT networks · RFID systems · Tag-information sampling problem · Communication cost

1 Introduction

Over the past dozen years, Radio Frequency Identification (RFID) technology has been widely applied in tracking moving objects [8,21,26], managing supply chains [13,20,22], and controlling warehouse inventory [2,9,14,23,25]. Conceptually, an RFID system in these applications consists the following components:

- RFID tags, each of which carries a unique 96-bit or 128-bit ID stored in its chip, are attached to different physical objects and serve as the unique identifiers of these objects. A tag also carries the tag-information which can be either the attribute data of the tagged object or the sensor data [3,12,15].
- RFID readers, each of which is deployed to a location of interest, are used for collecting the IDs and other related information from those tags within their range.

© ICST Institute for Computer Sciences, Social Informatics and Telecommunications Engineering 2020
Published by Springer Nature Switzerland AG 2020. All Rights Reserved
S. W. Loke et al. (Eds.): MONAMI 2020, LNICST 338, pp. 198–212, 2020.
https://doi.org/10.1007/978-3-030-64002-6_13

- A backend server connects to each reader in an RFID system for offering them with needed information storage and computation.

A fundamental yet important functionality needed in RFID systems is called tag-information sampling which is to randomly pick K tags from a large population S to construct a subset T, and then inform each tag in T of a unique order from $\{1, 2, ..., K\}$. More concretely, this problem requires to design a protocol P that effectively puts all the tags in S into a hat, then continuously determines the next tag t by randomly drawing a tag from the hat until K tags have been chosen, and inform each of these K tags of their ordering.

This function has a wide range of applications in many tag-management problems, such as monitoring and gathering tags' information. Because, when users need to analyze the status or characteristics of a large population S, it is time-consuming and sometimes unnecessary to collect the tag-information from every tag in S. In contrast, the tag-information from a random and small subset T is good enough. For example, we consider the type of RFID tags that are augmented with sensors, e.g., WISP tags [1]. This kind of tags can feedback their IDs as well as real-time sensor data related to the status of the tagged objects or surrounding environmental conditions [3, 12, 15]. In such scenario, when we need to periodically collect sensor data from a large tag population, it is common that we randomly choose a small number of tags at a time and collect their sensor data, due to the redundancy in environmental data (for example tags within in a small area sense the same temperature data). Tag-information sampling also plays an important role in IoT networks where massive data captured by various sensor-augmented RFID tags usually contains a large amount of redundancy, and must be smartly managed and timely analyzed [6, 7, 17, 24]. For other examples, please refer to [10, 15, 16, 22, 27].

There are a number of research works [3, 12, 19, 27] for collecting tags' information. However, these protocols work for collecting the information from either a tag population S or a specific tag subset B which is predetermined by users. This limitation incurs a high communication cost when we apply these protocols to solve the tag-information sampling problem. There are also some research works [10, 15] for collecting specific information, e.g., category information of the tagged objects, from a tag population which is pre-divided into multiple groups (subsets). However, these protocols still need to pre-set several groups (subsets), and only consider how to choose one tag randomly from a group each time. Therefore, these protocols are not suitable for solving the tag-information sampling problem.

For designing an efficient protocol for the tag-information sampling problem, we need to figure out the lower bound of communication cost when solving this problem and design a protocol that has a low communication cost. There are two technical challenges for achieving these two objectives. First, to obtain a lower bound, we need to analyze the essential information that must be transmitted between readers and tags such that the tag-information sampling problem is solved. This is not easy as we need to build a tricky process that transforms a protocol capable of solving the tag-information sampling problem into a coding process that represents any subset of a tag population. To the best of our knowledge, none of the existing works has achieved this goal, and there is no other exiting lower bound we can rely on. Secondly, we need to design a protocol, denoted by P_s and prove its efficiency. This is hard because we can not let the user pre-set a subset B of K tags, instead, we need to guarantee that every subset of K tags from S has an equal probability of being chosen. This point is even harder due to the extra requirement that each tag in T needs to be quickly informed with a unique order from $\{1, 2, ..., K\}$.

The rest of this paper is organized as follows. Section 2 defines the tag-information sampling problem. Section 3 presents the analysis of the lower bound of communication cost. Section 4 proposes an efficient protocol for this problem. Section 5 evaluates the performances of our protocol. Lastly, we conclude this paper in Sect. 6.

2   Problem Statement

We consider an RFID system that includes a reader R and a population S of N tags. All of the tags in S are within the interrogating range of reader R. Each tag t carries an ID, denoted by t^{ID}, which uniquely identifies the tagged object, and t^{ID} has already been collected by reader R and stored into the backend server. Each tag t also contains some kind of information (such as the attribute data of the object that tag t is associated, or the environmental data from the sensor installed on tag t) which the reader wants to collect periodically. We call this kind of information of t as its tag-information, denoted by t^{Info}. Then the tag-information sampling problem can be defined as follows.

Definition 1. *In an RFID system, let K be the pre-determined size of sampled subsets, then the tag-information sampling problem requires to design a protocol P between the reader R and tags such that the following two statements are satisfied at the end of protocol P.*

C-I: *A random subset T of K distinct tags is selected from the whole population S and every possible subset of K distinct tags has an equal probability of being chosen as T;*

C-: *Each tag in T is informed of a unique order ranging from 1 to K.*

3   Analysis of the Lower Bound on Communication Cost

When exploring the lower bound for solving this problem, we omit the communication cost between the reader R and backend server.[1] Because they are connected over a high-speed connection where the data rate is usually above 10Mit/s. For example, the IMPINJ R220 UHF RFID READER and ZEBRA

---

[1]   The reader R may transmit IDs and newly collected tag-information either to or from the backend server. or transmit newly collected tag-information to the backend server.

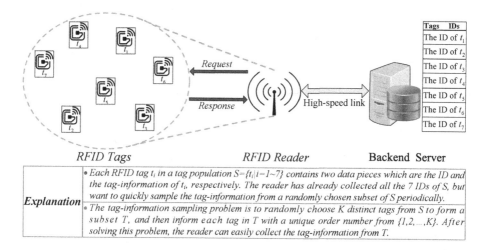

Explanation	• Each RFID tag t_i in a tag population $S=\{t_i|i=1\sim7\}$ contains two data pieces which are the ID and the tag-information of t_i, respectively. The reader has already collected all the 7 IDs of S, but want to quickly sample the tag-information from a randomly chosen subset of S periodically.
	• The tag-information sampling problem is to randomly choose K distinct tags from S to form a subset T, and then inform each tag in T with a unique order number from {1,2,...,K}. After solving this problem, the reader can easily collect the tag-information from T.

Fig. 1. An example of the tag-information sampling problem.

FX7500 RFID READER use Ethernet cable to join a network and connect to the backend server. In contrast, the reader R communicates with tags over a low-speed connection where the data rate ranges from 26.7 Kbit/s to 128 Kbit/s.

Before analyzing the lower bound, some symbols are defined as follows. We use T_{id} to denote a time frame for the reader R to broadcast a 96-bit array to all tags within its range. Thus, if reader R needs to send a total number of M bits to all tags during the execution of a protocol P, the communication cost and communication time of P are M and $\frac{MT_{\mathrm{id}}}{96}$, respectively. Let S denote a tag population of N tags, i.e., $S = \{t_i|i = 1 \sim N\}$, and K denote the size of the subset T. Without loss of generality, we assume that the ID of a tag is a 96-bit string, then set $\Gamma = 2^{96}$. Let U denote the universe of all the possible IDs, i.e., $U = \{0, 1, 2, ..., \Gamma - 1\}$. Lastly, t_i^{ID} is also used to represent a tag t, because t_i^{ID} is a unique identifier of tag t. Thus a tag population $S = \{t_i|i = 1 \sim N\}$ can also be represented by $S = \{t_i^{\mathrm{ID}}|i = 1 \sim N\}$.

The following theorem shows a nontrivial lower bound on the communication cost for any protocol P to solve the tag-information sampling problem. The road map of the proof is as follows. At first, based on the assumption that protocol P can randomly pick K tags from a tag population S, protocol P can be transformed into an encoding process that can represent S. Secondly, through analyzing the minimum number of bits required in the encoding process, we derive the lower bound on communication cost of P.

Theorem 1. *If a protocol P can solve the tag-information sampling problem by broadcasting $|P|$ bits from the reader R to all tags, then the following inequality is true:*

$$|P| \geq C_{lb} = \log_2(e)K, \tag{1}$$

where C_{lb} represents the lower bound of communication cost. Consequently, the communication time of protocol P can not be less than

$$T_{lb} = (C_{lb}T_{id})/96. \tag{2}$$

Proof. First, we analyze the general process when reader R solves the tag-information sapling problem by using a protocol P. Given a tag population S of N distinct IDs from the universe U ($S \subset U$), reader R takes S as the input to protocol P, and sends messages to tags. We can concatenate all of these messages into a single bit-string $\mathbb{M}$. Upon receiving $\mathbb{M}$, each tag $t \in S$ takes $\mathbb{M}$ and t^{ID} as the input to a decision function $Df()$ to decide whether t is chosen or not, and if so, which integer from $\{1, 2, ..., K\}$ is assigned to t. In general, the decision process of each tag $t \in S$ can be formulated as follows:

(1) If $\mathbf{Df}(t^{\mathrm{ID}}, \mathbb{M}) = K + 1$, tag t decides that it is not chosen;
(2) If $\mathbf{Df}(t^{\mathrm{ID}}, \mathbb{M}) = I \in \{1, 2, ..., K\}$, tag t decides that it is chosen and the unique integer assigned to t is I (when protocol P ends, tag t needs to send its tag-information in the I-th slot of the process that collects tag-information).

Based on the above, the transmitted message $\mathbb{M}$ actually is the parameter that decides how $\mathbf{Df}()$ maps every ID from U is mapped to the range $\{1, 2, ..., K\}$. A different value of $\mathbb{M}$ will lead to a different way that $\mathbf{Df}()$ maps IDs in U to $\{1, 2, ..., K\}$. Consider a specific value v of $\mathbb{M}$, let S_j represent the set of IDs in U that are mapped to $j \in \{1, 2, ..., K+1\}$, i.e., $S_j = \{t^{\mathrm{ID}} \in U | \mathbf{Df}(t^{\mathrm{ID}}, \mathbb{M}) = j\}$, and let x_i represent the size of S_j ($x_i = |\{S_j\}|$). Then it is clear that protocol P can use a value v to solve the tag-information sampling problem, when the tag population S contains exactly one ID from S_j for $j = 1, 2, ..., K$ and $N - K$ IDs from S_{K+1}. Because there are

$$Enum(v) = (\prod_{j=1}^{K} \binom{x_j}{1}) \times \binom{x_{K+1}}{N-K} \tag{3}$$

different sets that can be handled by a specific value v of $\mathbb{M}$, a value of $\mathbb{M}$ encodes $(\prod_{j=1}^{K} \binom{x_j}{1}) \times \binom{x_{K+1}}{N-K}$ different sets of N IDs from U.

Next, we simplify $Enum(v)$ in (3) as follows:

$$Enum(v) = (\prod_{j=1}^{K} \binom{x_j}{1}) \times \binom{x_{K+1}}{N-K}$$
$$\leq (\prod_{j=1}^{K} x_j) \times (x_{K+1})^{N-K}/(N-K)!, \tag{4}$$

where the inequality comes from the fact that $\binom{x_{K+1}}{N-K} = (x_{K+1})\underline{^{N-K}}/(N-K)! \leq (x_{K+1})^{N-K}/(N-K)!$. We then use the method of Lagrange multipliers to find the maximal value of (4), under the constraint that $\sum_{j=1}^{K+1} x_j \leq \Gamma$. More specifically, we set up a Lagrangian function:

$$\mathsf{L}(x_1, ..., x_{K+1}, \lambda) = (\prod_{j=1}^{K} x_j) \times (x_{K+1})^{N-K}/(N-K)! + \lambda(\sum_{j=1}^{K+1} x_j - \Gamma). \tag{5}$$

By taking derivative with respect to x_i $(i = 1, 2, ..., K + 1)$ and setting it equal to 0, it is easy to get the following equalities

$$\begin{cases} \prod_{j=1, j\neq i}^{K} x_j \times (x_{K+1})^{N-K} = \lambda, & \text{for } i = 1, 2, ..., K, \\ \prod_{j=1}^{K} x_j \times (N - K)(x_{K+1})^{N-K-1} = \lambda, & \text{for } i = K + 1. \end{cases}$$

Then based on the constraint $\sum_{j=1}^{K+1} x_j \leq \Gamma$, the maximum of (4) is achieved when $x_1 = x_2 = ..x_K = \Gamma/N$ and $x_{K+1} = \Gamma(N - K)/N$. Then, this indicates

$$Enum(v) \leq (\prod_{j=1}^{K} x_j) \times (x_{K+1})^{N-K}/(N - K)!$$
$$\leq [\Gamma/N]^K \times [\Gamma(N - K)/N]^{N-K}/(N - K)!. \tag{6}$$

Since there are $\binom{\Gamma}{N}$ different sets of N IDs to encode, and every single value v of the transmitted message $\mathbb{M}$ can encode at most $[\Gamma/N]^K \times [\Gamma(N - K)/N]^{N-K}/(N - K)!$, $\mathbb{M}$ must have at least $\frac{\binom{\Gamma}{N}}{[\Gamma/N]^K \times [\Gamma(N-K)/N]^{N-K}/(N-K)!}$ different values. Let $|\mathbb{M}|$ denote the number of bits contained in $\mathbb{M}$, the followings are true:

$$|\mathbb{M}| \approx -\log_2(N!) + K \log_2(N) + (N - K) \log_2(N/(N - K)) + \log_2((N - K)!)$$
$$\geq -\log_2(2\sqrt{2\pi N}(N/e)^N) + \log_2(\sqrt{2\pi(N - K)}((N - K)/e)^{N-K}) + K \log_2(N)$$
$$+ (N - K) \log_2(N/(N - K))$$
$$= K \log_2(e) + 0.5 \log_2((N - K)/N) - 1. \tag{7}$$

Note the first approximation in the above comes from the fact that $\Gamma \gg N$, and then $\Gamma^{\underline{N}} \approx \Gamma^N$. The inequality in the above is based on Stirling's Formula shown in Lemma 7.3 of [18]. We can obtain the lower bound shown in (1), because $0.5 \log_2((N - K)/N) - 1$ is comparatively smaller than $K \log_2(e)$.

Lastly, since reader R needs to send at least $C_{lb} = K \log_2(e)$ bits to tags, and T_{id} is a time frame for the reader R to broadcast a 96-bit array to all tags within its range, protocol P must have a communication time at least $\frac{C_{lb}T_{id}}{96}$.

4   Design of an Efficient Protocol for the Tag-Information Sampling Problem

In this section, we propose an efficient protocol, represented by P_s, which can solve the tag-information sampling problem by using a small communication cost. The basic idea of P_s is to design two separate phases: one phase, denoted as P_s-1, is for achieving the first requirement of Definition 1 (see C-I); and the other phase, denoted as P_s-2, is to satisfy the second requirement of Definition 1 (see C-II). In the following, we define there states of a tag t during the execution of P_s.

⋆ *UNSELECTED STATE*: A tag t is in this state if t does not know about whether it needs to report its tag-information. All of the tags in a population S are initialized to be in *UNSELECTED STATE*.

* *ACKNOWLEDGED STATE*: A tag t enters into this state if t is informed with a unique integer $I \in \{1, 2, ..., K\}$ and needs to report to R of its tag-information t^{Info} in the I-th slot of the subsequent process that collects tag-information.
* *INACTIVE STATE*: A tag t enters into this state if t knows that it does not need to report to R of its t^{Info} in the subsequent process that collects tag-information.

Obviously, when protocol P_s ends, every tag $t \in S$ is in either *ACKNOWLEDGED STATE* or *INACTIVE STATE*.

4.1 The Design and Analysis of the First Phase

This phase includes one simple communication round where each tag in population S used the parameters sent from reader R to compute a random hash function to determine whether it should remain in the *UNSELECTED STATE* or move to *INACTIVE STATE*. Given N and K, we describe the steps of the first phase below.

Step-1: The reader sends out a request with a random seed r to all tags.
Step-2: Upon receiving this random seed, each tag t computes a random number $h(t) = H(t^{\text{ID}}, r) \mod N$.
Step-3: If $h(t) < K$, tag t shall remain in *UNSELECTED STATE*, otherwise, t will enter the *INACTIVE STATE*.

The function $h()$ in step-2 is a hash function that maps tag t uniformly at random to an integer $h(t) \in \{0, 1, ..., N-1\}$. Thus, on average, there K tags from population S that are mapped to integers ranging from 0 to $K - 1$. For some random seeds, there may be more than K or less than K tags that are mapped to $\{0, 1, ..., K - 1\}$. However, reader R can avoid using these seeds, because it can pre-test a random seed to see if this seed picks K tags from S or not (R knows all the IDs of the tags in S).

Next, we analyze the theoretical performance of P_s-1. We first prove that P_s-1 satisfies the first requirement of Definition 1 in the following theorem.

Theorem 2. *Given a population S of N tags, after P_s-1 finishes, the probability that any K distinct tags in S are chosen to remain in the UNSELECTED STATE is equal $K!/N^{\underline{K}}$.*

Proof. Let $SP(i_1, i_2, .., i_K)$ represent the probability that tag $t_{i_1}, t_{i_2}, ..., t_{i_K}$ ($1 \leq i_1 < i_2 < ... < i_K \leq N$) are chosen to remain in the *UNSELECTED STATE* by P_s-1. Without loss of generality, we consider the first K tags: $t_1, t_2, ..., t_K$, and analyze $SP(1, 2, .., K)$. Because each tag $t \in S$ is mapped to an integer $h(t)$ in $\{0, 1, ..., K - 1\}$ independently and uniformly at random and reader R uses a random see that ensure that exactly K tags have their hashed integer less than K, the following is true:

$$SP(1, 2, .., K) = \frac{\mathbf{Pr}\left(h(t_1) < K, h(t_2) < K, ..., h(t_K) < K, h(t_{K+1}) \geq K, ..., h(t_N) \geq K\right)}{\mathbf{Pr}\left(\text{Only } K \text{ tags in } S \text{ have hashed integers less than } K\right)}$$

$$= \frac{(K/N)^K (1 - K/N)^{N-K}}{\binom{N}{K}(K/N)^K (1 - K/N)^{N-K}} = K!/N^{\underline{K}}. \tag{8}$$

We have the conclusion.

Next, we analyze the communication cost of P_s-1.

Theorem 3. *Given a population S of N tags, during the execution of P_s-1, the reader R needs to send $\log_2(N)$ bits to all tags.*

Proof. The only transmission cost in P_s-1 is for sending out a random seed r. Based on [4], we know a random universal hash function, which requires about $2 \times \log_2(N)$ bits to describe, can perform nearly as a truly random hash function in practice.

4.2   The Design and Analysis of the Second Phase

The second phase P_s-2 targets for the K tags that remain in the *UNSELECTED STATE* by the end of P_s-1, with the aim that each of them is informed of a unique order from $\{1, 2, ...K\}$ (see the second requirement of Definition 1).

P_s-2 consists of a number of communication rounds, each of which will let some tags in *UNSELECTED STATE* enter the *ACKNOWLEDGED STATE* by informing each of them with a unique order from $\{1, 2, ..., K\}$, until no tag is in *UNSELECTED STATE*. Let B represent the set of the K tags that stay in *UNSELECTED STATE* at the end of P_s-1. Detailed steps of P_s-2 are given below.

(1): If B is not an empty set, reader R starts a new communication round by broadcasting a request with two numbers $< |B|, r >$ where $|B|$ is number of tags in B and r is new random seed r.

(2): Upon receiving $<|B|, r>$, each tag t in *UNSELECTED STATE* computes a random number $f(t) = H(t^{ID}, r) \mod |B|$.

(3): Reader R knows all the IDs in set B, so reader R can also compute the random number $f(t)$ for each tag $t \in B$, and then construct a bit-array F with $|B|$ bits. Each bit $F[j], j \in \{0, 1, .., |B| - 1\}$ is set to '1' if there exists exactly one tag $t \in B$ that has $f(t) = j$; $F[j]$ is set to '0', otherwise.

(4): Reader R broadcasts the bit-array F out.

(5): Upon receiving F, each tag t in *UNSELECTED STATE* checks the $F(f(t))$. Then if $F(f(t)) = 1$ tag t shall take $Cnt(f(t)) + K - |B|$ as its order and enters the *ACKNOWLEDGED STATE*; Otherwise tag t remains in the *UNSELECTED STATE*. Note the $Cnt(f(t))$ represent the number of '1's in the subarray $F[0], F[1], ..., F[f(t)]$.

(6) Reader R deletes those tags that enter the *ACKNOWLEDGED STATE* from B, and go to step (1).

We use an example to explain how P_s-2 informs each tag in B with a unique integer. Suppose B contains 3 tags: t_1, t_2, t_3. In the first round, we assume that the hash values of these 3 tags are: $f(t_1) = 1$, $f(t_2) = 1$ and $f(t_3) = 2$, then R shall build a 3-bit array $F = $ "001" which is broadcasted out to all tags. After receiving $F = $ "001", tag t_3 finds out that $F[f(t_3)] = F[2]$ is equal to '1', thus t_3 will take $Cnt(f(t_3)) + K - |B| = Cnt(2) + 3 - 3 = 1 + 3 - 3$ as its integer and enters the *ACKNOWLEDGED STATE*. The other two tags: t_1 and

t_2 remain in the *UNSELECTED STATE*, as $F[f(t_1)] = F[(f(t_2)] = F[1] =' 0'$. equals $'0'$. At the end of this round, reader R deletes t_3 from B. In the second round, we assume that the hash values of the 2 tags in B are $f(t_1) = 1$ and $f(t_2) = 0$, then R shall build a 2-bit array $F =$ "11" and send it out. After receiving $F =$ "11", tag t_1 finds out that $F[f(t_1)] = F[1]$ is equal to $'1'$, then t_1 will take $Cnt(f(t_1)) + K - |B| = Cnt(2) + 3 - 2 = 2 + 3 - 2 = 3$ as its integer and enters the *ACKNOWLEDGED STATE*. Similar to tag t_1, t_2 takes $Cnt(f(t_2)) + K - |B| = Cnt(1) + 3 - 2 = 1 + 3 - 2 = 2$ as its integer and enters the *ACKNOWLEDGED STATE*. At the end of the second round, reader R deletes t_1 and t_2 from B, and then stops P_s-2 because B is empty.

Next, we analyze the theoretical performance of P_s-2. First, it is easy to observe from the above steps that all tags in B moves to the *ACKNOWLEDGED STATE*. Next, we analyze the integers that the K tags in B can get.

Theorem 4. *Each tag $t \in B$ can obtain a unique order from $\{1, 2, ..., K\}$ when t enters the ACKNOWLEDGED STATE.*

Proof. Without loss of generality, we assume that, in the first round, there are l tags $t_{i_1}, t_{i_2}, ..., t_{i_l}$ that enter the *ACKNOWLEDGED STATE*. So there will be l $'1'$s in the bit-array F sent from reader R. Then each of these tags shall have $Cnt(f(t_{i_1})) \neq Cnt(f(t_{i_2})) \neq .. \neq Cnt(f(t_{i_l}))$, and $\forall j \in \{1, 2, ..., l\}$, $Cnt(f(t_{i_j})) \in \{1, 2, ..., l\}$. Thus, we see that each t_{i_j}, $j \in \{1, 2, .., l\}$ gets a unique integer from $\{1, 2, .., K\}$.

Following a similar way, it is easy to prove that each of the l' tags that enter the *ACKNOWLEDGED STATE* in the second round can get a unique integer from $\{l + 1, l + 2, .., l + l'\}$.

Theorem 5. *During P_s-2, readers needs to send about $K \times e + \ln(K) \times 2\log_2(K)$ bits to all tags.*

Proof. In the first round, reader R needs to send two number $|B|$ and r to tags, each of which takes $\log_2(K)$ bits, and a bit-array of $|B|$ bits. Thus, R needs to send $2\log_2(K) + K$ bits.

A tag $t \in B$ is deleted from B in the first round if there does not exist another tag $t' \in B$ that has $f(t) = f(t')$. Then, the probability that t is deleted from B at the end of the first round is $(1 - 1/|B|)^{K-1} \approx e^{-1}$. Then, on average there are $(1 - e^{-1})K$ tags left in B ($|B| = (1 - e^{-1})K$) when the second round begins. In the second round, clearly, reader R still needs $2\log_2(K)$ bits for transmitting the new value of $|B|$ and a new random seed r, and then R sends out and a bit-array of $|B| = (1 - e^{-1})K$ bits. Thus, R needs to send $2\log_2(K) + (1 - e^{-1})K$.

Following a similar analysis, we know that the communication cost for the l-th round is $2\log_2(K) + (1 - e^{-1})l$. Since each round reduces the size of B by a fixed proportion $(1 - e^{-1})$, then after $\ln(K)$ rounds, B becomes empty. Therefore, the total number of bits that reader R sends to tags is $\ln(K) \times 2\log_2(K) + K + K(1 - e^{-1}) + ... + K(1 - e^{-1})^{\ln(K)} \leq K \times e + \ln(K) \times 2\log_2(K)$.

4.3   The Analysis of Protocol P_s

This section, we analyze the theoretical performance of protocol P_s.

Theorem 6. *The communication cost of protocol P_s is about 2 times of the lower bound C_{lb} shown in* (1).

Proof. Based on Theorem 3 and 4, we know that protocol P_s achieves the two requirements shown in Definition 1, and then solves the tag-information sampling problem. Next, based on Theorem 2 and 5, we see that protocol P_s has a communication cost of $\log_2(N) + K \times e + \ln(K) \times 2\log_2(K)$ bits. We compare this cost with the lower bound $C_{lb} = \log_2(e)K$ shown in Theorem 1 and obtain the following.

$$\frac{\log_2(N) + K \times e + \ln(K) \times 2\log_2(K)}{\log_2(e)K} \approx \frac{e}{\log_2(e)} \approx 2. \qquad (9)$$

In the above formula, we can use $\log_2(N)/K \approx 0$ because $\log_2(N)$ is usually much less than K in RFID systems. Through (9), we see the communication cost of protocol P_s is within a factor of 2 of the lower bound C_{lb}, which shows the efficiency of P_s.

5   Evaluation

In this section, the performance of the proposed P_s is evaluated and compared with the existing protocols through simulations.

5.1   Simulation Setting

The simulation parameter is set according to the specification of the EPCglobal C1G2 standard [5], which has been used widely to test protocols' performance in RFID systems [11,14,22,27]. Any two consecutive communications between readers and tags are separated by a time frame of $302\,\mu s$. The data rate of the link from readers to tags is set to 26.5 kbps. Thus, it takes the reader about $3897\,\mu s$ to broadcast out a 96-bit array to tags, i.e., $T_{id} = 3897\,\mu s$. As tags do not need to transmit any bits back to the reader, the data rate for the link from tags to the reader is not set.

We choose two state-of-the-art protocols which are the minimal Perfect hashing based Information Collection (PIC) in [27] and the Tag-Ordering Polling protocol (TOP) in [19], respectively. Because both of the two protocols require to preset a target T of a tag population S from which they collect the tag-information, we use them to solve the tag-information sampling problem in the following way:

(1) Let the reader R randomly generate a subset of K tags from S locally;
(2) Let R inform these K tags and then collect the tag-information from them by using either PIC or TOP.

Note that we set the length of the Bloom filter to be $24k$ in the following simulations when testing TOP [19]. This parameter setting is according to part A: Energy cost in section IV of [19]

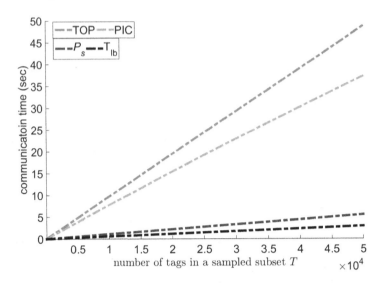

Fig. 2. Protocols' Performance in Scenario 1 where the number of tags in population S is fixed to 10^5 but the number of tags in a sampled subset T varies from 10^2 to 0.5×10^5 ($N = 10^5$ and $K \in [10^2, 0.5 \times 10^5]$).

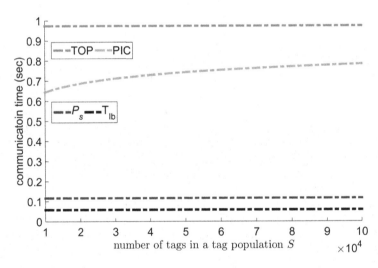

Fig. 3. Protocols' Performance in Scenario 2 where the number of tags in population S varies from 10^4 to 10^5 but the number of tags in a sampled subset is set fixed to 10^3 ($N \in [10^4, 10^5]$ and $K = 10^3$).

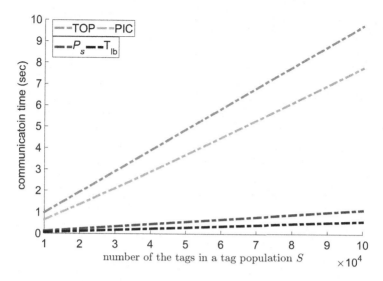

Fig. 4. Protocols' Performance in Scenario 3 where the number of tags in population S varies from 10^4 to 10^5 and the number of tags in a sampled subset is set equal to $0.1 \times N$ ($N \in [10^4, 10^5]$ and $K = 0.1 \times N$).

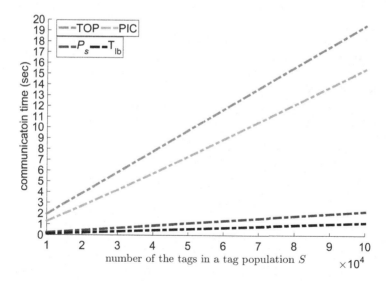

Fig. 5. Protocols' Performance in Scenario 4 where the number of tags in population S varies from 10^4 to 10^5 and the number of tags in a sampled subset is set equal to $0.1 \times N$ ($N \in [10^4, 10^5]$ and $K = 0.2 \times N$).

5.2 Simulation Results

We compare the performance of the three protocols in four different scenarios with different settings for K (the number of tags in a sampled subset T) and N (the number of tags in tag population S). All the simulation results in the following are the average outcome of 100 independent trials using MATLAB. In scenario 1, we set $N = 10^5$ but vary K from 10^2 to $5 * 10^5$. In scenario 2, we fix $K = 10^2$ but vary N from 10^4 to 10^5. For scenario 3, both N and K are varied in a way that $N \in \{10^3, 2 \times 10^3, .., 10^5\}$ and $K = 10^{-1} \times N$. Scenario 4 takes the same setting as scenario 4 except setting K to be equal $2 \times 10^{-1} \times N$. The communication time of the three protocols is presented in Fig. 2, 3, 4 and 5.

We can observe from the experiments that the communication time of P_s is the smallest among the three protocols. Indeed, it stays close the lower bound T_{lb}. Taking scenario 1 for example, when $K = 10^3$ and $N = 10^5$, the communication time of P_s is on 0.12 s, while the communication times of TOP and PIC are 0.98 s and 0.78s, respectively. This In scenario 3, when $K = 10^3$ and $N = 5 \times 10^4$, the communication time of P_s is only 0.56s, while the communication times of TOP and PIC are 4.87 s and 3.68 s, respectively. In summary, the proposed P_s has a communication time about 10%–20% of that of the other two protocols. The superiority of P_s as compared with other protocols can be explained in two angles. First, protocol P_s allows each tag in S to randomly decide to join in T or not (does not require to preset a subset T) locally, while the other protocols let the reader to globally pre-determine a subset of K tags and then send the information of this subset to tags. Secondly, protocol P_s smartly transmits a small number of bits by focusing on K tags out randomly chosen from S, while the other protocols need much more bits to take good care of every tag in S and inform them about which tags are in the pre-fixed subset and which are not.

Next, we see the ratio between the communication time of P_s and the lower bound T_{lb} in these four scenarios. Take scenario 1 for example, we see P_s uses a communication that is about 2 times of T_{lb}. In scenario 4, we also observe that P_s uses a communication that is about 2 times of T_{lb}.

6 Conclusion

This paper studies the problem of tag-information sampling problem in RFID systems, and obtains a lower bound of communication cost and proposes an efficient protocol P_s for this problem. The proposed protocol P_s has a communication cost that is not only much less than that of the state-of-art protocols but also proven to stay within a factor of 2 of the lower bound. Extensive simulations are conducted to evaluate the performance of the propose protocol P_s. The results show that P_s outperforms the state-of-art protocols.

Acknowledgements. This work was supported in part by the National Natural Sciences Foundation of China under Grants 61402008, 61702006 and 61672038, in part by the Provincial Key Research and Development Program of Anhui Province under Grants 202004a05020009 and 201904a05020071, in part by the Electronic Information and Control of Fujian University Engineering Research Center, Minjiang University, under Grant MJXY-KF-EIC1803, and in part by the Open Fund of Key Laboratory of Anhui Higher Education Institutes under Grant CS2020-006.

References

1. WISP: Wireless Identification and Sensing Platform (2011). https://sensor.cs. washington.edu/WISP.html
2. Bu, K., Xu, M., Liu, X., Luo, J., Zhang, S., Weng, M.: Deterministic detection of cloning attacks for anonymous rfid systems. IEEE Trans. Industr. Inf. **11**(6), 1255–1266 (2015)
3. Chen, S., Zhang, M., Xiao, B.: Efficient information collection protocols for sensor-augmented rfid networks. In: 2011 Proceedings IEEE INFOCOM. pp. 3101–3109. IEEE (2011)
4. Chung, K.M., Mitzenmacher, M., Vadhan, S.: Why simple hash functions work: exploiting the entropy in a data stream. Theory of Comput. **9**(1), 897–945 (2013)
5. EPCGlobal: EPC Radio-Frequency Identity Protocols Generation-2 UHF RFID Standard, Specification for RFID Air Interface Protocol for Communications at 860 MHz - 960 MHz. Technical Report (2018)
6. Gu, Y., Wang, Y., Liu, Z., Liu, J., Li, J.: Sleepguardian: An rf-basedhealthcare system guarding your sleep from afar. IEEE Network (2020)
7. Hu, H., Liu, Z., An, J.: Mining mobile intelligence for wireless systems: a deep neural network approach. IEEE Comput. Intell. Mag. **15**(1), 24–31 (2020)
8. Li, J., et al.: Psotrack: A rfid-based system for random moving objects tracking in unconstrained indoor environment. IEEE IoT J. **5**(6), 4632–4641 (2018)
9. Li, Q., et al.: Af-dcgan: Amplitude feature deep convolutional gan for fingerprint construction in indoor localization systems. IEEE Transactions on Emerging Topics in Computational Intelligence (2019)
10. Liu, J., Chen, S., Xiao, B., Wang, Y., Chen, L.: Category information collection in rfid systems. In: 2017 IEEE 37th International Conference on Distributed Computing Systems (ICDCS). pp. 2220–2225. IEEE (2017)
11. Liu, J., Chen, S., Xiao, Q., Chen, M., Xiao, B., Chen, L.: Efficient information sampling in multi-category rfid systems. IEEE/ACM Trans. Netwk. **27**(1), 159–172 (2018)
12. Liu, X., et al.: Fast rfid sensory data collection: trade-off between computation and communication costs. IEEE/ACM Trans. Netwk. **27**(3), 1179–1191 (2019)
13. Liu, X., et al.: Efficient unknown tag identification protocols in large-scale rfid systems. IEEE Trans. Parallel Distrib. Syst. **25**(12), 3145–3155 (2014)
14. Liu, X., et al.: Top-k queries for multi-category rfid systems. In: IEEE INFOCOM 2016-The 35th Annual IEEE International Conference on Computer Communications. pp. 1–9. IEEE (2016)
15. Liu, X., et al.: Efficient range queries for large-scale sensor-augmented rfid systems. IEEE/ACM Trans. Networking **27**(5), 1873–1886 (2019)
16. Liu, X., Yang, Q., Luo, J., Ding, B., Zhang, S.: An energy-aware offloading framework for edge-augmented mobile rfid systems. IEEE IoT J. **6**(3), 3994–4004 (2018)
17. Liu, Z., Ota, K.: Smart technologies for emergency response and disaster management. IGI Global (2017)
18. Mitzenmacher, M., Upfal, E.: Probability and computing: Randomization and probabilistic techniques in algorithms and data analysis. Cambridge university press (2017)

19. Qiao, Y., Chen, S., Li, T., Chen, S.: Tag-ordering polling protocols in rfid systems. IEEE/ACM Trans. Netwk. **24**(3), 1548–1561 (2015)
20. Reyes, P.M., Worthington, W.J., Collins, J.D.: Knowledge management enterprise- and rfid systems. Management Research Review (2015)
21. Shangguan, L., Jamieson, K.: The design and implementation of a mobile rfid tag sorting robot. In: Proceedings of the 14th Annual International Conference on Mobile Systems, Applications, and Services. pp. 31–42 (2016)
22. Wang, X., Liu, Z., Gao, Y., Zheng, X., Dang, Z., Shen, X.: A near-optimal protocol for the grouping problem in rfid systems. IEEE Trans. Mobile Comput. pp. 1–1 (2019). https://doi.org/10.1109/TMC.2019.2962125
23. Wang, X., Liu, Z., Gao, Y., Zheng, X., Chen, X., Wu, C.: Near-optimal data structure for approximate range emptiness problem in information-centric internet of things. IEEE Access **7**, 21857–21869 (2019)
24. Wu, C., Liu, Z., Zhang, D., Yoshinaga, T., Ji, Y.: Spatial intelligence toward trust-worthy vehicular iot. IEEE Commun. Mag. **56**(10), 22–27 (2018)
25. Xie, L., Han, H., Li, Q., Wu, J., Lu, S.: Efficiently collecting histograms over rfid tags. In: IEEE INFOCOM 2014-IEEE Conference on Computer Communications. pp. 145–153. IEEE (2014)
26. Xie, L., Sun, J., Cai, Q., Wang, C., Wu, J., Lu, S.: Tell me what i see: Recognize rfid tagged objects in augmented reality systems. In: Proceedings of the 2016 ACM International Joint Conference on Pervasive and Ubiquitous Computing. pp. 916–927 (2016)
27. Xie, X., Liu, X., Li, K., Xiao, B., Qi, H.: Minimal perfect hashing-based information collection protocol for rfid systems. IEEE Trans. Mob. Comput. **16**(10), 2792–2805 (2017)

Spectra Efficient Space Time Coding

Rui Yin[1]([✉]), Zhiqun Zou[1], Celimuge Wu[2], Hongjun Xu[3], and Chao Chen[4]

[1] School of Information and Electrical Engineering, Zhejiang University City College,
Hangzhou 310015, China
`yinrui@zucc.edu.cn`
[2] Graduate School of Informatics and Engineering, The University
of Electro-Communications, 1-5-1, Chofugaoka, Chofu-shi, Tokyo 182-8585, Japan
[3] School of Electrical, Electronic and Computer Engineering, KwaZulu-Natal
University, Durban, South Africa
[4] School of Information Science and Electronic Engineering, Zhejiang Gongshang
University, Hangzhou, China

Abstract. In this letter, a new *space time* (ST) coding scheme is proposed to improve the system *spectral efficiency* (SE). To improve the SE while achieving full diversity gain, the ST coded symbol transmission sequence (denoted as ST coding pattern in time domain) is exploited to improve the transmission rate. Since the orthogonal construction of the ST codes is preserved, the simple decoding scheme (linear maximum likelihood detector) is still applicable. Based on the analysis and Monte Carlo simulations, we demonstrate that the data rate increases by 25% and the its *bit error rate* (BER) is close to the conventional ST codes when 16-QAM or 16-PSK is used in the system.

Keywords: Spectrum efficiency · Space time coding · MIMO

1 Introduction

The rapid increase on personal intelligent terminals, such as tablets and smart phones, has led to the demand for high data rate with high reliability transmission in wireless communication systems [1]. To deal with such challenge, scholars and engineers have developed new technologies to improve the *spectrum efficiency* (SE) of the limited frequency resource. *Multiple input and multiple output* (MIMO) is one of them, which can improve the SE tremendously via introducing the spatial freedom. Specifically, the massive MIMO technique has become one of the key technologies for 5G system [2].

Theoretically, by using MIMO technique, both diversity and multiplex gain can be achieved to improve the transmit data rate and reliability. According to [3], there is a fundamental tradeoff between diversity and multiplex gain in MIMO system. To achieve these advantages in a practical MIMO system, Alamouti *space-time-block code* (STBC) has been proposed in [4]. In a conventional

S. W. Loke et al. (Eds.): MONAMI 2020, LNICST 338, pp. 213–225, 2020.
https://doi.org/10.1007/978-3-030-64002-6_14

Alamouti scheme [5], two antennas are deployed at a transmitter and two independent source symbols are transmitted via the antennas simultaneously over two consecutive time slots. The essence of the Alamouti scheme is that the encoding matrix maintains an orthogonal structure in two time slots, which allows a simple linear *maximum-likelihood* (ML) decoder in the quasi-static frequency flat Rayleigh block fading channels. Basically, Alamouti can achieve full diversity gain as demonstrated in [5]. But, it can not achieve full multiplex gain, which would reduce the transmission data rate.

To improve the SE of STBC, the efficiency of the STBC with *quadrature phase shift key* (QPSK) modulation has been investigated in [6]. Since the code efficiency is only 0.5, authors in [6] have used two QPSK constellations for STBC, which allows an additional bit to be sent. For QPSK based STBC, the SE increases by 0.5 bit/s/Hz. As an extension work of [7], the same strategy has been utilized when the number of transmission antenna is 4. In [8], a *space-time block coded spatial modulation* (STBC-SM) has been proposed, which combines *spatial modulation* (SM) and STBC to improve the SE. In the STBC-SM scheme, the transmitted symbols include not only the source information, but also the antenna indices information. As an extensional work of [8], a differential transmission scheme based on cyclic temporally and spatially modulated STBC has been developed in [9] to improve the SE. A high data rate STBC spatial modulation with cyclic structure has been proposed in [10]. In the scheme, a pair of transmit antennas is selected to send STBC symbols drawn from two different constellations, while the antenna pairs are moving cyclically along the total transmit antenna array. In [11], a constellation collaborated nonlinear orthogonal space-time block codes has been proposed to improve the BER performance. A corresponding fast maximum-likelihood detection scheme has been also proposed. Super-orthogonal space-time trellis codes have been applied in STBC-SM to further improve the SE in [12].

Most works mentioned above sacrifice either the diversity gain or the complexity of the detector at the receiver to achieve more SE. In this paper, we design a novel STBC scheme to improve the system SE while retaining the simple linear maximum likelihood detector and the diversity gain of the classic Alamouti scheme. The basic idea of the new scheme is to transmit more information by exploiting the sequence of transmitted symbols in time domain. As a result, additional bits can be transmitted.

The rest of the paper is organized as follows. In Sect. 2, a MIMO system with two transmit antennas and N_r receive antennas using Alamouti scheme is introduced. Section 3 proposes a novel space time coding scheme. Following this, *bit error rate* (BER) performance of the new scheme is analyzed in Sect. 4. Simulation results are demonstrated in Sect. 5 and we conclude in Sect. 6.

Notation: $|\cdot|$ and $\|\cdot\|_F$ denote the Euclidean and Frobenius norm operations, respectively. $(\cdot)^*$, $(\cdot)^T$ and $(\cdot)^H$ represent the complex conjugate, transpose and Hermitian operations, respectively.

2   Classic Alamouti Scheme

In the system, there are two transmit antennas and N_r antennas deployed at the receiver. The source bits are first divided into two streams. Each binary stream then goes through a modulator to map bits into symbols, x_1 and x_2. Each symbol contains $r = \log_2(M)$ bits, where M is the number of constellation points of QAM. Based on the Alamouti scheme, one transmission interval is divided into two consecutive time slots. Symbols x_1 and x_2 are transmitted via antenna 1 and antenna 2 at time slot one, and $-x_2^*$ and x_1^* are sent via two antennas at the consecutive time slot. Then, the received signals, $\mathbf{Y}^{(C)} = \left[\mathbf{y}_1^{(C)}, \mathbf{y}_2^{(C)} \right]$, are given by

$$\text{time slot 1}: \ \mathbf{y}_1^{(C)} = \sqrt{\frac{\rho}{2}} \left(\mathbf{h}_1 x_1 + \mathbf{h}_2 x_2 \right) + \mathbf{N}_1 \tag{1}$$

and

$$\text{time slot 2}: \ \mathbf{y}_2^{(C)} = \sqrt{\frac{\rho}{2}} \left(-\mathbf{h}_1 x_2^* + \mathbf{h}_2 x_1^* \right) + \mathbf{N}_2, \tag{2}$$

respectively. Herein, $\mathbf{h}_1$ is an $N_r \times 1$ vector to denote the channel gain from the first transmit antenna to N_r receive antennas. Similarly, $\mathbf{h}_2$ has the same dimension as $\mathbf{h}_1$ to represent the channel gain from the second transmit antenna to receive antennas. The upper symbol, C denotes 'classic'. In this paper, we assume that the channels are quasi-static frequency-flat Rayleigh fading channels. Therefore, $\mathbf{h}_1$ and $\mathbf{h}_2$ do not change in one transmission interval and the items in $\mathbf{h}_1$ and $\mathbf{h}_2$ are the complex Gaussian variables. $\mathbf{N}_1$ and $\mathbf{N}_2$ are $N_r \times 1$ noise vector with complex Gaussian distribution, $\mathcal{CN}(0,1)$. $\sqrt{\frac{\rho}{2}}$ is the average *signal-to-noise ratio* (SNR) at each receive antenna.

When the receiver has the *perfect channel state information* (CSI), it manipulates the received signals to yield

$$\mathbf{Y}_r = \begin{bmatrix} \mathbf{y}_1^{(C)} \\ -\left(\mathbf{y}_2^{(C)}\right)^* \end{bmatrix} = \begin{bmatrix} \mathbf{h}_1 & \mathbf{h}_2 \\ -\mathbf{h}_2^* & \mathbf{h}_1^* \end{bmatrix} \begin{bmatrix} x_1 \\ x_2 \end{bmatrix} + \begin{bmatrix} \mathbf{N}_1 \\ -\mathbf{N}_2^* \end{bmatrix}. \tag{3}$$

Define

$$\mathbf{H} \triangleq \begin{bmatrix} \mathbf{h}_1 & \mathbf{h}_2 \\ -\mathbf{h}_2^* & \mathbf{h}_1^* \end{bmatrix}. \tag{4}$$

Then, the receiver computes the following metric to have

$$\mathbf{Z} = \begin{bmatrix} z_1 \\ z_2 \end{bmatrix} = \mathbf{H}^H \mathbf{Y}_r. \tag{5}$$

Due to the orthogonal structure of the Alamouti code, the equalized symbols are calculated as

$$\hat{x}_1 = \frac{z_1}{\|\mathbf{h}_1\|_F^2 + \|\mathbf{h}_2\|_F^2},$$
$$\hat{x}_2 = \frac{z_2}{\|\mathbf{h}_1\|_F^2 + \|\mathbf{h}_1\|_F^2}.$$

Then, the receiver can recover the transmitted symbols via demodulating $\widehat{x}_1$ and $\widehat{x}_2$. According to [6], the encoded symbols are not independent in Alamouti scheme. Taking (1) and (2) as examples, symbols x_1 and x_2 are transmitted in the first time slot. Redundancy related to x_1 and x_2 are transmitted in the second time slot to exploit the diversity gain in spatial domain. Since the same information is transmitted in two consecutive time slots, SE is sacrificed. To make up this shortcoming, in next section, we propose a new scheme to exploit the sequence of the transmitted information in time domain so that one more bit can be carried.

3   Proposed STBC with Additional Spectral Efficiency

To improve the SE, another Alamouti coding pattern is designed by switching the transmitted symbols in two consecutive time slots. Then, the received signal, $\mathbf{Y}^{(N)} = \left[\mathbf{y}_1^{(N)}, \mathbf{y}_2^{(N)} \right]$, at the receiver is given by

$$\text{time slot 1}: \ \mathbf{y}_1^{(N)} = \sqrt{\frac{\rho}{2}} \left(-\mathbf{h}_1 x_2^* + \mathbf{h}_2 x_1^* \right) + \mathbf{N}_1, \tag{6}$$

and

$$\text{time slot 2}: \ \mathbf{y}_2^{(N)} = \sqrt{\frac{\rho}{2}} \left(\mathbf{h}_1 x_1 + \mathbf{h}_2 x_2 \right) + \mathbf{N}_2, \tag{7}$$

where the upper symbol, N, means 'new'. According to (1), (2), (6) and (7), it is observed that the only difference between the *new Alamouti coding pattern* (NAP) and the *classic Alamouti coding pattern* (CAP) is that $-x_2^*$ and x_1^* are transmitted in the first time slot, and x_1 and x_2 are transmitted in the second time slot. Therefore, the orthogonal structure is still preserved in NAP and the simple ML detector can be used to recover the transmitted symbols at the receiver.

In order to carry one more bit, transmitter can select either CAP or NAP scheme in each transmission interval based on the value of a variable, b. When b is equal to zero, CAP is selected. Otherwise, NAP scheme is chosen at the transmitter. The new transmission scheme is demonstrated in Fig. 1.

Fig. 1. Transmission with new STBC scheme

To recover the source symbols, the receiver applies the ML detection twice based on the NAP and CAP pattern, respectively. Assuming the symbols obtained based on NAP pattern are denoted as $\mathbf{x}^{(NAP)} = \left\{ x_1^{(NAP)}, x_2^{(NAP)} \right\}$. On the other hand, the symbols recovered based on CAP are represented as

$\mathbf{x}^{(CAP)} = \left\{ x_1^{(CAP)}, x_2^{(CAP)} \right\}$. Then, replace $\mathbf{a} = \{a_1, a_2\}$ of the following equation with $\mathbf{x}^{(NAP)}$ and $\mathbf{x}^{(CAP)}$,

$$\widehat{\mathbf{y}}_1 = \sqrt{\frac{\rho}{2}} \left(\mathbf{h}_1 a_1 + \mathbf{h}_2 a_2 \right), \tag{8}$$

$$\widehat{\mathbf{y}}_2 = \sqrt{\frac{\rho}{2}} \left(-\mathbf{h}_1 a_2^* + \mathbf{h}_2 a_1^* \right), \tag{9}$$

respectively, to obtain $\mathbf{Y}^{(CAP)} = \left[\widehat{\mathbf{y}}_1^{(CAP)}, \widehat{\mathbf{y}}_2^{(CAP)} \right]$ and $\mathbf{Y}^{(NAP)} = \left[\widehat{\mathbf{y}}_1^{(NAP)}, \widehat{\mathbf{y}}_2^{(NAP)} \right]$. Since the received signal, $\mathbf{Y}$, at the receiver is either equal to $\mathbf{Y}^{(C)}$ or $\mathbf{Y}^{(N)}$, the receiver compares the Frobenius norm $d^{(CAP)} = \left\| \mathbf{Y} - \mathbf{Y}^{(CAP)} \right\|_F^2$ and $d^{(NAP)} = \left\| \mathbf{Y} - \mathbf{Y}^{(NAP)} \right\|_F^2$. If $d^{(CAP)} < d^{(NAP)}$, then $\mathbf{x}^{(CAP)}$ and $b = 0$ are the outputs of the decoder. Otherwise, the decoder outputs $\mathbf{x}^{(NAP)}$ and $b = 1$. According to the above description, the detection scheme at the receiver is concluded in Table 1. Since one more bit is transmitted in the proposed scheme, the SE is improved by $1/\log_2(M)$ when M-ary modulation is used in the system.

Table 1. Detection scheme

Algorithm 1

1: Initialize two vectors, $\mathbf{x}^{(NAP)}$ and $\mathbf{x}^{(CAP)}$. Two matrices, $\mathbf{Y}^{(NAP)}$ and $\mathbf{Y}^{(CAP)}$;
2: Decode received signals based on CAP pattern and ML detection method and output $\mathbf{x}^{(CAP)} = \left\{ x_1^{(CAP)}, x_2^{(CAP)} \right\}$. Then calculate $\mathbf{Y}^{(CAP)}$ based on (10) and (14);
3: Decode received signals based on NAP pattern and ML detection method and output $\mathbf{x}^{(NAP)} = \left\{ x_1^{(NAP)}, x_2^{(NAP)} \right\}$. Then calculate $\mathbf{Y}^{(NAP)}$ based on (10) and (14);
4: Calculate $d^{(CAP)} = \left\| \mathbf{Y} - \mathbf{Y}^{(CAP)} \right\|_F^2$ and $d^{(NAP)} = \left\| \mathbf{Y} - \mathbf{Y}^{(NAP)} \right\|_F^2$;
5: **if** $d^{(CAP)} < d^{(NAP)}$ **then**
6:     $\mathbf{x}^{(CAP)}$ and $b = 0$;
7: **else**
8:     $\mathbf{x}^{(NAP)}$ and $b = 1$;
9: **end if**
10: Demodulate the output symbols based on the constellation of the modulation;

Comparing to the STBC-SM proposed in [8], the new scheme has the advantages on low detection complexity. At the transmitter, it only needs to swap the ST coded symbols of different slots, which is easy to be implemented in practice. At the receiver, the computational complexity is $O(4M)$ in Algorithm 1. On the other hand, the computational complexity at the receiver for STBC-SM is $O(cM^2)$, where c is the number of possible antenna combinations.

The proposed scheme can also be applied to the system with more than two transmit antennas. For example, the STBC $\mathcal{G}_4$ evaluated in [13] uses four transmit antennas and four consecutive time slots. Based on the algorithm 1, there exists 24 STBC patterns by swapping the STBC coded symbols of different time slots. Therefore, $1 \leq b \leq 4$ extra bits can be carried by the new scheme.

4   BER Performance of the Proposed Scheme

In this section, an asymptotic BER performance bound for the proposed scheme is analyzed when *M-ary phase shift keying* (MPSK) or *M-ary quadrature amplitude modulation* (MQAM) modulation are applied. The joint detection scheme represented in Table 1 includes estimation of two quantities: the index bit, b, and transmitted symbols. Therefore, the BER performance is decided by these two processes. Since it is hard to derive a closed-form expression for the joint detection, we assume that the index and symbol estimation processes are independent as [14] to derive a low bound on BER of the proposed scheme. Let p_i be the BER of index estimation given that the symbols are perfectly detected and p_s be the BER of symbol estimation given that the index is perfectly decoded. Then, the BER of the system is lower bounded by

$$p_b \geqslant 1 - (1 - p_i)(1 - p_s). \tag{10}$$

It is noteworthy that Algorithm 1 detects the index bit, b, and transmitted symbols jointly. As a result, the assumption of independent estimation processes is not realistic and cannot reach an accurate BER performance. But with this assumption, we can derive a closed-form BER lower bound for the proposed scheme as presented in (10).

First, we derive the BER of index bit estimation given that symbols, x_1 and x_2, are detected correctly. According to the appendix A, it is low bounded by (32).

Then, we derive the BER of transmitted symbols. Due to the orthogonality of the Alamouti STBC, an Alamouti scheme with two transmit and N_r receive antennas is equivalent to an *maximum ratio combination* (MRC) scheme with one transmit and $2N_r$ receive antennas with 3 dB loss [5]. Under the assumption that the index bit can be recovered correctly, the detection for symbols in our scheme is equal to the detection process for the Alamouti scheme. Therefore, the SER over a Rayleigh fading channel is given by [15]

$$
p_s^{(PSK)} \approx \frac{\alpha}{2c} \left\{ \begin{array}{l} (1 + s\,(0))^{-2N_r} + (1 + s\,(\alpha\pi))^{-2N_r} + \\ 2\sum_{k=1}^{c-1} \left(1 + s\left(\frac{k\alpha\pi}{c}\right)\right)^{-2N_r} \end{array} \right\} \tag{11}
$$

where $\kappa = \sin^2\left(\frac{\pi}{L}\right)$, $\alpha = \frac{M-1}{M}$, $s\,(\omega) = \frac{-\kappa\rho}{\sin^2\omega}$, c is a constant chosen for convergence, when M-ary PSK is used.

On the other hand, when M-ary QAM is used, the SER is expressed as

$$
p_s^{(QAM)} \approx
$$

$$
\frac{a}{c} \left\{ \begin{array}{l} \left(\frac{2}{bp+2}\right)^{N_r} - \frac{a}{2}\left(\frac{1}{bp+1}\right)^{N_r} + \\ (1-a)\sum_{i=1}^{c-1}\left(\frac{S\,(\theta_i)}{bp+S_i}\right)^{N_r} + \sum_{i=c}^{2c-1}\left(\frac{S\,(\theta)}{bp+S_i}\right)^{N_r} \end{array} \right\} \tag{12}
$$

where $a = 1 - \frac{1}{\sqrt{M}}$, $b = \frac{3}{M-1}$, $S\,(\theta_i) = 2\sin^2\theta_i$, $\theta_i = \frac{i\pi}{4n}$, and c is the number of summations. It is demonstrated that the difference between the simulated and theoretical SER for 4QAM configuration is only 0.0015 dB when c is greater than 10.

The BER, p_s, can be then derived from the approximate relationship as

$$
p_s \approx \frac{p_s^{(PSK)} \text{ or } p_s^{(QAM)}}{\log_2(M)}. \tag{13}
$$

Then, according to the (10), we can derive the BER of the proposed new scheme.

5   Numerical Results

In this section, the Monte Carlo simulation results are presented to demonstrate the performance of the proposed scheme. The 16-QAM and 16-PSK based STBC are used as references to validate that the BER of the proposed scheme is close to that of the conventional STBC. Assuming that the receiver has the accurate quasi-static frequency-flat Rayleigh fading channel information and the Gray coded M-QAM and M-PSK constellation points are used in the system. Figure 2 demonstrates the BER performance (SNR versus average BER) of the proposed scheme by the Monte Carlo simulation and analysis in (10) when 16AQM is used. It is evident that the formulated BER is the lower bound of the simulation results, which validate our analysis.

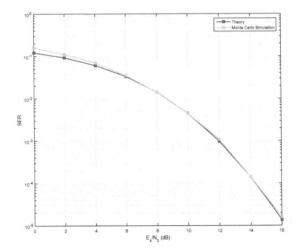

Fig. 2. Validation of analysis on BER for proposed scheme when 16-QAM is used

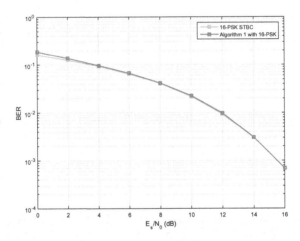

Fig. 3. Monte Carlo simulation results for the proposed and STBC schemes with 16-PSK

In Fig. 3 and 4, we compare the BER performance of the proposed scheme with the classic STBC scheme when 16-PSK and 16-QAM are used, respectively. We can observe that both schemes have the same slop which means our scheme can exploit the same diversity order as the classic STBC. Moreover, the BER performance of the new scheme is very close to that of the classic STBC. Therefore, without sacrificing the BER performance, the new scheme can improve the system SE by 25% when 16-QAM or 16-PSK is used in the system.

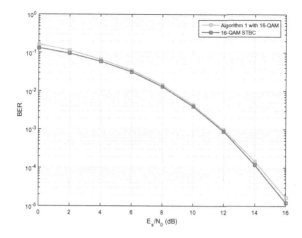

Fig. 4. Monte Carlo simulation results for the proposed and STBC schemes with 16-QAM

6 Conclusion

In this letter, a new STBC scheme is proposed to improve the transmission data rate while retaining the diversity gain of classic STBC scheme. Additional information bits are carried by using different STBC coding patterns in time domain. The efficiency of the scheme has been verified via both analysis and Monte Carlo simulation results. Its BER performance is close to the classic STBC scheme while 1 more bit can be transmitted in $2 \times N_r$ MIMO system. Moreover, the simple detection scheme at receiver is inherited from the classic STBC scheme. Therefore, the proposed scheme is an efficient and practical scheme for MIMO systems.

Acknowledgements. The authors would like to express our appreciation to the financial support of the National Natural Science Foundation of China (Grant No. 61771429), Zhejiang University City College Scientific Research Foundation (No. JZD18002).

A   Bit error rate on index bit

The classic Alamouti scheme and new Alamouti scheme can be described as the following formulas

$$\mathbf{y}_1{}^{(C)} = \sqrt{\tfrac{\rho}{2}}\left(\mathbf{h}_1 x_1 + \mathbf{h}_2 x_2\right) + \mathbf{N}_1, \qquad (14)$$

$$\mathbf{y}_2{}^{(C)} = \sqrt{\tfrac{\rho}{2}}\left(-\mathbf{h}_1 x_2{}^* + \mathbf{h}_2 x_1{}^*\right) + \mathbf{N}_2, \qquad (15)$$

while

$$\mathbf{y}_1{}^{(N)} = \sqrt{\tfrac{\rho}{2}}\left(-\mathbf{h}_1 x_2{}^* + \mathbf{h}_2 x_1{}^*\right) + \mathbf{N}_1, \tag{16}$$

$$\mathbf{y}_2{}^{(N)} = \sqrt{\tfrac{\rho}{2}}\left(\mathbf{h}_1 x_1 + \mathbf{h}_2 x_2\right) + \mathbf{N}_2, \tag{17}$$

where each entry of both $\mathbf{h}_i$ and $\mathbf{N}_i$ is distributed as $CN(0,1)$, $\mathbb{E}\left[|x_i|^2\right] = 1$. Let $\mathbf{Y}^{(C)} = \left[\mathbf{y}_1^{(C)}, \mathbf{y}_2^{(C)}\right]$, $\mathbf{Y}^{(N)} = \left[\mathbf{y}_1^{(N)}, \mathbf{y}_2^{(N)}\right]$ and $\mathbf{H} = [\mathbf{h}_1, \mathbf{h}_2]$. We derive the bit error rate of index bit estimation given that symbols, x_1 and x_2, are detected correctly. The *symbol error rate* (SER) of the index given the CSI can be expressed as

$$P_e\left(e \mid \mathbf{H}\right) = P\left(\mathbf{Y}^{(C)} \rightarrow \mathbf{Y}^{(N)}\right)$$
$$= P\left(\left\|\mathbf{Y} - \mathbf{Y}^{(N)}\right\|_F^2 < \left\|\mathbf{Y} - \mathbf{Y}^{(C)}\right\|_F^2\right) \tag{18}$$

Further we have

$$P\left(A + B \leq \left(\|\mathbf{N}_1\|_F^2 + \|\mathbf{N}_1\|_F^2\right)\right), \tag{19}$$

where

$$A = \left\|\sqrt{\tfrac{\rho}{2}}\mathbf{h}_1\left(x_1 + x_2^*\right) + \sqrt{\tfrac{\rho}{2}}\mathbf{h}_2\left(x_2 - x_1^*\right) + \mathbf{N}_1\right\|_F^2, \tag{20}$$

$$B = \left\|\sqrt{\tfrac{\rho}{2}}\mathbf{h}_1\left(x_1 + x_2^*\right) + \sqrt{\tfrac{\rho}{2}}\mathbf{h}_2\left(x_2 - x_1^*\right) + \mathbf{N}_2\right\|_F^2. \tag{21}$$

The equivalent model is given by

$$P_e\left(e \mid \mathbf{H}\right) =$$
$$P\left(\left\|\sqrt{\tfrac{\rho}{2}}\mathbf{h}_1 s_1 + \sqrt{\tfrac{\rho}{2}}\mathbf{h}_1 s_1 + \mathbf{N}_1\right\|_F^2 \leq \|\mathbf{N}_1\|_F^2\right), \tag{22}$$

where $s_1 = x_1 + x_2^*$, $s_2 = x_2 - x_1^*$.
Then we can get the following formulas,

$$P_e\left(e \mid \mathbf{H}\right) =$$
$$P\left(\begin{array}{c}\tfrac{\rho}{2}\|\mathbf{h}_1 s_1 + \mathbf{h}_2 s_2\|_F^2 + \\ 2\sqrt{\tfrac{\rho}{2}}\mathbb{R}\left\{\left(\mathbf{h}_1 s_1 + \mathbf{h}_2 s_2\right)\mathbf{N}_1{}^*\right\} \leq 0\end{array}\right), \tag{23}$$

$$P_e\left(e \mid \mathbf{H}\right) =$$
$$P\left(\mathbb{R}\left\{(\mathbf{h}_1 + \mathbf{h}_2)\,\mathbf{N}_1{}^*\right\} \geq \sqrt{\frac{\rho}{8}}\|\mathbf{h}_1 s_1 + \mathbf{h}_2 s_2\|_F^2\right). \tag{24}$$

According to the previous formulas, we can get the conclusion that $\mathbb{R}\left\{(\mathbf{h}_1 s_1 + \mathbf{h}_2 s_2)\,\mathbf{N}_1^*\right\}$ is distributed as $CN\left(0, \frac{1}{2}\|\mathbf{h}_1 s_1 + \mathbf{h}_2 s_2\|_F^2\right)$.

In order to normalize $\mathbb{R}\left\{(\mathbf{h}_1 s_1 + \mathbf{h}_2 s_2)\,\mathbf{N}_1^*\right\}$ and convert $P_e\left(e \mid \mathbf{H}\right)$ to Q function,

$$P_e\left(e \mid \mathbf{H}\right) =$$
$$P\left(\frac{\mathbb{R}\left\{(\mathbf{h}_1 s_1 + \mathbf{h}_2 s_2)\,\mathbf{N}_1{}^*\right\}}{\sqrt{\frac{1}{2}\|\mathbf{h}_1 s_1 + \mathbf{h}_2 s_2\|_F^2}} \geq \frac{\sqrt{\frac{\rho}{8}}\|\mathbf{h}_1 s_1 + \mathbf{h}_2 s_2\|_F^2}{\sqrt{\frac{1}{2}\|\mathbf{h}_1 s_1 + \mathbf{h}_2 s_2\|_F^2}}\right), \tag{25}$$

$$P_e\left(e \mid \mathbf{H}\right) = Q\left(\sqrt{\frac{\rho}{4}}\|\mathbf{h}_1 s_1 + \mathbf{h}_2 s_2\|_F^2\right). \tag{26}$$

Based on $\|A + B\|^2 \leq \|A\|^2 + \|B\|^2$,

$$P_e\left(e \mid \mathbf{H}\right) = Q\left(\sqrt{\frac{\rho}{4}}\|\mathbf{h}_1 s_1 + \mathbf{h}_2 s_2\|_F^2\right)$$
$$\geq Q\left(\sqrt{\frac{\rho}{4}\left(\|\mathbf{h}_1 s_1\|_F^2 + \|\mathbf{h}_2 s_2\|_F^2\right)}\right). \tag{27}$$

Based on Trapezoidal rule we have

$$P_e\left(e \mid \mathbf{H}\right) \geq$$
$$\frac{1}{2n}\left[\frac{1}{2}\exp\left(-\frac{\rho\left(\|\mathbf{h}_1 s_1\|_F^2 + \|\mathbf{h}_2 s_2\|_F^2\right)}{8}\right) + \sum_{k=1}^{n-1}\exp\left(-\frac{\rho\left(\|\mathbf{h}_1 s_1\|_F^2 + \|\mathbf{h}_2 s_2\|_F^2\right)}{8\sin^2\left(\frac{k\pi}{2n}\right)}\right)\right]. \tag{28}$$

We assume that $\gamma_1 = \rho\|\mathbf{h}_1\|_F^2$ and $\gamma_2 = \rho\|\mathbf{h}_2\|_F^2$,

$$P_e\left(e \mid \mathbf{H}\right) \geq$$
$$\frac{1}{2n}\left[\frac{1}{2}\exp\left(-\frac{\gamma_1\|s_1\|_F^2 + \gamma_2\|s_2\|_F^2}{2}\right) + \sum_{k=1}^{n-1}\exp\left(-\frac{\gamma_1\|s_1\|_F^2 + \gamma_2\|s_2\|_F^2}{2\sin^2\left(\frac{k\pi}{2n}\right)}\right)\right]. \tag{29}$$

Through the above formula, $P_e(e)$ can be computed as

$$P_e(e) \geq \int_0^\infty \int_0^\infty \frac{1}{2n} \left[\begin{array}{c} \frac{1}{2} \exp\left(-\frac{\gamma_1 \|s_1\|_F^2 + \gamma_2 \|s_2\|_F^2}{2} \right) \\ + \sum_{k=1}^{n-1} \exp\left(-\frac{\gamma_1 \|s_1\|_F^2 + \gamma_2 \|s_2\|_F^2}{2 \sin^2\left(\frac{k\pi}{2n}\right)} \right) \end{array} \right] \qquad (30)$$
$$f(\gamma_1) f(\gamma_2) \, d\gamma_1 \, d\gamma_2.$$

Define the moment generating function $M_s(s)$ as

$$M_s(s) = \int_0^\infty e^{-s\gamma} f_\gamma(\gamma) \, d\gamma = \left(\frac{1}{1+s\gamma} \right)^{N_R}. \qquad (31)$$

Put $P_e(e)$ into function $M_s(s)$, we finally have

$$P_e(e) \geq$$
$$\frac{1}{2n} \left[\begin{array}{c} \frac{1}{2} M_s\left(\frac{1}{2} |s_1|^2 \right) M_s\left(\frac{1}{2} |s_2|^2 \right) + \\ \sum_{k=1}^{n-1} M_s\left(\frac{1}{2 \sin^2\left(\frac{k\pi}{2n}\right)} |S_1|^2 \right) M_s\left(\frac{1}{2 \sin^2\left(\frac{k\pi}{2n}\right)} |S_2|^2 \right) \end{array} \right]. \qquad (32)$$

References

1. Andrews, J.G., et al.: What will 5G be? IEEE J. Selected Areas in Commun. **32**(6), 1065–1082 (2014)
2. Larsson, E., Edfors, O., Tufvesson, F., Marzetta, T.: Massive MIMO for next generation wireless systems. IEEE Commun. Magaz. **52**(2), 186–195 (2014)
3. Gesbert, D., Shafi, M., Shiu, D.: From theory to practice: an overview of MIMO space-time coded wireless systems. IEEE J. Sel. Area Commun. **21**(3), 281–302 (2003)
4. H. Jafarkhani, Space-time coding: theory and practice[M]. *Cambridge university press* (2005)
5. Alamouti, S.: A simple transmit diversity technique for wireless communications. IEEE J. Sel. Area Commun. **16**(8), 1451–1458 (1998)
6. Ling, Q., Li, T.: Efficiency improvment for Alamouti Codes. In: Proceedings of 40th IEEE CISS, Princeton. pp. 569–572 (2006)
7. Baloch, Z.A., Baloch, M.U., Hussain, N.: Efficiency improvement of space time block codes. Int. J Commun. Network Syst. Sci. **3**, 507–510 (2010)
8. Basar, E., Aygolu, U., Panayirci, E., Poor, H.V.: Space-time block coded spatial modulation. IEEE Trans. Commun. **59**(3), 823–832 (2011)
9. Helmy, A.G., Di Renzo, M., Al-Dhahir, N.: Differential spatially modulated space-time block codes with temporal permutations. IEEE Trans. Veh. Technol. **66**(8), 7548–7552 (2017)
10. Li, X., Wang, L.: High rate space-time block coded spatial modulation with cyclic structure. IEEE Commun. Letters **18**(4), 532–535 (2014)

11. Zhu, Y., Wang, W., Zhang, J., Zhang, Y.: Constellation collaborated nonlinear orthogonal space-time block codes with fast maximum likelihood detection. IEEE Trans. Vehic. Techn. **66**(1), 513–528 (2016)
12. Hua, Y., Zhao, G., Zhao, W., Jin, M.: Modified codewords design for space-time block coded spatial modulation. IET Commun. **11**(2), 249–257 (2017)
13. Tarokh, V., Jafarkhani, H., Calderbank, A.: Space-time block coding for wireless communications: performance results. IEEE J. Selected Areas in Commun. **17**(3), 451–460 (2017)
14. Mesleh, R., Haas, H., Sinanovic, S., Chang, A., Sangboh, Y.: Spatial modulation. IEEE Trans. Veh. Technol. **57**(4), 2228–2241 (2008)
15. Jafarkhani, H.: Space-Time Coding. Cambidge University Press, Theory and Practice (2005)

Emerging Technologies and Applications in Mobile Networks and Management

A Video Surveillance Network for Airport Ground Moving Targets

Xiang Zhang[1](✉) and Yi Qiao[2]

[1] University of Electronic Science and Technology of China, Chengdu, China
`uestchero@uestc.edu.cn`
[2] The Second Research Institute of the Civil Aviation Administration of China,
Chengdu, China
`qiaoyiqq@hotmail.com`

Abstract. In this paper we describe an airport ground movement surveillance network. Airport ground videos are captured by multiple cameras, and than transmitted to the airport control center based on the optical fiber network. On the high-performance servers in the control center, various intelligent applications process video data, visualize the processing results and provide them to the air traffic controllers as a reference for airport management. Moving object detection is the foundation of many video based intelligent applications in airport surveillance. We propose detecting the moving objects in the airport ground by the use of the prior knowledge, that is, the airport ground made of cement has a gray-white color distribution. Based on this fact, firstly we use a dual-mode Gaussian distribution to fit the color distribution of the ground. Next, based on the fitted distribution we build a prior model, where pixels near the class boundary are more likely to be classified as the foreground. Finally, the prior model is used to detect moving targets within a Bayesian classification framework. Experiments are conducted on the AGVS benchmark and the results demonstrate the effectiveness of the proposed moving object detection algorithm.

Keywords: Airport ground surveillance · Moving object detection

1 Introduction

With the continuous growth of civil aviation traffic, the airport ground is getting busier and crowded. The airport must be more intelligent to face operation and capacity challenges. Compared with the common Secondary Radar or Automatic Dependent Surveillance-Broadcast (ADS-B) [1], video data contains more information, so video based intelligent surveillance is more promising in the next generation of airport management system. Since the airport ground is very broad, it needs a network of multiple cameras to cover the whole monitoring area. Furthermore, the coding and transmission of video data must be considered in such a video surveillance system. In the control center, various intelligent applications

© ICST Institute for Computer Sciences, Social Informatics and Telecommunications Engineering 2020
Published by Springer Nature Switzerland AG 2020. All Rights Reserved
S. W. Loke et al. (Eds.): MONAMI 2020, LNICST 338, pp. 229–237, 2020.
https://doi.org/10.1007/978-3-030-64002-6_15

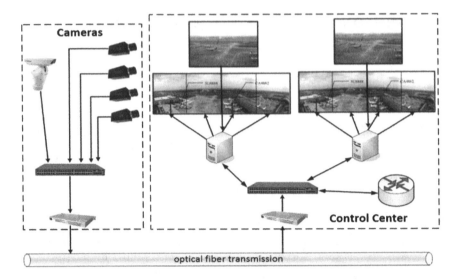

Fig. 1. Illustration of the airport ground video surveillance network.

can be developed based on video data, e.g. visual guidance and conflict alert. The foundation of most such applications is moving object detection [2], which aims to extract the moving targets on the ground from video sequences.

In this paper we present an airport ground movement surveillance network. Multiple cameras form a monitoring network covering the whole airport ground. Captured video data is transmitted to the airport control center based on a dedicated optical network. The video data format is H264. For various intelligent applications running in the control center, we propose a method of moving object detection which is specially used for ground surveillance. This method takes use of the prior knowledge in ground, that is, the airport ground made of cement has a gray-white color distribution. Based on this fact, firstly we use a dual-mode Gaussian distribution to fit the color distribution of the ground. Next, based on the fitted distribution we build a prior model, where pixels near the class boundary are more likely to be classified as the foreground. Finally, the prior model is used to detect moving targets within a Bayesian classification framework. Experiments are conducted on the AGVS benchmark [5] to evaluate the effectiveness of the proposed method.

The rest of the paper is organized as follows. The airport ground movement surveillance network is shortly described in Sect. 2. Section 3 presents details of the proposed moving object detection algorithm. Experimental results are shown in Sect. 4, followed by the conclusion in Sect. 5.

2   Proposed Surveillance Network

The airport ground movement surveillance network is shown in Fig. 1. Multiple cameras including both fixed and PTZ cameras, are installed around the airport.

Fig. 2. Spliced video in the airport ground video surveillance network.

Captured videos in the form of H264 are transmitted to the control center with a dedicated high-speed optical fiber network. In the control center, video data is processed and displayed on a large screen. Since the airport ground is very broad and the field of view of a single camera is limited, it is necessary to splice the videos based on the camera's geometry relationship. The spliced video is shown in Fig. 2. Based on the splice video, various intelligent applications can be developed. Next we introduce the proposed moving object detection algorithm, which is able to support high-precision upper applications.

3 Moving Object Detection

The most widely used strategy in moving object detection is unsupervised statistical modeling, which has been studied for more than twenty years. In recent years, the supervised moving object detection based on deep learning is rising, but this method has not met the requirements of real applications. Some statistical methods only model the background [3], while others build multi-layer models for the scene, such as bilayer modeling [4]. Our method belongs to the category of bilayer modeling. Since the prior knowledge of the airport ground is employed in our method, the proposed method is more accurate than the previous methods.

3.1 Overall Framework

First we give some notations. Let $\mathbf{Z}^t = \{\mathbf{z}_i^t\}$ be a frame at time t, each pixel $\mathbf{z}_i^t$ is a 3-tuple RGB vector, where i is the position index of pixels. For ease of notation, we may omit the superscript and subscript in case of no confusion. Let $\mathbf{L} = \{l_i\}$ be a binary silhouette map, where $l_i \in \{\mathcal{F}, \mathcal{B}\}$, with $\mathcal{F} = 1$ denoting foreground and $\mathcal{B} = 0$ referring to background. In the Bayesian classification framework, moving object detection is the Maximum Posterior Probability (MAP) estimation of $P(\mathbf{L}|\mathbf{Z})$

$$P(\mathbf{L}|\mathbf{Z}) \propto P(\mathbf{Z}|\mathbf{L})P(\mathbf{L}), \tag{1}$$

where $P(\mathbf{Z}|\mathbf{L})$ and $P(\mathbf{L})$ are the likelihood term and smoothness term, respectively. In our method, a prior model is presented and used in conjunction with

 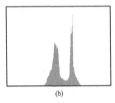 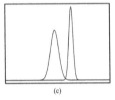 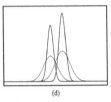

(a)   (b)   (c)   (d)

Fig. 3. (a) is one frame from sequence *S19* in the AGVS benchmark, and (b) is the gray histogram of (a). (c) is the fitted dual-model Gaussian distributions of (b). (d) shows the prior model with different σ.

the traditional bilayer model for classification. Therefore, the likelihood term in Eq. 1 consists of two terms

$$P(\mathbf{Z}|\mathbf{L}) = P_1(\mathbf{Z}|\mathbf{L})P_2(\mathbf{Z}|\mathbf{L}),\tag{2}$$

where $P_1(\mathbf{Z}|\mathbf{L})$ and $P_2(\mathbf{Z}|\mathbf{L})$ separately correspond to the prior model and the traditional bilayer mdoel. Next, we introduce each model in our method, the smoothness term and the optimization of Eq. 1.

3.2   Prior Model

The prior model is based on the prior knowledge in the ground, that is, miss-detections of moving object detection in ground surveillance are mainly caused by the camouflage phenomenon, which means the foreground and background share similar color distributions. Furthermore, the camouflage in ground surveillance occurs between the gray-white airport ground and airplanes dominated by white. In other words, the gray-white areas have a higher probability of camouflage occurrence. We compute the gray histogram of Fig. 3a, as shown in Fig. 3b. Figure 3a is from the AGVS benchmark, which is a special dataset for the research of airport ground surveillance. We can see that there are two significant peaks in the gray histogram. Because the airport ground is the main area in all videos of AGVS, we can infer that the two peaks in each histogram correspond to the gray and white areas of the airport ground, respectively. based on the least square method, we use a bimodal Gaussian distribution to fit the gray histogram

$$p_h(\mathbf{z}_i) = \sum_{r=1}^{2} \hat{\omega}_r \mathcal{N}(\mathbf{z}_i; \hat{\mu}_r, \hat{\sigma}_r),\tag{3}$$

where $\hat{\omega}_r$ is the weight of each Gaussian component, and $\hat{\mu}_r$ and $\hat{\sigma}_r$ are the mean and standard deviation of the ith Gaussian component.

We compute the dual-model Gaussian distribution of Fig. 3b, as shown in Fig. 3c. It can be seen that this bimodal model does reflect the probability of camouflage occurring in different gray pixels to a certain extent, because the largest camouflage probability is at the gray and white pixels of the ground, and the larger the gray difference from the ground pixel, the smaller the probability of camouflage occurrence. Next, we define the prior model as the conditional probability of σ

$$p_h(\mathbf{z}_i|\sigma) = \sum_{r=1}^{2} \hat{\omega}_r \mathcal{N}(\mathbf{z}_i; \hat{\mu}_r, \sigma), \tag{4}$$

where $\hat{\omega}_r$ and $\hat{\mu}_r$ are the same as in Eq. 3, σ is a variable parameter, and the two Gaussian components have the same σ. The prior model with different σ is shown in Fig. 3d. We can see that when σ is small, the camouflage probability of different pixels varies greatly (black curve), while when σ is large, the camouflage probability difference of pixels becomes small (red curve). When σ is infinite, the camouflage probability of all pixels is equal, which means this prior model does not work.

We have known that in the case of camouflage, classification tends to the background. The purpose of designing the prior model is to force the classification to the moving object when camouflage occurs, thus compensating the algorithm for the background bias. This is achieved by $P_1(\mathbf{Z}|\mathbf{L})$ in Eq. 2. Let $\alpha = \max[p_h(\mathbf{z}_i)]$ and β be the scale factor, first we define two probability items based on the prior model, $\beta(1 + p_h(\mathbf{z}_i|\sigma)/\alpha)$ and $\beta(1 - p_h(\mathbf{z}_i|\sigma)/\alpha)$. The scale factor β determines the absolute difference between the two probability terms. Next we construct $P_1(\mathbf{Z}|\mathbf{L})$ with the two probability items as

$$P_1(\mathbf{Z}|\mathbf{L}) = \prod_i [\beta(1 + \frac{p_h(\mathbf{z}_i|\sigma)}{\alpha})]^{l_n} [\beta(1 - \frac{p_h(\mathbf{z}_i|\sigma)}{\alpha})]^{1-l_n}. \tag{5}$$

In the framework of MAP, the meaning of Eq. 5 is that, if $\beta(1 + p_h(\mathbf{z}_i|\sigma)/\alpha)$ is larger than $\beta(1 - p_h(\mathbf{z}_i|\sigma)/\alpha)$, $\mathbf{z}_i$ is more likely to be classified as foreground. It can be seen that Eq. 5 does achieve our goal that the greater the camouflage probability, the higher the probability of being classified as foreground.

3.3   Traditional Bilayer Model

The traditional bilayer model is used in conjunction with the prior model for classification. We construct the bilayer model with the same manner as in [6], where a non-parametric model is separately kept for the background and foreground. Assuming the foreground probability and background probability based on the bilayer model are $p_f(\mathbf{z}_i)$ and $p_b(\mathbf{z}_i)$, respectively, the $P_2(\mathbf{Z}|\mathbf{L})$ in Eq. 2 is constructed as

$$P_2(\mathbf{Z}|\mathbf{L}) = \prod_i p_f(\mathbf{z}_i)^{l_n} p_b(\mathbf{z}_i)^{1-l_n}. \tag{6}$$

3.4   Smoothness Term and Optimization

The smoothness term allows to enforce the spatial coherence of pixel labels into the classification process. We use the Potts smoothness term as in [7]. Now we have all the probability terms in Eq. 1, and the MAP estimation of $P(\mathbf{L}|\mathbf{Z})$ is the final result of moving object detection. We convert the MAP estimation to an energy minimization problem. There have been many graph cut methods for energy minimization, and we use the α-expansion method in [8].

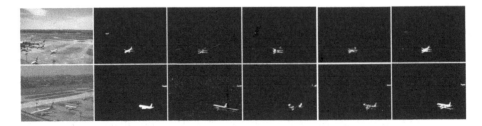

Fig. 4. Left to right: two frames in *S1* and *S21*, ground truth, KDE [12], KNN [10], Bodids [6] and the proposed method, respectively.

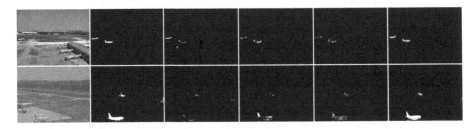

Fig. 5. Left to right: two frames in *S12* and *S20*, ground truth, SOBS [15], PBAS [14], CodeBook [11] and the proposed method, respectively.

4   Experimental Results

Comparative experiments are shown in this section. Ten state-of-the-art unsupervised algorithms with available public codes are chosen for comparison: SuB-SENSE [9], KNN [10], Bodids [6], CodeBook [11], KDE [12], ViBe [13], PBAS [14], SOBS [15], GMM [16], FGMM [17]. The AGVS dataset is used as the benchmark dataset. Next, we separately describe the experimental setting, qualitative analysis and quantitative analysis.

4.1   Experimental Setting

There are several parameters in the proposed method, e.g. $\hat{\omega}_1$, $\hat{\omega}_2$, $\hat{\mu}_1$, $\hat{\mu}_2$, α, β and σ. Among them, $\hat{\omega}_1$, $\hat{\omega}_2$, $\hat{\mu}_1$, $\hat{\mu}_2$ and α are learned from the gray histogram during the operation of the algorithm. Therefore, two parameter, β and σ, needs to be tuned in our method. An empirical way is adopted in our method to set the two parameters, that is, optional values of one parameter are tested while with the other parameter fixed, and we choose the one resulting in the best detection result by visual observation. With such a method, we set the two parameters as $\beta = 0.11$ and $\sigma = 3$.

4.2   Qualitative Analysis

The detection results of some algorithms are shown from in Fig. 4 and Fig. 5. Mild camouflage is shown in Fig. 4, where the white-dominated airplanes are

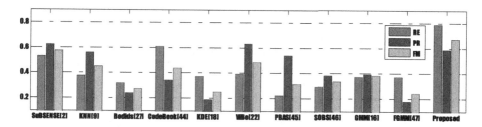

Fig. 6. Detection performance of 11 algorithms on AGVS.

moving on the gray area of the ground. We can see that the detection results by the proposed method are the most complete. The camouflage in Fig. 5 is more severe than in Fig. 4. The aircraft in Fig. 5 are all white, and the ground area they pass through is also bright white. Therefore, the detection defect of each comparison algorithm in Fig. 5 is very serious. The proposed method is effective for this severe camouflage, and its detection results are still the most complete. In fact, in addition to camouflage, Fig. 4 and Fig. 5 contain other challenges, e.g. shadow. It can be seen that the presented method is invalid for shadow.

4.3   Quantitative Analysis

We choose RE, PR and F-measure (FM) for quantitative comparison of detection accuracy:

$$RE = \frac{TP}{TP + FN}, \quad PR = \frac{TP}{TP + FP}$$

and

$$FM = \frac{2 \times RE \times PR}{RE + PR},$$

where TP, FP and FN are the numbers of true positives, false positives and false negatives, respectively. Higher RE means less detection defects, and higher PR indicates less detection noises. FM is the comprehensive result of RE and PR. When both RE and PR are close to 1, FM is also close to 1. When either RE or PR deteriorates, FM will also decrease.

Average RE, PR and FM of all methods on the AGVS dataset are shown in Fig. 6. PTZ videos are not considered, because unsupervised algorithms cannot deal with this problem. We can see that the proposed method has the best RE on all sequences, and compared with other algorithms, the RE is much improved. This means the defect detection due to camouflage is greatly improved by our method. Particularly, the presented method does not have the best PR on most sequences, which indicates the increase of false positives compared with other algorithms. As shown in Fig. 4, increased false positives are mainly the missclassified shadowed pixels. This problem may be resolved by using shadow removal as post-processing. Regarding with the computational time, our method can achieve the processing speed of 15 FPS on Intel i7 processor, which meets the requirements of practical applications.

5   Conclusion

An airport ground movement surveillance network was introduced in this paper. This system consisted of three parts, multiple cameras, optical fiber transmission and control center. There was multiple intelligent applications in the control center and moving object detection was the basis of most such applications. A new moving object detection algorithm was proposed by the use of the prior knowledge of airport ground. This method included a prior model and the traditional bilayer model, and the final classification was achieved via energy minimization. Experimental results on the AGVS benchmark demonstrated the effectiveness of the proposed method.

Acknowledgement. This work was supported by National Natural Science Foundation of China (U1733111, U19A2052), Key R&D projects in Sichuan Province (2020YFG0037), and Sichuan Science and Technology Achievement Transformation project (2020ZHCG0015).

References

1. Yang, H., Zhou, Q., Yao, M., Lu, R., Li, H., Zhang, X.: A practical and compatible cryptographic solution to ADS-B security. IEEE Internet Things J. **6**(2), 3322–3334 (2019)
2. Roy, S.M., Ghosh, A.: Foreground segmentation using adaptive 3 pahse background model. IEEE Trans. Intell. Transp. Syst. (2020, forthcoming)
3. Zhong, Z., Zhang, B., Lu, G., Zhao, Y., Xu, Y.: An adaptive background modeling method for foreground segmentation. IEEE Trans. Intell. Transp. Syst. **18**(5), 1109–1121 (2017)
4. Hao, J.Y., Li, C., Kim, Z., Xiong, Z.: Spatio-temporal traffic scene modeling for object motion detection. IEEE Trans. Intell. Transp. Syst. **14**(1), 295–302 (2013)
5. http://www.agvs-caac.com/
6. Sheikh, Y., Shah, M.: Bayesian modeling of dynamic scenes for object detection. IEEE Trans. Pattern Anal. Mach. Intell. **27**(11), 1778–1792 (2005)
7. Zabih, R., Kolmogorv, V.: Spatially coherent clustering using graph cuts. In: Proceedings of IEEE Conference on Computer Vision and Pattern Recognition (2004)
8. Boykov, Y., Veksler, O., Zabih, R.: Fast approximate energy minimization via graph cuts. IEEE Trans. Pattern Anal. Mach. Intell. **23**(11), 1222–1239 (2001)
9. Charles, P.L.S., Bilodeau, G.A., Bergevin, R.: SuBSENSE: a universal change detection method with local adaptive sensitivity. IEEE Trans. Image Process. **24**(1), 359–373 (2015)
10. Zivkovic, Z., Heijden, F.V.D.: Efficient adaptive density estimation per image pixel for the task of background subtraction. Pattern Recogn. Lett. **27**(7), 773–780 (2006)
11. Kim, K., Chalidabhongse, T.H., Harwood, D., Davis, L.: Real-time foreground-background segmentation using codebook model. Real-Time Imaging **11**, 172–185 (2005)
12. Elgammal, A., Duraiswami, R., Harwood, D., Davis, L.S.: Background and foreground modeling using non-parametric kernel density estimation for visual surveillance. Proc. IEEE **90**(7), 1151–1163 (2002)

13. Barnich, O., Droogenbroeck, M.V.: Vibe: a universal background subtraction algorithm for video sequences. IEEE Trans. Image Process. **20**(6), 1709–1724 (2011)
14. Hofmann, M., Tiefenbacher, P., Rigoll, G.: Background segmentation with feedback: the pixel-based adaptive segmenter. In: Proceedings of IEEE Workshop on Change Detection (2012)
15. Maddalena, L., Petrosino, A.: The SOBS algorithm: what are the limits? In: Proceedings of IEEE Workshop on Change Detection (2012)
16. Stauffer, C., Grimson, W.E.L.: Learning patterns of activity using real-time tracking. IEEE Trans. Pattern Anal. Mach. Intell. **22**(8), 747–757 (2000)
17. El Baf, F., Bouwmans, T., Vachon, B.: Type-2 fuzzy mixture of gaussians model: application to background modeling. In: Bebis, G., et al. (eds.) ISVC 2008. LNCS, vol. 5358, pp. 772–781. Springer, Heidelberg (2008). https://doi.org/10.1007/978-3-540-89639-5_74

Characterizing Latency Performance in Private Blockchain Network

Xuan Chen, Kien Nguyen$^{(\boxtimes)}$, and Hiroo Sekiya

Graduate School of Science and Engineering,
Chiba University, 1-33, Yayoi-cho, Inage-ku, Chiba-shi, Chiba, Japan
{chenxuan,nguyen}@chiba-u.jp, sekiya@faculty.chiba-u.jp

Abstract. There has recently been an increasing number of blockchain applications in different realms. Among the popular blockchain technologies, Ethereum is an emerging platform featuring smart contracts with the public Ethereum associated to the Ether currency. Besides, the private Ethereum has been gaining interest due to its applicability to the Internet of Things. An Ethereum blockchain network includes distributed records that are immutable and transparent through replicating among network nodes. Ethereum manages information in blocks that are submitted to the chain as transactions. This paper aims to characterize latency performance in the private Ethereum blockchain network. Initially, we clarify two perspectives of latency according to the lifecycle of transactions (transaction-oriented and block-oriented latency). We then construct a real private blockchain network with a laptop and Raspberry Pi 3b+ for the latency measurement. We write and deploy a smart contract to read and write data to the blockchain and measure the latencies in a baseline and realistic scenario. The experiment results reveal the latencies-hop correlation, as well as the latencies' relation in different workloads. Moreover, the blockchain network spends averagely 63.92 ms (except the mining time) to take one transaction into effect in one hop.

Keywords: Private blockchain · Ethereum · Latency · Transaction-oriented · Block-oriented

1 Introduction

Blockchain technology has been gaining popularity with the applications in many realms, including finance [1], healthcare [2], and the Internet of Things (IoT) [3]. A blockchain network is a distributed ledger, which can be replicated and shared among its nodes. Blockchain networks are transparent because any node can view all historical records. Also, the records are immutable because they are reserved eternally under 51% rule [4]. Thus, using blockchain, we can build a network that allows nodes to share information without trusting each other. All information submitted to a blockchain is formed as transactions. The mining nodes, which hold a full copy of the blockchain, can verify transactions and generate new blocks through the proof-of-work (PoW) consensus protocol. The blockchain networks

© ICST Institute for Computer Sciences, Social Informatics and Telecommunications Engineering 2020
Published by Springer Nature Switzerland AG 2020. All Rights Reserved
S. W. Loke et al. (Eds.): MONAMI 2020, LNICST 338, pp. 238–255, 2020.
https://doi.org/10.1007/978-3-030-64002-6_16

are divided into two categories: public and private. The former is known as a "permissionless" network. Anyone can join and leave a public blockchain network unrestrictedly. On the contrary, the latter is a "permissioned" network. Nodes need to be permitted by an administrator to join a private blockchain network [5].

The open-source Ethereum [6] is one of the most popular blockchain platforms. The public Ethereum network (Mainnet) is associated with the *Ether* cryptocurrency (i.e., similar to the well-known Bitcoin [7]). On the other hand, Ethereum allows users to deploy a private network with a self-configured genesis file. Ethereum features smart contracts that are self-executed computer programs without an external trusted authority. Ethereum executes the smart contracts in the Ethereum Virtual Machine (EVM) [8], in which the operations are activated by transactions. Once a node receives a new block, it verifies and runs functions triggered by the transaction. The blockchain mechanism ensures the execution outcomes are the same across nodes among a blockchain network.

The private Ethereum shows a substantial potential for the IoT system, which includes a group of devices. The devices typically cooperate and share information via wireless communication. In such a context, the smart contracts, which are immutable and transparent, can allow sharing information among trustless IoT nodes. Those characteristics significantly improve the IoT devices' cooperation [9]. Besides, the blockchain can extend the scalability of the IoT system with the distribution of records. It hence avoids a single point failure due to decentralized nature. One of the promising IoT applications for private Ethereum is in smart-home scenarios [10,11], which allows home appliances to store, share or modify states cooperatively. Therefore, it is crucial to understand the Ethereum performance for those scenarios.

In this research, we characterize the latency of information propagation in a private blockchain-based IoT scenario. We clarify latencies in two propagation steps as the transaction-oriented and block-oriented latency while ignoring the mining process time. We then investigate those latency values in a testbed. The testbed includes a laptop and four Raspberry Pi 3b+ aiming to mimic a home-based IoT application. The devices form a private Ethereum blockchain network wherein there is a preloaded smart contract to read and write strings to the blockchain. We measure the dissemination of writing-related transactions in a baseline and a realistic scenario. The measurement results show that the latency increases proportionally to the hop number in the realistic scenario. Besides, the transaction-oriented latency is lower than the block-oriented latency when the number of transactions is small. The opposite is observed when the number of transactions is relatively large. The total latency (without the mining time) indicates that the system spends averagely 63.92, 117.39, 172.38, and 229.21 ms to propagate a single transaction effectively in one, two, three, four hops, respectively.

The remainder of the paper is organized as follows. Section 2 presents related works. In Sect. 3, we introduce the background and our methodology. Section 4 describes the experiment setting and evaluation results. Finally, Sect. 5 concludes the paper and introduces the future works.

2   Related Work

The current IoT is constructed on a central server model, in which all devices have to connect to the server to ensure the authentication and communication [12]. The model may have issues, for example, when dealing with scalability [13]. Thus, it is essential to transfer a centralized model to a decentralized one [12]. The blockchain technology is attractive as one of the candidates for decentralizing IoT systems. In [14], the author discusses the possibility of blockchain to strengthen IoT. The work in [15] provides a comprehensive review and analysis of blockchain solutions for the IoT systems. It also shows the potential of integrating blockchain and IoT to solve current IoT issues.

There have already been many interested in combining the blockchain and IoT aiming to accelerate their adoption speeds [16]. In [3], the authors described a survey of the state-of-the-art combinations between the technologies. The blockchain enables a distributed peer-to-peer (P2P) network in which nodes don't need to trust other nodes through a trusted third party. This feature means that the nodes can reach a reconciliation faster and potentially increases the network scalability. Moreover, the utilization of smart contracts makes it possible for researchers and developers to fulfill the different demands of the IoT. With smart contracts, IoT devices can run multi-step processes automatically in a distributed method.

Up to date, there are many applications in which the blockchain has been beneficial for IoT networks. In [17], the authors proposed to use Ethereum to manage IoT devices. However, they only show proof of concept in a scenario with a limited number of IoT devices. In [11], the authors presented an overview of the private Ethereum blockchain-based smart home system (SHS). The SHS is defined as an integration of home appliances and sensors, which obtain and share information for each other. The presented SHS used a smart home miner to manage the private blockchain, and several non-mining sensors to deliver data to local storage. In [10], the authors presented a more realistic smart home application with a private Ethereum blockchain, which composes of four major components (i.e., temperature and humidity sensors, a smartphone-based visualization application, a Raspberry Pi 3b, and a computer). The Raspberry with sensors collects sensing data and calls a preloaded smart contract. The computer was used to manage a private blockchain. In both systems, there is always a computer to maintain the blockchain network. That is because IoT devices usually don't have enough capacity to conduct mining process nor store the full copy of the blockchain. However, both works did not investigate the performance of private blockchain. In [18,19], the authors introduce an architecture of a smart home containing several local private blockchain networks, which communicate with each other through an elected cluster header (CH). Each CH mines blocks and implement access control for its local private blockchain network.

Recently, there is an evaluation framework for analyzing private blockchains proposed in [20]. The authors divide a blockchain network into four layers. From top to bottom, they are application layer, execution engine layer, data model layer, and consensus layer. The authors use different workloads to evaluate different layers of a private blockchain. They evaluated latency ("the response time per transaction") in the application layer on three main blockchain platforms: Ethereum, Parity, and Hyperledger Fabric. In terms of latency, Parity has the lowest latency, and Ethereum has the highest. In [21], which is an extension of [20], the authors implemented different workloads with varying numbers of transactions to the application layer. They analyzed the performance of two platforms: Ethereum and Hyperledger Fabric. In both papers, they considered the response latency of transactions in a single node. In this work, we propose two different latency types according to the lifecycle of transactions. Those two latencies describe a full view of information propagation in a private blockchain network.

3 Background and Methodology

3.1 Background

Ethereum blockchain is essentially a transaction-based state machine [8]. The information of present state composes of account balances, data of smart contracts, etc. Any nodes in the blockchain network can submit transactions to modify the state machine. The submitted transaction on a node will broadcast to all other nodes. Each node maintains a transaction pool (txpool) to keep all pending transactions. A mining node will select some transactions from txpool to form a block and reach a consensus with the PoW algorithm [22]. After that, it will form and broadcast the block to other nodes. All other nodes need to confirm the correctness of the hash value contained in the block header. If the hash is validated, the block will be appended to the local blockchain database. When the block modification has been done by most of the nodes, they will reach a consensus for the state modification.

Geth [23] is the official implementation of Ethereum nodes. The nodes form the Ethereum blockchain network following the P2P networking protocols named DEVp2p [24]. Devp2p includes a node discovery protocol and a RLPx transport protocol, which are based on UDP, TCP, respectively (as shown in Fig. 1).

Node Discovery Protocol. Geth implements its node discovery protocol based on a Kademlia-like Distributed Hash Table (DHT) [25] for efficiently locating and storing content in a P2P network. In private Ethereum blockchain network, nodes are expected to join the network manually by the administrator, the node discovery protocol is used to routing peers.

Every node keep a 256-bit identity or "node ID" randomly generated from Secp256k1 elliptic curve [26]. The logical distance between two nodes is defined as the bitwise XOR of two nodes ID (a and b) as the following equation:

$$distance(a, b) = a \oplus b \tag{1}$$

Every node is also expected to maintain an Ethereum Node Records (ENR) containing up-to-date information of itself, including node ID, IP address, TCP

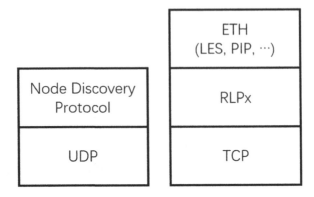

Fig. 1. Ethereum's DEVp2p protocols

and UDP port, etc. Nodes keep information about other nodes in their "neighborhood". The information of neighbor nodes are stored in a routing table. According to the integer value of the distance, Ethereum divides the routing table to several 'k-buckets.' For each $0 \le i < 256$, every node keeps a k-bucket for nodes of distance between 2^i and 2^{i+1} from itself. The current protocol uses $k = 16$, which means every k-bucket contains up to 16 node entries. The node entries are sorted in an update order – most recently updated at the tail and least recently updated at the head.

The RLPx Transport Protocol. The RLPx transport protocol is a TCP-based transport protocol used for communication among Ethereum nodes. Recursive Length Prefix (RLP) [27] is a protocol to encode arbitrarily nested arrays of binary data to serialize messages in Ethereum. Based on RLP, RLPx enables nodes to transfer encrypted, serialized data.

In RLPx, two nodes need to perform a two-phase handshake to initialize the session before transmitting essential messages. Figure 2 presents an overview of two handshakes. The first handshake pertains to the exchange of public keys that are used for the subsequent communication. The subsequent messages are therefore encrypted and authenticated. The second handshake pertains to the negotiation on the subsequent capabilities with a *Hello* message instantly after the first handshake.

An RLPx connection is established by creating a TCP connection and agreeing on a pair of an ephemeral key for further encrypted and authenticated communication. The process of creating a session keys between the 'initiator' (the node which opened the TCP connection) and the 'recipient' (the node which accepted it) is the first handshake. The initiator generates the ephemeral key with a shared secret and sends an *auth* message containing the encrypted shared secret to the recipient. The recipient decrypts and generates the same key with the shared secret. Then it responds an *auth − ack* message to the initiator. All messages following the first handshake are framed.

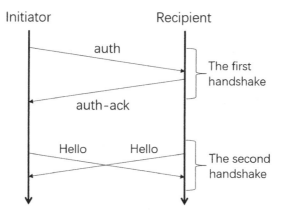

Fig. 2. Two handshakes in RLPx

After the ephemeral key is negotiated, both sides of the connection send a *Hello* message or a *Disconnect* message, which is considered the second handshake. The *Disconnect* message Inform the peer that a disconnection is imminent. The sender can append a single byte of reason code in the message on this disconnection. Alternatively, the *Hello* message exchanges their supporting capabilities and the corresponding version. Two sides of nodes negotiate which capability to use in the subsequent communication with *Hello* messages.

Ethereum Wire Protocol. Based on the RLPx protocol, Ethereum utilizes different capabilities in different clients or conditions. The most widely used subprotocol is the Ethereum Wire Protocol (ETH), which is used to exchange blockchain information between "full" nodes. The Light Ethereum Subprotocol (LES) is a protocol used by the "light" nodes, which only download block headers and fetch other parts of the blockchain on demand. It provides full functionalities of safely accessing the blockchain. Clients running LES do not mine blocks. Therefore they do not take part in the consensus process. The Parity Light Protocol (PIP) is a variation of LES for Parity Ethereum clients. We introduce the ETH in detail.

The latest version of ETH is *eth/64* at the time of writing. After the nodes agree to use ETH, they need to exchange *Status* messages. The *Status* message includes the Total Difficulty (TD) and the hash of their latest block. A node, which has a lower TD after exchanging the *Status* messages, will start synchronization immediately.

Transactions are propagated with one or more *Transactions* messages. Nodes utilize the *NewBlock*, and *NewBlockHashes* messages to propagate a new block. The *NewBlock* message includes the full block, which is sent to a small set of connected nodes (the square root of the total number of peers). Other peers are sent with a *NewBlockHashes* message, which contains the hash of

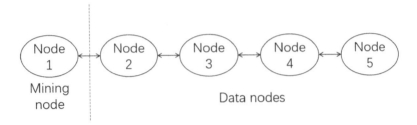

Fig. 3. The private blockchain structure in both experiments

the new block. Those peers can request the block body with *GetBlockBodies* message if they don't receive it from other nodes after a period of time.

3.2   Methodology

In the scope of this research, we consider the IoT-based application of the private Ethereum network. It is generally that some IoT devices may not have enough capacity to conduct the mining process. However, the mining process is indeed essential for the blockchain. Therefore, we come up with a scenario, as in Fig. 3, where a powerful node serves as the mining one for several other nodes. The nodes establish a blockchain network, which has a linear structure. In our work, rather than using the node discovery protocol, we create the connections manually. Node 1, which performs the mining tasks for the pending transactions, generates blocks for the other nodes. Except for Node 1, the other nodes submit transactions and wait for outcomes from the mining node. On creating a TCP connection between two nodes, they exchange existent information in k-bucket and initialize a blockchain connection on the ETH protocol. Transactions and blocks are propagated along with the blockchain connection, hop by hop.

We can present a lifecycle of a transaction following the three steps, as shown in Fig. 4. The lifecycle indicates the duration from the submitted moment to the time of becoming effective. First, transactions are submitted to the txpool, and then disseminated to the mining node. Second, the mining node executes the PoW algorithm and generates blocks. Note that the transactions involved in the mining process are packed into blocks. Third, the blocks are broadcasted and validated to all nodes in the blockchain network.

After the validation, the transactions will finally be efficacious. In this work, we intentionally ignore the period of the mining process and focus on the other two others, namely the propagation of transactions and the propagation of blocks. As indicated in Fig. 4, we define the leftmost process as transaction-oriented latency and the rightmost one as block-oriented latency. The transactions and blocks transmissions are triggered by *Transactions* and *NewBlock* messages, respectively. They are followed by several steps implemented in Geth. We analyze the Geth log at the highest verbosity to clarify the workflow of the two processes in the private Ethereum network. The definitions are presented as follows.

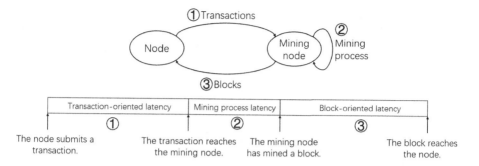

Fig. 4. Lifecycle of transactions in Ethereum blockchain network

Transaction-Oriented Latency. In Ethereum, the workflow of transmitting a transaction between a node and its peer is shown in Fig. 5. After a transaction is submitted to a node, it is pushed into a queue, waiting to be verified. When the node finishes the verification (i.e., at the *Promoted queued transaction* point), the transaction is submitted and added into the txpool (i.e., at the *Submitted transaction* point). Afterward, the node broadcasts the new transaction to its peer in *Transactions* message. The peer node first queues the received transaction at the *Pooled new future transaction* point. It then verifies the transaction after the *Promoted queued transaction* point. Subsequently, the transaction is added to the txpool of this peer. This peer repeats the process to propagate the transaction to the next peer. We define the transaction-oriented latency as the interval between the submission moment in one node and the promotion time in its peer. The transaction-oriented describes the time consumption for a transaction to be propagated in different hops. With a lower value of the transaction-oriented latency, a submitted transaction can reach the entire network quicker.

Block-Oriented Latency. The mining node selects transactions from txpool and packs them into a block, which is then propagated to its peer. Figure 6 shows the workflow of propagating a newly mined block, which begins at the *Mined potential block* point. Nodes in the network use the *NewBlock* message to send the full block to its peers at the *Propagated block* point. After the peer receives the block, the block is pushed into a queue at the *Queued propagated block* point. The peer imports the block at the *Importing propagated block* point then starts to process it. To reach all the nodes as soon as possible, the peer first passes the block to other nodes (i.e., at the *Propagated block* point). At this moment, the peer has already started repeating the block transmission process to the next peer. Then the peer verifies the block and inserts it in its local database at *Inserted block* point. The block finished its lifecycle at the *Imported new chain segment* point. The peer announces the ownership of the block to avoid duplicating transmission. We define the interval from mined a block to the import of the block in one of the peers as block-oriented latency.

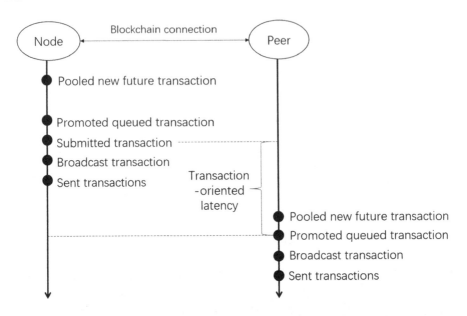

Fig. 5. The workflow of transmitting a new transaction in Geth

The block-oriented latency describes the time consumption for a block to be propagated in different hops. A block contains several verified transactions. After the block is propagated and appended to a peer, those transactions are formally accepted and come into effect. Thus, this latency describes how fast a block outstretches the network.

4   Evaluation

This section describes our evaluation of the two latencies. We first construct the experiment environment with several specific preparations. We then conduct experiments and report the results.

4.1   Experiment Setup

We build our testbed with a laptop computer and four IoT devices. Each IoT device is a single-board Raspberry Pi 3b+ that could run tasks as normal computers. The hardware configuration is shown in Table 1. Figure 7 shows the physical deployment of the devices. The devices connect to the same TPlink Wi-Fi router to build the underlying network. On top of the underlying network, we set up the Ethereum blockchain network using the software setting described in Table 2. We necessarily create a custom genesis file to launch the blockchain client in private deployment. Moreover, in the genesis file, we need to set a proper level of *difficulty*, which can ensure the data nodes receive responses in a reasonable time. Another critical parameter is the block gas limit,

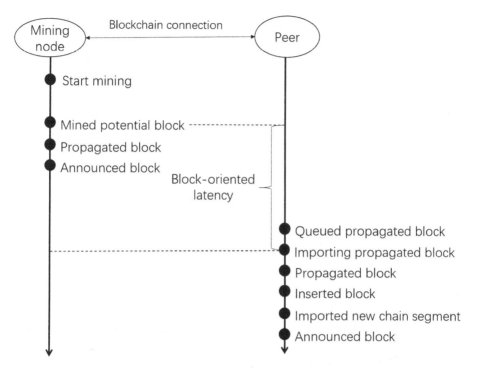

Fig. 6. The workflow of transmitting a new block in Geth

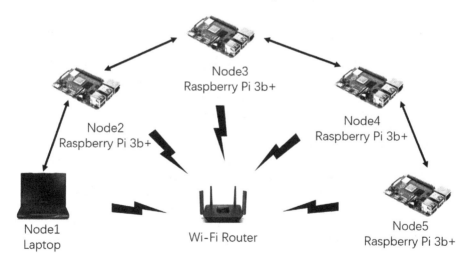

Fig. 7. Our deployment of the private block chain network (The lightning marks represent the underlying network connection, while the solid arrows represent the blockchain connection.)

Table 1. Hardware configuration

Raspberry Pi 3b+	
Processor	4x Cortex-A53 1.4 GHz
Memory	1 GB
Storage	16 GB MicroSDHC
Thinkpad laptop	
Processor	4x Corei5-7200U 2.5 GHz
Memory	8 GB and 2 GB Swap

Table 2. Software configuration

Thinkpad laptop	Ubuntu 16.04 LTS	Geth 1.9.10
Raspberry Pi 3b+	Ubuntu Mate 18.04	Geth 1.9.10

which allows the blocks contain sufficient transactions. Our private blockchain network has a linear structure that indicates by the arrows in Fig. 7. In this scenario, the laptop runs as a mining node, which has enough power to mine continuously. On the other hand, the Raspberry Pi 3b+ serves as a data node, which concentrates on information sharing. To run our experiments, we have to prepare two important issues as follows.

First, we deploy a smart contract written in Solidity [28] version 0.4.25. The smart contract, which simulates the reading and writing of information in the IoT system, has two functions, namely writing a string to the blockchain and reading the current string. Usually, Ethereum will charge the sender some *Ether* based on gas consumption and the gas price of the transaction. However, the nodes in a private network suppose to share information for free. In our private deployment, the gas price is set to zero. That means the nodes can submit transactions to write for free. Moreover, the reading function doesn't consume any gas. Thus, nodes can read the string from the smart contract without paying.

Second, we synchronize the system time on the nodes. We expect to measure the latency on the accuracy level of a millisecond. Thus, we choose *ntpdate* to synchronize the system time on all devices. The *ntpdate* command sets the local system time by polling the NTP (Network Time Protocol) servers specified to determine the correct time, which can adjust the time to microsecond accuracy. There are many target server can be utilized. We selected the closest available NTP pool server in Japan[1] as the synchronization target to get the highly accurate time. By running *ntpdate jp.pool.ntp.org* command several times, the time error can be adjusted less than one millisecond.

In our measurements, we use the Web3.js library [29] on every data node to send transactions. Those nodes call the writing function in a transaction. We preload a JavaScript file to the mining node. The file enables the start of a mining

---

[1] IP address: 133.243.238.243 or 133.243.238.163.

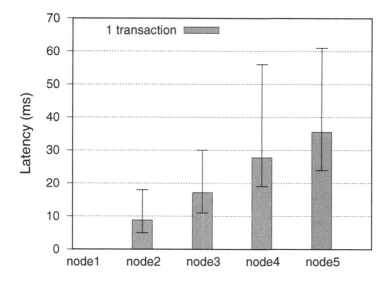

Fig. 8. Transaction-oriented latency in the baseline scenario

process after receiving a transaction. Moreover, it will stop mining after finish process all transactions in the txpool. Since the data nodes send transactions discontinuously in our scenario, this functionality can save computing power and reduce the number of empty blocks.

The *verbosity* is set to five in all nodes. That allows the Geth output has detailed information, including all steps (i.e., in Fig. 5 and Fig. 6) with a timestamp. We record those outputs from the console to a log file and collect them together with the *scp* (secure copy) tool. We then process the timestamp of the claimed steps for each type of latency using our self-written bash scripts. We calculate the minimum, average, and maximum value of different types of latency in each set of experiment.

4.2   Result

We first measure the so-called baseline scenario, which includes the transaction-oriented latency of transmitting a single transaction, and the block-oriented latency of transmitting an empty block. Then we add workloads to simulate latency in a realistic scenario. In transaction-oriented latency, we set two workloads: sending 10 and 100 transactions per time. We send transactions in each data node a hundred times for each workload. All transactions are sent without waiting until the previous one verified, and they arrive at the mining node within different hops. In block-oriented latency, we set three workloads: sending blocks containing 1, 10, and 100 transactions. The mining node collects transactions from data nodes and do the mining process. The latest block is propagated to data nodes within different hops. We send blocks from the mining node a hundred times for each workload. Because Geth will omit the verification process

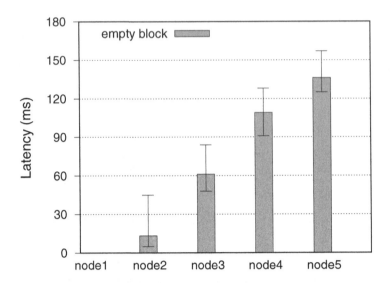

Fig. 9. Block-oriented latency in the baseline scenario

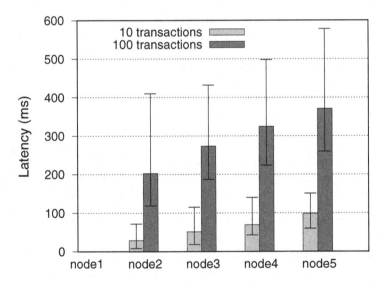

Fig. 10. Transaction-oriented latency in the realistic scenario

when receiving an empty block. We set the workload of transmitting blocks with one transaction to observe the time consumption to start the verification process.

Baseline Scenario. The results in the baseline shows the latency of conveying a minimal amount of information in this private blockchain network. For the transaction-oriented latency, we measure the time consumption for a

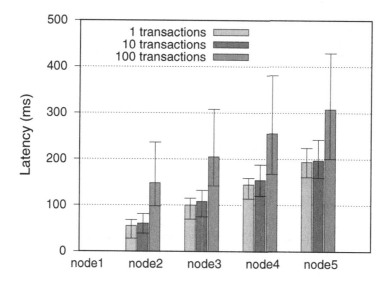

Fig. 11. Block-oriented latency in the realistic scenario

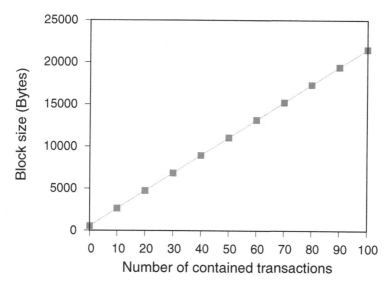

Fig. 12. Relationship between the block size and the number of transactions inside the block

transaction to be transferred from each data node to the mining node 100 times. Figure 8 shows the minimum, average, and maximum value of the measurement. The latency has a positive relationship with the number of hops. We notice that the average value increases approximately nine milliseconds for each hop. Since blockchain transfers messages via the network connection, we use *Ping* commands to assessed the RTT (Round Trip Time) between two devices 100 times. The average RTT is 5.047 ms (min: 2.33 ms, max: 21.3 ms), which means averagely a transaction consumes 4 ms to be processed and 5 ms to be transferred to the next node. Moreover, we notice the error bar extends in node 4 and node 5, especially the maximum value. It means the latency tend to diversify and become more significant with more hop.

For the block-oriented latency, we measure the time consumption for an empty block to be transferred from the mining node to each data node 100 times. We show the measurement results in Fig. 9. Again, the latency has a positive relationship with the number of hops. However, with no transaction, there is no need for confirmation process. Hence, the latency reflects transmitting a block header.

Realistic Scenario. The results in the realistic scenario show the latencies with workloads. For the transaction-oriented latency, we measure the time consumption of transmitting 10 and 100 transactions. Figure 10 shows the results of two workloads. Comparing to the baseline, we can see that at each node, processing more transactions spends more time. For each workload, the latency also has an approximately linear increase along with the number of hops. Notice that when we transfer ten times the transactions, the latency is not ten times the previous one. It is because the blockchain receives transactions continuously. They don't wait until a transaction is verified to accept the next one. Moreover, the error bar is bigger when the number of transactions is larger. The reason is related to the RTT. The blockchain network transmits each transaction independently. Therefore, there more transactions are sent, the more RTTs will be added to the latency. The RTT value is affected by the network condition. Thus, the latency is more diverse when transmitting more transactions.

For the block-oriented latency, we measure the time consumption of transmitting a block with 1, 10, and 100 transactions. Figure 11 shows the results of the latency in those three scenarios. Comparing to the baseline, we can observe that at each node, transmitting a block with more transactions spends more time (the relationship of block size and transaction is shown in Fig. 12). For each workload, the latency value linearly increases following the number of hops. A block with one transaction consumes approximately 50 ms more than an empty block. That is the time for the client to start the verification process. Moreover, the latency in the one transaction case is close to that in the 10 transactions scenario, which means to verify a transaction is quicker than initialize the verification process. Additionally, we can observe that, for the latency in 100 transaction-case. The first hop from the mining node to the data node consumes averagely 148.32 ms. Other nodes spend roughly 50 ms for each hop. It is because the first hop includes the verification time in the mining node, while the others don't. We also notice that the transaction-oriented latency is lower than the block-oriented latency when transmitting 1 or 10 transactions, while the block-oriented latency is more significant than the transaction-oriented latency when transmitting 100 transactions.

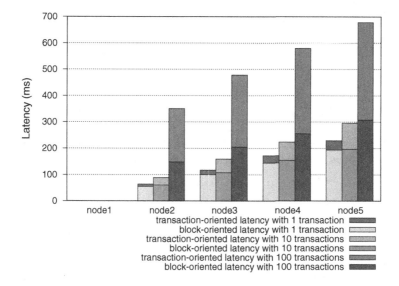

Fig. 13. The total latencies without mining time

Next, we consider the total latency (without the mining process) from submitting transactions to the transactions becomes effective. The total latency is a sum of the transaction-oriented latency and the block-oriented latency. The results are shown in Fig. 13, in which the private Ethereum blockchain consumes averagely 63.92, 117.39, 172.38, and 229.21 ms to propagate one transaction for one, two, three, four hops. Moreover, it also needs 350.83, 478.46, 579.44, and 678.27 ms to propagate 100 transactions for the same hop conditions. We can observe that the transaction-oriented latency is larger than the block-oriented latency when handling 100 transactions.

5   Conclusion and Future Work

The private blockchain network is the potential technology for many IoT applications; hence understanding the blockchain performance is essential. In this paper, we aim to characterize the latency in a real deployment of the private Ethereum. First, we have defined the two latency types (i.e., transaction-oriented and block-oriented latency) and their measurement methodology. We have then measured them in the baseline and realistic scenarios. The results give us an observation of the latencies' relationship. The transaction-oriented latency is lower than the block-oriented latency in the 1 or 10 transaction scenario. While the transaction-oriented latency becomes more significant than the block-oriented latency with the number of transactions increases to 100. Besides, we have considered the total latency, which integrates the two latencies without the consideration of mining latency. The private Ethereum blockchain consumes averagely 63.92, 117.39,

172.38, and 229.21 ms to spread one transaction for one, two, three, four hops, respectively. In the same scenario, the maximum total latency is less than 700 ms.

In the future, we plan to measure the performance of blockchain networks with a more complex structure and more nodes. We also plan to investigate the proof-of-authority (PoA) [30] consensus protocol, which doesn't require mining blocks, for the private Ethereum.

Acknowledgment. This work was supported by JSPS KAKENHI Grant Number 19K20251, 20H04174. Additionally, Kien Nguyen is supported by the Leading Initiative for Excellent Young Researchers (LEADER) program from MEXT, Japan.

References

1. Singh, S., Singh, N.: Blockchain: future of financial and cyber security. In: Proceedings of 2nd IEEE International Conference on Contemporary Computing and Informatics (IC3I), pp. 463–467 (2016)
2. Zīle, K., Strazdiņa, R.: Blockchain use cases and their feasibility. Appl. Comput. Syst. **23**(1), 12–20 (2018)
3. Christidis, K., Devetsikiotis, M.: Blockchains and smart contracts for the internet of things. IEEE Access **4**, 2292–2303 (2016)
4. Lin, I.C., Liao, T.C.: A survey of blockchain security issues and challenges. IJ Netw. Secur. **19**(5), 653–659 (2017)
5. Wüst, K., Gervais, A.: Do you need a blockchain? In: Proceedings of IEEE Crypto Valley Conference on Blockchain Technology (CVCBT), pp. 45–54 (2018)
6. Ethereum. https://ethereum.org/. Accessed 10 Mar 2020
7. Decker, C., Wattenhofer, R.: Information propagation in the bitcoin network. In: Proceedings of IEEE P2P 2013, pp. 1–10 (2013)
8. Wood, G., et al.: Ethereum: a secure decentralised generalised transaction ledger. Ethereum Project Yellow Paper **151**(2014), 1–32 (2014)
9. Xu, Q., Jin, C., Rasid, M.F.B.M., Veeravalli, B., Aung, K.M.M.: Blockchain-based decentralized content trust for docker images. Multimedia Tools Appl. **77**(14), 18223–18248 (2018)
10. Xu, Q., He, Z., Li, Z., Xiao, M.: Building an ethereum-based decentralized smart home system. In: Proceedings of IEEE 24th International Conference on Parallel and Distributed Systems (ICPADS), pp. 1004–1009 (2018)
11. Aung, Y.N., Tantidham, T.: Review of ethereum: smart home case study. In: Proceedings 2nd IEEE International Conference on Information Technology (INCIT), pp. 1–4 (2017)
12. Atlam, H.F., Alenezi, A., Alassafi, M.O., Wills, G.: Blockchain with internet of things: benefits, challenges, and future directions. Int. J. Intell. Syst. Appl. **10**(6), 40–48 (2018)
13. Beck, R., Stenum Czepluch, J., Lollike, N., Malone, S.: Blockchain-the gateway to trust-free cryptographic transactions (2016)
14. Kshetri, N.: Can blockchain strengthen the internet of things? IT Prof. **19**(4), 68–72 (2017)
15. Lo, S.K., Liu, Y., Chia, S.Y., Xu, X., Lu, Q., Zhu, L., Ning, H.: Analysis of blockchain solutions for IoT: a systematic literature review. IEEE Access **7**, 58822–58835 (2019)

16. Rathore, H., Mohamed, A., Guizani, M.: A survey of blockchain enabled cyber-physical systems. Sensors **20**(1), 282 (2020)
17. Huh, S., Cho, S., Kim, S.: Managing IoT devices using blockchain platform. In: Proceedings of IEEE 19th International Conference on Advanced Communication Technology (ICACT), pp. 464–467 (2017)
18. Dorri, A., Kanhere, S.S., Jurdak, R.: Blockchain in internet of things: challenges and solutions. arXiv preprint arXiv:1608.05187 (2016)
19. Dorri, A., Kanhere, S.S., Jurdak, R., Gauravaram, P.: Blockchain for IoT security and privacy: the case study of a smart home. In: 2017 IEEE International Conference on Pervasive Computing and Communications Workshops (PerCom Workshops), pp. 618–623. IEEE (2017)
20. Dinh, T.T.A., Wang, J., Chen, G., Liu, R., Ooi, B.C., Tan, K.L.: Blockbench: a framework for analyzing private blockchains. In: Proceedings of ACM International Conference on Management of Data, pp. 1085–1100 (2017)
21. Pongnumkul, S., Siripanpornchana, C., Thajchayapong, S.: Performance analysis of private blockchain platforms in varying workloads. In: Proceedings of 26th IEEE International Conference on Computer Communication and Networks (ICCCN), pp. 1–6 (2017)
22. Zheng, Z., Xie, S., Dai, H., Chen, X., Wang, H.: An overview of blockchain technology: architecture, consensus, and future trends. In: Proceedings of IEEE International Congress on Big Data (BigData Congress), pp. 557–564 (2017)
23. Go Ethereum (2013). https://geth.ethereum.org/. Accessed 12 Apr 2020
24. Devp2p (2020). https://github.com/ethereum/devp2p. Accessed: 13 Apr 2020
25. Maymounkov, P., Mazières, D.: Kademlia: a peer-to-peer information system based on the XOR metric. In: Druschel, P., Kaashoek, F., Rowstron, A. (eds.) IPTPS 2002. LNCS, vol. 2429, pp. 53–65. Springer, Heidelberg (2002). https://doi.org/10.1007/3-540-45748-8_5
26. Secp256k1. https://en.bitcoin.it/wiki/Secp256k1. Accessed 09 Apr 2020
27. RLP. https://github.com/ethereum/wiki/wiki/RLP. Accessed 11 Apr 2020
28. Solidity (2020). https://github.com/ethereum/solidity. Accessed 13 Apr 2020
29. Web3.js (2020). https://github.com/ethereum/web3.js/. Accessed 11 Apr 2020
30. Clique Poa Protocol (2020). https://github.com/ethereum/EIPs/issues/225. Accessed 11 Apr 2020

Energy Minimization for UAV Enabled Video Relay System Under QoE Constraints

Han Hu[1($\boxtimes$)], Cheng Zhan[2], and Jianping An[1]

[1] School of Information and Electronics,
Beijing Institute of Technology, Beijing, China
{hhu,an}@bit.edu.cn
[2] School of Computer and Information Science,
Southwest University, Chongqing, China
zhanc@swu.edu.cn

Abstract. With the explosive growth of mobile video services, unmanned aerial vehicle (UAV) is flexibly deployed as a relay node to offload cellular traffic or provide video services for emergency scenario without infrastructures. This paper proposes a novel design framework for UAV enabled video relay system with the aim of minimizing energy consumption of the UAV, subjecting to the QoE requirement of each GU. A dynamic resource allocation strategy is employed to model the UAV's power and bandwidth allocation and the optimization problem is formulated as a non-convex problem, via optimizing the transmit power and bandwidth allocation of the UAV jointly with the UAV trajectory. To tackle this non-convex problem, the original problem is decoupled into two sub-problems: bandwidth and transmit power allocation optimization, as well as UAV trajectory optimization. We propose an efficient iterative algorithm to obtain a Karush-Kuhn-Tucker (KKT) solution via solving the two sub-problems with successive convex approximation and alternating optimization techniques. Extensive simulations are conducted to evaluate the performance and the results demonstrate that with the proposed joint design, the UAV's energy consumption is significantly reduced, by up to 30%, and the QoE requirement for GUs can be well satisfied simultaneously.

Keywords: Unmanned aerial vehicle · Video relay system · Energy minimization · Quality of experience

1 Introduction

Recently, the global mobile data traffic has been dominated by mobile video streaming (e.g., Netflix and YouTube) [1], which is expected to grow due to the increasing use of higher resolution video formats e.g., 4K videos. On the other hand, the quality of experience (QoE) of end users will be degraded due

© ICST Institute for Computer Sciences, Social Informatics and Telecommunications Engineering 2020
Published by Springer Nature Switzerland AG 2020. All Rights Reserved
S. W. Loke et al. (Eds.): MONAMI 2020, LNICST 338, pp. 256–269, 2020.
https://doi.org/10.1007/978-3-030-64002-6_17

to the increased congestion brought by the growing popularity of video services, especially the cell edge users. As a result, recent researches have paid more attention on developing efficient solutions to meet the user's QoE requirement.

To tackle such issues, traditional solution is to deploy small-cell networks which consist of a large number of small base stations (SBSs). However, deploying a lot of fixed SBSs is cost-ineffective for scenarios with temporarily high user density or highly dynamic traffic demand [2]. Recently, unmanned aerial vehicles (UAVs) offer several opportunities for extending the coverage areas of current wireless networks, such as offloading overloaded traffic from existing cellular networks, or providing wireless video services as a relay node in infrastructure-less areas (e.g., due to disaster or maintenance), by relaying data from remote BSs [3]. Specifically, the channels between ground users (GUs) and the UAV have high probability to be line-of-sight (LoS) channels, where the transmission performance can be enhanced significantly [4]. Furthermore, since the UAV has high mobility, it is practical to deploy UAV flexibly and quickly for on-demand wireless systems, which is more suitable for the dynamic traffic demand scenario. In addition, the cost of deploying UAV is less expensive than that of deploying small-cell networks [5]. However, due to the flexible mobility of the UAV, the channel quality varies over time, which brings a great challenge to video services [6]. To tackle such challenge, dynamic adaptive video streaming over HTTP (DASH) is employed [7]. With DASH-based video streaming, the streaming media can dynamically select the most suitable video bitrate based on its instantaneous channel quality [8,9]. To be specific, DASH can adjust the video quality based on the available bandwidth or transmission rate between GUS and the UAV. This is a particularly useful feature for the UAV communication as the transmission rate of UAV-to-Ground (U2G) communication link may vary over time accordingly with time-varying channel quality. Average QoE was maximized for UAV-enabled DASH system in [9] by optimizing UAV's position and resource allocation without taking UAV's energy consumption into account.

Although DASH is adopted, new challenges arise for the UAV enabled video relay system. In particular, the UAV usually has very limited endurance since the onboard energy is limited, which requires to be efficiently utilized to prolong the UAV endurance. Compared to conventional terrestrial BSs, UAV flight (e.g., hovering or flying) incurs additional propulsion energy consumption. A fundamental tradeoff exists between maximizing QoE of GUs and minimizing UAV's energy consumption. Intuitively, if the UAV can fly closer to or even hover around each GU to provide video service with better channel quality, then the QoE of each GU increases. However, such trajectory leads to longer flying distance of the UAV, which will increase the UAV's energy consumption in general. It is difficult to achieve the optimal balance between maximizing QoE of GUs and minimizing UAV's energy consumption at the same time. Furthermore, the tradeoff between U2G channel quality and BS-to-UAV (B2U) channel quality for UAV relay platform should be investigated as the increment of U2G channel quality is generally at the cost of decrement of B2U channel quality. To provide energy efficient video services for GUs in UAV enabled relay system, the UAV's energy consumption should be minimized while ensuring the QoE requirement of GUs, via optimizing bandwidth and transmit power allocation jointly with UAV trajectory. The main contributions of this paper is summarized as follows:

- Firstly, we propose a novel design framework for UAV enabled video relay system to provide video services. An optimization problem for the UAV enabled video relay system is formulated with the aim of minimizing the UAV's total energy consumption subjecting to the QoE constraints of GUs, via optimizing the bandwidth and transmit power allocation jointly with the UAV trajectory.
- Secondly, the formulated problem is a non-convex optimization problem and it is difficult to obtain optimal solution directly. We decompose the original problem into two sub-problems, i.e., transmit power and bandwidth allocation optimization, and UAV trajectory optimization, and an efficient iterative algorithm is proposed by employing successive convex approximation (SCA) and alternating optimization techniques, which converges to a Karush-Kuhn-Tucker (KKT) solution.
- Lastly, extensive simulations are conducted to evaluate the performance under different settings, and the results demonstrate that the proposed joint design can reduce the UAV's total energy consumption, up to 30%, over benchmark schemes, and the QoE requirement for GUs can be well satisfied simultaneously.

2   System Model and Problem Statement

2.1   System Model

We consider an area in which the established BS is not functioning (e.g., due to disaster or maintenance). Such area may be a remote area, where there is no direct links between other BSs and the GUs. There are M existing BSs and K GUs in such area, denoted by $\mathcal{S} = \{s_1, s_2, \ldots, s_M\}$ and $\mathcal{U} = \{u_1, u_2, \ldots, u_K\}$, respectively. We employ a rotary-wing UAV as a aerial relay platform to provide video services from existing BSs to multiple GUs since rotary-wing UAV can hover over GUs to provide better video services. All BSs are assumed to have the same altitude H_B, and we denote $\mathbf{s}_m$ and $\mathbf{w}_k$ as the horizontal locations of BS s_m and GU u_k, respectively. For simplicity, the UAV is assumed to fly at a constant altitude of H. The initial/final locations are pre-determined to be the same, which is given as $\mathbf{q}_I \in \mathbb{R}^{2 \times 1}$. To facilitate the trajectory design of the UAV, the total time horizon is assumed to consist of $T > 0$ time slots, and δ_t is the time duration of the elemental time slot. Denote the horizontal location of UAV at time slot t as $\mathbf{q}[t] \in \mathbb{R}^{2 \times 1}$, then the UAV's flying trajectory can be denoted as the discrete set $\{\mathbf{q}[t], 0 \leq t \leq T\}$. As a result, the UAV velocity in time slot t is calculated as $\mathbf{v}[t] \triangleq \frac{\mathbf{q}[t+1]-\mathbf{q}[t]}{\delta_t}$, $\|\mathbf{v}[t]\| \leq V_{\max}, \forall t$, where $V_{\max}$ denotes the UAV's maximum speed.

The total bandwidth is denoted as B measured in hertz (Hz), and frequency division multiple access (FDMA) scheme is adopted by the UAV with dynamic bandwidth allocation among all BSs and GUs. In particular, at any time slot of the UAV flight period, the UAV communicates with multiple BSs and GUs simultaneously by assigning each BS or GU a fraction of the total bandwidth. Let $x_m[t] \geq 0$ represent the allocated fraction of bandwidth to BS $s_m, 1 \leq m \leq M$ at time slot t, and let $y_k[t] \geq 0$ represent the allocated fraction of bandwidth to GU $u_k, 1 \leq k \leq K$. Thus, we have $\sum_{m=1}^{M} x_m[t] + \sum_{k=1}^{K} y_k[t] \leq 1, \forall t$.

2.2   Channel Model

For B2U communication, the channel between the UAV and each BS is dominated by the LoS link as in [5,10]. At time slot t, the distance between the mth BS and UAV is calculated as $\hat{d}_m[t] = \sqrt{(H - H_B)^2 + \|\mathbf{q}[t] - \mathbf{s}_m\|}$. The channel power gain between the UAV and s_m at time slot t is then written as $\hat{\beta}_m[t] = \beta_0 \hat{d}_m^{-2}[t]$, where β_0 is channel power gain at 1 meter. Let P_B be the transmit power for each BS. Denote $\hat{R}_m[t]$ as the normalized instantaneous achievable rate of BS s_m for B2U communication in time slot t measured in bits/second/Hz (bps/Hz), then $\hat{R}_m[t]$ is written as $\hat{R}_m[t] = x_m[t] \log_2 \left(1 + \frac{P_B \gamma_0}{x_m[t]((H-H_B)^2 + \|\mathbf{q}[t] - \mathbf{s}_m\|^2)}\right)$ where $\gamma_0 \triangleq \frac{\beta_0}{BN_0}$, with N_0 denoting the power spectral density of noise at the receiver.

For U2G communication, signal reflection and scattering occurs in air-to-ground communication links [4]. Denote $\check{h}_k[t]$ as channel coefficient at time slot t between GU u_k and the UAV, then $\check{h}_k[t] = \sqrt{\check{\beta}_k[t]} \check{\rho}_k[t]$, where $\check{\beta}_k[t]$ and $\check{\rho}_k[t]$ represent for the large-scale coefficient and small-scale fading coefficient, respectively. In particular, we have $\check{\beta}_k[t] = \beta_0 \check{d}_k^{-\alpha}[t]$, where $\alpha \geq 2$ denotes the path loss exponent. Denote $p_k[t] \geq 0$ as the UAV transmit power allocated to GU s_k in time slot t, then $\sum_{k=1}^{K} p_k[t] \leq P_U, \forall t$, where P_U is the UAV's maximum allowable transmit power. As such, the normalized instantaneous achievable rate of GU u_k for U2G communication at time slot t, denoted by $\check{R}_k[t]$, measured in bits/second/Hz (bps/Hz), is then expressed as $\check{R}_k[t] = y_k[t] \log_2 \left(1 + \frac{p_k[t]\gamma_0 |\check{\rho}_k[t]|^2}{y_k[t](H^2 + \|\mathbf{q}[t] - \mathbf{w}_k\|^2)^{\alpha/2}}\right)$. Note that $\check{R}_k[t]$ is a random variable since $\check{\rho}_k[t]$ is a random variable. To tackle such issue, we focus on the average rate similar as in [11], defined as $\mathbb{E}[\check{R}_k[t]]$, which is approximated as $\mathbb{E}[\check{R}_k[t]] \approx y_k[t] \log_2 \left(1 + \frac{p_k[t]\gamma_0}{y_k[t](H^2 + \|\mathbf{q}[t] - \mathbf{w}_k\|^2)^{\alpha/2}}\right) \triangleq \tilde{R}_k[t]$, where $\tilde{R}_k[t]$ can be interpreted as an approximation of the average rate $\mathbb{E}[\check{R}_k[t]]$. It is shown in [11] that high accuracy can be achieved for such approximation, especially for rural or suburban environment.

2.3   Video Streaming and Energy Consumption Model

We consider a video-on-demand scenario. K GUs request for different video contents from BSs via the relay of UAV. The UAV fetches video contents from M BSs, and then forwards packets to K GUs. At each time slot t, the UAV can only relay the video data which has already been received from BSs. Thus, we have the following information-causality constraint by assuming that the processing delay at the UAV is one slot [5], i.e., $\sum_{n=0}^{t-1} \sum_{m=1}^{M} \hat{R}_m[n] \geq \sum_{n=1}^{t} \sum_{k=1}^{K} \tilde{R}_k[n], t = 1, 2, \ldots, T$.

We assume that the UAV enabled video relay system employs DASH for video streaming, which can dynamically adapt the video rate based on channel conditions. For simplicity, similar as in [12], the QoE (i.e. the utility) of users is modelled as a logarithmic function with transmission rate. In particular, the QoE utility of GU u_k is expressed as $\theta \log \beta \frac{\bar{R}_k}{r_k}$, where θ and β are positive constants which are different for various types of applications, and $\bar{R}_k \triangleq \frac{1}{T} \sum_{t=1}^{T} \tilde{R}_k[t]$ denotes the time-averaged transmission rate for GU u_k. r_k denotes the required playback rate for GU u_k, which depends on the physical capability of media outlet. As a result, we have $\theta \log \frac{\beta \sum_{t=1}^{T} \tilde{R}_k[t]}{T r_k} \geq U_k, \forall k$, where U_k represents the minimum QoE utility for GU u_k.

Typically, the UAV's energy consumption consists of both communication related energy consumption and propulsion energy consumption. The communication related energy consumption of the UAV can be calculated as $E_c(\{p_k[t]\}) \triangleq \sum_{k=1}^{K} \sum_{t=1}^{T} \delta_t p_k[t]$. On the other hand, the propulsion energy consumption of rotary-wing UAV was given in [11], i.e.,

$$
E_p(\{\mathbf{v}[t]\}) \approx \sum_{t=1}^{T} \delta_t \left(P_0 + \frac{3 P_0 \|\mathbf{v}[t]\|^2}{U_{tip}^2} + \frac{1}{2} d_0 \rho s A \|\mathbf{v}[t]\|^3 \right)
$$

$$
+ \sum_{t=1}^{T} \delta_t P_i \left(\sqrt{1 + \frac{\|\mathbf{v}[t]\|^4}{4 v_0^4}} - \frac{\|\mathbf{v}[t]\|^2}{2 v_0^2} \right)^{\frac{1}{2}}, \tag{1}
$$

where constants P_i and P_0 denote the hovering related induced power and blade profile, respectively. U_{tip} and v_0 denote the tip speed of rotor blade and mean rotor induced velocity when hovering. d_0 and s denote the fuselage drag ratio and rotor solidity. The air density and rotor disc area are denoted as ρ and A, respectively.

2.4   Problem Formulation

In this paper, our goal is to minimize the UAV's total energy consumption during a continuous period of T time slots, while ensuring that the target QoE utility for each GU is achieved, by jointly optimizing the UAV trajectory $\mathcal{Q} \triangleq \{\mathbf{q}[t]\}$ and bandwidth allocations $\mathcal{B} \triangleq \{x_m[t], y_k[t]\}$, as well as transmit power allocation $\mathcal{P} \triangleq \{p_k[t]\}$. Based on the various models derived above, the optimization problem can be expressed as follows:

$$(\text{P1}): \min_{\mathcal{Q}, \mathcal{B}, \mathcal{P}} \; E_c(\{p_k[t]\}) + E_p(\{\mathbf{v}[t]\})$$

$$\text{s.t.} \; \theta \log \frac{\beta \sum_{t=1}^{T} \tilde{R}_k[t]}{Tr_k} \geq U_k, \forall k, \tag{2}$$

$$\sum_{n=0}^{t-1} \sum_{m=1}^{M} \hat{R}_m[n] \geq \sum_{n=1}^{t} \sum_{k=1}^{K} \tilde{R}_k[n], t = 1, \ldots, T, \tag{3}$$

$$\sum_{m=1}^{M} x_m[t] + \sum_{k=1}^{K} y_k[t] \leq 1, \forall t, \tag{4}$$

$$x_m[t] \geq 0, y_k[t] \geq 0, \forall m, k, t, \tag{5}$$

$$\sum_{k=1}^{K} p_k[t] \leq P_U, \forall t, \tag{6}$$

$$\|\mathbf{v}[t]\| \leq V_{\max}, \forall t, \tag{7}$$

$$\mathbf{q}[0] = \mathbf{q}_I, \mathbf{q}[T] = \mathbf{q}_I. \tag{8}$$

In (P1), constraints in (2) impose a minimum QoE utility U_k for each GU u_k. Constraints in (3) are the information-causality constraints. Constraints in (4) and (5) are imposed due to dynamic bandwidth allocation scheme among all BSs and GUs. Constraints in (6)-(8) represent the UAV's physical constraints. Note that problem (P1) is non-convex which consists of coupled variables, and it is difficult to obtain the optimal solution of (P1) directly. In the following section, an effective method is proposed to obtain a sub-optimal solution to (P1) by iteratively solving its two sub-problems.

3   Proposed Solution

3.1   Bandwidth and Transmit Power Allocation

In this subsection, we consider the bandwidth and transmit power allocation with given UAV trajectory $\mathcal{Q}$. The UAV's propulsion energy consumption, i.e., E_p, is fixed due to the fixed trajectory $\mathcal{Q}$, and then problem (P1) reduces to:

$$(\text{P2}): \min_{\mathcal{B}, \mathcal{P}} \; E_c(\{p_k[t]\}) + E_p$$

$$\text{s.t. } (2) - (6).$$

Although UAV trajectory $\mathcal{Q}$ is given, problem (P2) remains non-convex since constraints (2) and (3) are still non-convex constraints. By employing the slack variables $\mathcal{W} \triangleq \{\omega_k[t], \forall k, t\}$, (P2) can be reformulated as

$$(P3): \min_{\mathcal{B},\mathcal{P},\mathcal{W}} \quad E_c(\{p_k[t]\}) + E_p$$

$$\text{s.t.} \quad (4) - (6),$$

$$\theta \log \frac{\beta \sum_{t=1}^{T} \omega_k[t]}{Tr_k} \geq U_k, \forall k, \tag{9}$$

$$y_k[t] \log_2 \left(1 + \frac{p_k[t]\gamma_0}{y_k[t](H^2 + \|\mathbf{q}[t] - \mathbf{w}_k\|^2)^{\alpha/2}} \right) \geq \omega_k[t],$$
$$\forall k, t, \tag{10}$$

$$\sum_{n=0}^{t-1} \sum_{m=1}^{M} x_m[n] \log_2 \left(1 + \frac{P_B \gamma_0}{x_m[n]((H - H_B)^2 + \|\mathbf{q}[n] - \mathbf{s}_m\|^2)} \right)$$
$$\geq \sum_{n=1}^{t} \sum_{k=1}^{K} \omega_k[n], t = 1, \dots, T. \tag{11}$$

Theorem 1. *Problem (P3) is equivalent to problem (P2).*

Proof. Considering problem (P3), it can be shown that in the optimal solution to (P3), equality holds in all constraints of (10), i.e., $\tilde{R}_k[t] = \omega_k[t], \forall k, t$. Since otherwise, we can decrease $p_k[t]$ to satisfy the equality, then the objective value of (P3) can be further reduced since E_c decreases while E_p keeps the same, and all other constraints are still satisfied. Therefore, in the optimal solution to problem (P3), $\tilde{R}_k[t] = \omega_k[t], \forall k, t$. By substituting $\omega_k[t]$ with $\tilde{R}_k[t]$ in (9) and (11), problem (P3) is the same as problem (P2), and the proof concludes. $\square$

Note (P3) is a standard convex optimization problem, where standard convex optimization techniques or existing solvers such as CVX[13] can be leveraged to solve (P3) efficiently.

3.2 UAV Trajectory Optimization

In this subsection, we focus on solving the sub-problem of UAV trajectory optimization problem with given bandwidth and transmit power allocation. As such, UAV's communication-related energy consumption, i.e., E_c, is fixed. This sub-problem is written as:

$$(P4): \min_{\mathcal{Q},\mathcal{V},\mathcal{W}} \quad E_c + E_p(\{\mathbf{v}[t]\})$$

$$\text{s.t.} \quad \theta \log \frac{\beta \sum_{t=1}^{T} \omega_k[t]}{Tr_k} \geq U_k, \forall k, \tag{12}$$

$$y_k[t] \log_2 \left(1 + \frac{p_k[t]\gamma_0}{y_k[t](H^2 + \|\mathbf{q}[t] - \mathbf{w}_k\|^2)^{\alpha/2}} \right) \geq \omega_k[t],$$
$$\forall k, t, \tag{13}$$

$$\sum_{n=0}^{t-1} \sum_{m=1}^{M} x_m[n] \log_2 \left(1 + \frac{P_B \gamma_0}{x_m[n]((H - H_B)^2 + \|\mathbf{q}[n] - \mathbf{s}_m\|^2)} \right)$$

$$\geq \sum_{n=1}^{t} \sum_{k=1}^{K} \omega_k[n], t = 1, \ldots, T. \tag{14}$$

$(7), (8),$

Problem (P4) is non-convex due to the non-convex objective function and both constraints (13) and (14) contain non-convex constraints. To tackle the non-convex term in $E_p(\{\mathbf{v}[t]\})$, slack variables $\mathcal{T} \triangleq \{\tau[t] \geq 0\}$ is introduced such that $\tau[t] = \left(\sqrt{1 + \frac{\|\mathbf{v}[t]\|^4}{4v_0^4}} - \frac{\|\mathbf{v}[t]\|^2}{2v_0^2}\right)^{1/2}$, and then we obtain $\frac{1}{\tau[t]^2} = \tau[t]^2 + \frac{\|\mathbf{v}[t]\|^2}{v_0^2}$. Define $E_p^\tau(\{\mathbf{v}[t]\}, \{\tau[t]\}) \triangleq \sum_{t=1}^{T} \delta_t \left(P_0 + \frac{3P_0\|\mathbf{v}[t]\|^2}{U_{tip}^2} + \frac{1}{2}d_0\rho s A \|\mathbf{v}[t]\|^3 + P_i\tau[t]\right)$, where $E_p^\tau(\{\mathbf{v}[t]\}, \{\tau[t]\})$ is joint convex with $\{\mathbf{v}[t]\}$ and $\{\tau[t]\}$, then (P4) is reduced to

$$(P5): \min_{\mathcal{Q}, \mathcal{V}, \mathcal{W}, \mathcal{T}} \quad E_c + E_p^\tau(\{\mathbf{v}[t]\}, \{\tau[t]\})$$

$$\text{s.t.} \quad \tau[t]^2 + \frac{\|\mathbf{v}[t]\|^2}{v_0^2} = \frac{1}{\tau[t]^2}, \forall t,$$

$$(7), (8), (12) - (14). \tag{15}$$

Note that problem (P5) remains non-convex since non-affine equality constraint exists in (15). To tackle such difficulty, we relax the equality constraint into the following inequality constraint, i.e.,

$$(P6): \min_{\mathcal{Q}, \mathcal{V}, \mathcal{W}, \mathcal{T}} \quad E_c + E_p^\tau(\{\mathbf{v}[t]\}, \{\tau[t]\})$$

$$\text{s.t.} \quad \tau[t]^2 + \frac{\|\mathbf{v}[t]\|^2}{v_0^2} \geq \frac{1}{\tau[t]^2}, \forall t,$$

$$(7), (8), (12) - (14). \tag{16}$$

Similar as that in Theorem 1, it is not difficult to see that at the optimal solution to (P6), equality holds in (16). Since otherwise, $\tau[t]$ can always be decreased until the equality is met, and the objective value will decrease since $E_p^\tau(\{\mathbf{v}[t]\}, \{\tau[t]\})$ is a monotonic increasing function with respect to $\tau[t]$. Therefore, solving problem (P5) is equivalent to solving problem (P6).

However, problem (P6) is still non-convex since non-convex constraints exist in (13), (14) and (16). To address such challenges, SCA technique is utilized to derive their convex approximations. Specifically, it can be shown that the first-order Taylor approximation of a convex function can be regarded as a global under-estimator [14], and $\tilde{R}_k[t]$ is convex with respect to term $\|\mathbf{q}[t] - \mathbf{w}_k\|^2$, then $\tilde{R}_k[t]$ can be lower-bounded at the given point $\mathbf{q}^r[t]$, as in [5,10,15], i.e.,

$$\tilde{R}_k[t] \geq y_k[t](A_k^r[t] - I_k^r[t](\|\mathbf{q}[t] - \mathbf{w}_k\|^2 - \|\mathbf{q}^r[t] - \mathbf{w}_k\|^2))$$
$$\triangleq \tilde{R}_k^{lb}[t] \tag{17}$$

where $I_k^r[t] = \frac{(\alpha/2)p_k[t]\gamma_0 \log_2 e}{(H^2+\|\mathbf{q}^r[t]-\mathbf{w}_k\|^2)(y_k[t](H^2+\|\mathbf{q}^r[t]-\mathbf{w}_k\|^2)^{\alpha/2}+p_k[t]\gamma_0)}$ and
$A_k^r[t] = \log_2\left(1 + \frac{p_k[t]\gamma_0}{y_k[t](H^2+\|\mathbf{q}^r[t]-\mathbf{w}_k\|^2)^{\alpha/2}}\right)$. The equality of (17) holds at the
point $\mathbf{q}[t] = \mathbf{q}^r[t]$ and both $\tilde{R}_k[t]$ and $\tilde{R}_k^{lb}[t]$ have identical gradient, i.e., $\nabla\tilde{R}_k[t] = \nabla\tilde{R}_k^{lb}[t], \forall k, t$.

Similarly, $\hat{R}_m[t]$ is lower-bounded as follows:

$$\hat{R}_m[t] \geq x_m[t](\hat{A}_m^r[t] - \hat{I}_m^r[t](\|\mathbf{q}[t] - \mathbf{s}_m\|^2 - \|\mathbf{q}^r[t] - \mathbf{s}_m\|^2))$$
$$\triangleq \hat{R}_m^{lb}[t] \tag{18}$$

where $\hat{A}_m^r[t] = \log_2\left(1 + \frac{P_B\gamma_0}{x_k[t]((H-H_B)^2+\|\mathbf{q}^r[t]-\mathbf{s}_m\|^2)}\right)$, $\hat{I}_m^r[t] = \frac{P_B\gamma_0 \log_2 e}{\hat{J}_m^r[t](x_k[t]\hat{J}_m^r[t]+P_B\gamma_0)}$, and $\hat{J}_m^r[t] = (H - H_B)^2 + \|\mathbf{q}^r[t] - \mathbf{s}_m\|^2$.

On the other hand, since terms $\|\mathbf{v}[t]\|^2$ and $\tau[t]^2$ are convex with $\mathbf{v}[t]$ and $\tau[t]$, respectively. By applying first-order Taylor expansion at local points $\mathbf{v}^r[t]$ and $\tau^r[t]$, we have

$$\|\mathbf{v}[t]\|^2 \geq \|\mathbf{v}^r[t]\|^2 + 2(\mathbf{v}^r[t])^T(\mathbf{v}[t] - \mathbf{v}^r[t]) \triangleq z_v^{lb}[t], \forall t, \tag{19}$$
$$\tau[t]^2 \geq (\tau^r[t])^2 + 2\tau^r[t](\tau[t] - \tau^r[t]) \triangleq z_\tau^{lb}[t], \forall t. \tag{20}$$

By substituting (17) and (18) into the left-hand sides(LHSs) of (13) and (14), respectively, and substituting (19) and (20) into the LHSs of (16), problem (P6) can be approximated as follows:

$$(P7): \min_{\mathcal{Q},\mathcal{V},\mathcal{W},\mathcal{T}} \quad E_c + E_p^\tau(\{\mathbf{v}[t]\}, \{\tau[t]\})$$

$$\text{s.t.} \quad z_\tau^{lb}[t] + \frac{z_v^{lb}[t]}{v_0^2} - \frac{1}{\tau[t]^2} \geq 0, \forall t, \tag{21}$$

$$\tilde{R}_k^{lb}[t] \geq \omega_k[t], \forall k, t, \tag{22}$$

$$\sum_{n=0}^{t-1}\sum_{m=1}^{M} \hat{R}_m^{lb}[n] \geq \sum_{n=1}^{t}\sum_{k=1}^{K} \omega_k[n], t = 1, \ldots, T,$$
$$(7), (8), (12). \tag{23}$$

Note that problem (P7) is now convex, and then CVX solvers and be utilized to solve (P7) efficiently.

3.3   Overall Iterative Algorithm, Convergence, and Complexity

Using the results obtained above, we propose an overall algorithm for computing the suboptimal solution to (P1) by employing SCA and alternating optimization techniques, where we summarize the details in Algorithm 1.

Algorithm 1. Iterative Bandwidth and Transmit Power Allocation, and Trajectory Optimization Algorithm for (P1)

1: Initialize $\mathcal{Q}^0$. Let $r \leftarrow 0$.
2: **repeat**
3:     Solve convex problem (P3) with CVX to obtain $\mathcal{B}^{r+1}$ and $\mathcal{P}^{r+1}$ with given $\mathcal{Q}^r$;
4:     Solve convex problem (P7) with CVX to obtain $\mathcal{Q}^{r+1}$ with given $\mathcal{B}^{r+1}$ and $\mathcal{P}^{r+1}$, as well as $\mathcal{Q}^r$;
5:     $r \leftarrow r + 1$;
6: **until** The objective value of (P1) converges

Theorem 2. *The proposed Algorithm 1 is convergent.*

Proof. Denote $E(\mathcal{B}^r, \mathcal{P}^r, \mathcal{Q}^r)$ as the objective value of problem (P1) in the rth iteration. Recall that the optimal solution $\mathcal{P}^{r+1}, \mathcal{B}^{r+1}$ is obtained by solving convex problem (P3), we have $E(\mathcal{B}^r, \mathcal{P}^r, \mathcal{Q}^r) \geq E(\mathcal{B}^{r+1}, \mathcal{P}^{r+1}, \mathcal{Q}^r)$. Denote E^{up} as the objective value of problem (P7), we have

$$E(\mathcal{B}^{r+1}, \mathcal{P}^{r+1}, \mathcal{Q}^r) \overset{(a)}{=} E^{up}(\mathcal{B}^{r+1}, \mathcal{P}^{r+1}, \mathcal{Q}^r)$$
$$\overset{(b)}{\geq} E^{up}(\mathcal{B}^{r+1}, \mathcal{P}^{r+1}, \mathcal{Q}^{r+1}) \overset{(c)}{\geq} E(\mathcal{B}^{r+1}, \mathcal{P}^{r+1}, \mathcal{Q}^{r+1}). \tag{24}$$

Recall that first-order Taylor expansions at given local points are tight in problem (P6), then (a) holds. (b) holds due to the fact that problem (P7) is optimally solved. Recall that the objective value of (P7) is an upper bound of that to (P6), then the inequality of (c) holds. As a result, we have $E(\mathcal{B}^r, \mathcal{P}^r, \mathcal{Q}^r) \geq E(\mathcal{B}^{r+1}, \mathcal{P}^{r+1}, \mathcal{Q}^{r+1})$. Therefore, the objective value of (P1) is non-increasing over iterations, which is lower bounded by a finite value. Furthermore, the first-order Taylor expansions have identical gradients as original functions. Therefore, Algorithm 1 converges to a KKT solution [5], i.e. the proposed Algorithm is convergent.

Note that Algorithm 1 requires alternatively solving problems (P3) and (P7), which are both standard convex optimization problems. Therefore, given the prescribed accuracy κ and let L be the number of iterations before convergence, then the computational complexity of Algorithm 1 is given by $O(LM^3K^3T^3)$[14], and L is in the order of $\log \frac{1}{\kappa}$.

4   Simulation Results

We consider a UAV enabled video relay system, which consists of $M = 2$ existing BSs and $K = 5$ GUs. The GUs are randomly located in a square area of 1.0×1.0 km^2, and the two BSs are located at the left/right side of this area, i.e., $\mathbf{s}_1 = [-500, 0]^T, \mathbf{s}_2 = [500, 0]^T$. $\mathbf{q}_I$ is set to be $[-200, 100]^T$. For the utility parameters, we set $r_k = 1$ Mbps, $\forall k$, and $\theta = 0.8$, similar to that in [12]. Furthermore, all GUs are assumed to have identical QoE requirements, i.e., $U_k = \bar{U}, \forall k$. In addition, similar as in [11], the rotary-wing UAV's propulsion energy parameters are set as $d_0 = 0.6, U_{tip} = 120, A = 0.503, \rho = 1.225, s = 0.05, v_0 = 4.03, P_0 = 79.8563, P_i = 88.6279$. We set $H = 100$ m, $H_s = 50$ m, $V_{\max} = 30$ m/s, $P_B = 1$ W, $P_U = 0.1$ W, $B = 1$ MHz, $\delta_t = 1$ s, $\alpha = 2.2$, $N_0 = -170$ dBm/Hz, $\beta_0 = -60$ dB.

The optimized trajectory under different QoE requirement $\bar{U}$ are shown in Fig. 1(a) with $T = 120$. It can be seen that with the increase of QoE requirement $\bar{U}$, the UAV can adjust its trajectory to move close to the BSs to obtain more video data, and then move closer to or even hover over GUs to provide better video service, as expected. When $\bar{U}$ decreases, the UAV trajectory shrinks and mainly consists of smooth curves. The reason is that the UAV does not have to move close to the BSs and GUs with low $\bar{U}$. Such trajectory will result in less energy consumption of the UAV since the smaller flying distance is needed to serve all GUs, and UAV's propulsion energy consumption achieves the smallest value with UAV speed around 12 m/s due to (1). This trend can also be observed in Fig. 1(b). If the QoE requirement $\bar{U}$ is sufficiently large, the UAV tends to fly over each BS and GU with the maximum speed. The reason is that the UAV should fly close to the BSs and GUs so that better communication channel are achieved for satisfying large QoE requirement.

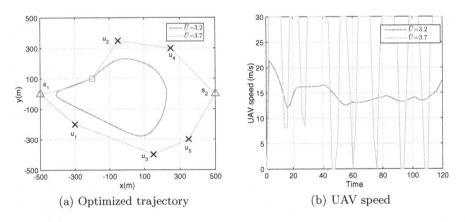

(a) Optimized trajectory   (b) UAV speed

Fig. 1. Optimized trajectories and UAV speed with different QoE requirement $\bar{U}$. The square denotes the initial and final UAV locations, and the triangles denote different existing BSs.

Figure 2 reflects the bandwidth and transmit power allocation with $T = 120, \bar{U} = 3.2$. From Fig. 2(a), it can be seen that the UAV only relays video data when the UAV flies sufficiently close to the corresponding GU. The UAV's transmit power is small since the QoE requirement for GUs $\bar{U}$ is small. The bandwidth allocation over each time slot for all GUs and BSs is shown in Fig. 2(b). The bandwidth is allocated to the BS if the UAV moves close to it such that more video data can be obtained. Such bandwidth allocation for all BSs is enough for each GU to achieve its QoE requirement. This is expected since the UAV relay's position can be dynamically adjusted to enhance the B2U and U2G links, respectively.

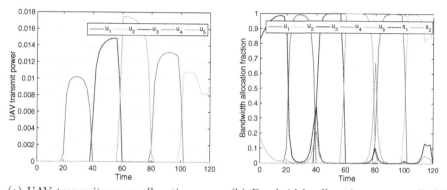

(a) UAV transmit power allocation among all GUs.

(b) Bandwidth allocation among all GUs and BSs.

Fig. 2. Bandwidth and transmit power with $T = 120, \bar{U} = 3.2$.

Finally, we compare the UAV's total energy consumption between our proposed scheme and three benchmark schemes, which are referred to *Static relaying benchmark* and *TSP benchmark*, as well as *QoE maximum benchmark*. In the static relaying benchmark, the UAV hovers over $\mathbf{q}_I$ all the time, and the resource allocation is optimized by solving (P2) with convex optimization technique. In the TSP benchmark, the UAV flies by following the TSP path to visit all GUs and BSs with maximum speed, and the resource allocation is optimized by solving (P2), similar as [16]. In the QoE maximum benchmark, the bandwidth and transmit power allocation are optimized jointly with UAV trajectory to maximize the minimum QoE among all GUs, similar as [10]. From Fig. 3, we can see that our proposed schemes can achieve lower energy consumption of the UAV than other benchmarks, and the gain are brought from the joint design of resource allocation and UAV trajectory.

In Fig. 3(a), it can be seen that the UAV's total energy consumption increases as T increases when $\bar{U} = 3.2$, and the achieved gain is remarkable with larger T. This is because the UAV's flying distance generally increases as T increases. When T is large enough, the UAV can hover over each BS to obtain more video data and hover above each GU in order to provide better video service. Figure 3(b) shows the impact of the QoE requirement $\bar{U}$ with different schemes when $T = 120$. The UAV's energy consumption increases when $\bar{U}$ increases since the UAV needs to to hover around each GU in order to provide better video service, which shows the trade off between minimizing the UAV's energy consumption and maximizing the QoE requirement. It is also observed that static relaying benchmark is not able to support larger QoE requirement, where such

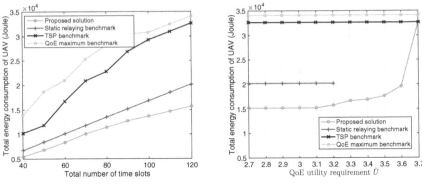

(a) Total energy consumption of the UAV versus T ($\bar{U} = 3.2$)

(b) Total energy consumption of the UAV versus $\bar{U}$ ($T = 120$)

Fig. 3. Total energy consumption of the UAV versus T or $\bar{U}$.

points do not appear in the figure. Furthermore, the performance of the three benchmarks varies a little. The reason is that the UAV trajectory is fixed, and the fixed propulsion energy dominates the UAV's energy consumption.

5   Conclusion

This paper considers a novel UAV enabled video relay system with a UAV relaying video data from multiple BSs to multiple GUs. The aim is to minimize the UAV's energy consumption of while guaranteeing the QoE constraint of each GU, via optimizing the bandwidth and transmit power allocation jointly with UAV trajectory. We propose an efficient iterative algorithm to obtain a KKT solution by using alternating optimization and SCA techniques, and the performance is evaluated numerically as compared to other benchmarks. The proposed design framework is general and can be applied to joint design resource allocation and UAV trajectory in other UAV enabled video streaming systems.

Acknowledgement. This work was supported by the National Natural Science Foundation of China under No. 61702426 and No. 61971457, Fundamental Research Funds for the Central Universities under Grant XDJK2019C084.

References

1. Cisco company: Visual networking index: Global mobile data traffic forecast update, 2016–2021 (2017)
2. Lyu, J., Zeng, Y., Zhang, R.: UAV-aided offloading for cellular hotspot. IEEE Trans. Wireless Commun. **17**(6), 3988–4001 (2018)
3. Chen, Y., Zhao, N., Ding, Z., Alouini, M.: Multiple UAVs as relays: multi-hop single link versus multiple dual-hop links. IEEE Trans. Wireless Commun. **17**(9), 6348–6359 (2018)

4. Khuwaja, A.A., Chen, Y., Zhao, N., Alouini, M.-S., Dobbins, P.: A survey of channel modeling for UAV communications. IEEE Commun. Surv. Tutor. **20**(4), 2804–
   2821 (2018)
5. Zeng, Y., Zhang, R., Lim, T.J.: Throughput maximization for UAV-enabled mobile
   relaying systems. IEEE Trans. Commun. **64**(12), 4983–4996 (2016)
6. She, C., Liu, C., Quek, T.Q.S., Yang, C., Li, Y.: Ultra-reliable and low-latency
   communications in unmanned aerial vehicle communication systems. IEEE Trans.
   Commun. **67**(5), 3768–3781 (2019)
7. Jiang, Z., Xu, C., Guan, J., Liu, Y., Muntean, G.: Stochastic analysis of DASH-
   based video service in high-speed railway networks. IEEE Trans. Multimedia **21**(6),
   1577–1592 (2019)
8. Gao, G., et al.: Optimizing quality of experience for adaptive bitrate streaming via
   viewer interest inference. IEEE Trans. Multimedia **20**(12), 3399–3413 (2018)
9. Hu, H., Zhan, C., An, J., Wen, Y.: Optimization for HTTP adaptive video streaming in UAV-enabled relaying system. In: Proceedings of IEEE ICC, Shanghai,
   China, pp. 1–6 (2019)
10. Wu, Q., Zhang, R.: Common throughput maximization in UAV-enabled OFDMA
    systems with delay consideration. IEEE Trans. Commun. **66**(12), 6614–6627 (2018)
11. Zeng, Y., Xu, J., Zhang, R.: Energy minimization for wireless communication with
    rotary-wing UAV. IEEE Trans. Wireless Commun. **18**(4), 2329–2345 (2019)
12. Zhang, W., Wen, Y., Chen, Z., Khisti, A.: QoE-driven cache management for
    HTTP adaptive bit rate streaming over wireless networks. IEEE Trans. Multi-
    media **15**(6), 1431–1445 (2013)
13. Grant, M., Boyd, S.: CVX: MATLAB Software for Disciplined Convex Program-
    ming. http://cvxr.com/cvx
14. Boyd, S., Vandenberghe, L.: Convex Optimization. Cambridge University Press,
    Cambridge (2004)
15. Zhan, C., Zeng, Y., Zhang, R.: Energy-efficient data collection in UAV enabled
    wireless sensor network. IEEE Wirel. Commun. Lett. **7**(3), 328–331 (2018)
16. Zhang, J., Zeng, Y., Zhang, R.: UAV-enabled radio access network: multi-mode
    communication and trajectory design. IEEE Trans. Signal Process. **66**(20), 5269–
    5284 (2018)

Adaptive Handover Scheme for Mulit-mode Device in Power Wireless Heterogeneous Networks

Weiping Shao[1], Donglei Zhang[2,3], Yang Lu[2,3], Yazhou Wang[5], Wei Bai[2,3(✉)], Ping Ma[4], and Shuiyao Chen[1]

[1] State Grid Zhejiang Electric Power Co., Ltd., Hangzhou, China
[2] Electric Power Intelligent Sensing Technology and Application State Grid Corporation Joint Laboratory, Beijing, China
[3] Global Energy Interconnection Research Institute Co., Ltd., Beijing, China
`baiwei@geiri.sgcc.com.cn`
[4] State Grid Shaoxing Electric Power Supply Company Shaoxing, Shaoxing, China
[5] Beijing University of Posts and Telecommunications, Beijing, China

Abstract. In smart grid systems, heterogeneous networks are considered as a promising solution to address the expeditious growth of mobile traffic. Considering the different user preferences, how to efficiently utilize the limited resource of small base stations (SBSs) becomes a challenge. In this paper, we investigate a joint handover and transmission strategy for users. We formulate the handover and transmission problem to minimize the service delay, which considers the overlapped coverage of SBSs and the limited capacity of backhaul link. To solve this NP-hard problem, we design a heuristic algorithm with two phases. In content caching phase, the contents are cached at SBSs according to the greedy algorithm. In content delivery phase, a transmission strategy is designed to meet the user demands for videos with different quality level. Simulation results show that our proposed algorithm has the advantage of reducing video delivery delay and saving the backhaul traffic compared with other algorithms.

Keywords: Smart grid networks · Heterogeneous small cell networks · Cooperative caching and transmission · Layered-video caching

1 Introduction

At present, the fifth generation network can be used as a new framework to enhance public utilities and smart grids [1]. However, the increasing traffic has put great pressure on the capacity of smart grid [2]. Small cell networks (SCNs) are one of the promising solutions to meet this increasing demands, where heterogeneous small base stations (SBSs) are densely deployed near users to improve area spectral efficiency and network capacity. However, the cost of deploying high-speed backhaul may hinder the densification of network [3].

© ICST Institute for Computer Sciences, Social Informatics and Telecommunications Engineering 2020
Published by Springer Nature Switzerland AG 2020. All Rights Reserved
S. W. Loke et al. (Eds.): MONAMI 2020, LNICST 338, pp. 270–283, 2020.
https://doi.org/10.1007/978-3-030-64002-6_18

Recently, various research has shown that the demands from users are usually focused on a few popular contents. Therefore, these popular contents can be proactively cached at the SBSs during off-peak hours, reducing the backhaul traffic caused by duplicate transmission [4]. In cache-enabled small cell networks, a key challenge is to determine which contents should be cached at each SBSs to improve the user experience, considering the content popularity and network topology. The works [5,6] analyze the optimal content caching strategy to minimize the download time of files. In work [7], the expected backhaul rate and the energy consumption is minimized via optimizing cache placement.

Furthermore, as the dense deployment of SBSs, cooperative cache has been proposed to efficiently utilize the limited cache capacity of SBSs [8–10]. In cooperative cache, users can be served by multiple nearby SBSs, and these SBSs can cache different contents to improve cache hit rate. In [8,9], the authors design a cooperative content caching and delivery policy in small cell network. In content caching phase, the network hasn't been congested, and each SBSs proactively stores contents according to the caching policy. In content delivery phase, the demands of users have been revealed, and the problem is to decide which place can serve the user requests. The work [10] explores cooperative cache in user-centric mobile networks, where the cache-enabled SBSs in user-centric cluster can cooperatively serve the user requests, and the cluster size shows a trade-off between caching diversity and spectrum efficiency.

Due to the heterogeneity of user devices and the variation of the wireless channel, users may have different preferences for video quality [11]. Scalable video coding (SVC) has been proposed to provide adaptive video streaming service, which allows temporal, spatial, and quality scalability [12]. In SVC, each video can be encoded into multiple layers, and the combination of these layers can achieve different video quality. The layer 1 is also called base layer that provides the lowest video quality. The high video quality can be achieved by adding the layer 2 up to the highest necessary layer. In work [13], the videos encoded by SVC are cached at base station to serve the user with different demands for video quality, and the author also proposes the content caching and transmission schemes for this scalable videos. The work [14] designs a cooperative caching algorithm for video encoding layers, where the multiple network operators can share their cached video layers to reduce the video delivery delay. The work [15] investigates a cooperative caching problem for video encoding layers in heterogeneous network. The author formulates the delay minimization problem and solves it by greedy algorithm.

Although much works have been done on layered video caching, they don't consider the properties of small cell networks, i.e., the overlapped coverage of SBSs and the limited capacity of backhaul link. In this paper, we design a cooperative caching and transmission strategy for video encoding layers, where the user can be served by multiple nearby SBSs and SBSs can cooperate with each other to minimize the video delivery delay. The main contributions of this paper are summarized as follows:

- We investigate the cooperative caching and transmission problem for SVC-encoded videos in small cell networks, and formulate the video delivery delay minimization problem considering the overlapped coverage of SBSs and the limited backhaul capacity.
- The delay minimization problem is NP-hard, we design a greedy caching algorithm to cache the video encoding layers at each SBS. After the content caching phase, we also design a content delivery algorithm to decide which place should serve the demands of users.
- The simulation results shows that our algorithm achieves lower delivery delay and saves the backhaul traffic compared with other algorithm.

The rest of this paper is organized as follows: Section 2 describes the caching and delivery model. Section 3 formulates the delay minimization problem and propose a heuristic algorithm to solve it. Section 4 presents simulation results. Finally, Sect. 5 concludes this paper.

2   System Model

2.1   Network Model

In the heterogeneous smart grid network, a macro base station (MBS) is connected with a remote video server, and M SBSs are deployed densely to serve N wireless users, as shown in Fig. 1. We denote the SBSs set as: $\mathcal{M} = \{1, 2, \ldots, M\}$, and the users set as: $\mathcal{N} = \{1, 2, \ldots, N\}$. The SBSs are connected with MBS via backhaul link, through which the cached contents can be shared to avoid requesting these contents from remote servers. The specific cooperation strategy will explain in the latter.

2.2   Scalable Video Coding and Caching

The SBSs are equipped with a cache of size C_m bits, which is filled in advance during off-peak hours, according to the popularity of the videos. Each user independently requests videos of interest from a library $\mathcal{V} = \{1, 2, \ldots, V\}$, where each video has the same size. We utilize SVC to encode each video content into multiple layers, $\mathcal{L} = \{1, 2, \ldots, L\}$, and the combination of these layers can achieve a certain quality level of corresponding video. For example, layer 1 provider the basic quality level 1, and the quality level 2 can be achieved by adding layer 2, and so on. Typically, the quality level q requires all the lower layer $1, 2, \cdots, q$ successfully decoded. We use L_{vl} to represent the layer l of video v, and V_{vq} to represent the qth quality level of video v. The size of layer L_{vl} is denoted as s_{vl}, which decreases with the increasing of the layer, i.e., $s_{v1} \geq s_{v2} \geq \cdots \geq s_{vL}$.

2.3   Requests and Cooperative Transmission

We assume the probability that users request the qth quality level of video v is known in advance, denoted by p_{vq}, which can be learned by analyzing the historical request patterns of users.

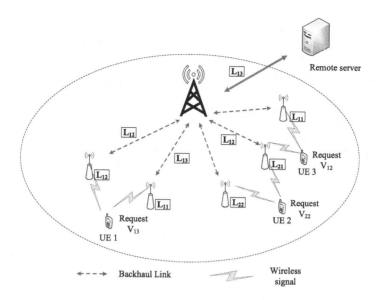

Fig. 1. A Smart Grid enabled heterogeneous network

As mentioned before, when a user requests video with quality level q, all the layers below q must be successfully received. To reduce the download delay, those layers are sent to the user at the same time. Thus the delivery delay of video is bounded by the maximum delivery delay among all the layers.

$$D_n^{vq} = \max_{1 \le l \le q} \left\{ d_n^{vl} \right\} \tag{1}$$

Where d_n^{vl} is the delivery delay of layer L_{vl}, and D_n^{vq} is the delivery delay of video V_{vq}.

In order to efficiently utilize the limited cache size of SBSs, the cached contents in SBS i can be shared with SBS j through the backhaul link. As illustrated in Fig. 1, the user 3 requests for video V_{12}, the layer L_{12} hasn't been cached in its nearby SBSs, then the SBS with layer L_{12} will send it to the nearest SBS of user 3, which will reduce the download delay compared with fetching L_{12} from the remote server. According to the different place where the user gets the requested content, we define the following three delivery modes.

- **Local delivery mode:** We denote the nearby SBSs set of user n as: $\mathcal{M}_n$. If the requested content of user n has been cached in the SBS m belonging to $\mathcal{M}_n$, this content is directly sent by SBS m. The download rate of this mode is given by

$$r_{mn}^w = W log_2 \left(1 + \frac{p_m g_{mn}}{I + \sigma^2} \right), \tag{2}$$

where g_{mn} is the channel coefficient from SBS m to user n, p_m is the transmission power of SBS m. In this paper, we assume that the simultaneous transmission at the same SBS is handled by orthogonal spectrum of the same bandwidth W, and the advanced inter-cell interference coordination (ICIC) technology has been used so that the interference I is a constant.

- **Backhaul delivery mode:** If the requested content of user n hasn't been cached in SBSs set $\mathcal{M}_n$, then the nearest SBS of user n will attempt to fetch this content through backhaul link and send it to user. This process will cause a larger delay compared with the local delivery. We use r_k^b to denote the download rate, where k represents the SBS that sends the requested content.
- **Remote delivery mode:** If there is no copy of the requested content in any SBS, the request file is fetched from the remote servers. This fetching will cause the slowest download rate r_0.

3 Problem Formulation and Solution

In this paper, our goal is to minimize the download delay of video with different quality level. To describe the video layers placement, we define the binary variables $x_m^{vl} \in \{0, 1\}$, where $x_m^{vl} = 1$ indicates that the layer L_{vl} is cached at the SBS m, and $x_m^{vl} = 0$ otherwise. The cache size constraint of SBS can be expressed as,

$$\sum_{v \in \mathcal{V}} \sum_{l \in \mathcal{L}} x_m^{vl} s_{vl} \leq C_m, \quad \forall m \in \mathcal{M}. \tag{3}$$

To describe the three mentioned delivery modes, we introduce the binary variables $\{y_n^{vl}, z_{kn}^{vl}\} \in \{0, 1\}$, where the binary variable $y_n^{vl} = 1$ is used to indicate that the layer L_{vl} is fetched from SBS in set $\mathcal{M}_n$, and the binary variable $z_{kn}^{vl} = 1$ is used to denote the layer L_{vl} is fetched from SBS k out of the set $\mathcal{M}_n$. The download rate in local delivery mode should be larger than backhaul delivery mode, then we have following constraint,

$$r_{mn}^w > \max(r_k^b), \quad \forall m \in \mathcal{M}_n. \tag{4}$$

The delay for user n receiving the layer L_{vl} can be expressed as:

$$d_n^{vl} = y_n^{vl} \min_{m \in \mathcal{M}_n} (x_m^{vl} \frac{s_{vl}}{r_{mn}^w}) +$$
$$(1 - y_n^{vl}) \sum_{k \in \mathcal{M} \setminus \mathcal{M}_n} z_{kn}^{vl} \frac{s_{vl}}{r_k^b} +$$
$$(1 - y_n^{vl}) \prod_{k \in \mathcal{M} \setminus \mathcal{M}_n} (1 - z_{kn}^{vl}) \frac{s_{vl}}{r_0}. \tag{5}$$

The first term is the delay of local delivery mode. If the nearby SBSs of user have cached the requested content, the closest SBS will send this content to user. The second term is the delay of backhaul delivery mode. If requested content has been cached in nearby SBSs, user will try to fetch it from other SBSs through backhaul link. The last term is the delay that the requested content is delivered from the remote server.

Generally, the capacity of the backhaul link of each SBS is limited. Therefore the upstream traffic of SBSs k can not greater than its backhaul capacity B_k.

$$\sum_{n \in \mathcal{N}} \sum_{v \in \mathcal{V}} \sum_{1 \leq l \leq q} z_{kn}^{vl} r_k^b \leq B_k, \quad \forall k \in \mathcal{M}. \tag{6}$$

The overall problem is minimal the delay when users request for video with different quality level. Given the probability p_{vq} that users request for video v with quality level q, the objective is to determine the cache placement of different layers x_m^{vl}, and the delivery modes of requested content $\{y_n^{vl}, z_{kn}^{vl}\}$.

$$\min_{x,y,z} \sum_{n \in \mathcal{N}} \sum_{v \in \mathcal{V}} \sum_{q \in \mathcal{Q}} p_{vq} \max_{1 \leq l \leq q} \{d_n^{vl}\} \tag{7a}$$

$$\text{s.t.} \quad \sum_{v \in \mathcal{V}} \sum_{l \in \mathcal{L}} x_m^{vl} s_{vl} \leq C_m, \quad \forall m \in \mathcal{M}, \tag{7b}$$

$$0 \leq y_n^{vl} \leq \min(\sum_{m \in \mathcal{M}_n} x_m^{vl}, 1), \quad \forall n, v, l, \tag{7c}$$

$$0 \leq z_{kn}^{vl} \leq x_k^{vl}, \quad \forall n, k, v, l, \tag{7d}$$

$$\sum_{n \in \mathcal{N}} \sum_{v \in \mathcal{V}} \sum_{1 \leq l \leq q} z_{kn}^{vl} r_k^b \leq B_k, \quad \forall k \in \mathcal{M}, \tag{7e}$$

$$r_{mn}^w > \max(r_k^b), \quad \forall m \in \mathcal{M}_n. \tag{7f}$$

$$x, y, z \in \{0,1\}. \tag{7g}$$

Constraint (7b) means that the cached contents of each SBS can't exceed its capacity C_m. Constraint (7c) and (7d) ensure the availability of the layers, i.e., the requested layers should be sent by the SBS that caches them. Constraint (7e) ensures that the upstream traffic of each SBS can't exceed its backhaul capacity B_k. Constraint (7f) limits the size of nearby SBS set $\mathcal{M}_n$.

This problem is NP-hard, which can be proved by reduction from the knapsack problem, and the latter can be expressed as follows. Given a knapsack with capacity W, and N items with non-negative weights $w_1, \cdots, w_N$ and values $v_1, \cdots, v_N$. The problem is to find a subset with largest value from items N, when the total weight of this subset does not exceed the capacity W. We consider a special case of our problem where each video encodes to one base layer and there are only one SBS in the network. Then this problem is to cache a subset of videos from $\mathcal{V}$ to achieve minimal delay under the constraint of caching size of SBS, which is the standard knapsack problem.

3.1 Proposed Greedy Layer Caching Algorithm

In this subsection, we will present the proposed greedy caching algorithm for the video layers caching problem, which can find a sub-optimal solution within polynomial time. We first give the expression of expected delay savings when adding a new content to the SBS cache. Then we design a greedy caching algorithm which caches the content with maximal delay savings in each iteration.

We define the set $\mathcal{X} = \{x_1^{11}, \ldots, x_m^{vl}, \ldots, x_M^{VL}\}$ to describe the cache placement, and $G(\mathcal{X}^*, x_m^{vl})$ represents the expected delay savings by adding new content x_m^{vl} to the last caching placement $\mathcal{X}^*$. To describe the delay savings, we introduce the variables $\{D_{nvl}^*, r_{vl}^*\}$ to record the state of the last caching placement, which are explained as follows.

- D_{nvl}^* is the last download delay for user n requesting the video v with quality level l.
- r_{vl}^* records the remaining number of users, and the layer l they requested is sent by the remote server.

When a new content x_m^{vl} is added into the caching placement $\mathcal{X}^*$, the SBS m can send this content to its nearby users $\mathcal{N}_m$, which may save the download delay when these users request for video V_{vl}, and this part of delay savings can be expressed as:

$$G_1 = \sum_{n \in \mathcal{N}_m} p_{vl} [D_{nvl}^* - D_{nvl}]^+, \tag{8}$$

where operation $[x]^+ \triangleq \max(x, 0)$, and D_{nvl} is the current download delay, which is bounded by the last download delay of video $V_{v(l-1)}$.

$$D_{nvl} = \max(\frac{s_{vl}}{r_{mn}^w}, D_{nv(l-1)}^*). \tag{9}$$

Note the SBS m can also send content x_m^{vl} to the remote users via backhaul link, which can save the delay compared with the remote delivery mode.

$$G_2 = p_{vl} \min(\frac{B_m}{r_m^b}, r_{vl}^*)(\frac{s_{vl}}{r_m^b} - \frac{s_{vl}}{r_0}). \tag{10}$$

Here, $\min(\frac{B_m}{r_m^b}, r_{vl}^*)$ is the number of users that they requested content is fetched from the SBS m via backhaul link.

By adding this two part of delay savings, $G(\mathcal{X}^*, x_m^{vl})$ can be expressed as follows.

$$G(\mathcal{X}^*, x_m^{vl}) = G_1 + G_2. \tag{11}$$

Next, we illustrate the greedy caching algorithm for the layer caching problem (7a) in Algorithm 1. This algorithm starts with the empty cache at each SBS. In each iteration, it adds the content $x_{m^*}^{v^* l^*}$ with maximum utility $U(x_m^{vl})$ to the SBS m until the caches of all SBSs are filled, and the utility is defined as the delay savings per bit.

$$U(x_m^{vl}) = \frac{G(\mathcal{X}^*, x_m^{vl})}{s_{vl}}. \tag{12}$$

After adding the content $x_{m^*}^{v^* l^*}$ to the cache of SBS m^*, the delay record $D_{nv^* l^*}^*$ and the remaining number of users $r_{v^* l^*}^*$ will be updated to record the state of current iteration.

Algorithm 1. Proposed Greedy Layer Caching Algorithm

Require: $\mathcal{N}_m$, p_{vl}, B_m, r_{mn}^w, r_m^b, r_0, s_{vl}.
Ensure: x_m^{vl}.
1: Initialization:
   $x_m^{vl} = 0$;
   $D_{nvl}^* = \dfrac{s_{vl}}{r_0}$, $D_{nv0}^* = 0$, $r_{vl}^* = N$;
2: **while** the caching space is not full **do**
3:     $(m^*, v^*, l^*) \leftarrow_{m,v,l} U(x_m^{vl})$, $x_{m^*}^{v^*l^*} = 1$;
4:     **for** each $n \in \mathcal{N}_{m^*}$ **do**
5:         **if** $\dfrac{s_{v^*l^*}}{r_{m^*n}^w} < D_{nv^*l^*}^*$ **then**
6:             $D_{nv^*l^*}^* = \max(\dfrac{s_{v^*l^*}}{r_{m^*n}^w}, D_{nv^*(l^*-1)}^*)$
7:         **end if**
8:     **end for**
9:     $r_{v^*l^*}^* = \max(r_{v^*l^*}^* - \dfrac{B_{m^*}}{r_{m^*}^b}, 0)$;
10: **end while**

3.2 Proposed Caching and Cooperative Delivery Algorithm

In the following, we will introduce the overall caching and cooperative delivery algorithm which gives the caching placement of video layers and the places that serve the requests of users.

In this algorithm, we first initialize the neighbor set M_n (N_m) of each user (SBS), which satisfies $r_{mn}^w > \max(r_m^b)$. Then, each SBS caches video layers x_m^{vl} according to the result of Algorithm 1. Finally, this algorithm will decide where to serve the requests of users. If a user n requests video V_{vq}, all the layers $l \leq q$ should be received to recover the original video. To get the layer L_{vl}, the user will first examine whether the nearby SBSs $m \in M_n$ have cached this layer. If not, the nearest SBS of this user will try to get this layer from remote SBSs through backhaul link. If the nearest SBS still can't get the layer L_{vl} from other SBSs, it will fetch this layer from the remote server. The delay for request r_{nvq} is the maximum download delay among all the layers $l \leq q$. The specific algorithm is shown in Algorithm 2.

4 Simulation Results

In this section, we evaluate the performance of the proposed layer caching and cooperative delivery algorithm. We consider a small cell network consisting of 13 uniformly distributed SBSs and 60 users. The video library V consists of 200 unique videos, and each video has $Q = 5$ quality levels by using SVC. For simplicity, we consider that each video has already been divided to equal size 40 MB, and the size of layers 1 to 5 is 20,5,5,5,5 MB. The popularity of the videos follows the Zipf distribution, and we assume the quality level of video requested by users follows a uniform distribution. Then the probability that users request

---

Algorithm 2. Proposed Layer Caching and Cooperative Delivery Algorithm

---

Require: $\mathcal{N}$, $\mathcal{M}$, g_{mn}, r_{nvq}, r_m^b, r_0, s_{vl}.
Ensure: x_m^{vl}, y_n^{vl}, z_{kn}^{vl}.

1: Initialization:
    Calculate $r_{mn}^w = W log_2 \left(1 + \frac{p_m g_{mn}}{I+\sigma^2}\right)$;
    Set $M_n = \emptyset$, $N_m = \emptyset$;
2: **for** each r_{mn}^w **do**
3:    **if** $r_{mn}^w > \max(r_m^b)$ **then**
4:       $\mathcal{M}_n \leftarrow M_n \cup m$, $\mathcal{N}_m \leftarrow N_m \cup n$;
5:    **end if**
6: **end for**
7: Obtain the caching placement x_m^{vl} by algorithm 1;
8: **for** each user request r_{nvq} **do**
9:    **for** $l = 1, \ldots, q$ **do**
10:      $r_n^{vl} = r_0$;
11:      **for** each SBS $m \in M_n$ **do**
12:         **if** $x_m^{vl} = 1$ **then**
13:           $r_n^{vl} = \max(r_{mn}^w)$, $y_n^{vl} = 1$;
14:           Go to step 22;
15:         **end if**
16:      **end for**
17:      **for** each SBS $k \notin M_n$ **do**
18:         **if** $x_k^{vl} = 1$ and $\sum_{n \in \mathcal{N}} \sum_{v \in \mathcal{V}} \sum_{1 \leq l \leq q} z_{kn}^{vl} r_k^b \leq B_k$ **then**
19:           $r_n^{vl} = \max(r_k^b)$
20:           $k^* \leftarrow_k (r_k^b)$, $z_{k^*n}^{vl} = 1$;
21:         **end if**
22:      **end for**
23:    **end for**
24:    $D_{nvq} = \max_{1 \leq l \leq q} \left(\frac{s_{vl}}{r_n^{vl}}\right)$;
25: **end for**

---

video v with quality level q can be expressed as:

$$p_{vq} = \frac{v^{-\delta}}{Q \sum_{i=1}^{V} i^{-\delta}}, \tag{13}$$

Where δ is the skew parameter. In this simulation, we generated 200 user requests r_{nvq} based on the popularity p_{vq} and calculated the corresponding performance indicators. The other settings of the simulation are summarized in Table 1.

We evaluate the performance in terms of average delivery delay and backhaul traffic load. The former is the average latency of delivering all the layers to decode the original video requested by the user, and the latter is defined as follows.

$$T_{bh} = s_{vl} \left(2 \sum_n \sum_k z_{kn}^{vl} + (1 - y_n^{vl}) \prod_k (1 - z_{kn}^{vl})\right). \tag{14}$$

The first term is the traffic caused by sharing layers over the backhaul link, and the last is caused by delivering layers from the remote server.

Table 1. Simulation parameters

Parameter	Value
Transmit power of SBSs p_m	200 mW
Path loss model	$140.7 + 36.7 \log_{10} d$
Bandwidth W	900 kHz
Noise power density σ^2	-174 dBm/Hz
Interference I	-100 dBm/Hz
Delivery rate over backhaul link r_m^b	5 Mbps
Delivery rate from remote server r_0	1 Mbps
Cache capacity of SBSs C_m	5%–35% (% of library size)
Backhaul capacity of SBSs B_m	10–80 MB
Zipf skewing parameter δ	0.3–1.0

For comparison, we implement the following three caching algorithm.

- *Most Popular Caching (MPC):* Each SBS independently caches layers of the videos with the highest popularity until the cache capacity is full.
- *Largest Content Diversity (LCD):* This algorithm try to cache more different layers in the network to achieve largest diversity. It traverses the video set V and caches the content in the SBS m with the maximum utility $U(x_m^{vl})$ each time.
- *Octopus:* We take the greedy idea of the proactive cache distribution algorithm in paper. Each user is associated with the closest SBS. Iteratively, it adds the layer with the maximum delay savings to the cache of SBSs, but does not consider the limited backhaul capacity.

We first compare the impact of different caching schemes on the average delivery delay in Fig. 2, where the default value is $C_m = 20\%$, $\delta = 0.6$, and $B_m = 20$ MB. It can be seen that our proposed algorithm always achieves the minimum delivery delay. This is because MPC redundantly caches the most popular content in each SBS, ignoring the cooperation opportunity between SBSs, and this can be seen from Fig. 2(c), the increasing of backhaul capacity has no impact on the delivery delay in MPC. Although LCD caches different contents as much as possible, it does not consider the popularity of the content. Thus from Fig. 2(b), the increasing of the Zipf parameter δ has no impact on the delivery delay in LCD. In Octopus, each user is only associated with the closest SBS, ignoring the overlapped coverage of SBSs, which leads to a larger delivery delay compared with our algorithm.

In addition, we can see that the marginal value of caching a new content becomes smaller as the cache size increases from Fig. 2(a). Therefore we should cache the content with more delay savings when the cache set is small. From Fig. 2(b), the average delivery delay decreases with the increasing of the Zipf skewing parameter δ, because the popularity is more concentrated in a few videos

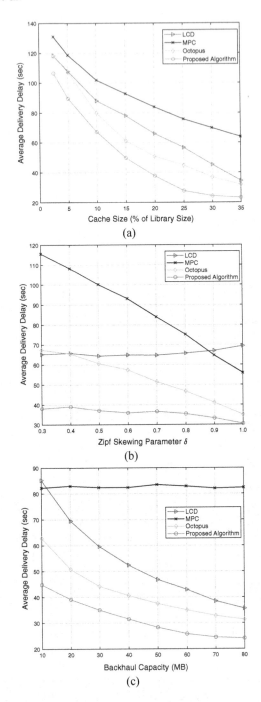

Fig. 2. The average delivery delay achieved by the different caching schemes as a function of (a) the cache sizes, (b) the skewing parameter δ of the Zipf distribution, and (c) the capacity of backhaul link.

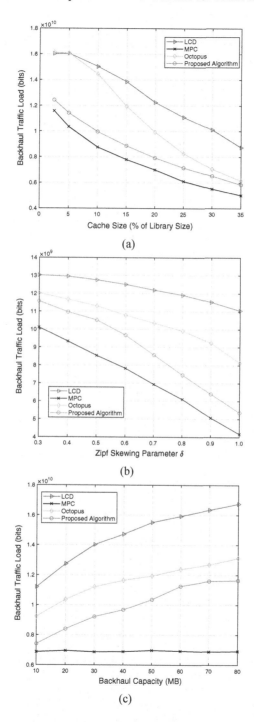

Fig. 3. The backhaul traffic load achieved by the different caching schemes as a function of (a) the cache sizes, (b) the skewing parameter δ of the Zipf distribution, and (c) the capacity of backhaul link.

with a larger δ. From Fig. 2(c), as the backhaul capacity increases, the delivery delay decreases, because the SBSs with larger backhaul capacity can share more cached contents, thus avoiding fetching them from the remote server.

Figure 3 compares the impact of different caching schemes on the backhaul traffic load. It can be seen that MPC scheme always achieves the minimum backhaul traffic, because there is no cooperation between SBSs in MPC, thus reducing the traffic caused by sharing contents over the backhaul link. However, as can be seen from Fig. 2, MPC will result in the largest delivery delay. LCD try to cache more different contents, which results in more frequent sharing of cached contents, and it achieves the maximum backhaul traffic in Fig. 3. Our proposed algorithm results smaller backhaul traffic compared with Octopus. Because users only associate with the closest SBS in Octopus, the cached contents in the nearby SBS should be delivered through the backhaul link, which results a larger backhaul traffic. In particular, we can see that our proposed algorithm have a larger gap between Octopus when cache size is small from Fig. 3(a).

5   Conclusion

In this paper, we design a cooperative caching and transmission strategy for video layers encoded by SVC. We formulate the problem to minimize the video delivery delay, where SBSs can share the cached content with each other and users can be served by multiple nearby SBSs. To solve this NP-hard problem, we design a heuristic algorithm with two phase. In content caching phase, a greedy algorithm is designed to cache the video encoding layers at each SBSs. After this phase, we also design a transmission strategy to deliver the cached video layers, which considers the limited capacity of backhaul link. Simulation results show that our proposed algorithm not only reduce the video delivery delay, but also save the backhaul traffic.

Acknowledgment. This work has been supported by STATE GRID Corporation of China science and technology project "Research and application on key technologies of power wireless heterogeneous network convergence" (5700-201919236A-0-0-00).

References

1. Anandakumar, H., Arulmurugan, R.: Next generation wireless communication networks for smart grid. In: 2019 Third International conference on I-SMAC (IoT in Social, Mobile, Analytics and Cloud) (I-SMAC), pp. 260–264 (2019)
2. Pei, Y., Zhang, H., Gu, X., Wang, H.: Research on power grid information model based on artificial intelligence. In: 2019 International Conference on Computer Network, Electronic and Automation (ICCNEA), pp. 321–328 (2019)
3. Asuhaimi, F.A., Bu, S., Klaine, P.V., Imran, M.A.: Channel access and power control for energy-efficient delay-aware heterogeneous cellular networks for smart grid communications using deep reinforcement learning. IEEE Access **7**, 133474–133484 (2019)

4. Baştuğ, E., Bennis, M., Debbah, M.: Cache-enabled small cell networks: modeling and tradeoffs. In: 2014 11th International Symposium on Wireless Communications Systems (ISWCS), pp. 649–653, August 2014
5. Shanmugam, K., Golrezaei, N., Dimakis, A.G., Molisch, A.F., Caire, G.: Femto-caching: wireless content delivery through distributed caching helpers. IEEE Trans. Inf. Theory **59**(12), 8402–8413 (2013)
6. Poularakis, K., Iosifidis, G., Argyriou, A., Tassiulas, L.: Video delivery over hetero-geneous cellular networks: optimizing cost and performance. In: IEEE INFOCOM 2014 - IEEE Conference on Computer Communications, pp. 1078–1086, April 2014
7. Gabry, F., Bioglio, V., Land, I.: On energy-efficient edge caching in heterogeneous networks. IEEE J. Sel. Areas Commun. **34**(12), 3288–3298 (2016)
8. Chen, Z., Lee, J., Quek, T.Q.S., Kountouris, M.: Cooperative caching and transmis-sion design in cluster-centric small cell networks. IEEE Trans. Wireless Commun. **16**(5), 3401–3415 (2017)
9. Jiang, W., Feng, G., Qin, S.: Optimal cooperative content caching and delivery pol-icy for heterogeneous cellular networks. IEEE Trans. Mob. Comput. **16**(5), 1382–1393 (2017)
10. Zhang, S., He, P., Suto, K., Yang, P., Zhao, L., Shen, X.: Cooperative edge caching in user-centric clustered mobile networks. IEEE Trans. Mob. Comput. **17**(8), 1791–1805 (2018)
11. Tran, T.X., Pandey, P., Hajisami, A., Pompili, D.: Collaborative multi-bitrate video caching and processing in mobile-edge computing networks. In: 2017 13th Annual Conference on Wireless On-demand Network Systems and Services (WONS), pp. 165–172, February 2017
12. Schwarz, H., Marpe, D., Wiegand, T.: Overview of the scalable video coding exten-sion of the H.264/AVC standard. IEEE Trans. Circuits Syst. Video Technol. **17**(9), 1103–1120 (2007)
13. Wu, L., Zhang, W.: Caching-based scalable video transmission over cellular net-works. IEEE Commun. Lett. **20**(6), 1156–1159 (2016)
14. Poularakis, K., Iosifidis, G., Argyriou, A., Koutsopoulos, I., Tassiulas, L.: Dis-tributed caching algorithms in the realm of layered video streaming. IEEE Trans. Mob. Comput. **18**(4), 757–770 (2019)
15. Zhang, T., Mao, S.: Cooperative caching for scalable video transmissions over het-erogeneous networks. IEEE Netw. Lett. **1**(2), 63–67 (2019)

A New Ultrasound Elastography Displacement Estimation Method for Mobile Telemedicine

Hong-an Li[1], Min Zhang[1], Keping Yu[2(✉)], Xin Qi[2], Li Zhen[3], Yi Gong[4,5], and Jianfeng Tong[6]

[1] College of Computer Science and Technology, Xi'an University of Science and Technology, Xi'an 710054, China
[2] Global Information and Telecommunication Institute, Waseda University, Tokyo 169-8050, Japan
keping.yu@aoni.waseda.jp
[3] School of Communications and Information Engineering, Xi'an University of Posts and Telecommunications, Xi'an 710121, China
[4] School of Information and Communication Engineering, Beijing University of Posts and Communications (BUPT), Beijing, China
[5] Global Big Data Technologies Center (GBDTC), University of Technology Sydney (UTS), Sydney, Australia
[6] School of Information Science and Technology, Northwest University, Xi'an 710127, China

Abstract. Traditional medicine requires doctors and patients to engage in face-to-face palpation, which is a great challenge in underdeveloped areas, especially in rural areas. Telemedicine provides an opportunity for patients to connect with doctors who may be thousands of miles away via mobile devices or the Internet. When using this method, elastography is a crucial medical imaging modality that maps the elastic properties of soft tissue, which can then be sent to doctors remotely. Ultrasound elastography has become a research focus because it can accurately measure soft tissue lesions. Displacement estimation is a key step in ultrasound elastography. The phase-zero search method is a popular displacement estimation method that is accurate and rapid. However, the method is ineffective when the displacement is more than a 1/4 wavelength. The block-matching method can address this shortcoming because it is suitable for large displacements, although it is not accurate. Notably, the quality-guided block matching method has exhibited good robustness under complex mutational conditions. In this paper, we propose a novel displacement estimation method that combines the block-matching method and the phase-zero search method. The block-matching method provides prior knowledge to increase the robustness of the phase-zero search under large displacement conditions. The experimental results show that our method exhibits stronger robustness, more accurate results, and faster calculation speed.

Keywords: Ultrasound elastography · Displacement estimated · Phase-zero search · Block-matching method

© ICST Institute for Computer Sciences, Social Informatics and Telecommunications Engineering 2020
Published by Springer Nature Switzerland AG 2020. All Rights Reserved
S. W. Loke et al. (Eds.): MONAMI 2020, LNICST 338, pp. 284–297, 2020.
https://doi.org/10.1007/978-3-030-64002-6_19

1 Introduction

In recent years, with the development of modern communication technology, telemedicine using mobile devices or the Internet has developed rapidly. This has brought great convenience to people in underdeveloped areas, even in rural areas. We can even conduct telemedicine consultations through mobile devices at home. We have seen national health authorities start to focus on E-health services such as E-health cards, electronic medical records and health portals, including the English NHS Direct Online, the German Telematics Platform, and the Danish Sundhed.dk. [1–3]. Blockchain technology is suitable for applications where independently managed biomedical/medical stakeholders (such as hospitals, suppliers, patients, and payers) wish to collaborate without ceding control to a centrally managed intermediary [4–7]. Traditional medicine relies on palpation to feel the size, shape or firmness of soft tissue, but this technique cannot provide accurate or concrete analysis. The firmness of biological soft tissue can provide important evidence for the early diagnosis of a nidus, especially for the diagnosis of tumors [8]. Ophir J. proposed the ultrasonic elastography method [9, 10], which is different from the traditional ultrasonic imaging method in that it can reflect the physical information of soft tissue through images, such as the Young's modulus. However, the traditional ultrasound imaging method provides only a reflection of the acoustic impedance of soft tissue. The conventional ultrasound imaging method has a limited ability to distinguish soft tissues with small differences in acoustic impedance, and it is prone to interference from various factors in the detection of deeper tissues of the body. Ultrasound elastography technology can address this deficiency. Ultrasound elastography has become a research topic of interest in the field of ultrasonic imagery both at home and abroad, and various improved ultrasonic imaging methods have emerged, such as O'Donnell M.'s envelope cross-correlation method [11], Sarvazyan A.P.'s method of shear wave elastography [12], Fatemi M.'s acoustic radiation imaging method [13], Varghese T.'s time-domain stretching method [14], and Sarvazyan A. P.'s alternating strain estimation method [15].

Using Ophir J.'s method, we can create a slight deformation of the tissue (1% to 2%) by applying a little pressure and collect an ultrasonic signal before and after the procedure through an ultrasonic device. Using a time-domain cross-correlation to compare the two sets of signals, we can obtain the displacement of each point in the tissue and calculate the displacement difference to obtain the tissue strain; the reciprocal of the strain is used to appropriately represent the physical attributes of the tissue. Although we cannot quantitatively measure the tissue elasticity with Ophir J.'s method, we can clearly distinguish tissues with different hardness levels. The accuracy of time-domain cross-correlation is subject to the ultrasonic frequency, the sampling rate and the signal-to-noise ratio and is more sensitive to the sampling rate when the signal-to-noise ratio is high.

In O'Donnell M.'s method, the signal envelope cross-correlation method is used to calculate the tissue displacement [11]. In this method, a Hilbert transform is performed on the collected RF to obtain the analytical signal, and the analytical signal is cross-correlated. By analyzing the phase of the analytical signal cross-correlation function, the displacement data of the tissue can be obtained. Due to the periodic characteristics of the phase, this method can only be used when the maximum displacement is less than a 1/4 wavelength. When the displacement is greater than a 1/4 wavelength, phase cancellation will occur and produce an incorrect displacement. To circumvent this limitation, Shiina T. proposed a CAM (Combined Autocorrelation Method) [16, 17], which expanded the application scope of the method. However, the CAM requires a large amount of computation and is greatly affected by noise.

The block-matching method is widely used in video compression and video tracking applications [18]. It divides the target frame into blocks of the same size. For each block, the best matching position is found in the reference frame (usually the adjacent frame of the target frame). There are many measures of matching degree, including SAD (Sum of Absolute Differences), MSD (Mean Square Differences) and NCC (Normalized Cross Correlation). The best matching location search methods include FS (Full Search), TSS (Three-Step Search), NTSS (New Three-Step Search), and 4SS (Four-Step Search) [19]. To narrow the search scope, the search can be carried out around the best matching position that has been calculated for the adjacent blocks. However, because this search method based on prior knowledge, it can lead to error accumulation and obtain intolerable error results. In this paper, a quality-guided block matching method is adopted to improve the computing speed and avoid the accumulation of errors.

In this paper, we take advantage of the technical merits of the quality-guided block matching method and the phase-zero search method. We combine these two popular methods into our new method to estimate the tissue displacement, achieving good experimental results. The structure of this paper is organized as follows. Section 1 introduces the current research background of ultrasound elastography in the E-health field. Section 2 presents the quality-guided block matching method and the phase-zero search method, and our algorithm framework is outlined. The experiments and analysis are presented in Sect. 3, and we compare our proposed model with two popular methods. Section 4 concludes this paper.

2 Algorithm Framework

2.1 Quality-Guided Block Matching

In our method, we take the sum of absolute differences (SAD) as the measurement of matching degree, and it is defined as follows:

$$SAD = \sum_{i=1}^{m} \sum_{j=1}^{n} |A(i,j) - B(i,j)| \tag{1}$$

where $m \times n$ is the size of the block, A is the block to be computed in the target frame and B is the block of the reference frame. Corresponding to the reference frames, the best matchable position in block $A(k, s)$ is:

$$B(k + p', s + q') = \arg\min(\sum_{i=k}^{k+m} \sum_{j=s}^{s+n} |A(i,j) - B(i+p, j+q)| \| p \in (-a, a), q \in (-b, b)) \tag{2}$$

where $(-a, a)$ is the transverse searching scope and $(-b, b)$ is the vertical searching scope. Meanwhile, we take the displacement of the points in block A as a vector (p', q'). On the basis of the traditional block searchin, which computes the displacement of every block by either row order or column order, using the result of the neighboring block of the current block as a reference computes the displacement of the current block. Due to the effect of noise, errors can accumulate continuously and even result in a large error if there is a displacement error in one block.

The quality-guided block matching method [20] does not calculate the blocks in the target frame in the order of row and column; it calculates the displacement of its neighbor block by referring to the block with the highest matching degree at a given point in time. Using this method can ensure that the more matchable block gets calculated first, and the block that has more noise and easily results in error is computed last, thus avoiding the transmission and accumulation of errors. The steps of this method are as follows:

Step 1. Select the starting block A and put it into the set S to calculate the displacement and matching degree of block A;

Step 2. Find the most matchable block in set S and take it as the current block. If there is more than one candidate, then randomly select from the candidates;

Step 3. Compute the displacement and matching degree of the current block;

Step 4. If there are neighboring blocks of the current block that have not been computed, go to Step 5; otherwise, go to Step 7;

Step 5. If the neighboring block chosen in the last step was not in set S, initialize the neighboring block with the displacement and matching degree of the current block, put it into set S and go to Step 4. If it was in set S, go to Step 6;

Step 6. If the matching degree of neighboring block is higher than the current block, go to Step 4; otherwise, update the displacement and matching degree of the neighboring block with that of the current block and go to Step 4;

Step 7. Remove the current block from set S;

Step 8. If set S is not empty, go to Step 2, otherwise the steps are finished.

2.2 Phase-Zero Search

The phase-zero search first calculates the analytical form of the two frames of signals before and after palpation, and then, it calculates the position of the phase-zero crossing by using the cross-correlation of the analytical signals, i.e., the position of the maximum value of the cross-correlation function.

The bandpass of the two signals $x_1(t)$ and $x_2(t)$ are described as:

$$\tilde{x}_1 = A(t - \tau_1)e^{-i\omega_0\tau_1}, \quad \tilde{x}_2 = A(t - \tau_2)e^{-i\omega_0\tau_2} \tag{3}$$

The complex cross-correlation functions of the two signals are described as:

$$\tilde{C}(t) = \frac{1}{T}\int_0^T \tilde{x}_1(\tau)\tilde{x}_2^*(t + \tau)d\tau \tag{4}$$

When t is 0, we can obtain the simplified form of the above expression:

$$\tilde{C}(0) = \Gamma_{AA}(\tau)e^{i\omega_0\tau} \tag{5}$$

where $\Gamma_{AA}(\tau)$ is an autocorrelation function of the signal envelope. The time delay of signals $x_1(t)$ and $x_2(t)$ can be described with the above phase-zero search:

$$\tau_{BB} = \frac{\phi(0)}{\omega_0} = \frac{\tan^{-1}\left(\frac{Im(\tilde{C}(0))}{Re(\tilde{C}(0))}\right)}{\omega_0} \tag{6}$$

The displacement is:

$$d = \tau_{BB} \cdot c \tag{7}$$

where c is the ultrasonic propagation velocity in the medium.

This method can obtain equal accuracy with oversampling by a lower calculation and cause phase cancellation, resulting in a miscalculation of time delay when the displacement is more than a half phase. Combining block-matching with a phase-zero search can obtain an accurate displacement field after first computing a rough displacement with block-matching that limits the error no more than a half phase. To clearly reflect the physical characteristic of the tissue, we compute the strain field from the displacement field with the gradient method. The algorithm framework is as follows (Fig. 1):

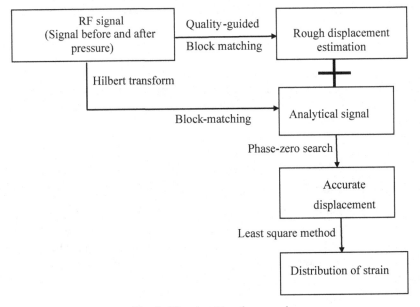

Fig. 1. The algorithm framework

3   Experiment and Analysis

A two-dimensional soft tissue model was created using Abaqus software, and this model contained circular tissue that was four times harder than the surrounding tissue. Then, a 2% deformation is generated in the model, and a simulated RF signal is generated by the consistent displacement generated by the deformation. In this set of simulation data, the central frequency of the signal is 5 MHz, the sampling rate is 20 MHz, and the maximum displacement is greater than twice the length of the ultrasonic wave. The CAM [16, 17] and the traditional TDE (Time Delay Estimation) algorithm [21] are classical and popular methods of the current displacement estimation methods. Therefore, this paper uses these methods as a comparative experiment.

3.1 Combined Autocorrelation Method

To maintain simplicity, we consider only the axial displacement of the tissue (that is, along the direction of the beam). Supposing that the signal distortion caused by tissue deformation (the decorrelation of speckle structure) is locally ignored, the RF signal measured before and after distortion can be modeled as

$$x(t) = u(t)e^{-j(\omega_0 t - \theta)}$$
$$y(t) = u(t - \tau)e^{-j[\omega_0(t-\tau)-\theta]} \tag{8}$$

where they are complex expressions and u, ω_0 and τ represent the envelope, the carrier angular frequency and the time shift, respectively. We define the complex cross-correlation function between $x(t)$ and $y(t + nT/2)$ as

$$R_{xy}(t; n) = \int_{-t_0/2}^{t_0} x(t + v)y(t + nT/2 + v) * dv$$
$$= R_u(t; \tau - nT/2)e^{-j\omega_0(\tau - nT/2)}$$
$$(n = \ldots - 2, -1, 0, 1, 2 \ldots) \tag{9}$$

where T is an ultrasonic period and $R_u(t; \tau)$ represents the autocorrelation function of the envelope. For the special case of, $n = 0$ Eq. 9 becomes:

$$R_{xy}(t; 0) = \int_{-t_0/2}^{t_0/2} x(t + v)y(t + v) * dv = R_u(t; \tau)e^{-j\omega_0\tau} \tag{10}$$

This expression corresponds to the output of the autocorrelation operator of a traditional Doppler system. The difference is that the Doppler method uses a moving average filter instead of averaging the subsequent sequence. If the displacement δ is less than a quarter of the wave length, the displacement can be obtained by the phase shift $\phi = \omega_0\tau$:

$$\delta(t) = \frac{\phi}{2\pi}\lambda = \frac{\omega_0\tau}{2\pi}\lambda \tag{11}$$

It is impossible to estimate δ unambiguously from Eq. 10 except by using a priori knowledge about displacement or the standard simple form of expansion (only extending the aliasing limit from $\lambda/4$ to $\lambda/2$).

To avoid fuzziness, the envelope correlation coefficient $C_u(t; n)$ defined by Eq. 12 is adopted, but it also brings a certain amount of calculation.

$$C_u(t; n) = \frac{|R_{xy}(t; n)|}{|x(t)||y(t + nT/2)|} \tag{12}$$

According to Eqs. 9 and 12, the two sets C_u and ϕ can be obtained for every time t:

$$\{C_u(t)\} = \left\{ C_u^{-M}, \ldots, C_u^{-1}, C_u^0, C_u^1, \ldots, C_u^N \right\}$$
$$\{\phi(t)\} = \{\phi^{-M}, \ldots, \phi^{-1}, \phi^0, \phi^1, \ldots, \phi^n\} \tag{13}$$

where $C_u^n = C_u(t; n)$ and ϕ^n is the phase of $R_{xy}(t; n)$. If M and N are designated large enough, a component of $\{\phi(t)\}$, ϕ^k will not be wrapped because if it comes from the two sequences $x(t)$ and $y(t + kT/2)$, the displacement t between the two sequences is less than $\lambda/4$. Meanwhile, C_u^n becomes the maximum at $n = k$. Therefore, the first step is to determine the maximum value of C_u^n at n, after which the unwrapped phase shift can be obtained as $\phi(n) = \arctan(R_{xy}(n))$, and the displacement δ can be calculated from Eq. 11. Finally, the strain along the beam direction $s(t)$ can be calculated as follows:

$$s(t) = \frac{d\delta}{dt} \tag{14}$$

From the perspective of envelope correlation, the first step is similar to the speckle tracing algorithm. The first and second steps can occur simultaneously through autocorrelation processing, and C_u is computed only a few times; that is, $N + M + I$ determines the unwrapped region. So the processing speed is faster than the speckle tracking, and the correlation coefficient is calculated by changing τ many times.

In practice, as shown in Fig. 2, by using multiple autocorrelation processing units in parallel, it should be possible to perform real-time processing similar to traditional Doppler methods.

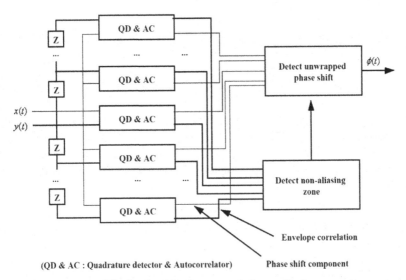

Fig. 2. Combined autocorrelation method

3.2 Time Delay Estimation

Time delay estimation is used to calculate the time delay of a reference signal and a contrast signal in a period of time. As shown in Fig. 3, the time shift exists between the reference signal and the contrast signal. The present TDE method has good performance under high Signal to Noise Ratio (SNR). However, with the decrease of signal correlation, the performance decreases, so the robustness is poor.

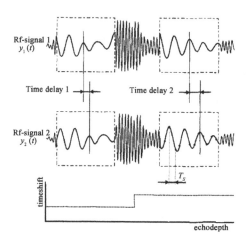

Fig. 3. Reference signal and delay signal

Because the tissue vibration is small and its orders of magnitude are usually measured in microns, the sampling frequency of common ultrasonic equipment cannot meet the requirement. Therefore, a signal interpolation algorithm must be used to improve the estimation accuracy of displacement. The interpolation algorithm is an important function approximation method. The spline interpolation finds a set of fitting polynomials according to the existing data points. In the fitting process, a polynomial is used to fit the curves for adjacent data points, which is mostly used in signal processing.

In signal processing, the mutual transformation of continuous and discrete signals is a basic task, and the spline interpolation is the most suitable method. Schoenberg proposed the theoretical basis of spline interpolation and introduced the B-spline curve. Spline curves are represented by piecewise polynomials and connected together smoothly. Connection points are called nodes. For an n-order spline interpolation, each segment of its polynomial is an n-order, and each segment of the curve requires $n + 1$ coefficients. The curvature of a cubic spline curve is the smallest, so it is mostly used in practice.

Let Δ be a division of $[a, b]$, $\Delta \cdot a = x_0 < x_1 < \cdots < x_n = b$. If $S(x)$ satisfies:

a. $S(x) \in C^2[a, b]$;
b. $S(x_i) = f(x_i), i = 0, 1, 2, 3, 4$;
c. $S(x)$ is a polynomial of degree no greater than three in all subintervals and is a polynomial of degree of at least one subinterval; then $S(x)$ is a cubic spline function that divides Δ.

The cubic spline interpolation is typically used in signal processing because of the balance between computation and accuracy. With spline interpolation, the discrete signal can be expressed in a continuous form as a polynomial. Then, the original signal can be interpolated by increasing the sampling frequency or by directly applying the polynomial coefficient to the delay calculation.

The cubic spline is a piecewise cubic polynomial, and the first and second derivatives of the node are continuous. The sampling result of signal $r(i\Delta t)$ can be expressed as

$$r(i\Delta t) = p_i(t) = a_1 t^3 + b_1 t^2 + c_i t + d_i \tag{15}$$

The third-order interpolation of the original data can obtain a balance between performance and computation. The interpolation effect at a third order and above cannot be optimized; the error increases and the computational efficiency decreases.

Let the reference signal and the contrast signal be $x_1(n)$ and $x_2(n)$ respectively; the expressions are as follows:

$$x_1(n) = s(n) + v_1(n), \quad x_2(n) = s(n) + v_2(n) \tag{16}$$

The correlation function of the two signals is

$$R_{12}(\tau) = |E(x_1(n)x_2(n-\tau))| = R_{ss}(\tau - D) + R_{sv_1}(\tau - D) + R_{sv_2}(\tau) + R_{v_1 v_2}(\tau) \tag{17}$$

where $v_1(n)$ and $v_2(n)$ are noises; D is the time difference of reaching the sensor. In engineering, the noise is independent of the signal, that is,

$$R_{12}(\tau) = Rss(\tau - D) \tag{18}$$

From the properties of related functions, the function reaches the maximum value at $\tau = D$:

$$D = \arg\{\max[Rss(\tau - D)]\} \tag{19}$$

where arg represents the independent variable of the function; max denotes the maximum value of the function. The estimated value of D is obtained from the above equation when the cross-correlation function is maximized. Based on this theory, the time-domain cross-correlation is used to estimate the vibration displacement of the organization.

$$R(\tau) = \frac{\sum\limits_{i=0}^{T-1} s_1(\tau)s_2(\tau+i)}{\sqrt{\sum\limits_{k=0}^{T-1} [s_1(\tau+k)]^2 \sum\limits_{j=0}^{T-1} [s_2(\tau+j)]^2}} \tag{20}$$

where S_1 is the reference RF signal; S_2 is the signal after vibration; T is the window size in the time domain; τ is the axial time point, and the range of τ is determined by the longitudinal length of radio frequency echo data and the prior knowledge of compression. This formula can be used to calculate the cross-correlation peak of the two segments before and after compression, so the displacement of the tissues before and after compression at different depths can be obtained by the offset of the cross-correlation peak along the time axis.

3.3 Estimation of Longitudinal Displacement

In the TDE method, RF signals are initially oversampled. When looking for the peak of the cross-correlation function, the parabolic interpolation method is adopted. Figures 4 (a), (b) and (c) show the displacement field calculated by the TDE method, the CAM method and our method, respectively, and Fig. 4 (d) shows the comparison between the displacement distribution of the three methods on a longitudinal line and the real displacement distribution.

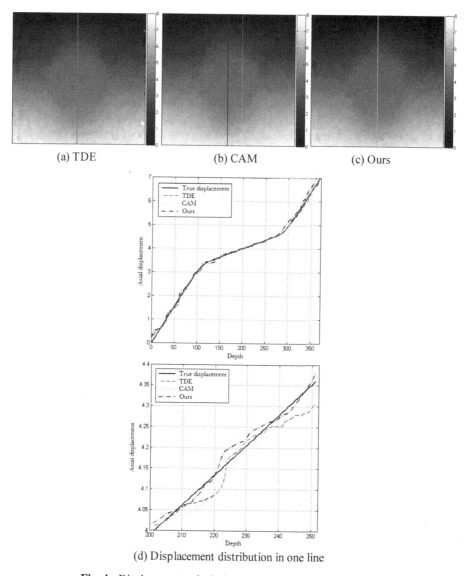

(a) TDE   (b) CAM   (c) Ours

(d) Displacement distribution in one line

Fig. 4. Displacement calculation comparison of three methods

It can be seen that the method in this paper is closer to the real displacement distribution because the method in this paper takes the displacement of the neighboring points as the prior information when calculating the displacement of a certain point, which not only improves the accuracy but also greatly reduces the search scope, thus reducing the amount of calculation and speeding up the calculation speed. To obtain the same result as the method in this paper, the TDE method needs to carry out oversampling with a very large amount of computation. There are also many redundant cross-correlation calculations in the CAM method, and the half wavelength limitation cannot be broken. To quantitatively analyze the accuracy of the three methods, we define the displacement difference of the calculation results as:

$$\sigma = \sqrt{\frac{\sum_{i=1}^{n} (result_i - true_i)^2}{n}} \tag{21}$$

where $result$ is the displacement field calculated, and $true$ is the error of the three methods, n is the number of samples. These results are shown in Table 1, which are 0.1156, 0.0798 and 0.0657, respectively. Obviously, the Displacement field error of this method is the smallest, which indicated that the calculation result of this method is more accurate. This is shown in Fig. 4, the method in this paper is closer to the real displacement distribution.

Table 1. Three methods of displacement field error

Method	TDE	CAM	Ours
Displacement field error	0.1156	0.0798	0.0657

3.4 Strain Estimation

To clearly indicate the physical characteristic of the tissue, we compute the tissue strain on the basis of the gained displacement field with the least square method, namely, the tissue strain is represented by a gradient. Figures 5 (a), (b), (c) separately represent the results of the TDE, the CAM and the method in this paper. As seen from the figure, the result obtained by the method in this paper is smoother, and the diseased tissue is easier to distinguish. Figure 5 (d) shows the strain distribution at the midline position.

A comparative transport rate (CNR) is adopted to quantitatively analyze the lesion degree resolution of the tissue of each method:

$$CNR = \frac{m_b - m_t}{\sqrt{(\sigma_b^2 + \sigma_t^2)/2}} \tag{22}$$

where m_b, σ_b are the mean and standard deviation of the background, and m_t, σ_t are the mean and standard deviation of the target. These are shown in Table 2. The CNRs of the three methods are calculated as follows: 7.67, 26.08, 157.06. Obviously, after comparison, the CNR of our method is the highest, which is the same as that shown in Fig. 5.

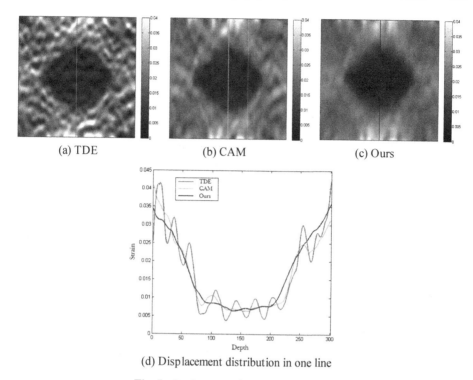

(a) TDE   (b) CAM   (c) Ours

(d) Displacement distribution in one line

Fig. 5. Strain comparison of three methods

Table 2. Three methods of comparative transport rate

Method	TDE	CAM	Ours
CNR	7.67	26.08	157.06

4 Conclusion

This paper presents a new displacement estimation method for ultrasound elastography, namely, the QGBM + PS method. The experimental results show that this method can accurately and efficiently calculate the displacement field and effectively solve the error transmission problem when using prior information. In the future, this method will be further optimized. For example, in the QGBM method, the determination of block size can be adaptive. In the PS method, the results can be calculated by an iterative method to make the results more accurate. In addition, a GPU array can be used to accelerate the method to meet real-time requirements [22, 23]. With the development of modern communication technology, telemedicine using mobile devices or the Internet will become more popular.

Acknowledgments. This work was supported in part by the Natural Science Basic Research Plan in Shaanxi Province of China (2019JM-162), and in part by the Japan Society for the Promotion of Science (JSPS) Grants-in-Aid for Scientific Research (KAKENHI) under Grant JP18K18044.

References

1. Andreassen, H.K., Bujnowska-Fedak, M.M., Chronaki, C.E., et al.: European citizens use of E-health services: a study of seven countries. BMC Public Health **7**(53), 1–7 (2007)
2. Hongan, L., Min, Z., Keping, Y., et al.: Combined forecasting model of cloud computing resource load for energy-efficient IoT system. IEEE Access **7**, 149542–149553 (2019)
3. Liu, Z., Dong, M., Gu, B., et al.: Fast-start video delivery in future internet architectures with intra-domain caching. Mob. Netw. Appl. **22**(1), 98–112 (2017)
4. Kuo, T.T., Hsu, C.N., Ohno-Machado, L.: Model chain: decentralized privacy-preserving healthcare predictive modeling framework on private block chain networks, pp. 1–13 (2016). https://www.healthit.gov/sites/default/files/10-30-ucsd-dbmi-onc-blockchain-challenge.pdf
5. Liu, Z., Feng, J., Ji, Y., et al.: EAF: energy-aware adaptive free viewpoint video wireless transmission. J. Netw. Comput. Appl. **46**, 384–394 (2014)
6. Hongan, L., ZhuoMing, D., Jing, Z., Zhanli, L.: A retrieval method of medical 3D models based on sparse representation. J. Med. Imaging Health Inf. **9**(9), 1988–1992 (2019)
7. Kuo, T.T., Kim, H.E., Ohno-Machado, L.: Blockchain distributed ledger technologies for biomedical and health care applications. J. Am. Med. Inform. Assoc. **24**(6), 1211–1220 (2017)
8. Yan, F., Song, Z., Du, M., Klibanov, A.L.: Ultrasound molecular imaging for differentiation of benign and malignant tumors in patients. Quant. Imaging Med. Surg. **8**(11), 1078–1083 (2018)
9. Gennisson, J.L., Deffieux, T., Fink, M., et al.: Ultrasound elastography: principles and techniques. Diagn. Interv. Imaging **94**(5), 487–495 (2013)
10. Ophir, J., Cespedes, I., Ponnekanti, H., et al.: Elastography: a quantitative method for imaging the elasticity of biological tissues. Ultrason. Imaging **13**(2), 111–134 (1991)
11. O'Donnell, M., Skovoroda, A.R., Shapo, B.M., et al.: Internal displacement and strain imaging using ultrasonic speckle tracking. IEEE Trans. Ultrason. Ferroelectr. Freq. Control **41**(3), 314–325 (1994)
12. Sarvazyan, A.P., Rudenko, O.V., Swanson, S.D., et al.: Shear wave elasticity imaging: a new ultrasonic technology of medical diagnostics. Ultrasound Med. Biol. **24**(9), 1419–1435 (1998)
13. Fatemi, M., Greenleaf, J.F.: Ultrasound-stimulated vibro-acoustic spectrography. Science **280**(5360), 82–85 (1998)
14. Varghese, T., Ophir, J.: Enhancement of echo-signal correlation in elastography using temporal stretching. IEEE Trans. Ultrason. Ferroelectr. Freq. Control **44**(1), 173–180 (1997)
15. Sarvazyan, A.P.: A new approach to remote ultrasonic evaluation of viscoelastic properties of tissues for diagnostics and healing monitoring. In: Abstract of ARPA/ONR Medical Ultrasonic Imaging Technology Workshop 1, pp. 24–26 (1995)
16. Shiina, T., Doyley, M.M., Bamer, J.C.: Strain imaging using combined RF and envelope autocorrelation processing. In: Ultrasonics Symposium 2, pp. 1331–1336 (1996)
17. Shiina, T., Yamakawa, M., Nitta, N., et al.: Clinical assessment of real-time, freehand elasticity imaging system based on the combined autocorrelation method. In: IEEE Symposium on Ultrasonics, Honolulu, USA, pp. 664–667 (2003)
18. Gyaourova, A., Kamath, C., Cheung, S.C.: Block matching for object tracking. Department of Computer Science, University of Nevada, Reno, pp. 1–15 (2003)
19. Nie, Y., Ma, K.K.: Adaptive rood pattern search for fast block-matching motion estimation. IEEE Trans. Image Process. **11**(12), 1442–1449 (2002)

20. Chen, L., Treece, G.M., Lindop, J.E., et al.: A quality-guided displacement tracking algorithm for ultrasonic elasticity imaging. Med. Image Anal. **13**(2), 286–296 (2009)
21. Ke, C., Jiangli, L., Guanxiong, H.: Tissue motion estimation based on ultrasound RF signal and TDE algorithm. J. Xihua Univ. (Nat. Sci. Ed.) **36**(4), 1–4 (2017)
22. Liu, Z., Cheung, G., Ji, Y.: Optimizing distributed source coding for interactive multiview video streaming over lossy networks. IEEE Trans. Circuits Syst. Video Technol. **23**(10), 1781–1794 (2013)
23. Qingfang, L., Baosheng, K., Keping, Y., Xin, Q., Jing, L., Shoujin, W., Hongan, L.: Contour-maintaining-based image adaption for an efficient ambulance service in intelligent transportation systems. IEEE Access **8**, 12644–12654 (2020)

Author Index

Printed in the United States
By Bookmasters